Object-Oriented Programming: Using C++ for Engineering and Technology

Object-Oriented Programming: Using C++ for Engineering and Technology

GORAN SVENK

DELMAR

THOMSON LEARNING ™

Australia • Canada • Mexico • Singapore • Spain • United Kingdom • United States

DELMAR

THOMSON LEARNING

Object-Oriented Programming: Using C++ for Engineering and Technology
By Goran Svenk

Executive Director:
Alar Elken

Executive Editor:
Sandy Clark

Senior Acquisitions Editor:
Gregory L. Clayton

Senior Development Editor:
Michelle Ruelos Cannistraci

Executive Marketing Manager:
Maura Theriault

Channel Manager:
Fair Huntoon

Marketing Coordinator:
Brian McGrath

Executive Production Manager:
Mary Ellen Black

Production Manager:
Larry Main

Senior Project Editor:
Christopher Chien

Art/Design Coordinator:
David Arsenault

Technology Project Manager:
David Porush

Technology Project Specialist:
Kevin Smith

Senior Editorial Assistant:
Dawn Daugherty

NOTICE TO THE READER

CONTENTS

PREFACE

For over a decade, C++ has been one of the most popular and widely used programming languages. It is used for computer applications development in a broad variety of fields in both industry and business. C++ and its predecessor, C, have been dominant programming languages in diverse areas of engineering and engineering technology; such as, control systems, telecommunications, computer-aided design, and embedded systems. Estimates suggest that there are several million C++ programmers worldwide. The C++ standard, ratified in 1998, has made it easier to teach, learn, and develop applications using C++.

INTENDED AUDIENCE

This book is ideal for students in engineering, engineering technology, computer science, or computer studies technology programs who have completed a procedural programming course using C language. It contains many practical examples from electrical engineering, and therefore relates well to students in electrical engineering or electronics technology programs. *Object-Oriented Programming: Using C++ for Engineering and Technology* is aimed specifically at intermediate-level programmers. This book is also intended for programmers, engineers, or anyone who is familiar with C and wants to learn C++. Those who already have had experience with C++ will find the latest developments in C++ programming useful.

ABOUT THIS BOOK

C++ is a general-purpose programming language that supports low-level programming, procedural (structured) programming, object-oriented programming (OOP), and generic programming. The authors of C++ books, therefore, have faced a difficult challenge when making a decision about the approach to use. A common dilemma when writing a C++ book is whether the book should present a pure object-oriented approach, or a hybrid approach balancing procedural programming with OOP. In most of the engineering schools, students are required to successfully complete procedural programming using C prior to taking a C++ course. Most of the C++ textbooks, however, use the hybrid approach and contain a significant amount of redundant material for those who have completed a C course. This results in an unnecessarily lengthy text that discourages students from learning new OOP concepts.

This textbook's author has taught C++ to engineering students for more than eight years. He has been searching for a C++ book that uses a pure object-oriented approach and contains program examples from a variety of engineering disciplines. Not being able to find such a textbook, the author decided to write a book that met these requirements. *Object-Oriented Programming: Using C++ for Engineering and Technology* uses a pure object-oriented approach to teach C++ and avoids redundant material for those who have already completed a C course. The book also discusses the differences between C and C++. It contains many practical examples from the electrical and computer engineering disciplines. The text is based on the C++ programming language as defined by the ANSI/ISO C++ standard.

BOOK ORGANIZATION

The book is organized into 12 chapters. The introductory chapters (Chapters 1 through 3) discuss both the differences between C and C++ and the C++ enhancements to procedural programming in C. The remaining chapters (Chapters 4 through 12) present OOP concepts with a rich collection of program examples. The chapters are organized in the following manner:

- **Chapter 1, Moving from C to C++**, addresses the fundamental differences between C and C++ and discusses both namespaces and C++ input/output.

- **Chapter 2, C++ Function Enhancements**, explains the advantages of C++ functions over C functions and discusses C++ function enhancements.

- **Chapter 3, Pointers, References, and Dynamic Memory Allocation**, emphasizes the use of pointers and references and discusses the concept of dynamic memory allocation and its implementation in C++.

- **Chapter 4, Classes and Objects**, explains the key OOP concepts and terminology and introduces C++ expanded structures, classes, and mechanisms of creating and destroying class objects.

- **Chapter 5, Classes: Advanced Topics**, explains the procedures of passing and returning objects from functions and discusses copy constructors, *friend* functions and *friend* classes, *static* class members, the *this* pointer, and *const* member functions.

- **Chapter 6, Operator Overloading**, discusses all aspects of operator overloading and demonstrates practical examples of programs that implement operator overloading.

- **Chapter 7, Inheritance**, addresses the most important aspects of the implementation of inheritance; such as, constructing and destroying derived class objects, using multiple-direct and multiple-indirect inheritance, and overriding and dominating inherited class members.

- **Chapter 8, Composition**, discusses and demonstrates some practical examples of composition, as well as program examples that combine composition and inheritance.

- **Chapter 9, Polymorphism and Virtual Functions**, explains the difference between static and dynamic binding and addresses the importance of both *virtual* functions and abstract base classes when implementing run-time polymorphism.

- **Chapter 10, Templates**, explains class templates, containers and iterators, and introduces the STL library.

- **Chapter 11, Exception Handling**, describes and demonstrates the exception-handling mechanisms and tools in C++.

- **Chapter 12, File I/O**, discusses the steps in C++ file I/O processing and demonstrates some commonly used C++ techniques when processing sequential and random-access files.

FEATURES

The text uses a pure object-oriented approach to teach the essentials of programming using C++. It also discusses the C++ enhancements to procedural programming in C. This text could be used as a learning tool, or as a valuable reference sourcebook. It includes many practical examples from the electrical and computer engineering disciplines. The text presents many aspects of software engineering and program design using C++.

Every chapter is divided into sections. To make the text more readable, code listings, figures, tables, and important programming tips are set off from the text using different graphic styles. Program examples are numbered for easy reference to specific lines in the text. Short code segments are inserted directly into the text without line numbers.

The book uses a wide spectrum of pedagogical features, such as

- **A set of chapter objectives and a table of contents** at the beginning of every chapter.

- **Programming tips and important notes** that are emphasized.

- **Program examples** in every chapter to exhibit specific programming concepts and C++ tools.

- **Case studies** that solve typical problems in a variety of engineering disciplines. The problems are analyzed and the programs are developed in logical steps using pseudocode and flowcharts.

- **Chapter summaries** of key points.

- **End-of-chapter review questions and problems** follow every chapter to check the understanding of the material covered. Some problems require an analysis and tracing of program segments, while the others require writing, modifying, or troubleshooting code segments. Answers to the odd-numbered questions are provided at the end of the text.

- **Programming projects** at the end of every chapter that require complete solutions to typical engineering problems using the programming tools and techniques discussed in that particular chapter.

- An accompanying **CD-ROM** contains the C++ compiler (Microsoft Visual C++, Learning Edition) and source code files for all program examples and case studies in the text.

The following **conventions** are used to make the text more readable

- Important terms and definitions are shown using a bolded text font (e.g. **multiple inheritance, abstract class**).

- C++ keywords and standard library functions are shown in a bolded and italicized font (e.g., ***new, static, push_back()***).

- User-defined identifiers and functions are shown in Courier font (e.g., `amplifier`, `getCurrent()`).

- Keywords with the prefix "non"- will be shown in italicized text font. Italicized text font is also used to emphasize important concepts or words (e.g., *non-friend, parent class*).

SUPPLEMENTS

To supplement this text, an **Instructor's Manual**, (ISBN#:0-7668-3895-1) contains solutions to the programming projects and exercises. This manual also includes necessary information about different C++ compilers.

ABOUT THE AUTHOR

The author is a professor in the Faculty of Technology at Seneca College and a group facilitator for software engineering in the School of Electronics and Computer Engineering Technology. He has taught a variety of courses in computer science and control systems at colleges and universities for over 18 years. He has also been responsible for course and curriculum development for a number of programming languages (Pascal, C, C++, Visual Basic, and JAVA).

Goran Svenk
Toronto, 2002

ACKNOWLEDGMENTS

I would like to thank Greg Clayton and Michelle Ruelos Cannistraci , my editors, and all the crew at Delmar Learning—Larry Main, Christopher Chien, David Arsenault, and Jennifer Luck—for their support and constant encouragement. It has been a pleasure to work with them.

I would also like to express my gratitude to Professor Len Klochek and Professor Martyn McKinney, my colleagues from Seneca College, for their extraordinary effort and contributions in making this a better book. Professor Klochek's technical review of the manuscript and his suggestions were exceptionally helpful to me when preparing the final version of this book.

I would also like to thank the following reviewers for their very constructive comments:

Richard L. Henderson, DeVry University, Kansas City, MO

Deneil Lutter, DeVry University, Kansas City, MO

Bud Berges, DeVry University, Calgary, Alberta

Len Klochek, Seneca College, Toronto, Ontario

DEDICATION

To My Parents, Djuja and Anton Svenk

CHAPTER 1

MOVING FROM C TO C++

OBJECTIVES

- To understand the differences between C and C++

- To be able to use C++ input/output and formatting

- To understand the *namespace* mechanism and to be able to define and use namespaces

- To become familiar with the C++ standard

CHAPTER CONTENTS

INTRODUCTION

Although C++ evolved from C, it is considered to be a different programming language. Many programmers also consider C++ as a superset of C. C++ adds new, enhanced features to some important C concepts such as functions, pointers, and structures. Unlike C, which is a pure structured (procedural) language, C++ also provides another approach to programming called **object-oriented programming**. Object-oriented programming is more efficient when dealing with large, complex projects and requires a different way of visualizing solutions to programming problems.

Instead of C's standard I/O functions, C++ uses different tools to get input and produce output. C++ also provides a new tool called a *namespace* to prevent errors that may occur when linking multiple files containing source code into one application. This chapter will first address the fundamental differences between C and C++. It will then discuss the concepts of C++ input/output and namespaces.

1.1 DIFFERENCES BETWEEN C AND C++

C has been used for almost three decades and has been the most popular structured programming language in engineering. Its structured approach, however, limits its use in large and complex projects. The main reasons for expanding C and creating C++ were the following:

- To provide a new approach to programming (object-oriented programming) that would overcome the limits of C's structured approach when dealing with large and complex programming problems.

- To design new programming tools that would help programmers write code quickly and efficiently, as well as help improve maintainability of large projects.

- To design a more rigid programming language that would require programmers to follow certain strict rules, thus reducing chances for making errors.

- To create a highly extendable programming language.

- To enhance some important C concepts such as functions, pointers, and structures and make these tools even more powerful.

These five reasons for creating C++ are fundamental to the differences between C and C++.

When problems in programming exceed a certain size, C's structured approach makes such programs hard to design and maintain. C++'s object-oriented approach is much more efficient when dealing with large and complex programming problems. Using object-oriented tools when developing a large project decreases the program's development time and improves its maintainability.

C is less rigid than C++. For example, C does not require programmers to specify a function type or function arguments when writing function prototypes. There are many other examples of C's lack of rigidity that will be discussed in this book. A flexible programming language like C allows the compiler to make certain decisions for programmers. This is a disadvantage because the compiler may make an incorrect guess as to the programmer's intention, leading to increased errors. C++ is much more rigid than C and forces programmers to follow very strict rules when writing code.

C++ is much larger (provides more programming tools) and more complex than C. C may also be defined as a subset of C++. Any C++ compiler can therefore compile C programs as well, with very few coding changes. The relationship between C and C++ can be graphically represented, as shown in Figure 1.1. A small circle representing C is located almost entirely within a large circle representing C++. Only a small component of C does not also belong to C++.

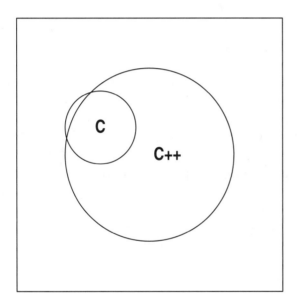

Figure 1.1 *Graphical representation of the relationship between C and C++.*

C is very efficient when solving small and simple programming problems. C++ is the language of choice when dealing with large and complex problems. There is no reason to use C++'s advanced tools in small and simple programs—it may even needlessly increase their complexity.

1.1.1 THE C++ STANDARD AND COMPILERS

Many different C++ compilers are used in industry and schools today. Different versions of Borland C++, Microsoft Visual C++, and Borland C++ Builder are commonly used. Some of the compilers may be older than the current ANSI/ISO C++ standard that was published in 1998. Programmers, therefore, may experience problems when attempting to use some standard libraries and advanced C++ tools that might not be supported by the compiler they use. It is important to check whether the compiler complies with the C++ standard before designing programs.

An electronic copy of the C++ standard document (entitled *Programming Languages–C++, reference number: ISO/IEC 14882:1998*) can be ordered from the following web site:

http://www.ansi.org/

It should be noted that the text in this book complies with the current ANSI/ISO C++ standard. Some of the program examples, however, may not compile if older or nonstandard compilers are used. In most cases, just minor modifications should be made to successfully compile these programs. The necessary compiler information will be provided to the readers where appropriate.

1.1.2 C++ COMMENTS

Writing comments throughout code is good programming practice. It improves program readability and provides help when maintaining programs. C++ provides a new comment style, in which each comment line begins with two forward slashes (//) and continues until the end of the line is reached. Unlike the comment style in C, the C++ comment style does not use any special symbol(s) to end a comment line or a comment block. The compiler ignores text that follows two forward slashes until the end of the current line.

C++ also supports C's commenting style, in which /* marks the beginning of a comment and */ ends the comment. The following fragment illustrates both commenting styles:

```
/* This is the old C commenting style, in which
multiple comment lines (a comment block) begin
with a forward slash followed by an asterisk and
end with an asterisk followed by a forward slash. */


//This is the new C++ commenting style, in which each
//line begins with two forward slashes without end symbols.
```

C++ programmers may use both commenting styles. C's commenting style is appropriate for lengthy multiple-line comments, while the new C++ commenting style is appropriate for single-line comments.

1.1.3 HEADER FILES

The C++ library is a collection of files, called **header files**, containing definitions and declarations of programming entities such as functions, data types, and constants. The *#include* preprocessor directive, followed by a header file name, is placed at the beginning of a program to include the contents of that header file in the program. The preprocessor substitutes the *#include* directive with a copy of a file whose name is specified in the directive. A standard library header file name is enclosed in angle brackets (< >).

The C language requires that all header files have an **.h** extension. The C++ standard does not require any extension for standard header files. The following code fragment demonstrates the differences between C and C++ **#include** directives:

```
#include <stdio.h>       //Includes C's standard header file
#include <iostream>      //Includes C++'s standard header file
```

In addition to using standard library header files, programmers can also create their own header files, called **user-defined header files**. A user-defined header file should also have an **.h** extension. The **#include** preprocessor directive is also used to include user-defined header files. Unlike standard library header files whose names are enclosed in angle brackets, names of user-defined header files should be enclosed in double quotes. The following fragment illustrates this syntax:

```
#include <iostream>      //Includes a standard header file
#include "myheader.h"    //Includes a user-defined header file
```

Enclosing a user-defined header file name in double quotes causes the preprocessor to first search for the file in the same directory where the source file being compiled is stored. If the user-defined header file is not found in this directory, the pre-processor continues to search the specified path for standard library header files. The search mechanism varies between C++ implementations and computer systems that are used to run programs.

Note: Appendix C contains a list of the C++ standard library header files with a brief description of each file.

1.1.4 DATA TYPES

In addition to C's five basic data types (*char*, *int*, *float*, *double*, and *void*), C++ also provides a new data type named *bool*. Values of the *bool* type—also called **Boolean values**—can be *true* or *false*. These values are commonly used in logic operations.

A value of the *bool* type can be converted to a value of the *int* type. The keywords *true* and *false* have predefined numeric values—*true* is numerically one and *false* is numerically zero. The following code fragment demonstrates a function that returns a value of the *bool* type:

```
bool fun(float x, float y )     //Function returns true or false
{
      bool answer;      //Variable answer of bool type is instantiated
      if(x<y && x>0)
          answer=true;   //true is assigned to answer
```

```
    else
        answer=false;   //false is assigned to answer
    return answer;

}
```

This function instantiates an `answer` variable of the ***bool*** type. The `answer` variable is assigned ***true*** or ***false*** depending on a value of the ***if*** condition. The function returns the value of `answer`.

The ***bool*** type is preferred over the ***int*** type, which is used in C when creating variables that indicate a ***true*** or ***false*** state. Using ***bool*** values makes a program more readable and its logic clearer. In addition to improving the program's clarity, the ***bool*** type consumes less memory than the ***int*** type.

Both C and C++ permit values of one type to be mixed with values of another type in expressions or assignment statements. The following rules of **automatic data type conversions** are applied when this situation occurs:

1. Values of different types are first converted to the largest data type used in an **expression** and then the expression is evaluated.

2. A value on the right side of an **assignment statement** is converted to the data type on the left side.

The following code fragment demonstrates the rules of automatic data type conversions:

```
int a=2;
float b=3.12;
double c=1.9999, d;
d=a/b*c;        //Values of a and b are temporarily converted to double
a=c;            //Value of c is temporarily converted to int
```

Values of `a` and `b` are first temporarily converted to ***double*** (the largest type in the expression `a/b*c`) and then the expression is evaluated. The value of `c` is temporarily converted to ***int*** (data type on the left side of the assignment statement) before assigning `c` to `a`. As a result of this conversion, the `a` variable is set to 1 because the decimal part of 1.9999 is truncated.

The compiler performs data type conversions automatically before evaluating expressions and performing assignments. It should be noted that values of variables are temporarily converted for the expression evaluation only. The values stored in memory, however, remain unchanged. These automatic type conversions may be a source of logic errors. The C++ compiler warns programmers each time a type conversion occurs. These warnings indicate that something unusual has happened and may help programmers prevent some types of logic errors (e.g., by using a **type cast**). It should be noted that a type cast is an explicit data type change that is requested by the programmer. The following code segment demonstrates the C-style type cast that can also be used in C++:

```
int a=9, b=10;
float percent;
percent=a/b*100;          //assigns 0.0 to percent
//Use type cast to change a to float before performing division.
percent=(float)a/b*100;  //assigns 90.0 to percent
```

The expression on the right side of the first assignment statement (a/b*100) uses three integer values and, therefore, is evaluated as *int* (an integer division 9/10 = 0). The value of this expression is then converted to *float* (0.0) before assigning to percent. The expression in the second assignment statement uses an explicit type cast to temporarily convert a to *float*. The b variable is then temporarily converted to *float* automatically by the compiler before a real division (9.0/10.0 = 0.9) is performed. A correct value is assigned to percent (90.0) as a result of using type cast.

In addition to the C-style type cast, C++ also provides the following cast operators:

- *static_cast* – for standard type conversions
  For example: static_cast<float>(a) converts a to *float*

- *const_cast* – for casting constants

- *reinterpret_cast* – for nonstandard type conversions

The use of C++ cast operators will be demonstrated in program examples in later chapters.

A variable in C does not necessarily have to store its declared type of data. Unlike C, *C++ is more rigid in its data type checking*. Although C++ still enables mixing or assigning values of different data types, a type cast must be used in some cases before a value can be assigned.

1.1.5 RESOLVING SCOPE AND VARIABLE DECLARATIONS

Variables in C and C++ can be declared **globally** (outside function definitions, usually before *main()*) and **locally** (within a function). The C++ standard differs from the C standard in regard to local declarations as follows:

- Local variables in standard C have to be declared after the opening brace ({) that indicates the beginning of a function definition, or after the opening brace that indicates the beginning of a block within the function definition.

- Local variables in C++ can be declared anywhere within the body of a function or within a block, *as long as they are declared before being used.*

Both C and C++ allow local and global variables to have the same names. Both languages also allow the same names of two or more local variables declared within the same function as long as they are declared within different blocks.

When using two or more variables with the same name in a C program, the most locally declared variable is only accessible at any time. A global variable cannot, therefore, be accessed within a function or a block within the function that uses a local variable with the same name as the global variable.

C++ provides the **scope resolution operator** (::), which can be used to access global variables that have same names as local variables. The following code segment demonstrates the use of the scope resolution operator:

```
int x=1;              //global variable
int  main()
{
      int x=2;        //local variable
      ::x=8;          //assigns 8 to the global variable
      {                       //beginning of a block
          int x=3;            //new local variable whose scope
                              //is the inner block
          cout<<x;            //prints value of local variable (3)
          cout<<::x;          //prints value of global variable (8)
      }
      cout<<x;                //prints value of local variable (2)
      return 0;
}
```

This code segment instantiates a global variable named x and initializes it to 1. It also instantiates two local variables with the same name and initializes them to 2 and 3 respectively. It should be noted that the third variable declared within the block that is in the *main()* function is visible only to that block. When using x within the block, the most local variable that is initialized to 3 is accessed. When using x outside the block, the local variable that is declared at the beginning of *main()* and initialized to 2 is accessed. To access x declared globally, the variable name is preceded by the scope resolution operator (i.e., ::x). Be aware that this code fragment also uses two C++ output statements to print values of x declared locally as well as globally (cout<<x; and cout<<::x;). C++ input and output will be discussed in Section 1.2.

Although using global variables is not good programming practice, the scope resolution operator that C++ provides may help when resolving conflicts similar to the one demonstrated in the preceding code segment.

1.1.6 CONSTANTS

C uses the *#define* preprocessor directive to create **constants**. C++ uses the *const* keyword to declare constants. The general format of a constant declaration in C++ is shown in Figure 1.2.

```
const data_type constant_name = value;
```

Figure 1.2 *General format of a constant declaration.*

Unlike constants created using *#define*, constants declared using *const* must have a data type specified and a value assigned by the assignment operator. If a constant data type is omitted, C++ assumes *int*. The following code fragment demonstrates C and C++ constants:

```
//C constants
#define MAX_SPEED 100
#define MESSAGE "Switch printer on!"
#define RATE 1.15


//C++ constants
const int MAX_SPEED=100;
const char MESSAGE[]="Switch printer on!";
const float RATE=1.15;
```

Creating constants using the *#define* preprocessor directive has the following disadvantages compared to creating constants using *const*:

- **#define** does not perform type checking
- **#define** cannot be debugged (i.e., the value of the constant cannot be checked)

Unlike preprocessor, which processes *#define* directives, the compiler that processes *const* declarations does type checking on the constant. The C++ compiler reserves a storage space in memory for a constant and makes its value **read-only**. While debugging code, values of constants created by *const* can be checked, which helps to detect logic errors caused by incorrect constants values.

The following code fragment demonstrates some common errors when declaring constants in C++:

```
const PI=3.14159265;      //LOGIC ERROR: C++ assumes that PI is int
const float X;            //SYNTAX ERROR: X is not assigned a value
```

A value of type *double* (3.14159265) is assigned to the PI constant, however a data type is not specified for PI. If a constant's type is missing, C++ assumes type *int*—therefore, the value stored in memory allocated for PI is the integer 3. To prevent a data type conversion like the one demonstrated in this example, a constant must be declared with a data type that matches the type of the value assigned to the constant. *Not assigning a value to a constant when it is declared causes a syntax error.*

1.2 C++ INPUT/OUTPUT

1.2.1 C++ I/O METHODS

C's standard input/output (I/O) functions (e.g., *scanf()* and *printf()*) cannot supply the necessary I/O in C++ when writing object-oriented programs. C++ provides different I/O methods than C, based on the use of streams, objects, and operators.

A **stream** is a sequence of data. Streams can be input streams or output streams. An **input stream** is a sequence of data that flows from an input device (such as a keyboard, disk drive, or network card) to main computer memory. In an **output stream**, data flows from main memory to an output device (such as a display screen, disk drive, network card, or printer).

When performing I/O operations, C++ commonly uses two standard **objects** called *cin* and *cout*. These two objects are defined within the *std* namespace in the *iostream* header file. Note that the namespace mechanism will be discussed in Section 1.3. The *cin* object is the console input device (usually a keyboard). The *cout* object refers to the console output device (usually a display screen). The concept of objects will be introduced in Chapter 4.

C++ uses the following two **operators** to perform I/O operations:

- the **stream insertion operator <<** (usually used with **cout**)
- the **stream extraction operator >>** (usually used with **cin**)

The stream operators << and >> are defined in the *iostream* header file. The stream insertion operator inserts data into an output object that is named on the left side of the operator. For example,

```
cout<<"OOP USING C++";
```

instructs the computer to send a string "OOP USING C++" to the *cout* object (usually a display screen).

The stream extraction operator extracts data from an input object named on the left side of the operator and stores data into a memory location of an object that is specified on the right side of the operator. For example,

```
cin>>score;
```

instructs the computer to extract a value from the **cin** object (usually a keyboard that the user uses to enter data) and store the value into a memory location that is reserved for the score variable. The concept of C++ I/O is illustrated in Figure 1.3.

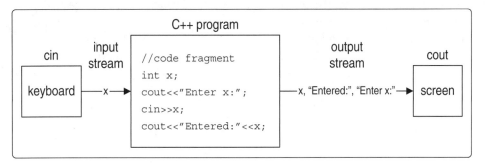

Figure 1.3 *Sample demonstration of C++ I/O.*

Values are extracted from an input stream and inserted into an output stream in a specific order that a C++ program dictates. The code segment in Figure 1.3, for example, inserts values into the **cout** stream in the following order: first, the string "Enter x:"; second, the string "Entered:"; and last, the value of x is inserted.

A single **cin>>** or **cout<<** statement can be used to input or output more than one value as demonstrated in Program Example 1.1.

PROGRAM EXAMPLE 1.1: PROG1_1

```
1 //PROG1_1: Program demonstrates C++ I/O.
2 #include <iostream>
3 using namespace std; //cout and cin are defined in std
4
5 int main()
6 {
7     float length, width, area;
8     cout<<"Enter length and width => ";          //output
9     cin>>length>>width;                           //input
10    area=length*width;
11    cout<<"Area = "<<area;                   //output
12    return 0;
13 }
```

This program first displays the string "Enter length and width =>" on a standard output device (line 8). The program is then paused until the user enters the values of width and length (line 9). Between the two input values, the user should enter a whitespace, or hit the *Enter* key. To complete the input and proceed with program execution, the user must hit the *Enter* key. The stream extraction operator puts the two values entered into the length and width variable, respectively. The program computes area (line 10) and at the end displays the value of area preceded with a string "Area = " (line 11). A sample run of PROG1_1 is shown in Figure 1.4.

```
Enter length and width => 2.3 4.7

Area = 10.81
```

Figure 1.4 *Sample run of PROG1_1.*

It should be noted that the data extraction (input) operation using >> is terminated by a whitespace or the *Enter* key (same as with C's *scanf()*). If an input value should include a whitespace, a library function (e.g., *getline()* or *get()*) should be used instead of the stream extraction operator to get input.

The *get()* function (defined in *iostream*) is used to get a single character, including a whitespace. This function is called with the *cin* object as shown in the following code segment:

```
char ch;
cout<<"Enter a character";
ch=cin.get();    //Returns a character entered by the user
                 //and assigns to ch.
```

The *getline()* function (defined in *iostream*) is used to get a sequence of characters (a string) that can include whitespace(s). The following code segment demonstrates an example of this function call:

```
char message[50];
cout<<"Enter a message";
cin.getline(message,50); //Gets a string and puts into message
cout<<"The message entered: "<<message;
```

It should be noted that the *getline()* function requires two arguments: a string name and the size of the string.

C++ I/O methods have the following important advantages over C I/O methods:

- Unlike C's standard I/O library functions that only work with built-in data types, C++'s stream extraction and stream insertion operators can work with any data type, including user-defined data types (demonstrated in Chapter 6).

- Data types of values being entered or displayed/printed do not have to be specified.

- C++ provides more powerful formatting tools than C.

1.2.2 C++ FORMATTING

C++ provides a variety of **manipulators** to control the format of the output produced by a program. Output stream manipulators can be categorized into the following three groups:

1. Numeric base manipulators

2. Character control manipulators

3. Format control manipulators

The stream insertion operator is used to insert manipulators into the output stream (*cout*). All values that are inserted into the output stream after specific manipulators are inserted will be displayed in the specified format (with the exception of the *setw()* manipulator) . Commonly used C++ output stream manipulators are shown in Table 1.1.

Numeric base manipulators are used to set a numeric base (decimal, hexadecimal, or octal) prior to displaying integer numbers. Integer numbers are normally output in base 10. Inserting one of the base manipulators into the output stream, however, changes subsequent integer output to that base. Floating point numbers are unaffected by the numeric base manipulators. The following code segment demonstrates these manipulators:

```
int x=10, y=11, z=12, q=13;
cout<<hex<<x<<' '<<y;   //prints a b
cout<<z<<' '<<dec<<q;   //prints c 13
```

Note that x, y, and z are printed as hexadecimal values, because *hex* is inserted into the output stream before x, y, and z are inserted. The *dec* manipulator is inserted before q, thus causing q to be displayed as a decimal value.

Table 1.1 C++ Output Stream Manipulators

Manipulator	Description
Numeric Base Manipulators	
dec	Sets decimal base
hex	Sets hexadecimal base
oct	Sets octal base
Character Control Manipulators	
endl	Inserts a new-line character '\n' and flushes the buffer
ends	Inserts a null character '\0'
flush	Flushes the buffer
Format Control Manipulators	
setw(int)	Sets the field width for a single output field
setprecision(int)	Sets the floating point precision
setiosflags(flag)	Sets the output format flags
resetiosflags(flag)	Resets the output format flags
setfill(char)	Sets the fill character

Character control manipulators manipulate a sequence of characters by inserting a new-line character **\n** (*endl*) or a null character **\0** (*ends*) and flushing the output buffer (*endl* and *flush*). Note that the *endl* manipulator simultaneously inserts a new-line character and flushes the output buffer before a value is printed in a new line. The following code segment demonstrates *endl*:

```
cout<<"Speed = "<<sp<<endl;
```

Cursor is moved down one line and to column 1 after the value of sp is output.

Format control manipulators control the output by setting the width of a field in which a value is displayed (*setw()*), setting the precision of floating point numbers (*setprecision()*), aligning a value within a field, or performing some other formatting operations (*setiosflags()* and *resetiosflags()*). Unlike numeric base and character control manipulators that are defined in the *iostream* header file, format control manipulators are defined in the *iomanip* header file.

The *setw()* manipulator has an integer argument that specifies the width of a field in which a value is displayed. This is the **only manipulator that is reset each time after a value is displayed** and should be specified for each value individually. For example,

```
cout<<setw(6)<<x<<setw(6)<<y;
```

displays x and y values in 6 spaces. Unused spaces within the specified field will be blank by default. If the requested width of a field is smaller than the value to be displayed, the compiler will ignore the **setw()** manipulator and display the entire value without blank spaces. For example,

```
int x=12345;
cout<<setw(3)<<x;   //prints 12345
```

prints all five digits of x, although the field width is set to 3.

The **setprecision()** manipulator uses an integer argument to set a number of digits after the decimal point when printing/displaying floating point numbers. If all values that a program outputs have the same precision, **setprecision()** should be inserted only once before a first value is inserted into an output stream. For example,

```
cout<<setprecision(2);
cout<<x<<y<<z;
```

prints values of x, y, and z with two digits after the decimal point. By default, floating point numbers are displayed with six decimal digits.

The **setiosflags()** and **resetiosflags()** manipulators are used to set or reset format states that are specified by **format flags** as shown in Table 1.2. One **setiosflags()** or **resetiosflags()** manipulator can be used to set or reset as many different formats (format state flags) as necessary. For example,

```
cout<<setiosflags(ios::left|ios::scientific|ios::showpos);
```

justifies values to the left within a specified field, sets the scientific notation for floating point numbers, and indicates that a +/- sign is displayed before a number. Note that format flags are separated by a pipe | within **setiosflags()**.

Table 1.2 C++ Format State Flags

Format Flag	Description
ios::left	Sets left justification within a field
ios::right	Sets right justification within a field
ios::dec	Sets decimal numeric base
ios::hex	Sets hexadecimal numeric base
ios::oct	Sets octal numeric base
ios::showbase	Shows a numeric base before a number
ios::uppercase	Shows uppercase letters in hexadecimal values
ios::showpos	Shows a positive/negative sign before a number
ios::fixed	Shows decimal numbers with a fixed decimal point
ios::scientific	Shows decimal numbers in scientific notation

16

The *setfill()* manipulator fills in unused spaces within a specified field with a character that is passed to the manipulator. For example,

```
int x=13;
cout<<setfill('$')<<setw(6)<<x; //print $$$$13
```

fills in four unused spaces with a $ sign. In Program Example 1.2, PROG1_2 demonstrates various format control manipulators and format state flags.

PROGRAM EXAMPLE 1.2: PROG1_2

```
1   //PROG1_2 demonstrates C++ formatting.
2   #include <iostream>
3   #include <iomanip>
4   using namespace std;
5
6   void print()
7   {
8       cout<<hex<<setw(5)<<11<<endl;
9   }
10
11  int main()
12  {
13      cout<<setw(20)<<"C++ FORMATTING"<<endl;
14      cout<<"Integer numbers:\n";
15      cout<<173<<endl;
16      print();
17      cout<<setiosflags(ios::left|ios::uppercase);
18      cout<<setw(6)<<15<<dec<<15<<endl;
19      cout<<"\nFloating point numbers:"<<endl;
20      cout<<resetiosflags(ios::left);
21      cout<<setiosflags(ios::fixed|ios::showpos);
22      cout<<setprecision(2)<<setw(15)<<123.6789<<endl;
23      cout<<setfill('*')<<resetiosflags(ios::fixed);
24      cout<<setw(15)<<123.6789;
```

```
25      return 0;
26 }
```

The ***main()*** function of PROG1_2 calls the `print()` function that sets a hexadecimal numeric base (line 8). An integer value of 15 is inserted into the output stream after the `print()` function is called and before the ***dec*** manipulator is inserted. It is therefore displayed as a hexadecimal value F (line 18). If a function inserts specific format control manipulators (with the exception of ***setw()***), the output produced by subsequent function calls will also be manipulated by these manipulators (unless functions insert their own manipulators). By default, numeric values and strings are **right-justified** within a field set by ***setw()***. The ***setiosflags()*** and ***resetiosflags()*** manipulators are used to change justification (i.e., set a new alignment or reset current; lines 17 and 20). These manipulators are also used to change a notation in which floating-point values are displayed. In this program, the fixed decimal point notation is set first (line 21). Resetting the fixed decimal point notation (line 23) sets the scientific notation. PROG1_2 produces the output shown in Figure 1.5.

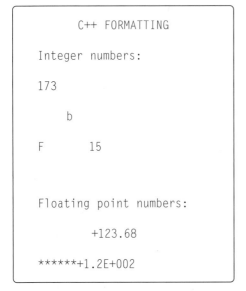

```
        C++ FORMATTING

  Integer numbers:

  173

          b

  F        15



  Floating point numbers:

          +123.68

  ******+1.2E+002
```

Figure 1.5 *Output produced by PROG1_2.*

The main advantage of C++ formatting (over C formatting) is that it only needs to be done once (except ***setw()***) in instances where all output values are required to have the same format. C requires that each value be formatted individually, even if the same format is used for all values. C++ formatting also provides more options than C formatting.

1.3 NAMESPACES

C++ provides numerous tools for programmers to assist in developing or maintaining large programs. Teams of programmers that produce source code in multiple files develop most real-life C++ applications. These files (modules) that may have been designed by different programmers are eventually linked together into the final application. When developing projects composed of multiple source files, errors may occur if duplicate identifiers (names of variables, constants, functions, structures, *typedefs*, etc.) are used in the same global scope that is shared by all modules. A function may be declared with the same name in more than one file, for example, causing an error when linking these files. C++ provides a mechanism called a ***namespace*** to prevent errors that may occur when linking multiple modules (source files and libraries).

The ***namespace*** keyword is used to group together logically related programming entities such as variables, objects, functions, and structures. Programming entities that are grouped within one namespace share a common **namespace name**. By using namespaces, a program can be divided into sections (scopes), each of which uses its own identifiers. The identifiers that are declared and used in one namespace will not be in conflict with identical identifiers used in another namespace. The general format of a namespace declaration is shown in Figure 1.6.

```
namespace namespace_name    {


        //body of the namespace


        //that contains declarations


        //and definitions


    }
```

Figure 1.6 *General format of a **namespace** declaration.*

The namespace mechanism is similar to structures in C that group together related variables. Unlike C structures that can contain only variables, however, namespaces can contain other programming entities as well—such as functions and classes—which will be introduced in Chapter 4.

Programming entities declared within a namespace are called **namespace members**. A namespace member identifier has a namespace scope; that is, the identifier is only visible within its namespace. As a result, there will be no conflict and an error will not occur if the same identifiers (variable names and function names) are used in different namespaces.

Please note that unlike a structure declaration, a namespace declaration is not completed by a semicolon. The following code fragment illustrates a namespace declaration:

```
namespace Sample {        //namespace declaration
       int i;
       float f;
       void display() { cout<<i<<f; }
       float getf() { return f; }

    }
```

`Sample` is the name (identifier) of this namespace, while variables `i` and `f` and functions `display()` and `getf()` are its members. If another `display()` function is declared in a different namespace and used in the same program as the `display()` function from the `Sample` namespace, an error will not occur.

One way of accessing namespace members outside the namespace is by preceding a member identifier with its namespace name followed by the scope resolution operator. For example, outside the `Sample` namespace its members can be accessed as follows:

```
Sample::i=33;
Sample::f=1.23;
float x=Sample::getf();
Sample::display();
```

A namespace should be given a name that has not been previously used as a global identifier. A namespace can also be **unnamed** (anonymous namespace). An unnamed namespace has no identifier.

 NOTE: All unnamed namespaces in one program share the same global scope within the same compilation unit. Duplicate member identifiers must therefore be avoided.

A compilation/translation unit (part of a program or an entire program) can be organized into as many different namespaces (scopes) as necessary, including a global (unnamed) namespace such as the one shown in Figure 1.7.

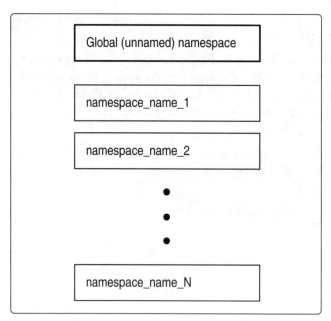

Figure 1.7 *Compilation unit consisting of multiple namespaces.*

A namespace can also be declared within another namespace (**nested namespaces**).

When used within an outer namespace, a member identifier of an inner namespace must be preceded with its namespace name followed by the scope resolution operator.

Program Example 1.3 demonstrates named and unnamed namespaces.

PROGRAM EXAMPLE 1.3:PROG1_3

```
1 //PROG1_3: Program demonstrates named and unnamed namespaces.
2 #include <iostream>
3 using namespace std;
4
5 namespace Circle {    //named namespace declaration
6     const double PI=3.14159265;
7     float r;    //radius of a circle
8     float a;    //area of a circle
9     float area(){ return PI*r*r;} //Computes and returns area
10    void print(){ cout<<"Area = "<<a<<endl;} //Prints area
11 }
```

```
12
13  namespace {     //unnamed namespace declaration
14     float a=0;     //total area
15     void print(){ cout<<"\nTotal area = "<<a;} //Prints total area
16  }
17  int main()
18  {
19     for(int i=0; i<3; i++)
20     {
21         cout<<"Enter radius of circle #"<<(i+1)<<" => ";
22         cin>>Circle::r;
23         Circle::a=Circle::area();
24         Circle::print();   //Calls print() from Circle
25         a=a+Circle::a;
26     }
27     print();                //Calls print() from unnamed namespace
28     return 0;
29  }
```

This program declares two namespaces—a namespace named Circle (lines 5–11) and an unnamed namespace (lines 13–16). Two identical identifiers are declared within both namespaces—a variable named a and a function named print() (lines 8, 10, 14, and 15). Duplicate identifiers are intentionally used in this program to demonstrate that an error does not occur if identical identifiers are declared and used in two or more namespaces that have different names (one namespace can be unnamed). Each time a member of the Circle namespace is used (accessed) in **main()**, this member is preceded with Circle followed by the scope resolution operator (lines 22–25). Members of the unnamed namespace are accessed in **main()** directly by using their identifiers (lines 25 and 27). A sample run of PROG1_3 is shown in Figure 1.8.

```
Enter radius of circle #1 => 1

Area = 3.14159

Enter radius of circle #2 => 2

Area = 12.5664

Enter radius of circle #3 => 3

Area = 28.2743


Total area = 43.9823
```

Figure 1.8 *Sample run of PROG1_3.*

Repetitive use of a namespace name followed by :: each time a preceding member of a namespace is listed is often not convenient, particularly if they are used frequently. To eliminate this redundant syntax, C++ provides the ***using*** directive, the general format of which is shown in Figure 1.9.

```
using namespace namespace_name;
```

Figure 1.9 *General format of the **using** directive.*

If the ***using*** directive with a specific namespace_name is placed at the beginning of a source code file, then all members of the specified namespace can be used in that file without preceding each member with the namespace_name followed by ::. Note that all previous program examples contain the following ***using*** statement after the ***#include<iostream>*** preprocessor directive:

```
using namespace std;
```

The ***iostream*** standard header file declares the ***std*** namespace. The entire content of ***iostream*** is defined within ***std***. Members of ***std***, such as the frequently used ***cin, cout,*** and ***endl,*** are therefore accessed as shown in the following code fragment:

```
std::cin>>x;
std::cout<<"VALUE ="<<x<<std::endl;
```

It is much more convenient to place ***using namespace std;*** at the beginning of a file rather than precede ***cin, cout,*** and all other members of ***std*** with ***std::*** each time these members are used.

The *using* directive can be used to specify individual members of a namespace that are going to be used in a file, rather than the entire content of the namespace. For example,

```
using std::cin;
using std::cout;
using std::endl;
```

specifies that *cin*, *cout*, and *endl* from the *std* namespace are used in the file. This eliminates the need for inserting *std::* before a member name when these members are used. Many programmers prefer this method, by which individual namespace members are specified rather than the entire namespace. To make the code smaller, however, the program examples in this book will use the *using* directive that specifies the entire *std* namespace.

In addition to built-in namespaces such as *std*, the *using* directive can also be used to specify user-defined namespaces, such as those demonstrated in Program Example 1.4.

PROGRAM EXAMPLE 1.4: PROG 1_4

```
1 //PROG1_4: Program demonstrates using directives.
2 #include <iostream>
3 using namespace std;          //predefined namespace
4
5 namespace Rectangle {         //user-defined namespace
6     float length;
7     float width;
8     void area(){ cout<<"Area = "<<(length*width); }
9 }
10 using namespace Rectangle;    //Specifies user-defined namespace
11
12 int main()
13 {
14     cout<<"Enter length => ";
15     cin>>length;
16     cout<<"Enter width => ";
17     cin>>width;
```

```
18    area();
19    return 0;
20 }
```

The *using* directive is used to specify the *std* predefined namespace (line 3) and a user-defined namespace named Rectangle (line 10). Be aware that using namespace Rectangle; must be placed after the Rectangle's definition (lines 5–9). Members of *std* (*cin* and *cout*), as well as members of Rectangle (length, width and area()), are accessed in *main()* without its namespace name and the scope resolution operator preceding them. A sample run of PROG1_4 is shown in Figure 1.10.

```
Enter length => 2.2
Enter width => 3.3
Area = 7.26
```

Figure 1.10 *Sample run of PROG1_4*

PROG1_5 is a modified version of PROG1_4 without the *using* directives. Members of the *std* and Rectangle namespaces, therefore, must be preceded with *std::* and Rectangle:: every time when used in *main()*, as in Program Example 1.5.

PROGRAM EXAMPLE 1.5: PROG1_5

```
1  //PROG1_5: Program demonstrates code without the using directive.
2  #include <iostream>
3
4  namespace Rectangle {
5      float length;
6      float width;
7      void area(){ std::cout<<"Area = "<<(length*width); }
8  }
9
10 int main()
11 {
12     std::cout<<"Enter length => ";
13     std::cin>>Rectangle::length;
14     std::cout<<"Enter width => ";
15     std::cin>>Rectangle::width;
```

```
16    Rectangle::area();
17    return 0;
18 }
```

 Tip: Using namespaces prevents errors when linking together code modules or libraries that declare identical identifiers (names of variables, functions, etc.).

 Tip: Use the *using* directive to reduce the amount of coding—i.e., to avoid redundant coding (preceding a namespace member name with its namespace name followed by :: when using this member).

SUMMARY

1. C++ provides new object-oriented programming tools to decrease the development time and improve maintainability of large programs.

2. C++ is more rigid than C and forces programmers to follow strict rules when writing code, thus preventing some types of errors.

3. C++ can be defined as a superset of C. Therefore, any C++ compiler can compile C programs as well with very few coding changes.

4. The programmers should check if the compiler they use complies with the C++ standard before designing programs.

5. In addition to C's commenting style, C++ also provides a new commenting style, in which each line begins with two forward slashes.

6. C++ does not require any extension for standard library header files, while a **.h** extension is required for user-defined header files.

7. C++ provides a data type named **bool** for the **true** and **false** Boolean values.

8. In addition to the C-style type cast, C++ also provides the **static_cast,** **const_cast,** and **reinterpret_cast** operators when performing typecasting.

9. C++ provides the scope resolution operator (::), which can be used to access global variables that have the same names as local variables.

10. C++ uses the **const** keyword when declaring constants. Unlike constants created using the **#define** directive, types and values of constants created using **const** can be checked.

11. C++ I/O methods are based on the use of input/output streams, objects (usually **cout** and **cin**) and operators. The stream extraction operator (>>) and stream insertion operator (<<) can be used to input/output values of any type, including user-defined types.

12. C++ provides a large collection of output stream manipulators to format an output. Numeric base manipulators (*dec*, *hex*, and *oct*) are used to set a numeric base for integer numbers. Character control manipulators (*endl*, *ends*, and *flush*) manipulate a sequence of characters. Commonly used format control manipulators are *setw( )*, *setprecision( )*, *setfill( )*, *setiosflags( )*, and *resetiosflags( )*.

13. C++ provides namespaces to prevent errors when linking together code modules or libraries that may declare identical identifiers (names of variables, functions, structures, etc.). A namespace can be named or unnamed (global namespace). Duplicate identifiers can be declared in two or more different named namespaces.

14. The *using* directive is used to avoid redundant coding. Placing the *using* directive with a specific namespace name eliminates the need for preceding namespace members to be listed with namespace name followed by the scope resolution operator.

EXERCISES

Identify and correct the errors in the code segments in Exercises 1.1 through 1.7.

1.1 `cout<<setprecision()<<x<<y;`

1.2 `cout<<"Enter a value";`

`cin<<x;`

1.3 `cout<<setprecision(4)setw(10)<<x;`

1.4 `cout<<setiosflags(ios::left,ios::fixed)<<x;`

1.5 `const char PLANGUAGE = "C++";`

1.6 `const int SIZE;`

1.7 `namespace sample {`

`    int a;`

`    print() { cout<<sample::a<<sample::b;`

`    };`

Determine the output produced by the code segments in Exercises 1.8 through 1.11. Assume default settings if not otherwise specified.

1.8   `cout<<setw(7)<<setfill('*')<<"C++";`

1.9   `cout<<setw(5)<<13<<hex<<setw(5)<<13;`

1.10   `x=2.3489;`
`cout<<setiosflags(ios::left|ios::fixed|ios::showpos);`
`cout<<setw(10)<<setprecision(2)<<x;`

1.11   `cout<<setiosflags(ios::uppercase|ios::hex);`
`cout<<11<<endl<<15;`

PROGRAMMING PROJECTS

1.1   Create a program that obtains the following values from the user:

a) an integer number

b) a floating point number

c) a string up to 20 characters long

The program should display the values entered using the following formats:

a) the integer number should be displayed as a decimal, hexadecimal, and octal value, left justified within a field, the width of which is 6.

b) the floating point number should be displayed with a +/- sign and two digits after the decimal point using the fixed decimal point and scientific notation.

c) the string should be displayed right justified in a field, the width of which is 25; unused spaces within the field should be filled with a $ character.

1.2   Design a named namespace that contains three variables used to store three sides of a box, as well as a function that computes and prints the volume of a box. Design an unnamed namespace, which contains two functions that compare three sides of a box and display the smallest and largest side, respectively. Create a program that uses all members defined in both namespaces.

1.3   Design a program that draws a rectangle based on the user's input. The user should enter the length and width of a rectangle, as well as characters that will be used to draw the borders of the rectangle and to fill the rectangle, respectively. A sample run of the program is shown in Figure 1.11.

```
Enter length and width => 10 7
Ender border and fill characters => C +

        CCCCCCCCCC
        C++++++++C
        C++++++++C
        C++++++++C
        C++++++++C
        C++++++++C
        CCCCCCCCCC
```

Figure 1.11 *Sample run of Program Project 1.3.*

CHAPTER 2

C++ FUNCTION ENHANCEMENTS

OBJECTIVES

- To introduce the advantages of C++ functions over C functions
- To become familiar with *inline* functions
- To understand default arguments
- To be able to use function overloading and function templates

CHAPTER CONTENTS

INTRODUCTION

C programs are designed as collections of functions (built-in or user-defined). Functions are the most important tool of the C language. C++ has enhanced this tool by adding new concepts such as function overloading, default arguments, and function templates. C++ programming also provides a new kind of function called the *inline* function. C++ is much more rigid than C when handling function prototypes, and its rigidity may prevent some types of errors. This chapter will address the advantages of C++ functions and discuss C++ function enhancements.

2.1 C++ PROTOTYPING

C is less rigid than C++ when dealing with **function prototypes**. Lack of rigidity within a programming language is a distinct disadvantage that leads to increased errors. A rigid programming language forces programmers to follow very strict rules when coding, thus preventing some of the types of errors discussed in this section. It should be noted that in C/C++ programming, function prototypes are required for all user-defined functions unless they are defined before being called.

A function's prototype provides the compiler with information needed to compile the program successfully. The prototype consists of the following three elements: the function's **name**, its **return type**, and a **list of parameters**. Identifiers for the function parameters are optional in the function prototype, however, a data type should be specified for each parameter. If the function's return type is not specified, both C and C++ assume type *int*. For this reason, the following three function prototypes are equivalent:

```
int calc(int x, float y);      //These function prototypes are
int calc(int, float);    //equivalent in C and C++.
calc(int, float);
```

The following are the differences between C and C++ when handling function prototypes:

- If no value is returned in the function definition, C ignores the *int* return type; that is, the *void* return type does not need to be specified if a *return* statement is missing.

- If no value is returned in the function definition, C++ requires the *void* return type.

- C treats missing parameters in the function's prototype as **unspecified**. If parameters are not specified in the function's prototype, any number of values (or no value) can be passed to the function when it is called.

- C++ treats missing parameters in the function's prototype as *void*—i.e., the function without parameters. No value can be passed to the function when it is called.

If C++ programmers want to create functions with an unspecified number of parameters of any type, they place ellipses (**...**) at the end of the parameter list. For example, if the function prototypes are given,

```
void fun1();
void fun2(int, …);
```

one should assume the following function calls:

```
fun1(8, 3.7,-1.3);       //No problem in C; an error in C++.
fun1();   //No problem in C and C++.
fun2(8, 3.7, -1.3 );     //A valid function call in C++.
fun2(1, "C++");     //A valid function call in C++.
```

C++ treats `fun1()` as a function without parameters, and `fun2()` as a function with unspecified parameters. An attempt to pass values to the function `fun1()` when it is called, therefore, causes an error in C++. When calling the function `fun2()`, any number of values of any type can be passed.

 Note: The first parameter in `fun2()` is specified as an integer, therefore the first value passed to the function should be an integer or an automatic type conversion may occur.

Variable-length parameter lists are used when passing different numbers of arguments to the function at different places in the program. There is little need, however, to use unspecified parameter lists in C++. C++ provides more efficient and enhanced tools (which will be discussed later in this chapter) to accomplish what is accomplished in C with variable-length parameter lists.

Considering the differences discussed so far, it is clear that C++ is much more rigid than C when handling function prototypes. It requires all elements of the function prototype to be explicitly specified. A request to create a function with an unspecified number of parameters should be explicit as well. The rigidity protects against possible errors.

C++ provides the following advantages over and improvements in C functions:

- Inline functions
- Passing references to functions
- Default arguments
- Function overloading
- Function templates

2.2 INLINE FUNCTIONS

2.2.1 USING C MACROS

The calling of a normal function involves a series of instructions that are processed by the CPU. These instructions push function arguments onto the stack, allocate local variables, return from the function, and keep track of the memory location where the program execution resumes. This function-call, run-time overhead decreases the speed of the program, particularly when the function is called frequently.

C offers a tool called a **macro** to eliminate the function-call overhead. The *#define* preprocessor directive is used to create macros. A macro can be implemented with or without parameters. The general format of a **parameterized macro** is shown in Figure 2.1.

```
#define macro_identifier(parameters) substitution_text
```

Figure 2.1 *General format of a parameterized macro.*

The macro parameters are enclosed in parenthesis and separated by commas. Unlike functions, neither macros nor their parameters have a type.

The preprocessor handles macros before the program is compiled. It simply replaces the `macro_identifier` with its `substitution_text` every time the identifier is used in the code. The process is essentially an **expansion of the macro** within the code. If a macro has parameters, they are replaced with actual arguments in the substitution text first and then the macro is expanded in the code. Consider Program Example 2.1, which uses macros.

PROGRAM EXAMPLE 2.1: PROG2_1

```
1   //PROG2_1: Program demonstrates parameterized macros.
2   #include <iostream>
3   using namespace std;
4   #define AREA(ln,wd) (ln)*(wd)          //Parameterized macros
5   #define PRINT(x) cout<<"\tArea = "<<(x)<<endl
6
7   int main()
8   {
9       float length=3.0, width=4.0, a;
10      cout<<"Computing the area of a rectangle:"<<endl;
11      cout<<"\nLength = "<<length;
12      cout<<"\tWidth = "<<width;
13          a=AREA(length, width);          //Macros are expanded here.
14          PRINT(a);
15      cout<<"\nAfter incrementing length and width by 1:"<<endl;
16      cout<<"\nLength = "<<(length+1);
17      cout<<"\tWidth = "<<(width+1);
18          a=AREA(length+1, width+1);     //Macros are expanded here.
```

E
X
A
M
P
L
E

```
19        PRINT(a);
20        return 0;
21 }
```

This program uses two parameterized macros called AREA and PRINT. They are expanded in the code as follows:

```
a = (length) * (width);            //Line 13
cout<<"\tArea = "<<(a)<<endl;      //Line 14
a = (length + 1) * (width + 1);    //Line 18
cout<<"\tArea = "<<(a)<<endl;      //Line 19
```

The output of PROG2_1 is shown in Figure 2.2.

```
Computing the area of a rectangle:

Length = 3           Width = 4             Area = 12

After incrementing length and width by 1:

Length = 4           Width = 5             Area = 20
```

Figure 2.2 *Output produced by PROG2_1.*

Please note that there is no semicolon at the end of the macro definition (lines 4 and 5). It is, however, needed in the code after the macro identifier to separate its call from the subsequent program statement (lines 13, 14, 18, and 19). Also notice that each macro parameter is enclosed in parenthesis in the substitution text (lines 4 and 5). It may seem unnecessary, but it is good programming practice to enclose all macro parameters in parentheses to prevent errors. Assume, for example, that the macro AREA is defined in PROG2_1 as follows:

```
#define AREA(ln,wd)   ln*wd
```

The output of PROG2_1, in this case, is shown in Figure 2.3.

```
Computing the area of a rectangle:

Length = 3           Width = 4             Area = 12

After incrementing length and width by 1:
                                                          Error!
Length = 4           Width = 5             Area = 8  ←
```

Figure 2.3 *Output produced by PROG2_1, when macro parameters are not enclosed in parentheses.*

It is obvious that the program produces an incorrect result. The area following incrementing length and width is equal to 8 in this case, instead of 20. This error is caused by the macro expansion in the code as follows:

```
a = length + 1 * width + 1;
```

The multiplication operator has higher precedence than the addition operator and the expression evaluates to 8. This type of a logic error is not easy to detect because macros are preprocessor directives and cannot be debugged interactively. Programmers should test their programs carefully when using macros.

If substitution text is longer than one line, a backslash should be placed at the end of the line and continued on the next line, as shown in the following example:

```
#define DISPLAY    cout<<"The program PROG2_1 is designed to "; \
                   cout<<"demonstrate parameterized macros.";    \
                   cout<<"\nInline functions are more powerful";\
                   cout<<" than macros."
```

Note that the macro DISPLAY used in this example has no parameters. It should also be noted that there is no semicolon after the last line of the macro. The semicolon will be used after DISPLAY in the code.

The primary benefit of using macros instead of normal functions is that the function-call overhead described at the beginning of this section is eliminated, which may increase the speed of the program. The size of the program may be increased as well, however, because a macro expansion causes duplicate code. Macros can also be a source of logic errors that are difficult to detect.

2.2.2 USING INLINE FUNCTIONS

While macros eliminate the function-call overhead in C, C++ offers a more powerful tool called *inline* **functions** to achieve this benefit. Unlike macros that are handled by the preprocessor, the compiler handles *inline* functions. The way the compiler handles *inline* functions is similar to the way the preprocessor handles macros—i.e., the compiler substitutes an *inline* function call with the function's code. To create an *inline* function, the *inline* keyword should precede the function's return type in the function definition, as shown in Figure 2.4.

The programmer's request to create a function as an *inline* function instructs the compiler to replace the function call with a copy of the function's code. The C++ compiler, however, may ignore an *inline* request and compile the function as a normal *non-inline* function. It should be noted that cases when an *inline* request might be ignored are discussed at the end of this section. Good candidates for *inline* functions are small, frequently called functions.

```
inline return_type function_name(parameter list)
{
    //body of the function

}
```

Figure 2.4 *General format of an **inline** function definition.*

PROG2_2 (see Program Example 2.2) is a modified version of PROG2_1, in which the macros AREA and PRINT are replaced with the ***inline*** functions area() and print().

PROGRAM EXAMPLE 2.2: PROG2_2

```
1   //PROG2_2: Program demonstrates inline functions.
2   #include <iostream>
3   using namespace std;
4   inline float area(float ln, float wd)      //inline function
5   {
6       return ln * wd;
7   }
8   inline void print(float x)   //inline function
9   {
10      cout<<"\tArea = "<<x<<endl;
11  }
12
13  int main()
14  {
15      float length = 3.0, width = 4.0,  a;
16      cout<<"Computing the area of a rectangle:"<<endl;
17      cout<<"\nLength = "<<length;
18      cout<<"\tWidth = "<<width;
19          a = area(length, width);      //area() is expanded here
20          print(a);        //print() is expanded here
21      cout<<"\nAfter incrementing length and width by 1:"<<endl;
```

```
22   cout<<"\nLength = "<<(length+1);
23   cout<<"\tWidth = "<<(width+1);
24      a = area(length+1, width+1);  //area() is expanded here
25      print(a);                     //print() is expanded here
26   return 0;
27 }
```

Notice that both *inline* functions `area()` and `print()` are defined before the ***main()*** function (lines 4–11). An *inline* function should be defined before it is called. The compiler **expands** an *inline* function (substitutes a copy of the function's code) at the location of each function's call in the program. For example, the statement that calls the *inline* function `area()`,

```
a = area(length+1, width+1);
```

is substituted with:

```
a = (length+1)*(width+1);
```

Extra parentheses are not required to enclose function arguments within the body of the function to ensure a proper *inline* expansion. Using *inline* functions prevents problems such as those previously discussed and shown in Figure 2.3. PROG2_2 produces the same output as PROG2_1, shown in Figure 2.2.

Inline functions have the following significant advantages as compared with macros:

- Programmers can debug them interactively in order to detect logic or run-time errors.

- Expanding *inline* functions is less prone to errors than expanding macros. Programmers do not require extra parentheses to ensure proper *inline* expansion.

- When handling *inline* functions, the compiler also performs all necessary data type conversions. The preprocessor is not capable of doing type conversions.

TIP: Use *inline* functions rather than parameterized macros to reduce the function-call overhead.

Inline functions, compared to normal *non-inline* functions, can reduce the program execution time—i.e., increase the speed of the program. A negative side effect of using *inline* functions is that inserting multiple copies of a function's code into the program can make the program larger. When choosing between *inline* or *non-inline* functions, programmers should consider the tradeoff between the speed and the size of the program.

The C++ standard does not require the compiler to accept *inline* requests. If the compiler does not comply with the *inline* request, it compiles a function as a normal *non-inline* function. Most C++ compilers generate a warning message to notify the programmer that the *inline* request is not accepted and explain the reason. The following functions are usually not expanded *inline*:

- Large functions
- Functions containing loops
- Functions containing *switch* or *goto* statements
- Recursive functions
- Functions containing *static* variables

Inline functions become very important when designing classes and object-oriented programs. These will be discussed in Chapter 4.

2.3 DEFAULT ARGUMENTS

A C++ function can have a variable number of arguments when called during run-time. It is accomplished by using ellipses (...) and an unspecified parameter list (discussed in Section 2.1), or more conveniently by assigning default values to the function's arguments. These arguments are called **default arguments** and they are specified in the function prototype, or the header of the function definition if the function prototype is not used. Values assigned to default arguments can be constants, global variables, or function calls. Default arguments can be used with both *inline* and *non-inline* functions.

A function can have all arguments specified as default arguments, as shown in the following example:

```
void fun1(char x='$', int y=1, float z=3.14);
```

The fun1() function has three default arguments, and may be called with zero, one, two, or three arguments, as follows:

```
fun1();                 //All defaults are used -
                        //same as: fun1('$', 1 , 3.14);
fun1('+');              //First default is overridden -
                        //same as: fun1('+', 1, 3.14);
fun1('%', 9);           //First and second default are overridden -
                        //same as: fun1('%', 9, 3.14);
fun1('&', 9, 6.28);     //All defaults are overridden
```

If a function has both default and non-default arguments, the non-default arguments must be listed first in the function's parameter list. *The default arguments must always be to the right of those specified as non-default arguments in the parameter list.* Some of the following function prototypes (or calls) that use default arguments are valid—others are invalid.

```
int calc(int a, int b=0, int c=1); //VALID function prototype
    x=calc(5);                      //VALID function call
    x=calc(5, -1);                  //VALID function call
    x=calc(5, -1, 9);               //VALID function call
    x=calc(5, , 9);                 //INVALID function call! ERROR #3
    x=calc();                       //INVALID function call! ERROR #2
void showError(int x, char * message="Memory allocation error!");
                                    //VALID function prototype
    showError(1);                   //VALID function call
    showError(2,"File opening error!");//VALID function call
    showError();                    //INVALID function call! ERROR #2
    showError("Division by 0!");    //INVALID function call! ERROR #2
void fun(float a, int b = 0, char c); /INVALID! ERROR #1
void fun(float a, char c, int b = 0);  //VALID prototype
```

These examples show the following common programming errors when using default arguments:

- ERROR #1: Placing a default argument to the left of a non-default argument in the parameter list of the function prototype
- ERROR #2: Not passing values to all non-default arguments when calling functions
- ERROR #3: Attempting to skip a default argument in the middle of an argument list when calling functions

PROG2_3, shown in Program Example 2.3, demonstrates a practical use of default arguments when solving the problem shown in Figure 2.5.

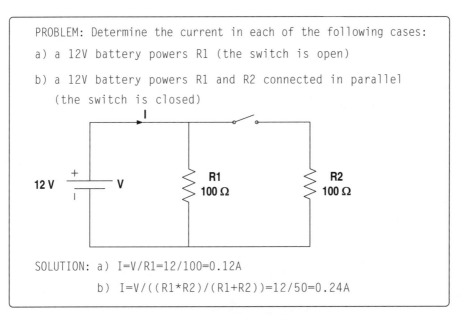

PROBLEM: Determine the current in each of the following cases:

a) a 12V battery powers R1 (the switch is open)

b) a 12V battery powers R1 and R2 connected in parallel
   (the switch is closed)

SOLUTION: a) I=V/R1=12/100=0.12A

b) I=V/((R1*R2)/(R1+R2))=12/50=0.24A

Figure 2.5 *Visual representation of the problem for PROG2_3.*

PROGRAM EXAMPLE 2.3: PROG2_3

```
1  //PROG2_3: Program demonstrates a use of default arguments.
2  #include <iostream>
3  using namespace std;
4  const float volt = 12.0;      //battery's voltage
5  float current(float r1, float r2=0); //Uses a default argument
6
7  int main()
8  {
9     cout<<"\t*** Device resistance = 100 Ohms *** \n"<<endl;
10    cout<<"\tSwitch open:   Current[A] = "<<current(100)<<endl;
11    cout<<"\tSwitch closed: Current[A] = "<<current(100, 100);
12    return 0;
13 }
14
15 float current(float r1, float r2) //Computes and returns current
16 {
```

```
17    float totR;          //equivalent resistance in parallel
18    if(r2 != 0)          //if r2 is not equal to default value
19    {
20        totR = (r1*r2)/(r1+r2);
21        return volt/totR;
22    }
23    else if(r1!=0)       //prevents run-time error
24        return volt/r1;
25    else
26        return 0;
27 }
```

PROG2_3 is used to compute the current for a circuit consisting of a 12 V battery and a device, or two identical devices connected in parallel (the switch opened/closed), for which the resistance is given. The battery first powers one device and then two devices connected in parallel. The program uses a function named current() that computes and returns current in both cases. The current() function uses a default argument for the second device resistance (line 5). This function is called first to compute the current for one device (line 10). The default value (= 0) for the second argument, which is used in this case, indicates that the second device is not connected to the battery. The current() function is then called in line 11 to compute the current for two devices connected in parallel. The default value of the second argument is overridden by a value of the second device resistance.

The practical use of default arguments in this example is to enable function calls with variable number arguments—i.e., to process a different number of devices by the current() function. The default value of the second argument is used as a flag to instruct the current() function to compute the current for either one or two devices. The output produced by this program is shown in Figure 2.6.

```
***Device resistance = 100 Ohms***

Switch open:    Current[A] = 0.12
Switch closed:  Current[A] = 0.24
```

Figure 2.6 *Output produced by PROG2_3.*

The solution demonstrated in PROG2_3 can also be used as an alternative to function overloading, which is discussed in the following section. C++ programmers should decide when it is appropriate and beneficial to use default arguments. Good candidates for default arguments are

- Arguments of frequently called functions that have the same value most of the time.

- Arguments used as flags when selecting an option. For example, if a default value is used when a function is called, it might instruct the function to use the previously selected option.

 TIP: Use default arguments rather than ellipses (...) when designing functions with a variable number of arguments.

2.4 FUNCTION OVERLOADING

Unlike C, C++ enables the same name to be used for two or more different functions. This concept is called **function overloading.** Functions that share the same name are called **overloaded functions**.

Overloaded functions require different parameter lists. The C++ compiler can overload two or more functions, if they meet at least one of the following requirements:

- Have a different number of parameters, as shown in the following example:

```
int fun1(int);
int fun1(int, float);
int fun1(int, float, int);
```

- Have the same number of parameters, then:

    a. Parameter types should be in a different order, as in:

```
void fun2(char, int, float);
void fun2(int, char, float);
void fun2(float, char, int);
```

    b. At least one parameter type should be different, as in:

```
void fun3(int, char);
void fun3(double, char);
```

It is not possible to overload functions by changing their return types. If two or more functions have the same parameter lists, they must have different names, although they might have different return types. The following, for example, is not a correct function overloading:

```
int fun(double, int);
double fun(double, int);
```

When using function overloading, the compiler checks the function's arguments on each call to determine which function to use.

In Program Example 2.4, PROG2_4 uses two functions to sort integer and floating point arrays, respectively. Both functions perform the same task and even use the same sorting algorithm. The only difference between the two functions is the **type** of array. It is therefore a good idea to use the same name for both functions.

PROGRAM EXAMPLE 2.4: PROG2_4

```
1   //PROG2_4: Program uses overloaded functions to sort arrays.
2   #include <iostream>
3   #include <iomanip>
4   using namespace std;
5   const int size = 10;
6
7   void sort(int arr[]);          //overloaded function
8   void sort(float arr[]);
9
10  int main()
11  {
12      int nums1[size]={3,9,1,-5,0,1,-3,4,6,7};
13      float nums2[size]={9.1,-0.7,4.6,0.3,9.9,1.1,3.2,-1.2,6.7,-4.9};
14          sort(nums1);           //Calls overloaded function
15          sort(nums2);
16      cout<<" Sorted   arrays:"<<endl;
17      for(int j=0; j<size; j++)
18              cout<<setw(5)<<nums1[j]<<setw(8)<<nums2[j]<<endl;
19      return 0;
20  }
21  void sort(int arr[])           //Sorts an integer array
22  {
23          int temp;
24          for(int j =1; j<size; j++)
25              for(int k =0; k<size-1; k++)
26                  if(arr[k]>arr[k+1])
```

```
27                     {
28                         temp = arr[k];
29                         arr[k] = arr[k+1];
30                         arr[k+1] = temp;
31                     }
32 }
33
34 void sort(float arr[])        //Sorts a floating-point array
35 {
36    float temp;
37    for(int j =1; j<size; j++)
38       for(int k =0; k<size-1; k++)
39          if(arr[k]>arr[k+1])
40          {
41                temp = arr[k];
42                arr[k] = arr[k+1];
43                arr[k+1] = temp;
44          }
45 }
```

This program declares and initializes an integer array nums1 (line 12) and a floating point array nums2 (line 13). It then calls the overloaded sort() function and first passes nums1 (line 14) and then nums2 (line 15) to the function. The compiler checks the array type to determine which version of the overloaded function to use. The program at the end displays both arrays in ascending order, as shown in Figure 2.7.

```
        Sorted arrays:

          -5        -4.9
          -3        -1.2
           0        -0.7
           1         0.3
           1         1.1
           3         3.2
           4         4.6
           6         6.7
           7         9.1
           9         9.9
```

Figure 2.7 *Output produced by PROG2_4.*

The C++ compiler uses **function name mangling** to implement function overloading. The compiler creates a function's **signature** and uses that signature to identify the function. A function's signature is usually a combination of the function's name used in the source code to identify the function and the letters representing its parameter types. There is no standard for function name mangling. Different compilers might perform function name mangling in different ways.

When overloaded functions are called in a program, the compiler checks the number of arguments and their types on each call. It then searches for a function's signature that matches that argument list in order to know which version of the overloaded function to use. If the compiler is *confused* when deciding which version of the overloaded function to use, it produces an error message. There are several possible sources of **ambiguity** *(or compiler confusion)* when using function overloading. The most common sources of ambiguity are

- Automatic type conversions
- Using default arguments
- Using references as function parameters
- Calling overloaded functions

 NOTE: Ambiguity must be eliminated in order to compile a program successfully.

The following examples demonstrate ambiguity when using function overloading:

```
//Functions fun1() and fun2() are overloaded as follows:
```

```
    void fun1(float);
    void fun1(double);
    void fun2(int=1);
    void fun2();
//Assume these declarations:
    int x=3;
    float y=4.4;
    double z=5.5555;
//Calling overloaded functions:
    fun1(y);    //Valid call; fun1(float) is called
    fun1(z);    //Valid call; fun1(double) is called
    fun1(x);    //Ambiguity: x can be converted to float or double
    fun2(x);    //Valid call; fun2(int) is called
    fun2();     //Ambiguity: default argument can be used
```

The fun1() function is overloaded properly, because its parameter is of a different type in each version—i.e., types *float* and *double*, respectively. When this function is called and an argument of either of these two types is passed, the compiler is able to call a correct version of fun1(). If the function is called and an integer value is passed, however, it causes ambiguity because the integer value could be converted to either type *float* or type *double*. The compiler does not know which version of fun1() to use.

The fun2() function is overloaded properly because the first version of fun2() has an integer parameter, while the second version has no parameters. Please note that the first version can also use a default argument. This causes ambiguity if fun2() is called and no value is passed to it. The compiler does not know which version of fun2() to select because the first version uses the default value in this case and the second version does not need any value. If fun2() is called and an integer value passed, there is no ambiguity because only the first version of the function can be used.

Function overloading is a powerful programming tool. It may reduce the complexity of a program, particularly of large programs. When designing functions in C that perform identical operations on different data types, different functions must be created for each type and each function must have a different name. This adds complexity to the program because programmers must remember several functions' names. In C++, only one function name needs to be used, leaving the compiler to select the correct version of the function. Function overloading is widely used when designing C++ classes and object-oriented programs.

 TIP: It is not good programming practice to use the same name for functions that perform logically different operations.

2.5 FUNCTION TEMPLATES

Function overloading is commonly used when designing functions that perform similar operations. These functions should operate on either a different number of arguments or different data types. PROG2_4 demonstrates function overloading and uses two versions of the overloaded sort() function. Both versions apply the same programming logic to perform identical operations on different data types. C++ offers a more efficient and convenient tool called a **function template** to solve problems similar to that illustrated in PROG2_4.

A function template serves as a function pattern, which defines a set of operations that can be applied to different data types. It uses user-defined identifiers instead of specific data types. When a function defined as a template is called, arguments of specific data types are passed to it. The compiler automatically generates a complete version of the function that operates on that specific set of data types. A function that the compiler generates using a function template is called an **instance** of the function template or a **template function**.

To design a function template, the general format shown in Figure 2.8 is used. A function template definition begins with keyword *template*. It is followed by angle brackets (< >) used to enclose a list of function **formal type parameters**. Each formal type parameter in the list must be preceded by either the *class* or *typename* keyword and separated by a comma. Spacing between an angle bracket and a function's return type, as well as the *template* keyword is optional.

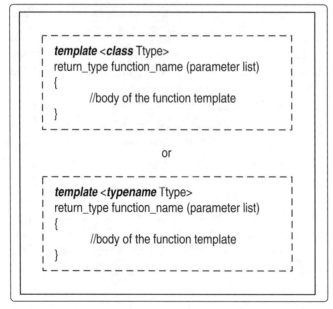

Figure 2.8 *General format of function templates.*

`Ttype` is a formal type parameter that serves as a placeholder for a specific data type. Any valid C++ identifier can be used to name a formal type parameter. When the compiler generates a template function—i.e., an instance of the function template— it replaces all formal type parameters throughout the function with actual data types used in the function call.

As shown in Program Example 2.5, PROG2_5 is an improved version of PROG2_4, which uses a function template instead of the overloaded `sort()` function.

PROGRAM EXAMPLE 2.5: PROG2_5

```
1  //PROG2_5: Program demonstrates a use of a function template
2  //to sort arrays of different types.
3  #include <iostream>
4  #include <iomanip>
5  using namespace std;
6  const int size = 10;
7
8  template<class arrType>       //Function template definition
9  void sort(arrType arr[])
10 {
11    arrType temp;
12    for(int j =1; j<size; j++)
13       for(int k=0; k<size-1; k++)
14           if(arr[k]>arr[k+1])
15           {
16                 temp = arr[k];
17                 arr[k] = arr[k+1];
18                 arr[k+1] = temp;
19           }
20 }
21 int main()
22 {
23 int nums1[size]={ 3,9,1,-5,0,1,-3,4,6,7 };
24 float nums2[size]={9.1,-0.7,4.6,0.3,9.9,1.1,3.2,-1.2,6.7,-4.9};
25    sort(nums1);                //template function call
```

```
26    sort(nums2);                    //template function call
27 cout<<" Sorted   arrays:"<<endl;
28 for(int j=0; j<size; j++)
29    cout<<setw(5)<<nums1[j]<<setw(8)<<nums2[j]<<endl;
30 return 0;
31 }
```

The `sort()` function template is designed as a general procedure that can be used to sort arrays of different data types such as *char*, *int*, *float*, *double*, etc. It is first used in *main()* to sort an integer array `nums1` (line 25) and then a floating point array `nums2` (line 26). The compiler automatically generates two template functions and replaces a formal type parameter `arrType` with the *int* and *float* types, respectively.

PROG2_5 produces the same output as PROG2_4 shown in Figure 2.7. Please note that the formal type parameter `arrType` is used in this example as a placeholder for an array type in the function parameter list and as a placeholder for a data type of a local variable `temp`.

In general, the formal type parameters can be used as placeholders for

- A function's return type
- Data types of function parameters
- Data types of local variables

Note that the function template in PROG2_5 uses only one formal type parameter. A list of formal type parameters, however, may include as many type parameters as needed. Consider the following example:

```
template <class T1, class T2, class T3>
T1 fun(T1 x, T2 y, T3 z);
```

A function template called `fun()` in this example uses three formal type parameters T1, T2, and T3. It may be called as follows:

```
double a=1.3333;
float b=7.3;
int c=8;
a=fun(a, b, c);    //template function call
cout<<fun(c, b, a);//template function call
```

Note that the compiler automatically generates two instances of the function template `fun()`, because the argument list types are different on each call.

A function template overloads itself automatically relative to a specific set of data types. However, it may be overloaded explicitly in a manner similar to normal functions. If a function template is overloaded, it means that there is a non-template function that shares the same name with the function template. This non-template function overrides or hides the template for that specific argument list. PROG2_6, shown here in Program Example 2.6, demonstrates function template overloading.

PROGRAM EXAMPLE 2.6: PROG2_6

```
1  //PROG2_6: Program demonstrates function template overloading.
2  #include <iostream>
3  #include <iomanip>
4  using namespace std;
5
6  template<class vType> //function template
7  void display(vType x)
8  {
9     cout<<"  X = ";
10    cout<<setw(8)<<x<<endl;
11 }
12
13 void display(char c) //Overloads function template
14 {
15    cout<<'*'<<c;
16 }
17
18 int main()
19 {
20    char *cp = "TEMPLATE";
21    int a = 3;
22    float b = 5.6;
23    double c = 1.3333;
24
25    for(int i = 0; i<8; i++)
26        display(cp[i]); //Calls function that overrides template
```

```
27
28    cout<<'*'<<endl;
29    display(a);   //Calls template function, version #1.
30    display(b);   //Calls template function, version #2.
31    display(c);   //Calls template function, version #3.
32    return 0;
33 }
```

This program uses a function template named display() (lines 6–11). The template has a formal type parameter vType, which can be replaced with any type when a template function is called. The program also uses a normal non-template function with the same name display() (lines 13–16). The non-template function has a parameter of type *char*. If display() is called with an actual argument of type *char* (line 26), it invokes the non-template function that overloads the function template for this particular type. If display() is called with an argument of any other type, such as *int*, *float*, or *double* as shown in this example (lines 29–31), the compiler automatically generates and invokes a correct version of a template function. The program produces the output shown in Figure 2.9.

```
*T*E*M*P*L*A*T*E*
        X =         3
        X =       5.6
        X = 1.3333
```

Figure 2.9 *Output produced by PROG2_6.*

 NOTE: A list of the formal type parameters of a function template may include built-in types in addition to the user-defined types.

The use of function templates is the preferred approach over explicit function overloading because this approach implements function overloading automatically and saves programming time when coding. It also reduces the size of the source code. A function template may be overloaded if it is needed to define a specific operation that differs from the general operation that the template defines. The same concept that is used to design function templates can be used to design **class templates** as well. Class templates are discussed in greater detail in Chapter 10.

C++ enhancements such as *inline* functions, default arguments, function overloading, and function templates make C++ functions more powerful and efficient than C functions. Additional C++ function advantages, such as passing references to functions or returning references from functions, are discussed in the next chapter.

SUMMARY

1. C++ is more stringent than C when handling function prototypes. It requires all elements of a function's prototype to be specified explicitly. This strictness may protect programs against some errors.

2. Calling a normal function causes run-time overhead, which may decrease the speed of a program. C++ offers *inline* functions that are more powerful than macros in C to eliminate the function-call overhead.

3. The compiler replaces an *inline* function call with a copy of the function's code. When using *inline* functions, programmers should consider the tradeoff between the speed and size of the program.

4. Default arguments can be used to design functions that have a variable number of arguments when called at run-time. They should always be to the right of those specified as non-default in the parameter list.

5. Functions that perform similar operations may share the same name. These functions are called overloaded functions. They must differ by their parameter lists.

6. The compiler uses function name mangling when overloading functions. It creates function signatures.

7. There might be several sources of ambiguity when using overloaded functions. Ambiguity must be eliminated in order to compile programs successfully.

8. When designing functions that perform identical operations on different data types, function templates should be used.

9. The compiler uses a function template to generate a correct version of a template function—i.e., an instance of the function template. It substitutes formal type parameters used in the function template by specific data types passed to the function when it is called.

10. A function template may be overloaded by a non-template function in order to define a specific operation that differs from the general operation that the template defines.

EXERCISE

EXERCISES

Define *inline* functions that can replace macros in Exercises 2.1 through 2.5.

2.1 `#define PERIMETER(width,length) (2*(width)+ 2*(length))`

2.2 #define PRINT(width, length) cout<<"Width = "; \
            cout<<setw(5)<<(width)<<endl<<"Length = "; \
            cout<<setw(5)<<(length)<<endl

2.3 #define MAX(x,y) (x)>(y)?(x):(y)

2.4 #define PAUSE cout<<"Hit any key to continue!"; getch( )

2.5 #define MAGNITUDE(x,y) sqrt(x*x+y*y)

Design prototypes of the functions that can overload functions given in Exercises 2.6 through 2.9, and change one argument to a default argument.

2.6 int fun1(int, float);

2.7 void fun2(char, int, float);

2.8 float fun3(double, double);

2.9 void fun4(int, int, char *);

The function prototypes or calls in Exercises 2.10 through 2.15 may contain errors. Identify the errors, if any.

2.10 fun1(float, int=0);   //function prototype

2.11 void fun2(int, …);   //function prototype
        fun2();   //function call #1
        fun2(3, "C/C++");   //function call #2
        fun2(-1, '$', 3.9);   //function call #3

2.12 int fun3(int, float=0, float);   //function prototype

2.13 double fun4(int, float=0);   //function prototype
        cout<<fun4(1);   //function call #1
        double x = fun4(1, 3.3)   //function call #2
        double y = fun4();   //function call #3

2.14
```
void display(char *course = "C++"); //function prototype
    display();                  //function call #1
    display('C');               //function call #2
    display("JAVA");            //function call #3
```

2.15
```
int fun5(float, int=0);      //function prototype #1
int fun5(float);             //function prototype #2
int fun5(int);               //function prototype #3
```

Design function templates for the functions in Exercises 2.16 through 2.20. Use formal type parameters where appropriate.

2.16
```
float magnitude(float x, float y)
{
    return sqrt(x*x + y*y);
}
```

2.17
```
int counter(float a[], float x, int n)
{
    int count=0;
    for(int j=0; j<n; j++)
    {
        if(a[j]==x)
        count++;
    }
    return count;
}
```

2.18
```
void swap(int *x, int *y)
{
    int temp;
    temp = *x;
    *x = *y;
    *y = temp;
}
```

2.19
```
float average(float a[], int n)
{
     float total=0;
     for(int k=0; k<n; k++)
          total=total+a[k];
     return total/n;
}
```

2.20
```
int maxIndex(double a[], int n)
{
     int k=0;
     for(int j=0; j<n; j++)
          if(a[j]>a[k])  k=j;
     return k;
}
```

PROGRAMMING PROJECTS

2.1 Modify PROG2_3 (see Program Example 2.3) and change both arguments of the current() function to default arguments. Let the user chose either default values of the device resistance or enter his/her own values. The program should compute and display a value of the current in each case.

2.2 Design two C++ functions that compute and return y for the functions $y=f1(x)$ and $y=f2(x)$ shown in Figures 2.10 and 2.11. Create a program that uses both functions to compute y for two sets of values of x as follows:

a. $-10 \leq x \leq 10$, increment = 1

b. $-5.0 \leq x \leq 5.0$, increment = 0.5

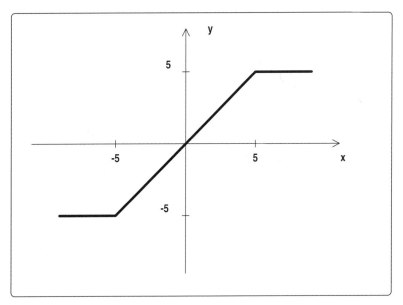

Figure 2.10 *Function* y = f1(x).

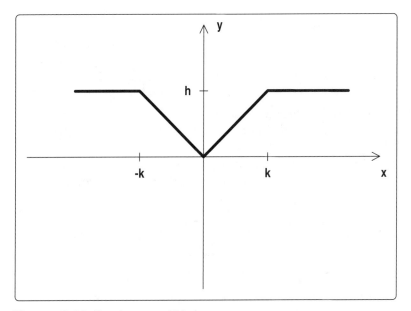

Figure 2.11 *Function* y = f2(x).

Note that the parameters h and k for the function f2(x) should be specified by the user. The program should display the values of x and corresponding values of y for both functions in a table like format. It is required to use at least one of the C++ function enhancements discussed in this chapter.

2.3 Design a C++ function that computes and returns y for the function y=f(x) shown in Figure 2.12.

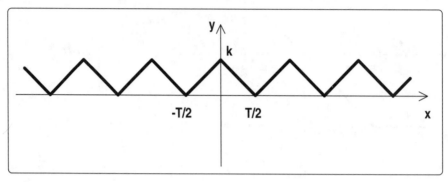

Figure 2.12 *Function* y = f(x).

Create a program that obtains the values of x and function parameters k and T from the user. The program uses the function to compute y for given x. It outputs the values of x and corresponding values of y in a table like format.

2.4 Design a function template that can be used to search an array for a value. The array and the value to be searched for should be passed to the template function. It may be multiple matches found as a result of the search operation. The template function should return the number of matches found. Create a program to test the function template and use arrays of types **char, int,** and **float**.

2.5 Design a program that can help to reduce the cost of floor tiling. Assume that only square tiles of the same size are used to tile a floor. The program should use the following **inline** functions:

    a. A function that computes and returns a number of tiles needed to tile the floor for given floor's length and width, and a tile's size (ln, wd, and s in Figure 2.13).

    b. A function that computes and returns the wasted area of tiles (the shadowed area in Figure 2.13) for given dimensions of the floor, the tile's size, and the number of tiles needed to tile the floor.

Assume that the tiles of three different sizes are available—for example, 10 cm, 15 cm, and 18 cm. The program should obtain the floor's length and width from the user. It should use **inline** functions to compute a number of tiles needed to tile the floor as well as the wasted area of tiles for each size available. The program should also compare the wasted areas and output the tile's size that produces the smallest wasted area. It should use a *non-inline* function to perform this task.

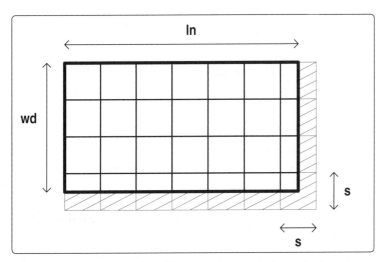

Figure 2.13 *Tiling the floor (the wasted area of tiles is shadowed).*

2.6 Design the following *Guess The Numbers* game. A 4-digit number should be guessed. Duplicate digits should be excluded. For example, 4018 is a valid number while 3319 is invalid. The player should guess a number randomly generated by the computer.

When the game starts, the player should enter his or her first guess. The program then displays how many of the guessed digits are correct and how many of them are in the right position. It helps the player to reduce the number of attempts to guess the number. The player keeps guessing until the number is guessed successfully or the number of attempts exceeds 10. The program should display an appropriate message at the end of the game and the number of attempts used to guess the number.

A sample run of the program is shown in Figure 2.14. Assume that the random number to be guessed is 4018.

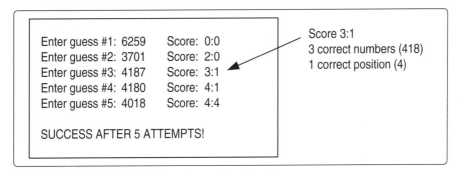

Figure 2.14 *Sample run of the* Guess The Numbers *program.*

A modular approach should be applied when designing the program—i.e., appropriate functions should be designed to perform all operations needed to solve this problem.

2.7   Design a function that uses the Trapezoidal Rule to approximate a definite integral:

$$\int_a^b f(x)\,dx = \frac{h}{2}\left[f(a)+f(b)+2\sum_{i=1}^{n-1} f(x_i)\right]$$

where $h=(b-a)/n$. Note that the interval $[a,b]$ is divided into n subintervals. The function should have the following parameters: the interval's endpoints a and b, and the number of subintervals n. As the number of subintervals increases, so will the accuracy of the approximation.

Create a program that uses this function to compute a voltage across capacitor at different values of time t. The capacitor voltage is given by the expression:

$$v_c(t) = \frac{1}{C}\int_{t_0} i_c\,dt + V_0$$

Assume that the value of capacitance is $C=0.1\,\mu F$, and capacitor current is given by the expression:

$$i_c(t) = 0.5e^{-t/10^{-6}}$$

The user should input the time interval $[t_0,t]$, initial voltage V_0, and number of subintervals n. The program should compute and display the values of capacitor voltage at different values of time within the specified interval.

CHAPTER 3

Pointers, References, and Dynamic Memory Allocation

OBJECTIVES

- To understand the differences between C and C++ pointers
- To be able to use references as independent variables and function parameters
- To be able to return references by functions
- To be able to use pointers and references with constants
- To understand the difference between static and dynamic memory allocation
- To be able to allocate, process, and deallocate dynamic arrays

CHAPTER CONTENTS

INTRODUCTION

C pointers are very powerful. At the same time, if they are not used properly they are prone to producing unpredictable results, including system crashes. C++ enhances C pointers and provides increased security because of its rigidity. In addition, C++ provides a new kind of pointer called a **reference**. References have advantages over regular pointers when passed to functions.

While Sections 3.1.1 and 3.1.2 provide a brief review of pointers, the reader should already be familiar with the basic concepts of C pointers. This chapter will emphasize the use of pointers and references in C++. It will also discuss the concept of dynamic memory allocation and its implementation in C++.

3.1 C++ POINTERS

3.1.1 REVIEWING THE FUNDAMENTALS OF POINTERS

A **pointer** is a variable that is used to store a memory address. This address can be a location of one of the following in memory:

- Variable
- Pointer
- Function

It is said that a pointer *points to* a variable, a function or another pointer. The major benefits of using pointers in C/C++ are

- To support dynamic memory allocation
- To provide the means by which functions can modify their actual arguments
- To support some types of data structures such as linked lists and binary trees
- To improve the efficiency of some programs

To avoid serious problems such as system crashes, it is very important to ensure that pointers are used correctly. A **pointer variable** is declared using the general format shown in Figure 3.1.

```
data_type  *variable_name;
```

Figure 3.1 *General format of a pointer variable declaration.*

A pointer type (data_type in Figure 3.1) specifies the type of variable to which the pointer points. This type can be any valid C/C++ type including *void* and user-defined types as shown in the following example:

```
int *ptr1;      //can point to any variable of type int
```

```
double *ptr2;    //can point to any variable of type double
void *ptr3;      //can point to a variable of any type
Robot *ptr4;     //can point to any variable of the user-defined
                 //type named Robot
```

 NOTE: A *void* pointer is a pointer variable that can point to a variable of any type, including user-defined types.

The following two operators are used with pointers:

1. **indirection** operator (*)

2. **address-of** operator (&)

The & operator returns the memory address of its operand. The * operator precedes a pointer and returns the value of a variable, the address of which is stored in the pointer. The following code fragment illustrates a use of both pointer operators.

```
float x=1.23, y;
float *pt;       //pt can point to any variable of type float
pt=&x;           //places the memory address of x into pt
cout<<*pt;       //prints the value of x: 1.23
```

The operation that the * operator performs on a pointer (accessing the value the pointer points to) is also described as *dereferencing the pointer*. A *void* pointer cannot be dereferenced, therefore the following code fragment produces an error.

```
void *pt1;       //pt1 is a void pointer
int *pt2;        //pt2 is an integer pointer
int x=3,y,z;
pt1=pt2=&x;      //pt1 and pt2 point to x
y=*pt1;          //ERROR! pt1 cannot be dereferenced.
z=*pt2;          //CORRECT! pt2 is dereferenced and the value of x
                 //is placed into z.
```

Pointer expressions comply with the same rules as any other C/C++ expression. Pointers can be used as operands in **assignment**, **arithmetic**, and **comparison expressions**. Please note that some operators are not used with pointers. The only two arithmetic operations that can be performed on pointers, for example, are addition and subtraction. The following code fragment demonstrates some pointer expressions:

```
float f=13.3;    //Assume: the address of f is 1000 and
```

```
                        //the size of float is 8 bytes
float *ptr1,*ptr2;
ptr1=&f;
ptr2=ptr1;           //assigning pointers: ptr1 and ptr2 point to f
ptr1--;              //decrementing ptr1
cout<<ptr1;          //The value of ptr1 is 992 (=1000-8)
ptr2=ptr2+5;         //adding 5 to ptr2 and assigning result to ptr2
cout<<ptr2;          //The value of ptr2 is 1040 (=1000+5*8)
if (ptr1==ptr2)   //comparing pointers by equality
    cout<<"Both pointers contain the same memory address.";
```

A pointer can point to another pointer, as illustrated in the following example:

```
float a=0.99, *b, **c;
b=&a;                //pointer b points to variable a
c=&b;                //pointer c points to pointer b
cout<<**c;           //dereferencing pointer c two times to access a
```

When declaring a pointer that points to another pointer, two asterisks must precede the pointer name.

In addition to accessing **array** elements using subscripts, array elements can also be accessed using pointers. Because an array name returns the starting address of the array (the address of the first element of the array), *an array name can also be used as a pointer to the array.* Figure 3.2 illustrates two different ways of accessing array elements.

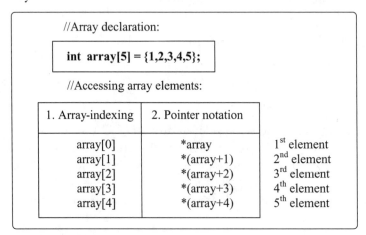

Figure 3.2 *Two ways of accessing array elements.*

Accessing array elements using pointers can be faster than array indexing.

A **string** is equivalent to a character pointer. Operations with strings are often performed by using pointers. The following code fragment demonstrates the use of a character pointer to process a string:

```
char   scientist[13]="Nikola Tesla";

char   *cptr;

cptr = scientist; //cptr is set to the address of scientist

cout<<*(cptr+2);  //prints the third character 'k'

cout<<cptr;        //prints the entire string "Nikola Tesla"
```

Pointers to functions will be discussed in Chapter 9 when implementing dynamic binding (late binding).

3.1.2 DIFFERENCES BETWEEN C AND C++ POINTERS

Although the concept and use of pointers is similar in C and C++, C++ handles pointers in a different and more efficient way than C. C++ offers extended features for enhanced implementation.

The most important difference between C and C++ pointers is that C++ is much more strict when dealing with pointer types. This is especially apparent in the implementation of *void* pointers. A *void* pointer can point to a variable of any type. Consider the following example:

```
int ivalue=13;

float fvalue=8.3;

int *iptr;

float *fptr;

void *vptr;

fptr=&ivalue;     //ERROR! A float pointer cannot point to an
                        //integer variable.

iptr=&ivalue;     //CORRECT

vptr=&ivalue;     //CORRECT

vptr=&fvalue;     // CORRECT

iptr=fptr;        //ERROR! A float pointer cannot be assigned to
                        //an integer pointer.

vptr=fptr;        //CORRECT

vptr=iptr;        //CORRECT
```

Both C and C++ do not permit the direct assigning pointers of different types. C can accomplish that indirectly, however, through a *void* pointer. For example,

```
mytype1 *ptr1;
mytype2 *ptr2;
void *vptr;
//Assume all pointers have been initialized at this point.
vptr = ptr1;
ptr2 = vptr;                // No problem in C; Invalid in C++.
```

In this example, `ptr1` and `ptr2` are pointers of different types and they are assigned to each other indirectly through a `vptr` *void* pointer. As mentioned earlier, C is not as strict as C++. It will permit the manipulation of data like that shown in the previous example. This kind of flexibility could become a source of errors. A C++ compiler will always produce an error message when assigning pointers of different types to each other through a *void* pointer. For the previous example, pointers of different types can be assigned to each other by using a **type cast** as follows:

```
ptr2 = (mytype2 *) ptr1;     //type cast ptr1 to match the type of
                             //ptr2 before assigning ptr1 to ptr2
```

The type of the `ptr1` pointer has to be changed to match the type of the `ptr2` pointer before assigning it to `ptr2`.

3.2 REFERENCES

C++ provides new kinds of variables called **references.** A reference is an implicit pointer that is automatically dereferenced. References also act as alternative names for other variables. They are easier to work with than pointers, as it is not necessary to use the `*` operator to get to a value, which is pointed to by a reference.

A reference can be used in three different ways:

- Created as an independent variable
- Passed to a function or
- Returned by a function

Passing references between functions is a powerful and very important use of references.

3.2.1 REFERENCES AS INDEPENDENT VARIABLES

References can be created as independent variables. To create a reference variable, the & operator has to be put before the variable name when it is declared. The & operator is an example of an overloaded operator. An overloaded operator performs different operations depending on the context of the expression in which it is used. This operator could be used as the *address of* or *bitwise AND* operator, as well as the operator that designates reference variables. The type of reference variable should be the same as the type of the variable to which it points. *If used as independent variables, reference variables have to be initialized when declared.* The general format of a reference variable declaration is shown in Figure 3.3.

```
data_type & reference_name = variable_name;
```

Figure 3.3 *General format of a reference variable declaration.*

Here is an example of an independent reference variable called `refnum`, which is declared as follows:

```
float num = 7.3;
float & refnum = num;    //There is no & before num.
                         //A space between & and refnum is optional.
```

The `refnum` reference is initialized to `num` and it acts as an alias for `num`. Any manipulation of the `refnum` reference (for example, changing its value) will also be automatically done to the `num` variable that it references. The example shown in Figure 3.4 demonstrates the differences between pointers and references.

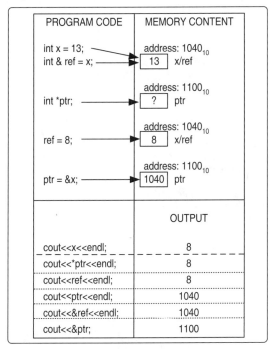

Figure 3.4 *References versus pointers.*

The code fragment uses a `ptr` pointer variable and a `ref` reference variable, both pointing to the same `x` variable. The `x` variable and `ref` reference both refer to the same memory location, whose address is 1040_{10}. Unlike the `ref` reference, however, the `ptr` pointer requires a storage space to store the address (1040_{10}) of the `x` variable to which it points. That storage space is at the address 1100_{10}. To get the value of the `x` variable, either the `ptr` pointer or `ref` reference can be used. Unlike the `ptr` pointer, the `ref` reference is automatically dereferenced. Note, there is no `*` *operator* used with `ref` to get the value of `x`. The most important differences between pointers and references, as well as the restrictions that apply to references, are shown in Table 3.1.

Table 3.1 Differences Between Pointers and References

RESTRICTIONS	Reference	Pointer
It reserves a space in the memory to store an address that it points to or references.	NO	YES
It has to be initialized when it is declared.	YES	NO
It can be initialized at any time.	NO	YES
Once it is initialized, it can be changed to point to another variable of the same type.	NO	YES
It has to be dereferenced to get to a value it points to.	NO	YES
It can be a NULL pointer/reference.	NO	YES
It can point to another reference/pointer.	NO	YES
An array of references/pointers can be created.	NO	YES

PROG3_1, demonstrated in Program Example 3.1, uses an independent reference variable.

PROGRAM EXAMPLE 3.1: PROG3_1

```
1  //PROG3_1: Program demonstrates a use of an independent
2  //         reference variable.
3  #include <iostream>
4  using namespace std;
5
6  int main()
7  {
```

```
8    int i = 13;
9    int &iref = i;              //declaring a reference variable
10   cout<<"The value is => "<<iref;
11   i--;
12   cout<<"\nAfter decrementing => "<<iref<<endl;
13   iref = 99;
14   cout<<"The value is now => "<<i;
15   return 0;
16 }
```

The iref independent reference variable in this example serves as another name for the i variable (line 8). These two variables are equivalent from a practical point of view. The output produced by PROG3_1 is shown in Figure 3.5.

```
The value is => 13
After decrementing => 12
The value is now => 99
```

Figure 3.5 *Output produced by PROG3_1.*

Because of the practical reasons and restrictions mentioned in Table 3.1, most programmers feel that there is no reason to use references as independent variables. They can also add complexity to a program.

3.2.2 PASSING REFERENCES TO FUNCTIONS

C++ supports the following three methods for passing values to functions: by **value,** by **address,** and by **reference.** When passed to functions, references have a clear advantage over pointers. Program Example 3.2 exhibits PROG3_2's use of a function with two references as parameters.

PROGRAM EXAMPLE 3.2: PROG3_2

```
1  //PROG3_2: Program demonstrates functions with
2  //          references as parameters.
3  #include <iostream>
4  #include <iomanip>
5  #include <cstdlib>
6  #include <ctime>
```

```
7   using namespace std;
8   const long NUM = 1000000;
9   const int RANGE = 100;
10
11  void odd_even(int x, int &ce, int &co)
12  {                        //references as parameters
13    if ((x % 2)==0)
14        ce++;
15    else
16        co++;
17  }
18
19  int main()
20  {
21    int num,i;
22    float perc_even;        //even numbers percentage
23    float perc_odd;         //odd numbers percentage
24    int counteven = 0;      //even numbers counter
25    int countodd = 0;       //odd numbers counter
26    srand(time(0));    //Initializes random number generator
27
28    for(i=0; i<NUM; i++)
29    {
30        num = 1+rand()%RANGE;//Generates a random number num
31        odd_even(num, counteven, countodd);    //Checks num and
32    }                        //increments even/odd counter
33
34    perc_even=static_cast<float>(counteven*100)/NUM;
35    perc_odd = static_cast<float>(countodd*100)/NUM;
36    cout<<setiosflags(ios::fixed)<<setprecision(4);
37    cout<<"The percentage of even numbers => "<<perc_even<<"%";
38    cout<<"\nThe percantage of odd numbers  => "<<perc_odd<<"%";
39    return 0;
40  }
```

A sample run of PROG3_2 is shown in Figure 3.6.

```
The percentage of even numbers => 49.9966%
The percentage of odd numbers => 50.0034%
```

Figure 3.6 *Output produced by PROG3_2.*

PROG3_2 generates a sequence of 1,000,000 pseudorandom integer numbers with a range from 1 to 100, and computes and displays a percentage of even and odd numbers in that sequence. This program could be used as a method to evaluate the efficiency of a random generator, which is frequently used in simulation programs. The program uses the `odd_even()` function with the references `ce` and `co` as parameters representing even and odd number counters (lines 11–17). The `counteven` and `countodd` counter variables are declared in *main( )* (lines 24, 25). They are passed **by reference** to the `odd_even()` function as well as an integer number generated by the random generator (line 31). The function checks whether the number passed to it is odd or even and increments a value of either the `ce` or `co` counter (lines 13–16). Changing the values of the `co` and `ce` references will automatically affect the values of the `countodd` and `counteven` variables in *main()*.

Passing a reference to a function is like passing the address of the variable used as the argument in the function call. When the reference is used within the function—e.g., `co`—the compiler automatically uses the `countodd` variable, which is referenced by `co`.

Reference parameters can be preceded with *const* to prevent a function from changing them inadvertently, as is shown in the following example:

```
void fun(const int &cref)
{
    cout<<cref/15;              //NO PROBLEM
    cref++;         //ERROR! Cannot modify a const reference.
}
```

In PROG3_2, pointers, rather than references, can be used as parameters of the `odd_even()` function without changing the logic of the program. To illustrate, the function could be defined as follows:

```
void odd_even(int x, int *ce, int *co)   //Pointers as function
{                                        //parameters
    if((x % 2)==0)
        *ce++;          //a pointer has to be dereferenced
    else
        *co++;
}
```

Because ce and co are now pointers, the * operator has to be used to manipulate the values to which they point. This is not necessary, however, where ce and co are references. In fact, it is illegal to use the * operator with references.

If pointers are used as function parameters, the function call has to be changed as well by preceding the arguments with the & operator. PROG3_2 illustrates this with the odd_even() function called as follows:

```
odd_even(num, &counteven, &countodd);
```

Although pointers as function parameters have the same effect as references, references as function parameters have several advantages.

- The code is cleaner, because it is not necessary to use the * operator.

- The programmer does not have to remember to pass the address of the function argument.

- Unlike passing with a pointer, no memory location is required and no copy of the function argument is made when using a reference. This becomes very important when objects are passed to functions (see Chapter 5).

 TIP: Use references rather than pointers when passing variables to functions by address.

3.2.3 RETURNING REFERENCES BY FUNCTIONS

A function may return a reference. This is particularly important when overloading some types of operators—e.g., *inserter* and *extractor* (operator overloading is discussed in Chapter 6). Returning a reference by a function also permits the function to be called from the left side of the assignment operator. Consider Program Example 3.3.

PROGRAM EXAMPLE 3.3: PROG3_3

```
1   //PROG3_3: Program demonstrates a function returning
2   //         a reference.
3   #include <iostream>
4   using namespace std;
5   const int SIZE = 6;
6
7   int & put_val(int a[], int n) //function returns a reference
8   {
9      if(n>=SIZE || n<0)
10     {
```

```
11          cout<<"Outside of boundaries!";
12          exit(1);
13      }
14      return a[n];
15 }
16
17 int main()
18 {
19      int array[SIZE];
20      for(int i=0; i<SIZE; i++)
21          put_val(array, i)=i*2; //function call is on the left
22      for(int j=0; j<SIZE; j++)
23          cout<<"array["<<j<<"] = "<<array[j]<<endl;
24      return 0;
25 }
```

The output produced by this program is shown in Figure 3.7.

```
array[0] = 0
array[1] = 2
array[2] = 4
array[3] = 6
array[4] = 8
array[5] = 10
```

Figure 3.7 *Output produced by PROG3_3.*

The put_val() function has two arguments—an integer array (a) and an integer value (n) representing the array index (lines 7–15). The function returns a reference to the a[n] array element. This reference is used in *main()* on the left side of the assignment statement (line 21), as follows:

```
put_val(array,i) = i*2;
```

This assigns a value to the array element specified by the i index. The statement above is equivalent to the assignment statement, which assigns values directly to the array elements, as follows:

```
array[i] = i*2;
```

The solution demonstrated in PROG3_3 uses the `put_val()` function to assign values to the array elements. This approach is less error prone than a direct assignment. The function `put_val()` checks at run-time that the array boundaries are not exceeded before it returns a reference to an array element. This prevents run-time errors such as array overflows or underflows (caused by assigning a value to an array element specified by the index that is outside of the boundaries of the array).

3.3 USING REFERENCES AND POINTERS WITH CONSTANTS

If the *const* keyword is applied to references and pointers, one of the following four types can be created:

- A reference to a constant
- A pointer to a constant
- A constant pointer
- A constant pointer to a constant

By preceding a reference type with the *const* keyword**, a reference to a constant** is created. It is a read-only alias, which cannot be used to change the value it references; however, a variable that is referenced by this reference can be changed.

Consider the following code example:

```
int x=8;
const int & xref=x;      //A reference to a constant
x=33;
cout<<xref;              //Displays 33
xref=15;       //ERROR! Cannot modify a reference to a constant.
```

The x variable in this example can be changed. However, its `xref` reference cannot be modified even though both x and `xref` refer to the same memory location. `xref` is a read-only reference and cannot be used to change the x variable that it references.

The following code example demonstrates the use of a **pointer to a constant**:

```
const double *pt;       //A pointer to a constant
double x=3.3, y=4.4;
pt=&x;
cout<<*pt;              //Displays 3.3
pt=&y;
cout<<*pt;              //Displays 4.4
```

```
    *pt=5.05;//ERROR! Cannot modify a pointer to a constant.
```

The `pt` pointer to a constant used in this example can store different addresses—that is, it can point to different variables. It cannot, however, be used to change a value, which is stored at the address to which it points.

A pointer to a constant should be distinguished from a **constant pointer**, which is demonstrated in the following example:

```
    int var1=15, var2=8;
    int * const cpt=&var1;    //A constant pointer to an integer
    *cpt=34;
    cout<<var1;               //Displays 34
    cpt=&var2;     //ERROR! A constant pointer cannot be changed.
```

A constant pointer can be used to change the value it points to; however, it cannot be changed to point to another value—i.e., the address stored in a constant pointer cannot be changed.

The following example demonstrates the use of a constant pointer to a constant:

```
    const int value1=11, value2=22;
    const int *cptc=&value1;     //A constant pointer to a constant
    *cptc=33;                    //ERROR! Cannot modify a constant.
    cout<<*cptc;                 //Displays 11
    cptc=&value2;
    cout<<*cptc;                 //Displays 22
```

A constant pointer to a constant cannot be used to change the constant value to which it points. It can, however, be changed to point to another constant of the same type.

A summary of the differences between these four types is shown in Table 3.2.

Table 3.2 Four Types of Pointers/References with Constants

Type/Feature	Reference to a Constant	Pointer to a Constant	Constant Pointer	Constant Pointer to a Constant
It can be changed to point to another value.	NO	YES	NO	YES
It can be used to change the value it points to.	NO	NO	YES	NO
The value it points to can be changed.	YES	YES	YES	NO

3.4 DYNAMIC MEMORY ALLOCATION

Managing memory efficiently is an important goal that programmers should aim for when designing their programs. A well-designed program will use only as much memory as it needs to at any time during execution of the program. The amount of memory available depends on the RAM physical limit, as well as the operating system used.

3.4.1 STATIC VERSUS DYNAMIC MEMORY ALLOCATION

Static memory allocation is a technique that uses the explicit variable and fixed-size array declarations to allocate memory. An amount of memory allocated using this technique is reserved when a program is loaded into the memory. If static/fixed-size arrays are used, a program could fail when running on some computer systems that lack enough memory, or the program could reserve an excessive amount of memory and make it difficult to run any other programs at the same time.

Consider the following example. Suppose a program needs to be written to process an inventory of computer parts. Assume also that the data needed for each part are stored in the following structure:

```
struct comp_part {          //a structure comp_part definition
    char code[7];
    char description[30];
    int on_stock;
    int sold;
    float price;
};
```

If the maximum number of parts to be processed is 100, an array that will store the parts data could be declared as follows:

```
comp_part  list[100];    //a static array declaration
```

The list array is an example of a **static array**. It allocates 100 structure variables that are fixed until the array goes out of scope. If only 10 parts are to be processed during an execution of the program, 90 blocks of memory are reserved but not used. On the other hand, if more than 100 parts need to be processed, there will be no space in memory available.

Dynamic memory allocation is a technique used to efficiently solve this problem. It is the process of allocating memory **at run-time**. A program that uses dynamic memory allocation allocates exactly the amount of memory needed during its execution. A region of memory called **heap** is used to allocate memory dynamically. It is a pool of free memory locations that are not being used by any program. Memory allocated in the heap during a program execution has to be returned back to the heap when the program is finished.

The C programming language uses functions such as ***malloc(), calloc(), realloc()***, and ***free()*** to implement dynamic memory allocation. C++ provides more efficient and convenient ways to allocate memory. In C++, the memory can be allocated and freed at run-time using the ***new*** and ***delete*** operators.

The general format of an expression that uses the ***new*** operator is shown in Figure 3.8.

```
new data_type;
```

Figure 3.8 *The* **new** *expression.*

In Figure 3.8, `data_type` is a type of a variable that is dynamically allocated. The variable type specified by `data_type` could be any built-in type or user-defined type such as `comp_part`, as defined in the previous example. The ***new*** operator allocates a block of memory in the heap, the size of which is equal to the size of `data_type`. The ***new*** expression is commonly used in an assignment statement, which uses a pointer variable (Figure 3.9).

```
pointer_var = new data_type (initial_value);
```

Figure 3.9 *General format of an assignment statement with the* **new** *expression.*

The pointer variable on the left side of the assignment statement in Figure 3.9 has to be of the same type as specified by `data_type`. The pointer is used to store the address of the memory block allocated by the ***new*** operator. It is also used to access the dynamically allocated memory block. An initial value is optional and it has to be put in the brackets. If the ***new*** operator fails to allocate memory as requested—i.e., there is not enough memory available in the heap—it returns a null pointer. This can be used to design an error checker for a memory allocation error.

The ***delete*** operator is the complement of the ***new*** operator. It is used to free all of the heap memory allocated by the ***new*** operator. The memory released by the ***delete*** operator is then available to other programs that are running on the same system, as well as the program that had been using it. The general format of the ***delete*** expression is shown in Figure 3.10.

```
delete pointer_var;
```

Figure 3.10 *The* **delete** *expression.*

Consider the following code example:

```
float *fpt = new float(0.0);    //Allocates a float variable
                                     //and initializes to 0.0
if(fpt==0)                      //Checks for a memory allocation error
{                                    //Can be changed to if(!pt)
    cout<<"Memory allocation error.";
    exit(1);
}
*fpt=3.45;                      //Uses pointer to access memory
cout<<*fpt;
delete fpt;                     //Frees memory allocated dynamically
```

In this example, an `fpt` pointer is used to store an address of a *float* variable allocated using the *new* operator. The variable is initialized to 0.0 explicitly by the *new* expression. An *if* statement is used as a memory allocation error checker. It checks for a null pointer (0), which is returned by the *new* operator if memory allocation fails. To access the newly allocated memory, the `fpt` pointer is used to assign or read a value. If the dynamically allocated memory is not needed, it should be returned to the heap using the *delete* operator.

When dynamic memory allocation is used extensively, which is common in large programs, an error called **memory leaking** may occur. This is a very common type of error and failing to prevent it could result in a memory resource problem. The following code fragment demonstrates a memory leak:

```
float *ptr = new float; //Allocates first block
*ptr = 7.9;             //Accesses first block
ptr = new float;        //Allocates second block
*ptr = 5.1;             //Accesses second block
```

A `ptr` pointer points to a dynamically allocated block of memory. It is first used to put a value into that memory block and then set to point to another block of memory that is dynamically allocated as well. The first memory block is not deleted, however its address is lost because the pointer contains the address of the second block. If the pointer is set to point to another block of memory without the *delete* statement that frees the previous block, it causes a **memory leak**. The program does not use the first block or return it back to the heap. Figure 3.11 illustrates this example.

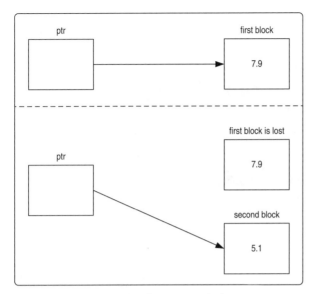

Figure 3.11 *Example of a memory leak.*

3.4.2 DYNAMIC ARRAYS

As opposed to a static array, in which size is fixed, a **dynamically allocated array** may have a variable size. At run-time (during program execution), the size of a dynamic array may vary in order to store exactly as many values as needed. Dynamic arrays are allocated in C++ using the ***new*** operator and deallocated using the ***delete*** operator in much the same way as single variables. After a dynamic array is allocated, it is processed in a manner similar to a static array.

 NOTE: As in C, an array name serves as a pointer to the array.

To dynamically allocate a ***single-dimensional array***, the general form of the ***new*** statement is used, as shown in Figure 3.12.

```
pointer_var = new data_type[size];
```

Figure 3.12 *Allocating a single-dimensional dynamic array.*

The size of a dynamic array can be specified by using an integer constant, an integer variable, or an expression, which is evaluated to an integer value at run-time. The amount of memory allocated to store a dynamic array, as specified by its size, may change each time the program is running.

To deallocate a dynamically allocated single-dimensional array, the form of the ***delete*** expression shown in Figure 3.13 is used.

```
delete []pointer_var;
```

Figure 3.13 *Deallocating a single-dimensional dynamic array.*

By putting the array subscript operator (**[ ]**) between *delete* and the array name, the entire array will be deleted from the heap.

Program Example 3.4 demonstrates the use of the *new* operator in PROG3_4 to allocate a single-dimensional array at run-time.

PROGRAM EXAMPLE 3.4: PROG3_4

```
1   //PROG3_4: Program demonstrates a single-dimensional
2   //           dynamic array.
3   #include <iostream>
4   #include <iomanip>
5   using namespace std;
6
7   int main()
8   {
9     int *ptr, n=10;
10    ptr = new int[n];   //Allocates an array dynamically
11    if(!ptr)            //Checks for a memory allocation error
12    {
13       cout<<"Memory allocation error!";
14       exit(1);
15    }
16    for(int i=0; i<n; i++)
17    {
18       ptr[i]=(i+1)*2;        //Initializes the array
19       cout<<setw(4)<<ptr[i];     //Displays its values
20    }
21    delete []ptr;         //Deletes the array from the heap
22    return 0;
23  }
```

Memory contents during execution of PROG3_4 are shown in Figure 3.14. The dynamically allocated memory state is shown before freeing (using ***delete***). The output is also shown. The addresses of the ptr pointer (1100_{10}) and of the dynamic array (3300_{10}) are assumed.

 NOTE: The size of integer, which depends on the compiler used, is assumed to be four bytes.

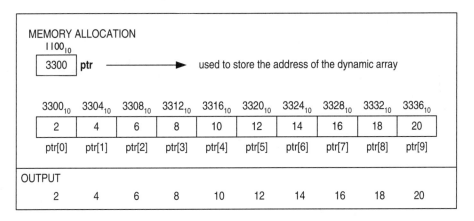

Figure 3.14 *Memory allocation and output produced by PROG3_4.*

In this example, an n variable initialized to 10 (line 9) is used to specify the size of the dynamic array. The pointer returned by the ***new*** operator and assigned to the ptr pointer (line 10) points to the first element of the array. The ptr pointer serves as the name of the dynamically allocated array, therefore the dynamic array is accessed and its values are processed through the ptr pointer (lines 18, 19). This program could be redesigned to set the value of n at run-time, based on input from the user, to determine the size of the dynamic array.

Program Example 3.5 shows PROG3_5 as a modified version of PROG3_4, in which the size of the dynamic array is determined at run-time based on input from the user.

PROGRAM EXAMPLE 3.5: PROG3_5

```
1   //PROG3_5: Program demonstrates a dynamic array, where
2   //the size is determined at run-time.
3   #include <iostream>
4   #include <iomanip>
5   using namespace std;
```

```
6
7   int main()
8   {
9     int *ptr, n;
10    cout<<"Enter how many even numbers to generate => ";
11    cin>>n;              //Gets the size of the array from the user
12    ptr=new int[n];      //Allocates the array dynamically
13    if(!ptr)             //Checks for a memory allocation error
14    {
15        cout<<"Memory allocation error!";
16        exit(1);
17    }
18    cout<<"\n\tEven numbers are: \n"<<endl;
19    for(int i=0; i<n;i++)
20    {
21        ptr[i]=(i+1)*2;
22        cout<<setw(4)<<ptr[i];
23    }
24    delete []ptr;        //Frees dynamically allocated memory
25    return 0;
26 }
```

A sample run of PROG3_5 is shown in Figure 3.15.

```
Enter how many even numbers to generate => 8

    Even numbers are:

2    4    6    8    10    12    14    16
```

Figure 3.15 *Sample run of PROG3_5.*

The *new* and *delete* operators can be used to allocate and deallocate **dynamic multidimensional arrays** in addition to dynamic single-dimensional arrays. Program Example 3.6 uses PROG3_6 to demonstrate a two-dimensional dynamic array.

PROGRAM EXAMPLE 3.6: PROG3_6

```
1   //PROG3_6: Program demonstrates a two-dimensional dynamic array.
2   #include <iostream>
3   #include <iomanip>
4   using namespace std;
5   void memError()
6   {
7     cout<<"Memory allocation error!";
8     exit(1);
9   }
10
11  int main( )
12  {
13    int rows, columns, i, j;
14    int **p2d;                  //Declares a pointer to pointer
15    cout<<"Enter a number of rows => ";
16    cin>>rows;
17    cout<<"\nEnter a number of columns => ";
18    cin>>columns;
19
20    p2d=new int*[rows];         //Sets up an array of row elements
21                                              //of pointers
22    if(!p2d)                    //Checks for an allocation error
23        memError( );
24    for(i=0; i<rows; i++)
25    {
26        p2d[i] = new int [columns];   //Sets up the columns
27        if(!p2d[i])             //Checks for an allocation error
28            memError();
29    }
30    cout<<"\n***MULTIPLICATION TABLE***"<<endl;
```

```
31    for(i=0; i<rows; i++)
32    {
33        for(j=0; j<columns; j++)
34        {
35            p2d[i][j]=(i+1)*(j+1);     //Initializes the array
36            cout<<setw(5)<<p2d[i][j]; //Displays its values
37        }
38        cout<<endl;
39    }
40
41    for(i=0; i<rows; i++)
42        delete [] p2d[i];      //Deletes the columns
43    delete [] p2d;            //Deletes the rows
44    return 0;
45 }
```

A sample run of this program is shown in Figure 3.16.

```
Enter a number of rows => 5
Enter a number of columns => 4
***MULTIPLICATION TABLE***
      1    2    3    4
      2    4    6    8
      3    6    9   12
      4    8   12   16
      5   10   15   20
```

Figure 3.16 *Sample run of PROG3_6.*

The program uses a pointer to a pointer called p2d to allocate a two-dimensional array dynamically. As stated before, an array name also acts as a pointer to the array—i.e., the array name points to the first element of the array. A two-dimensional array could be viewed as an array of single-dimensional arrays. To allocate a two-dimensional dynamic array, therefore, a pointer that points to an array of pointers is used. Each of the pointers that are elements of the array point to one row/array in the two-dimensional array, as shown in Figure 3.17.

When the program executes, it uses the p2d *two-star pointer* and the ***new*** operator to allocate an array of pointers—the number of elements being equal to the number of rows of the two-dimensional array (line 20). It then uses a loop to dynamically allocate the two-dimensional array (lines 24–29). The two-dimensional dynamic array is initialized and processed in a manner similar to a static two-dimensional array (lines 31–39). At the end of the program, the entire two-dimensional array should be deleted by deleting the array of pointers as well as the two-star pointer (lines 41–43).

3.5 CASE STUDY: LOTTERY RANDOM NUMBER GENERATOR

This case study demonstrates the use of the ***new*** and ***delete*** operators to allocate and deallocate a two-dimensional dynamic array, which is used to store any number of sets of randomly generated LOTO 6/49 numbers (6 numbers ranging from 1 to 49 within each set). It also demonstrates a method to process a dynamic two-dimensional array—e.g., check for duplicate values in each row and sort the values of each row.

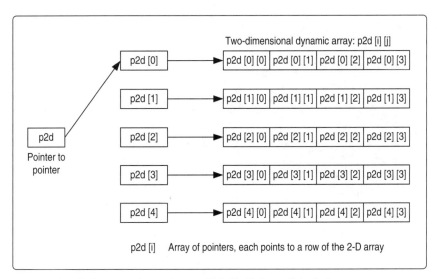

Figure 3.17 *Pointer relationships in PROG3_5 for a (5 * 4) dynamic array.*

PROBLEM DESCRIPTION

The program should randomly generate sets of tickets of six numbers ranging from 1 to 49, as requested by the user, excluding any duplicate numbers within each set. The program should display the numbers in a table format, sorted in ascending order within each set. The program should also check to see how many times a number chosen by the user occurred in all sets.

INPUT/OUTPUT

Requested **input** from the user:

1. A number of sets/tickets

2. A number to be checked for occurrences

Requested **output**:

1. A table containing randomly generated numbers sorted in an ascending order within each row

2. The number of occurrences of a user-chosen number

 NOTE: One row of the table represents one set of LOTO 6/49 numbers.

PSEUDOCODE

- **User-defined functions:**

1. void initArray(int ** table, int numSets);

    //INITIALIZES ARRAY BY 0s

    START

    I=0

    J=0

    FOR I<NUMSETS

        FOR J<COLUMNS

            TABLE[I][J]=0

            J=J+1

        END FOR

        I=I+1

    END FOR

    STOP

2. void genLOTO(int ** table, int numSets);

    //RANDOMLY GENERATES LOTTERY NUMBERS

    START

```
            I=0
            J=0
            FOR I<NUMSETS
                  FOR J<COLUMNS
                        DO WHILE IS_DUPLICATE() RETURNS 1
                              GENERATE NEWNUM (EXECUTE RAND())
                        END DO
                        TABLE[I][J]=NEWNUM
                        J=J+1
                  END FOR
                  I=I+1
            END FOR
            STOP
```

3. `int isDuplicate(int ** table, int rowNum, int newNum);`

```
      //CHECKS FOR DUPLICATE NUMBERS IN A ROW
      START
      I=0
      FOR I<COLUMNS
            IF TABLE[ROWNUM][I]=0
                  RETURN 0
            END IF
            IF TABLE[ROWNUM][I]=NEWNUM
                  RETURN 1
            END IF
            I=I+1
      END FOR
      RETURN 0
      STOP
```

4. `void  sortRow(int ** table, int rowNum);`

```
      //SORTS NUMBERS IN A ROW IN AN ASCENDING ORDER
      START
      I=0
      J=0
```

```
                FOR I<COLUMNS-1
                    FOR J<COLUMNS-1
                        IF TABLE[ROWNUM][J]>TABLE[ROWNUM][J+1]
                            TEMP=TABLE[ROWNUM][J]
                            TABLE[ROWNUM][J]=TABLE[ROWNUM][J+1]
                            TABLE[ROWNUM][J+1]=TEMP
                        END IF
                        J=J+1
                    END FOR
                    I=I+1
                END FOR
                STOP
5. void printLOTO(int **, int);
    //DISPLAYS LOTTERY NUMBERS IN A TABLE-LIKE FORMAT
    START
    PRINT "************ THE NUMBERS ARE : ************"
    I=0
    J=0
    FOR I<NUMSETS
        INSERT 2 TABS
        FOR J<COLUMNS
            PRINT TABLE[I][J]
            INSERT 1 TAB
            J=J+1
        END FOR
        INSERT NEW LINE
        I=I+1
    END FOR
    STOP
6. int numOccure(int ** table, int num, int numSets);
    //COUNTS A NUMBER OF OCCURENCES
    START
    COUNT=0
```

```
       I=0
       J=0
       FOR I<NUMSETS
              FOR J<COLUMNS
                     IF TABLE[I][J]=NUM
                            COUNT=COUNT+1
                     END IF
                     J=J+1
              END FOR
              I=I+1
       END FOR
       RETURN COUNT
       STOP
```

7. `inline void memError();`

```
       //HANDLES MEMORY ALLOCATION ERROR
       START
       PRINT "MEMORY ALLOCATION ERROR"
       EXECUTE EXIT()
       STOP
```

FLOWCHARTS

Figures 3.18, 3.19, and 3.20 show flowcharts of the *main( )* function.

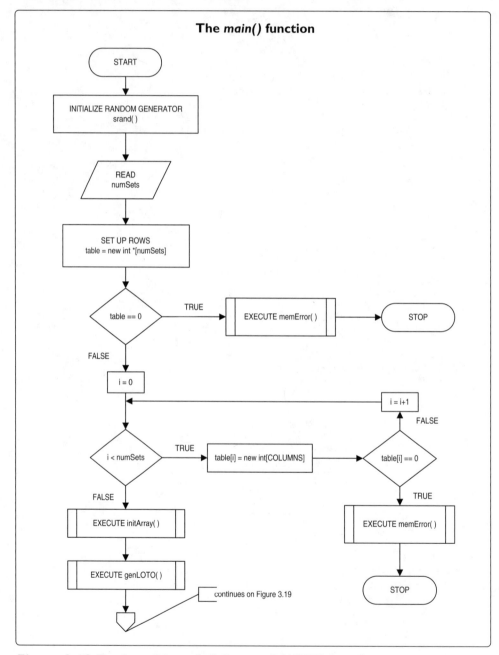

Figure 3.18 *Flowchart of the main( ) function of CASEST3 (part 1).*

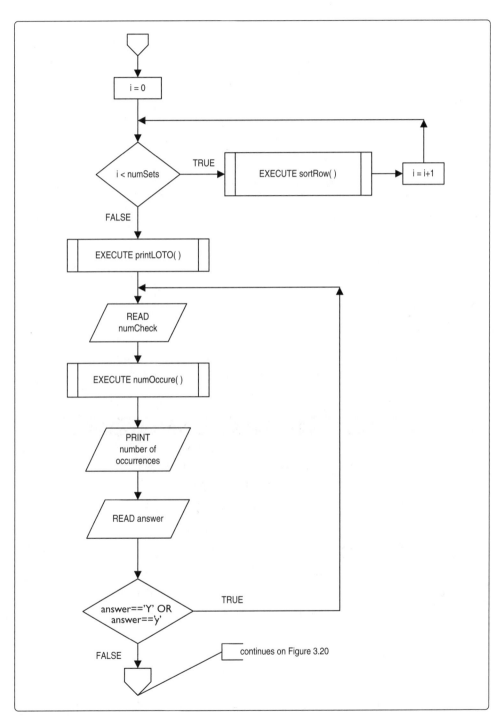

Figure 3.19 *Flowchart of the **main()** function of CASEST3 (part 2).*

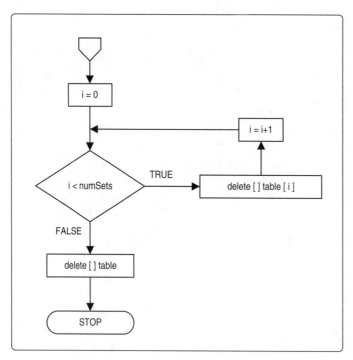

Figure 3.20 *Flowchart of the **main( )** function of CASEST3 (part 3).*

SOURCE CODE

PROGRAM EXAMPLE 3.7: CASE STUDY SOURCE CODE

```
1  //CASEST3: Program uses a 2-D dynamic array to store any
2  //number of sets of randomly generated LOTO 6/49 numbers.
3  #include <iostream>
4  #include <cstdlib>
5  #include <ctime>
6  using namespace std;
7  const int COLUMNS = 6;      //a number of columns
8  const int MAXNUM = 49;      //the largest number to be generated
9
10 void initArray(int **,int);       //Initializes array
11 void genLOTO(int **,int);         //Generates LOTO numbers
12 int isDuplicate(int **,int,int); //Checks for duplicate numbers
13 void sortRow(int **,int);         //Sorts a row
```

```
14  void printLOTO(int **,int);  //Prints LOTO numbers
15  int numOccure(int **,int,int);  //Returns a number of occurrences
16  inline void memError()  //Handles a memory allocation error
17  {
18    cout<<"Memory allocation error!";
19    exit(1);
20  }
21
22  int main()
23  {
24    int **table;      //a pointer that points to a 2-D array
25    int numSets;      //a number of sets/rows
26    int numCheck;     //a number to be checked
27    int i;
28    char answer;
29
30    srand((unsigned)time(0));  //Initializes the random generator
31    cout << "How many sets of LOTO 6/49 numbers? => ";
32    cin >> numSets;          //Gets the number of sets
33
34    table = new int *[numSets];       //Sets up the rows
35    if(!table)            //Checks for an allocation error
36      memError();
37    for (i = 0; i < numSets; i++)
38    {
39      table[i] = new int[COLUMNS];     //Sets up the columns
40          if(!table[i])     //Checks for an allocation error
41              memError();
42    }
43
44    initArray(table,numSets);
45    genLOTO(table,numSets);
46
```

```
47   for (i = 0; i < numSets; i++) {
48       sortRow(table, i);        //Sorts numbers in a row
49   }
50   printLOTO(table,numSets);
51
52   do{              //Checks for the number of occurrences
53       cout << "\n\nEnter a number to be checked => ";
54       cin>>numCheck;           //Gets a number to be checked.
55       cout << "\n\n\n   Number:\t\tOccurrence:\n\n";
56       cout << "\t" << numCheck << "\t\t\t";
57       cout<<numOccure(table, numCheck, numSets) << endl;
58       cout<<"\n\n\nAnother number to check? (Y/N) => ";
59       cin>>answer;
60   }while(answer=='Y'||answer=='y'); //Loop back if answer is y/Y
61
62   for(i=0;i<numSets;i++)
63       delete []table[i];           //Deletes columns
64   delete []table;          //Deletes rows
65
66   return 0;
67 }
68 void initArray(int **table, int numSets)
69 {
70   for (int i = 0; i < numSets; i++)
71       for (int j = 0; j < COLUMNS; j++)
72           table[i][j] = 0;          //Initialize the array by 0s
73 }
74 void genLOTO(int **table, int numSets)
75 {
76   int newNum;               //random number
77   for (int i = 0; i < numSets; i++) {
78       for (int j = 0; j < COLUMNS; j++) {
79           do {
```

```
80        newNum = rand()%MAXNUM + 1; //Generates a random number
81            }while (isDuplicate(table, i, newNum));
82            //Loop back, if the number is a duplicate
83            table[i][j] = newNum; //Stores the number into the array
84        }
85    }
86 }
87 int isDuplicate(int **table, int rowNum, int newNum)
88 {
89    for (int i = 0; i < COLUMNS; i++) {
90        if (table[rowNum][i] == 0)
91            return 0;
92        if (table[rowNum][i] == newNum)
93            return 1;   //Returns 1 if a duplicate number is found
94    }
95    return 0;    //Returns 0 if a duplicate number is not found
96 }
97 void sortRow(int **table, int rowNum)
98 {
99    int temp;
100   for (int i = 0; i < COLUMNS - 1; i++) {
101       for (int j = 0; j < COLUMNS - 1; j++) {
102           if(table[rowNum][j] > table[rowNum][j+1])
103           {
104               temp = table[rowNum][j];
105               table[rowNum][j] = table[rowNum][j+1];
106               table[rowNum][j+1] = temp;
107           }
108       }
109   }
110 }
111 void printLOTO(int **table, int numSets)
112 {
```

```
113    cout<<endl;
114    cout<<"\t\t********** THE NUMBERS ARE : **********\n"<<endl;
115    for (int i = 0; i < numSets; i++) {
116        cout<<"\t\t";
117        for (int j = 0; j < COLUMNS; j++) {
118            cout << table[i][j] << '\t';
119        }
120        cout <<endl;
121    }
122 }
123 int numOccure(int **table, int num, int numSets)
124 {
125    int count = 0;    //Counts a number of occurences
126    for (int i = 0; i < numSets; i++) {
127        for (int j = 0; j < COLUMNS; j++) {
128            if (table[i][j] == num)
129                count++;
130        }
131    }
132    return count;
133 }
```

OUTPUT

Output produced by this program is shown in Figure 3.21.

```
How many sets of LOTO 6/49 numbers? => 7
**********  THE NUMBERS ARE:  **********
    4      15      18      30      37      47
    1       3      15      21      22      47
    2       4      14      15      17      19
   22      28      31      42      48      49
    2      17      19      26      39      42
    6      11      17      18      37      49
    4       9      14      18      29      33


Enter a number to be checked => 13


   Number:               Occurrence:
     13                       0


Another number to check? (Y/N) => N
```

Figure 3.21 *Sample run of CASEST3.*

CONCLUSION

CASEST3 uses structured methodology and C++ dynamic memory allocation to allocate, process, and deallocate a two-dimensional array. The array is dimensioned as [rows]*[6], where the number of rows is specified by the user at run-time. The program demonstrates the efficiency of memory management when using C++ dynamic memory allocation.

SUMMARY

1. C++ is much more stringent than C when dealing with pointer types. It does not permit an assignment of pointers of different types to each other through a *void* pointer.

2. A reference is an implicit pointer that is automatically dereferenced. It can be passed to a function, returned by a function, or used as an independent variable.

3. Unlike pointers, references have to be initialized when they are declared. Once a reference is initialized to a variable, it cannot be changed to point/refer to another variable. Its address is the same as the address of the variable to which it refers. An array of references cannot be created.

4. If used as function parameters, references have several advantages over pointers. When passed to functions, they produce much cleaner and less error-prone code than pointers.

5. Returning a reference from a function permits the function to be called from the left side of the assignment operator.

6. If the **const** keyword is applied to references and pointers, it may result in one of the following four types: a reference to a constant, a pointer to a constant, a constant pointer, or a constant pointer to a constant.

7. When a program uses static arrays, it could fail if there isn't available memory to store the array. While statically allocating enough memory will prevent this, the program may use memory inefficiently by reserving memory that is never used.

8. A program that uses dynamic memory allocation allocates exactly as much memory as needed during its execution. A region of memory called heap is used to allocate memory dynamically.

9. An amount of memory allocated dynamically at run-time has to be returned back to the heap when it is not needed, or a memory leak may occur.

10. C++ provides a more efficient and convenient way to implement dynamic memory allocation than C. It uses the **new** and **delete** operators to allocate and free memory at run-time.

11. Pointers are needed to implement dynamic memory allocation.

12. A dynamic array may have a variable size unlike a static array, where size is fixed.

13. The **new** and **delete** operators can be used to allocate and free both single-dimensional and multidimensional dynamic arrays.

EXERCISES

Identify the errors in the code segments in Exercises 3.1 through 3.9.

3.1
```
int &refs[4]={1,2,3,4};
cout<<refs[2];
```

3.2
```
float f=3.14;
const float &fref=f;
fref=6.28;
```

3.3
```
int x=13;
int &ref1=x;
int &&ref2=ref1;
cout<<ref1<<endl;
cout<<ref2;
```

3.4
```
float x=1.99;
int &ref=x;
cout<<ref;
```

3.5
```
double v1, v2;
double *const dp=&v1;
*dp=1.33;
v2=0.66;
dp=&v2;
cout<<*dp;
```

3.6
```
int *ipt=new int(0);
 if (*ipt==0)
   cout<<"Memory allocation error";
```

3.7
```
float *fp;
fp=new char;
```

3.8
```
int **ipt=new int[x];
```

3.9
```
char stfun(char * pstr, int n)
 {
     int i;
     char *cp = new char[n+1];
```

```
            for(i=0; i<n; i++)
                cp[i] = pstr[i];
            cp[i+1]='\0';
            return cp;
        }
```

Determine the output produced by the code segments in Exercises 3.10 through 3.13.

3.10
```
int x=13;      //Assume x is stored at address 0x0064fe00
int &ref=x;
cout<<&ref<<endl;
cout<<&x;
```

3.11
```
int x=13;
int &ref1=x;
int &ref2=ref1;
cout<<hex<<ref1<<endl;
cout<<ref2;
```

3.12
```
void cube(int &x)
{
  x = x * x * x;
}
void output()
{
  int num = 2;
  cube(num);
  cout<<"The value of num is "<<num;
}
```

3.13
```
void fswap(float &x, float &y)
{
  float z;
  z=x;
  x=y;
```

```
  y=z;
}
void output()
{
  float a=2.3, b=3.4;
  cout<<setw(5)<<a<<setw(5)<<b<<endl;
  fswap(a,b);
  cout<<setw(5)<<a<<setw(5)<<b;
}
```

3.14 Fill in the missing code fragments where indicated in the following program:

```
//The program uses a dynamic array to store any number of
//values as requested by the user. It obtains the values from the
//user and then displays the largest value.
#include <iostream>
using namespace std;
float greatest(float *ptr, int count)
{
    float gr = ptr[0];
  int i;
    for(i=1;i<count;i++)
        if(ptr[i]>gr)
    //MISSING STATEMENT
        return gr;
}
int main()
{
    int num, j;
    cout<<"How many values? ";
    cin>>num;
    float *ptr = new _____;        //MISSING CODE
    if( _____ )                    //MISSING CODE
    {
```

```
            cout<<"Allocation error!";
            exit(1);
        }
        for(j=0;j<num; j++)
        {
            cout<<"\nEnter value #"<<(j+1)<<" : ";
            cin>>_____;                    //MISSING CODE
        }
        cout<<"\n\nThe largest value is: "<<greatest(ptr,num);

        delete []ptr;
        return 0;

    }
```

PROGRAMMING PROJECTS

3.1 Design a program that uses a dynamic array to store a number of resistors requested by the user. It will first obtain the resistor values from the user and then display all of the values sorted in descending order. The program will also compute and display the parallel and series resistances.

3.2 Given the following structure definition,

```
struct comp_part {
char description[10];
 int quantity;
};
```

design a program that uses the structure type above to store computer parts data. The program will prompt the user to enter a computer's part description and quantity. The user should be able to enter as many parts as needed. When the user chooses to stop the data entry, the program will display all of the parts entered, sorted by quantity in ascending order. The program should use dynamic memory allocation to allocate as many memory blocks as needed to store the parts data as requested by the user at run-time.

3.3 An ac current is described by the following equation:

$$i(t) = I_M \sin (2\pi ft + \varphi)$$

EXERCISE

where I_M is the maximum value, f is the frequency, and φ is the phase shift of the current. Design a program that simulates an analog-to-digital conversion. The program computes the current at various values of time t given in seconds for the number of time samples requested by the user. It should use a two-dimensional dynamic array to store the values of the current and corresponding values of time t.

Assume f = 60 Hz

The following input is requested from the user:

- the maximum value of the current I_M

- the phase shift φ

- the number of time samples within one cycle nt

The program should first compute a $tinc$ (time increment) and then compute the values of time t and corresponding values of the current for the required number of time samples.

 **NOTE:** $tinc=(1/f)/nt$

The program should output the values of the current for all time samples in a table format. It should also use the values of the current stored in the two-dimensional array to present the current graphically in text mode. An example of the output could be as shown in Figure 3.22.

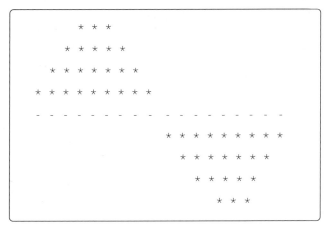

Figure 3.22 *Sample output produced by Program 3.3.*

 NOTE: In the example above nt =18. Each value of the current is represented by a corresponding number of asterisks.

3.4 A thermocouple is a device that converts temperature into an electrical signal. It is used as a sensor to measure temperature. Assume that the thermoelectric voltage measurements at various temperatures for a chromel/constantan thermocouple are given as shown in the following table:

Thermoelectric voltage values at different temperatures

Voltage (mV)	12.9	21.1	28.7	37.2	45.3	53.1
Temperature (°C)	200	300	400	500	600	700

Design a program that computes the coefficients a and b of a linear equation for this thermocouple by using the least-squares approximation. The linear equation is given as follows:

T = a * V + b

where T is the temperature, V the voltage, and a and b the coefficients that are computed using the following formulas:

$$a = (n * (\Sigma(V_i * T_i)) - (\Sigma V_i) * (\Sigma T_i)) / (n * (\Sigma(V_i * V_i)) - (\Sigma V_i)^2)$$
$$b = (\Sigma T_i - a * (\Sigma V_i)) / n$$

NOTE: n is the number of measurements, and V_i and T_i are the measured values of voltages and temperatures, where i varies from 1 to n, and Σ is the *sum* of operator.

The program should use a two-dimensional dynamic array to store the measured voltages and temperatures obtained from the user. The user should be able to enter any number of measured values and not be limited to the number of values shown in the table above. After the user has entered all the values of the measured voltages and temperatures, the program computes the a and b coefficients. It then displays the linear equation for the thermocouple used in the experiment. The program should also test the equation and use it to compute a temperature for a given voltage. An example of the output of the program is shown in Figure 3.23

```
The thermocouple equation:

    T = 12.44 * V + 39.79


        ***TEST***


Enter voltage (mV):2
Temperature (°C) = 64.67
```

Figure 3.23 *Sample output produced by Program 3.4.*

3.5 Design a program that uses a two-dimensional dynamic array to store the values of temperature, humidity, and barometric pressure for different days. The array should be dimensioned as [3] * [noDays], where noDays (the number of days) is specified by the user at run-time. The program should do the following:

- Get the number of days from the user

- Dynamically allocate a two-dimensional array

- Get the values of temperature, humidity, and barometric pressure for each day from the user and store these values into the three rows of the array

- Sort the values in each row in descending order

- Compute the average value of each row (i.e., the average temperature, humidity, and air pressure)

- Display the values of temperature, humidity, and barometric pressure after sorting, as well as their average values

EXERCISE

CHAPTER 4

CLASSES AND OBJECTS

OBJECTIVES

- To understand the differences between procedural and object-oriented approaches to programming

- To introduce expanded structures

- To be able to design classes and control access to class members

- To understand the mechanisms of creating and destroying class objects

- To be able to allocate and deallocate class objects dynamically

- To be able to design and use constructor and destructor functions

CHAPTER CONTENTS

INTRODUCTION

This chapter is a turning point in the book. It will introduce readers who have developed programming skills and logic based on procedural concepts to a new approach to programming, called **object-oriented programming (OOP)**. The chapter will discuss key OOP concepts and terminology and will focus first on the differences between the procedural and OOP approaches to programming. In addition, the chapter will introduce C++ expanded structures, classes, and mechanisms of creating and destroying class objects.

4.1 PROCEDURAL VERSUS OBJECT-ORIENTED PROGRAMMING

Procedural/structured programming technology, which produced the C programming language, provides tools to solve a broad variety of problems in engineering and technology. Its efficiency, however, is significantly decreased if used in large and complex programs.

C++ also supports procedural technology. It provides an additional approach to programming, however, called object-oriented programming (OOP). OOP technology is much more efficient than procedural technology when dealing with large and complex programming problems. Its approach to problem solving is similar to the logic applied when solving real-life problems and is quite different from *artificial* procedural logic. Although OOP logic is more *natural*, programmers who have used procedural methodology for years often have difficulties adopting this logic.

The programmer who uses procedural programming techniques is focused on a program's functionality—i.e., procedures/functions to be followed in order to solve a problem. How to represent the data is not his or her primary concern; therefore, a procedural program can be described as a collection of functions or procedures with an open flow of data among them. This concept is illustrated in Figure 4.1.

Applying procedural or structured concepts in a large, complex program may lead to a variety of problems such as

- Difficulty in maintaining and modifying the program
- Many details easily can disorganize and overload the programmer
- Difficulty in debugging the program and following its logic
- Creation of logic errors such as inadvertent data modification

OOP technology provides the tools needed to overcome these problems. Its concepts are based on the use of objects. An **object** is a single entity that groups together related data and functions that operate on that data as shown in Figure 4.2.

 NOTE: Another definition of an object as an instance of a class is discussed in Section 4.3.

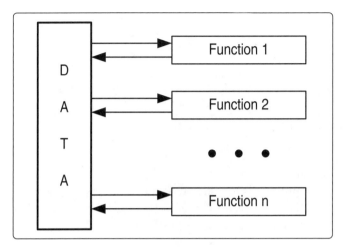

Figure 4.1 *Illustration of a procedural program.*

Some functions can be used as utility functions within the object while the others serve as interface functions to communicate with other objects within a program.

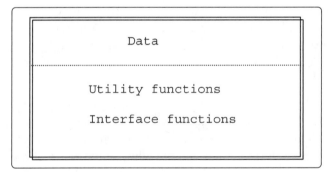

Figure 4.2 *An object's representation.*

Objects can be found everywhere in real life. They may be physical objects such as a computer or a spacecraft, or nonphysical objects such as an e-mail message or a vector in mathematics. An **OOP program** can be described as a collection of objects that communicate with each other through their interface functions. The communication between objects is commonly described as *sending messages to objects.* Figure 4.3 illustrates this concept.

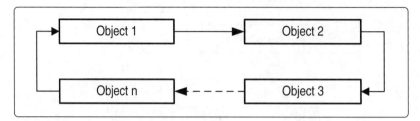

Figure 4.3 *Illustration of an OOP program.*

As opposed to procedural programming, in which the programmers are focused on procedures, object-oriented programming is focused on data and the operations to be performed on the data. OOP technology implements the following important concepts, which will be discussed in detail in Chapters 4 through 9:

- Encapsulation

- Inheritance

- Polymorphism

Encapsulation is the concept of binding together data and functions into one capsule or object. This concept is also known as **data abstraction.** Its implementation enables **data hiding,** which means an object can hide its data from the rest of the program and provide access to the data only through its interface functions. This reduces the possibility of inadvertent data modification and various kinds of logic errors.

OOP technology facilitates code reusability much more efficiently than procedural technology. **Inheritance** is one of the most important OOP tools in the implementation of code reusability. When using inheritance, new code can be derived or inherited from existing code. This reduces the amount of coding and the size of the program.

Polymorphism is the concept of using the same functions on different types of objects. This OOP tool enables C++ programmers to reduce program development time.

This book uses short program examples, no longer than a few hundreds of lines of code, to demonstrate the methodology and application of OOP tools. The real power and advantage of OOP techniques (over procedural techniques), however, can only be efficiently demonstrated in large and complex programs exceeding tens of thousands of lines of code. There is no reason to use OOP methodology in small and simple programs. It may even needlessly increase their complexity.

 NOTE: OOP concepts such as encapsulation, inheritance and polymorphism should be used in large programs to reduce their size and complexity. Procedural methodology should be used in small and simple programs.

OOP techniques have evolved from the concept of data structures introduced in C. C++ has expanded C structures to include both data and functions. It also provides a new kind of structure called the **class.** The next section will discuss the differences between structures in C and C++.

4.2 C++ STRUCTURES VERSUS C STRUCTURES

Structures are used in C programming to group related variables together. Variables that are elements or members of a structure can be of different data types. The member variables share a common structure variable name. Using structures may simplify a program's logic as well as its processing. Consider the following structure and variable declarations:

```
struct circuit {                        //structure declaration
    char description[10];
    int quantity;
    float impedance;
};

//structure variable declarations in C
struct circuit amplifier, speaker;
```

Note that `circuit` is the structure tag name in this example, while `amplifier` and `speaker` represent two structure variables. Every *struct* `circuit` structure variable consists of three member variables: `description`, `quantity`, and `impedance`. Figure 4.4 shows the `amplifier` structure variable as it appears in memory. It is assumed that the size of *int* and *float* are four and eight bytes, respectively.

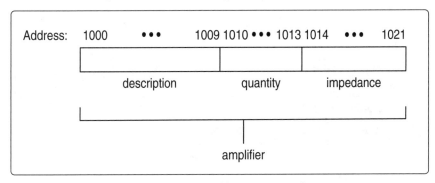

Figure 4.4 `amplifier` *structure variable as it is stored in memory.*

When declaring structure variables in C, the *struct* keyword must precede structure tag names each time to specify the variable type. To avoid this redundancy, C programmers may use the *typedef* statement. Unlike C, C++ keeps track of all user-defined data types such as structures, unions, enumerations, classes, etc., as soon as they are declared. It is not necessary, therefore, to use the *struct* keyword in C++ when declaring structure variables. A structure tag name is sufficient to specify a variable type as shown in this example:

```
//structure variable declarations in C++
circuit amplifier, speaker;
```

To access any member variable, a dot separator (.) is used to separate the structure variable name from its member variable as shown in the following examples:

```
speaker.impedance = 8;
amplifier.quantity = 1;
cout<<amplifier.description;
```

The benefits of grouping related data together are obvious. For example, if it is necessary to pass 10 **related** variables to a function, it is much easier to group them together into a structure and then pass one structure variable instead of passing 10 individual variables.

Consider PROG4_1, which simulates a battery's operation (Figure 4.5) in Program Example 4.1.

```
PROBLEM:    Compute for how long a battery can deliver
            a certain amount of current I to a device
            (load) at the rated voltage. The battery's
            voltage Vb and capacity (ampere-hour rat-
            ing), as well as the impedance Z of the
            device are given.


SOLUTION:   If given Vb=12 V, capacity=20 Ah, Z=50 Ω,
            I=Vb/Z=12/50=0.24 A
            Time=capacity/I=20/0.24=83.33 h
```

Figure 4.5 *The problem for PROG4_1.*

PROGRAM EXAMPLE 4.1: PROG4_1

```
1 //PROG4_1: Program simulates a battery's operation and uses a
2 //          data structure.
3 #include <iostream>
4 #include <iomanip>
```

```
5 using namespace std;
6 struct Battery {        //structure declaration
7     float voltage;
8     float capacity;
9 };
10  void setValues(Battery &);   //reference to a structure as a
11  void getValues(Battery &);   //function parameter
12  float getHours(Battery &, float);
13
14  int main()
15  {
16      float imp=50;      //device impedance
17      Battery b;         //structure variable
18      setValues(b);      //passing structure variable by reference
19      cout<<endl;
20      getValues(b);
21      cout<<"Device can be powered "<<getHours(b,imp)<<" hours.";
22      return 0;
23  }
24
25  void setValues(Battery &rb) //Gets battery's voltage and
26  {                          //capacity from the user
27      cout<<"Enter battery's voltage: ";
28      cin>>rb.voltage;
29      cout<<"Enter battery's capacity: ";
30      cin>>rb.capacity;
31  }
32
33  void getValues(Battery &rb) //Displays battery voltage and
34  {                          //capacity
35      cout<<setiosflags(ios::fixed)<<setprecision(1);
36      cout<<"Voltage = "<<rb.voltage<<" [V]"<<endl;
37      cout<<"Capacity = "<<rb.capacity<<" [Ah]"<<endl;
```

E X A M P L E

```
38 }
39
40 float getHours(Battery &rb, float imp) //Computes and returns
41 {                                      //the time
42        float current = rb.voltage/imp;
43      return rb.capacity/current;
44 }
```

The program defines a structure type named Battery, which consists of two members: voltage and capacity (lines 6–9). The *main()* function instantiates a b structure variable of the Battery type (line 17). Please note that b represents a battery as a voltage source. The *main()* then calls the setValues() and getValues() functions to obtain a battery's voltage and capacity from the user and display their values, respectively (lines 18, 20). It then calls the getHours() function to compute and display how long a device with a given impedance can be powered on by the battery (line 21). Note that all three functions have a Battery reference as a parameter. When each of these functions is called, the b structure variable is passed by reference to the function. The reference, which is named rb, serves as another name for b. It is used to access the memory locations of the battery's voltage and capacity using the rb.voltage and rb.capacity syntax.

A sample run of PROG4_1 is shown in Figure 4.6.

```
Enter battery's voltage: 12
Enter battery's capacity: 20

Voltage = 12.0 [V]
Capacity = 20.0 [Ah]
Device can be powered 83.3 hours.
```

Figure 4.6 *Output produced by the program PROG4_1.*

The Battery structure type is globally declared in PROG4_1 and then used in all of its functions. If it is necessary to modify the Battery structure—i.e., to add some new members, or delete the existing member(s)—it may require a modification of all functions that use that type. The user-defined functions in PROG4_1 are related because they process the same data. It would be convenient to group them together into the same structure with the data they process, and C++ provides this capability.

The structure type has been expanded in C++. It can also include functions as structure members along with the data they process. The general format of a C++ structure is shown in Figure 4.7.

```
struct tag_name {

public:

        //public data and functions

private:

        //private data and functions

};
```

Figure 4.7 *General format of expanded structures.*

Structure members (variables or functions) that follow the ***private*** keyword are private to that structure—i.e., they can be accessed only by other members of the same structure. Public structure members can be used/accessed outside the structure.

 NOTE: *public* and *private* access specifiers are discussed in more detail in the next section.

PROG4_2 is a modified version of PROG4_1, as shown in Program Example 4.2. It uses an expanded `Battery` structure that includes functions as its members.

PROGRAM EXAMPLE 4.2: PROG4_2

```
1   //PROG4_2. An improved version of the program PROG4_1,
2   //           which uses an expanded Battery structure.
3   #include <iostream>
4   #include <iomanip>
5   using namespace std;
6
7   struct Battery {
8     void setValues()      //functions as public structure members
9     {
```

```
10      cout<<"Enter battery voltage: ";
11      cin>>voltage;
12      cout<<"Enter battery capacity: ";
13      cin>>capacity;
14    }
15    void getValues( )
16    {
17      cout<<setiosflags(ios::fixed)<<setprecision(1);
18      cout<<"Voltage = "<<voltage<<" [V]"<<endl;
19      cout<<"Capacity = "<<capacity<<" [Ah]"<<endl;
20    }
21    float getHours(float imp)
22    {
23      float current=voltage/imp;
24      return capacity/current;
25    }
26 private:
27    float voltage;              //private data members
28    float capacity;
29 };
30
31 int main()
32 {
33    float imp=50;
34    Battery b;
35    b.setValues();      //calling a structure member function
36    cout<<endl;
37    b.getValues();
38    cout<<"Device can be powered "<<b.getHours(imp)<<" hours.";
39    return 0;
40 }
```

User-defined functions in PROG4_2 are defined as ***public*** members of the Battery structure. It should be noted that the ***public*** keyword is not placed prior to the functions' definitions. It is not necessary because the ***public*** access specifier is the default for structures and may be omitted when defining those structures.

Data members `voltage` and `capacity` are ***private*** to the `Battery` structure and hidden from the rest of the program. They can be accessed only by the structure member functions.

Functions that are members of a structure are called outside the structure using a structure variable and the dot operator (.) as shown in Figure 4.8. The statements that call structure member functions in PROG4_2 are shown on lines 35, 37, and 38.

```
struct_var.function_name();
```

Figure 4.8 *Calling a structure member function.*

It is not necessary to pass the structure member variables as arguments to the functions that are members of the same structure. Note that the functions that are members of the `Battery` structure have direct access to the `voltage` and `capacity` structure data members.

Grouping related functions and data they operate upon together into one unit or structure has the following important advantages:

- Simplification of the program's logic and reduction of its complexity

- Easier modification and maintenance of the program (If it is necessary, for example, to add new data or delete the existing data, all functions affected by that change are within the same structure.)

- Protection of data from inadvertent changes

 NOTE: C++ structures have the following advantages over C structures:

- A C++ structure may contain both functions and data, unlike C structures that contain data only.

- Data can be protected or hidden by using the ***private*** access specifier.

- It is not necessary to use the ***struct*** keyword when instantiating variables.

The next section will discuss **classes**—the single most important C++ programming tool that has evolved from the concept of structures.

4.3 CLASSES

The *class* is a foundation of OOP. It is very similar to the expanded structures that group related data and functions together.

The general format of a class declaration is shown in Figure 4.9.

```
class class_name {

private:
    //private variables and functions

public:
    //public variables and functions

} object_list;
```

Figure 4.9 *General format of a C++ class.*

Any valid C++ identifier can be used as `class_name`. Most programmers begin `class_name` with an uppercase letter to improve the program readability and distinguish the class type from other data types. Note that `object_list` is optional in the class declaration. Functions and variables declared inside the class are called **class members**. There are two kinds of class members:

- Member variables, also called data members
- Member functions

C++ uses classes to create objects. *An object is an instance of a class.* Class data members can be viewed as the object's **attributes** or **properties**, while member functions describe its **behavior** or **methods**. For example, a spacecraft is an object with attributes such as velocity, acceleration, and position. Functions that manipulate the spacecraft's attributes describe its behavior.

The *class* keyword can also be used to create a **forward reference** to inform the compiler that the identifier that follows is a class type. Where a class name or identifier precedes the class definition, a forward reference is required. For example,

```
class Spacecraft; //forward reference
```

where `Spacecraft` is a class name/identifier.

An object of the `Spacecraft` class can be declared or instantiated as follows:

```
Spacecraft challenger;   //challenger is an object of
                         //the class Spacecraft
```

The definition of the `Spacecraft` class describes all attributes and behavior of the `challenger` object. Every time a class object is declared, a block of memory is allocated to store the values of all data members of that class. Each object has its own values (attributes or properties). A class object is similar to a structure variable.

4.3.1 ACCESSING CLASS MEMBERS

C++ provides three ways of accessing class members. The way a class member is accessed is specified by one of the following member **access specifiers**:

- *private*
- *public*
- *protected*

Both data members and member functions can have *private*, *public*, or *protected* access. It should be noted that the *private* data members or member functions can only be accessed by other members of the same class. The *public* class members can be accessed by members of its class as well as members of any other class and non-member functions, including *main( )*. The *protected* access specifier will be introduced in Chapter 7 when dealing with inheritance.

An access specifier followed by a colon should be placed before a class member declaration. Members with the same access should be grouped together and listed after their access specifier.

Data members are usually kept *private* to the class, meaning they are hidden from the rest of the program. The interface between the class and other classes or non-member functions, including *main( )*, should be established through *public* member functions. The *private* member functions serve only as utility functions for other member functions of the same class.

Unlike structure members, the **default** access specifier for class members is *private*. If the *private* members are listed first in a class definition, the access specifier can be omitted. To improve clarity, the program should explicitly use *private* to denote access.

Consider the following class definition:

```
1  class Jet {
2     float acc, vel, dis;   //acceleration, velocity, displacement
3     float getTime(){       //Computes the time during which
4        return vel/acc;     //the jet is being accelerated
5           }
6  public:
7     void setValues(float x, float y) {
8        acc=x;   vel=y;     //Sets the acceleration and velocity
9           }
10 float getDisplacement() {
```

```
11          return (vel*getTime())/2;      //Returns the displacement
12    }                                     //of the jet
13 };
```

Please note that an access specifier is missing before the data members `acc`, `vel`, and `dis` declarations (line 2). By default, they are *private*. The `getTime()` function is also *private* and it serves as a utility function for the `getDisplacement()` function, which calculates the jet's displacement (line 11). Member `setValues()` and `getDisplacement()` functions are defined as *public* members of the `Jet` class. They can therefore be accessed outside the class through a class object using the general format shown in Figure 4.10.

```
object.class_member
```

Figure 4.10 *Accessing class members using an object of the class.*

It should be noted that an object is not needed to access a class member by another member of the same class (line 11).

Assume the following *main()* function that uses the `Jet` class:

```
1 int main()
2 {
3   Jet plane;                //Instantiates an object
4   plane.setValues(40, 65);    //Calls a member function
5   cout<<"The time during which the plane ";
6   cout<<"is being accelarated = ";
7   cout<<plane.getTime();       //ERROR!!!
8   cout<<"\n The plane's displacement = ";
9   cout<<plane.getDisplacement();
10 return 0;
11 }
```

The *main()* function instantiates an object of the `Jet` class named `plane` (line 3). It then uses the object to call class member functions (lines 4, 7, and 9). An error occurs in line 7 because the `getTime()` function is *private* to the class and cannot be called outside the class.

 NOTE: The default access specifier for class members is *private*, while for structure members it is *public*.

TIP: When designing classes, all data members should be kept *private*. The *public* member functions should be used to initialize, modify, and get the values of *private* data members.

4.3.2 MEMBER FUNCTIONS

A **member function** is a function that is a member of a class. Member functions are usually used to manipulate class data members, and in most cases provide the only way to access the *private* class data.

While a class object does not contain copies of member functions' code, class objects can hold data members and have ownership of member functions' calls. If a program instantiates 10 objects of a class, for example, there will be 10 copies of the class member variables in memory and only one copy of each member function's code. Remember that an object is needed to call member functions outside the class. The process of calling member functions is discussed in more detail in Chapter 5.

A member function can be either an *inline* or *non-inline* function. To create an *inline* member function, it is only necessary to place the function's definition inside the class. It is not necessary to use the *inline* keyword in this case, as is the case with non-member functions. Some functions—long functions, recursive functions, and functions containing loops or *static* variables—cannot be expanded *inline*. If a member function falls into one of these categories and its definition is placed within the body of the class, the compiler will usually issue a warning message and process the function as a *non-inline* member function.

Non-inline member functions have their prototypes inside the class and definitions outside the class. To define a *non-inline* function outside the class, the general format shown in Figure 4.11 is used.

```
return_type class_name::function_name(parameters)
{
        //Body of the function
}
```

Figure 4.11 *General format of a* non-inline *member function definition.*

When defining a *non-inline* member function (outside the class), the class name followed by the scope resolution operator (::) must be placed in front of the function's name to identify the function as a member of its class. It is not required to place the class name and the :: operator in front of the function's name in the function prototype (inside the class).

In Program Example 4.3, PROG4_3 uses a class named `Resistor`, containing *inline* and *non-inline* member functions to solve the problem shown in Figure 4.12.

```
PROBLEM:   Color bands are used to designate a resistor's
           value and tolerance. Compute the resistance R
           of a resistor, given four color bands, where
           the fourth band represents the resistor's
           tolerance.

SOLUTION:  Shown below is a table with colors and
           corresponding integer values as follows:
```

BAND 1-3		BAND 4	
COLOR	VALUE	COLOR	VALUE
BLACK	0	GOLD (±5%)	10
BROWN	1	SILVER (±10%)	11
RED	2	NONE (±20%)	12
ORANGE	3		
YELLOW	4		
GREEN	5		
BLUE	6		
VIOLET	7		
GRAY	8		
WHITE	9		

```
           Assume the following color bands:

               YELLOW-VIOLET-ORANGE-GOLD
```

$$R = (\ band1*10 + band2\ )\ *10^{band3}$$
$$R = (4*10+7)*10^3\ =\ 47,000\ \Omega \pm 5\%$$

Figure 4.12 *The problem for PROG4_3.*

PROGRAM EXAMPLE 4.3: PROG4_3

```
1  //PROG4_3:  Computes the resistance for specified color bands.
2  //          Uses a class with inline and non-inline
3  //          member functions.
4  #include <iostream>
5  #include <cmath>
6  using namespace std;
7  class Resistor {
8  private:
9     int band1, band2, band3, band4;
10    int resistance;
11 public:
12    void getValues();        //non-inline function prototype
13    void calcResistance() {  //inline function definition
14       resistance=(((band1*10)+band2)*pow(10,band3));
15    }
16    void printResistance();  //non-inline function prototype
17 };                          //End of class definition
18
19 void Resistor::getValues()  //non-inline function definition
20 {
21    cout<<"\t\tCOLORS:";
22    cout<<"\n\n 0==BLACK  1==BROWN   2==RED   3==ORANGE"<<endl;
23    cout<<" 4==YELLOW 5==GREEN   6==BLUE" <<endl;
24    cout<<" 7==VIOLET 8==GRAY    9==WHITE"<<endl;
25    cout<<"10==GOLD   11==SILVER 12==NONE\n\n"<<endl;
26    cout<<"Please select first band (1-9) ==> ";
27    cin >> band1;
28    cout<<"Please select second band (1-9) ==> ";
29    cin >> band2;
30    cout<<"Please select third band (1-9) ==> ";
```

```
31    cin >> band3;
32    cout << "Please select tolerance/fourth band (10-12) ==> ";
33    cin >> band4;
34 }
35 void Resistor::printResistance()
36 {                              //non-inline function definition
37    char *tolerance;
38
39    calcResistance();          //Calls a member function
40
41    if( band4 == 10 )
42       tolerance = "+/- 5%";
43    if( band4 == 11 )
44       tolerance = "+/- 10%";
45    if( band4 == 12 )
46       tolerance = "+/- 20%";
47
48    cout<<"\n\n The resistance is "<<resistance<< " ohms";
49    cout<<" with "<< tolerance<<" tolerance." << endl;
50 }
51
52 int main()
53 {
54    Resistor res;            //Instantiates an object
55    res.getValues();         //Calls a member function
56    res.printResistance();   //Calls a member function
57    return 0;
58 }
```

A sample run of PROG4_3 is shown in Figure 4.13.

```
                    COLORS:

   0==BLACK    1==BROWN    2==RED     3==ORANGE
   4==YELLOW   5==GREEN    6==BLUE
   7==VIOLET   8==GRAY     9==WHITE
   10==GOLD    11==SILVER  12==NONE


   Please select first band (1-9) ==> 4
   Please select second band (1-9) ==> 7
   Please select third band (1-9) ==> 3
   Please select tolerance/fourth band (10-12) ==> 10


   The resistance is 47000 ohms with +/- 5% tolerance.
```

Figure 4.13 *Sample run of PROG4_3.*

The Resistor class contains two *non-inline* functions: getValues() and printResistance(). The prototypes of these two functions are placed inside the body of the class (lines 12 and 16), while their definitions are outside the class (lines 19–34 and 35–50). The primary reason to define these two functions outside the class is their size. Taking definitions of longer functions outside the class is good programming practice—it improves program clarity and makes it easier to understand the content of the class.

The Resistor class also contains a calcResistance() *inline* function. The definition of this function is inside the class (lines 13–15). The body of the calcResistance() function contains one statement (line 14). Due to its brevity, this function is a good candidate for an *inline* function.

The *main()* function instantiates a res object of the Resistor class. The res object is used to store values of four color bands of a resistor and its resistance. The *main()* function then uses res to call the getValues() function (line 55) to obtain values of the resistor's color bands from the user. The same object is used to call printResistance() (line 56) to calculate and print the resistance and tolerance for the given color bands. The calcResistance() function, which calculates resistance, serves as a utility function for printResistance() (line 39).

It should be noted that the getValues() function should have been checked for errors to make sure that the values entered by the user were within the required range. To minimize program size, error checking was eliminated in this example.

4.3.3 ALLOCATING OBJECTS AT RUN-TIME

A class object or an array of objects can be dynamically allocated at run-time in the same way as ordinary variables of built-in types. A pointer of the class type and the *new* operator are needed to perform this operation. The *delete* operator is used to free memory dynamically allocated to store class object(s).

PROG4_3 allocates one object of the Resistor class at compile time. It can be redesigned to allocate and process, at run-time, any number of objects/resistors requested by the user. Assuming the Resistor class is the same as in PROG4_3, the *main()* function may be redefined as follows:

```
1   int main()
2   {
3     int num, i;
4     cout<<"How many resistors? ";
5     cin>>num;
6
7     Resistor *ptres=new Resistor[num];    //Allocating objects
8                                            //dynamically
9     if(!ptres)
10    {
11        cout<<"Memory Allocation Error!";
12        exit(1);
13    }
14    for(i=0; i<num; i++)
15    {
16        cout<<"\nResistor # "<<(i+1)<<endl;
17        ptres[i].getValues();
18        ptres[i].printResistance();
19    }
20    delete []ptres;
21    return 0;
22 }
```

The *main()* function uses a Resistor-type ptres pointer to store an address of a memory block allocated by the *new* operator (line 7). This block of memory pointed to by ptres is allocated in the heap and used to store an array of num objects of the `Resistor` class. The number of objects, `num`, is specified by the user at run-time. The `ptres` pointer is then used to access individual objects in order to call member functions (lines 17 and 18). Memory allocated in the heap should be released when it is not needed using **delete** (line 20).

4.4 CONSTRUCTOR AND DESTRUCTOR FUNCTIONS

4.4.1 CONSTRUCTORS

Initializing variables before they are used is a common programming practice. There are instances when it must be done; for example, initializing counters and totals to 0. When working with classes, it is even more important to properly initialize class objects prior to their use.

PROG4_3 uses the `getValues()` member function to initialize a class object. C++, however, provides a special kind of member function called the **constructor function,** which is a more convenient tool to perform initialization than using functions such as the `getValues()` function. A constructor function can perform any kind of operation—just like any other member function. It is a common programming method, however, to use constructors to initialize class data members.

A constructor function has the following properties or characteristics:

- It has the same name as the class for which it is designed.
- It has no return type, not even **void**.
- It can have arguments, including default arguments.
- Unlike other member functions, it is never explicitly called. A constructor function is automatically called whenever an object is declared.

When using constructors, it is also important to know the following:

- Constructors should be **public**, so they can be called outside the class—including **main( )**.
- A class can have as many constructors as necessary—i.e., they can be overloaded.
- Constructors cannot be inherited (inheritance will be discussed in Chapter 7).
- Each class should have its own constructors.

A common programming error is an attempt to directly initialize class data members within the class, as shown in the following example:

```
class Battery {
    float voltage = 12.0;   //ERROR! This cannot be done here.
    float capacity;
```

```
public:
    // member functions
};
```

The initialization should be done by a constructor function. A constructor for the Battery class may be designed as follows:

```
Battery ()                          //default constructor
{
    voltage = 12.0;
    capacity = 30.0;
}
```

This constructor function is called a **default constructor**, because it assigns default values to the class data members. Notice that the function has the same name as the class, it has no return type, and it has no parameters. When an object of the class is declared, the constructor is automatically called.

```
Battery bt;            //Calling default constructor
```

A constructor function can have parameters. For example, the following is a Battery constructor that may take two arguments when called:

```
Battery(float v, float c)        //constructor with arguments
{
    voltage = v;
    capacity = c;
}
```

When calling this constructor, two arguments should be passed to the function. It is accomplished as shown in the following example:

```
Battery bt(12.0, 30.0);          //Calling constructor and passing
                                 //arguments
```

A constructor function may use default arguments, as shown in the following example of the Battery constructor:

```
Battery(float v = 12.0, float c = 30.0)      //constructor with
{                                            //default arguments
    voltage = v;
    capacity = c;
}
```

This constructor function may be called with or without passing arguments as follows:

```
Battery bt1;              //Uses default values
Battery bt2(5.0, 20.0);  //Overrides default values
```

Memory contents when instantiating `bt1` and `bt2` objects are shown in Figure 4.14.

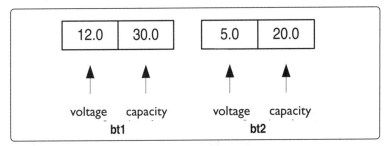

Figure 4.14 *Memory contents when instantiating* `bt1` *and* `bt2` *objects.*

The use of constructors with default arguments eliminates the need for constructor overloading. For example, instead of two overloaded constructor functions such as `Battery(float v, float c)` and `Battery()`, a single constructor function with default arguments `Battery(float v=12.0, float c=30.0)` could be used.

C++ also provides a special kind of constructor function that is used when creating copies of class objects. This function is called the **copy constructor** and it is discussed in Chapter 5.

4.4.2 THE CLASS DESTRUCTOR

Constructor functions do their *construction job* when class objects are instantiated. Although they commonly initialize class objects, constructors are also frequently used to perform other operations as well—an example of which is dynamically allocating memory for class data members. There is a need, therefore, to do a *cleaning* when objects are destroyed. For example, memory dynamically allocated by the constructor when an object is created should be released when that object is destroyed.

C++ provides a special member function called the **destructor function** that is the complement of a constructor function. It is automatically called when an object is destroyed. The destructor function is needed to clean up the class object when it goes out of scope. Unlike constructors, a class can have only one destructor—there are many ways to construct objects but only one way to destroy them.

A destructor function has the following properties:

- Its name is the tilde (~) character followed by the class name.
- It cannot have a return type.
- It cannot have arguments.
- It is automatically called when an object goes out of scope.

Consider a class with the following skeleton:

```
class ErrMessage {
    char *mes;
public:
    ErrMessage(char *em) {              //constructor
            mes=new char[strlen(em)];   //Allocates memory dynamically
            strcpy(mes, em);            //Initializes data member
    }

            //other member functions
};
```

The ErrMessage class uses a constructor with a string as an argument. The constructor dynamically allocates memory, the size of which is equal to the length of the em string that is passed to the constructor. It uses the mes member pointer to store the address of that memory block. This class needs a destructor function to free dynamically allocated memory when a class object goes out of scope. Its destructor may be defined as follows:

```
~ErrMessage() { delete []mes; }         //destructor
```

In Program Example 4.4, PROG4_4 uses a Battery class similar to the expanded structure from PROG4_2. In addition to the member functions used in the structure, the Battery class contains an overloaded constructor and a destructor function.

PROGRAM EXAMPLE 4.4: PROG4_4

```
1   //PROG4_4: Demonstrates a use of the overloaded constructor and
2   //          destructor functions.
3   #include <iostream>
4   #include <iomanip>
5   using namespace std;
6
7   class Battery {
8   private:
9     float voltage;
10    float capacity;
11  public:
12    Battery() {   //default constructor
```

```
13        voltage=12;
14        capacity=20;
15    }
16    Battery(float v, float cp) {      //constructor with arguments
17        voltage=v;
18        capacity=cp;
19    }
20    void getValues(){
21        cout<<setiosflags(ios::fixed)<<setprecision(1);
22        cout<<"Voltage = "<<voltage<<" [V]"<<endl;
23        cout<<"Capacity = "<<capacity<<" [Ah]"<<endl;
24    }
25    float getHours(float imp) {
26        float current=voltage/imp;
27        return capacity/current;
28    }
29    ~Battery(){ cout<<"\nBattery discharged!!!"; }   //destructor
30 };
31
32 int main()
33 {
34    float imp=100;             //device impedance
35    {
36        Battery b1;            //Calls default constructor
37        cout<<"First battery: "<<endl;
38        b1.getValues();
39        cout<<"Device can be powered "<<b1.getHours(imp);
40        cout<<" hours."<<endl;
41    }                          //Calls destructor to destroy b1
42    Battery b2(12,10);         //Calls constructor with arguments
43    cout<<"\n\nSecond battery: "<<endl;
44    b2.getValues();
45    cout<<"Device can be powered "<<b2.getHours(imp);
```

Page 130

```
46    cout<<" hours."<<endl;
47    return 0;    //Calls destructor to destroy b2
48 }
```

Notice that the Battery class can use one constructor with default arguments instead of two overloaded constructors. The only purpose of designing a destructor function for the Battery class in this example is to demonstrate the destructor's calls.

The *main()* function contains a block of code between lines 35 and 41 that is separated from the rest of the code. This block calls the default constructor to initialize the b1 object (line 36). The end of the block (line 41) is the end of lifetime of the b1 object. The destructor is automatically called at that point because b1 goes out of scope. It displays the message Battery discharged!!! The b2 object is instantiated outside the block (line 42). The second constructor with arguments initializes b2. The end of *main()* (line 48) marks the end of lifetime of b2. The destructor is called again—this time to *clean-up* b2—and displays Battery discharged!!!.

The output produced by PROG4_4 is shown in Figure 4.15.

```
First battery:
Voltage = 12 [V]
Capacity = 20.0 [Ah]
Device can be powered 166.7 hours.

Battery discharged!!!

Second battery:
Voltage = 12.0 [V]
Capacity = 10.0 [Ah]
Device can be powered 83.3 hours.

Battery discharged!!!
```

Figure 4.15 *Output produced by PROG4_4.*

NOTE: A class can have as many constructors as necessary, but only one destructor.

TIP: Class objects should be initialized by constructors. A destructor should be used to free memory dynamically allocated by a constructor.

4.5 CASE STUDY: DATA ENCRYPTION

This case study demonstrates the use of OOP methodology in implementing a simple data encryption/decryption technique. The encryption technique uses the X-OR bitwise operator and a random generator. A class is designed to group all related variables and functions together. Practical use of constructor and destructor functions is also demonstrated. The constructor is used to dynamically allocate memory and initialize class data members, while the class destructor is used to free memory allocated by the constructor.

PROBLEM DESCRIPTION

The program should first obtain a message up to 80 characters long from the user and then encrypt the message. It should then offer the user an option to either view the encrypted message or view the original message. The original message should be password protected—that is, the user should enter a correct password in order to view the original message. The number of attempts to enter the password should be limited to three.

INPUT/OUTPUT

Requested **input** from the user:

1. A message up to 80 characters long

2. A selection of one of the following options:

   • View the encrypted message

   • View the original message

   • Exit the program

3. If the option to view the original message is selected, a password up to six characters long should be required.

Requested **output**: The encrypted or original message, based on the user's selection.

PSEUDOCODE

Design the Encryption class with the following skeleton:

• **Data members (*private*):**

1. `char * message;`   //a message to be encrypted/decrypted

2. `char password[7];` //a password to decrypt the message

3. `int mask;`   //a mask to encrypt the message

• **Member functions (*public*):**

1. `Encryption(char *tmes);`

   //ALLOCATES MEMORY DYNAMICALLY TO STORE message AND

```
//INITIALIZES message, password AND mask.
START
N = LENGTH OF TMES (EXECUTE STRLEN())
MESSAGE = ADDRESS OF NEW CHAR[N+1]
IF MESSAGE==0
    PRINT "MEMORY ALLOCATION ERROR"
    EXECUTE EXIT()
    STOP
END IF
MESSAGE = TMES
PASSWORD = " "
GENERATE MASK (EXECUTE RAND())
STOP
```

2. ~Encryption();

```
//RELEASES DYNAMICALLY ALLOCATED MEMORY AND
//PRINTS "MESSAGE DESTROYED!".
START
DELETE MESSAGE
PRINT "MESSAGE DESTROYED"
STOP
```

3. void encryptDecrypt();

```
//ENCRYPTS message
START
I=0
FOR I<LENGTH OF MESSAGE
    MESSAGE[I] = MESSAGE[I] XOR MASK
    I=I+1
END FOR
STOP
```

4. `bool getPassword();`

//GETS **password** FROM THE USER AND RETURNS TRUE IF CORRECT,

//OR FALSE IF INCORRECT

START

COUNTER=3

PASS="SENECA"

DO WHILE COUNTER>0 AND PASS!=PASSWORD

    PRINT "ENTER PASSWORD"

    READ PASSWORD

    IF PASSWORD != PASS

        PRINT "INVALID PASSWORD"

        PRINT COUNTER-1 "ATTEMPTS LEFT"

    END IF

    COUNTER=COUNTER-1

END DO

IF PASSWORD=PASS

    RETURN TRUE

ELSE

    RETURN FALSE

STOP

5. `getOption();`

//PROMPTS THE USER TO SELECT EITHER VIEWING THE ENCRYPTED

//MESSAGE, OR THE ORIGINAL MESSAGE AND EXECUTES THE OPTION

//SELECTED BY THE USER.

//A FLOWCHART IS SHOWN IN FIGURE 4.16.

FLOWCHARTS

Figures 4.16 and 4.17 show flowcharts of the `Encryption::getOption()` member function and the *main()* function, respectively.

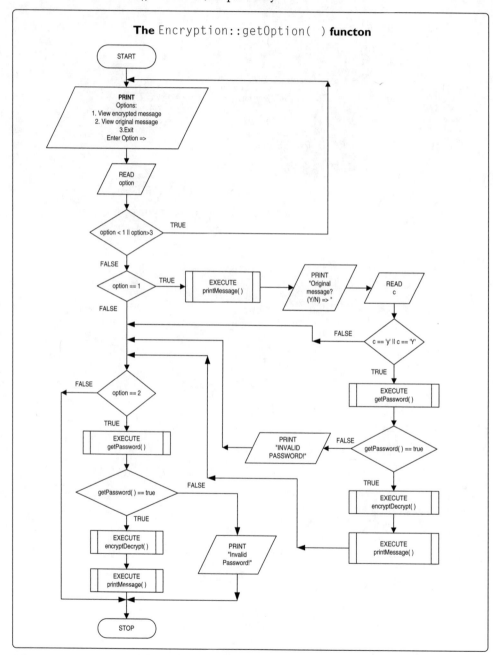

Figure 4.16 *Flowchart of the* `Encryption::getOption()` *function.*

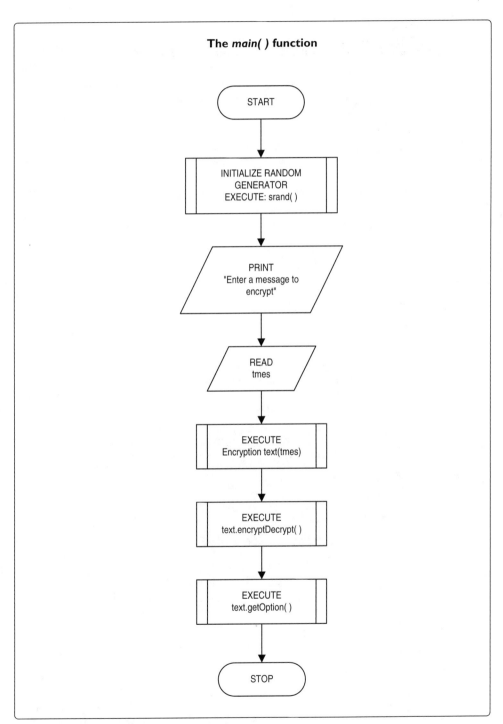

Figure 4.17 *Flowchart of the* **main( )** *function.*

SOURCE CODE

PROGRAM EXAMPLE 4.5: SOURCE CODE FOR CASEST4

```cpp
1   //CASEST4: Program demonstrates a data encryption technique and
2   //          a class with a constructor and destructor.
3   #include <iostream>
4   #include <cstdlib>
5   #include <ctime>
6   using namespace std;
7
8   class Encryption {
9     char *message;
10    char password[7];
11    int mask;
12  public:
13    Encryption(char *);        //constructor
14    ~Encryption(){             //destructor
15       delete []message;
16       cout<<"\nMessage destroyed!\n";
17    }
18    void encryptDecrypt();
19    bool getPassword();
20    void getOption();
21    void printMessage() {
22       cout<<"\n\nMessage: "<<message<<endl;
23    }
24  };
25  Encryption::Encryption(char *tmes)
26  {                              //Allocates memory dynamically
27    int n=strlen(tmes);        //and initializes data members
28    message = new char[n+1];
29    if(!message) {
30       cout<<"Memory Allocation Error!";
```

```
31        exit(1);
32    }
33    strcpy(message,tmes);
34    strcpy(password," ");
35    mask = rand();
36 }
37
38 void Encryption::encryptDecrypt()    //Encrypts/decrypts a
39 {                                    //message
40    for (int i=0; i<strlen(message); i++)
41    {
42        message[i] ^ = mask;
43    }
44 }
45
46 bool Encryption::getPassword()        //Gets password from the user
47 {                                     //and checks if correct
48    int cnt=3;
49    char pass[7]="SENECA";
50    do
51    {
52       cout<<"\nEnter password => ";
53       cin>>password;
54       if(strcmp(pass, password))
55       {
56            cout<<"\nInvalid Password! ";
57            cout<<(cnt-1)<<" attempt(s) left!\n";
58       }
59       cnt--;
60    }while(cnt>0 && strcmp(pass, password));
61
62    if(!strcmp(pass,password))
63        return true;
```

```
64    else
65        return false;
66  }
67  void Encryption::getOption()      //Gets a selection from the user
68  {                                  //and executes the operation
69     int option;                     //selected by the user
70     char c;
71
72     do
73     {
74        cout<<"\nOptions:";
75        cout<<"\n\t1. View encrypted message";
76        cout<<"\n\t2. View original message";
77        cout<<"\n\t3. Exit";
78        cout<<"\n\n\tEnter Option => ";
79        cin>>option;
80
81     }while (option<1 || option>3);
82
83     if(option==1)
84     {
85        printMessage();
86        cout<<"\n\nDisplay original message? (y/n) => ";
87        cin>>c;
88        if(c=='y'||c=='Y')
89        {
90            if(getPassword())
91        {
92            encryptDecrypt();
93            printMessage();
94        }
95        else
96            cout<<"\n\nInvalid password!\n";
```

```
97          }
98      }
99      if(option==2)
100     {
101         if(getPassword())
102         {
103             encryptDecrypt();
104             printMessage();
105         }
106         else
107             cout<<"\nInvalid password!\n";
108     }
109     }
110
111     int main()
112     {
113         char tmes[81];
114         srand(time(0));
115         cout<<"\nEnter a message to encrypt (up to 80 ";
116         cout<<"characters):\n => ";
117         cin.getline(tmes,80);
118
119         Encryption text(tmes);    //Instantiates an object
120
121         text.encryptDecrypt();    //Calls member functions
122         text.getOption();
123
124         return 0;
125     }                            //Executes the destructor
                                     //automatically
```

A sample run of CASEST4 is shown in Figure 4.18.

```
        Enter a message to encrypt (up to 80 characters):
        => DELMAR

Options:
        1. View encrypted message
        2. View original message
        3. Exit

        Enter Option => 1

Message: 54=<0||

Display original message? (y/n) => y

Enter password => SENECA

Message: DELMAR

Message destroyed!
```

Figure 4.18 *Sample run of CASEST4.*

CONCLUSION

CASEST4 applies an object-oriented approach in implementing a simple data encryption/decryption technique. A more sophisticated encryption algorithm can be developed, but is beyond the focus of this chapter. The `Encryption` class uses constructor and destructor functions to dynamically allocate and deallocate memory. This class can be expanded by adding a copy constructor (discussed in Chapter 5).

SUMMARY

1. C++ provides a different approach to programming from the procedural C. It is called object-oriented programming (OOP).

2. OOP technology is much more efficient than procedural programming technology when dealing with large and complex programs.

3. Unlike procedural programming that is focused on procedures or functions, OOP is focused on data and operations to be performed on the data.

4. An object is a single entity that groups together related data and functions that operate on the data.

5. The three most important OOP concepts are encapsulation, inheritance, and polymorphism.

6. C++ has expanded C structures to include both data and functions.

7. The **struct** keyword can be omitted when declaring structure variables in C++.

8. Data can be hidden within a structure by using the **private** access specifier.

9. A class is similar to an expanded structure that groups related data and functions together.

10. An object is an instance of a class.

11. There are two kinds of class members: data members and member functions.

12. The default access specifier for class members is **private**, while it is **public** for structure members.

13. A member function can be either an *inline* or *non-inline* function.

14. A class object or an array of objects can be allocated or destroyed at run-time by using the **new** and **delete** operators.

15. C++ classes use special member functions called the constructor functions to initialize class objects. A class can have as many constructors as necessary.

16. A constructor is automatically called when an object is instantiated.

17. A special member function called the destructor function is used to "clean up" class objects. A class can have only one destructor.

18. The class destructor is automatically called when an object goes out of scope.

19. If a constructor dynamically allocates memory, the class destructor should be used to free that memory.

EXERCISES

State the output produced by the programs in Exercises 4.1 and 4.2.

4.1
```cpp
#include <iostream>
using namespace std;
class Pixel{
    int x, y;
public:
    Pixel(){ x=1; y=0; }
    ~Pixel(){cout<<"Pixel "<<x<<','<<y<<" is deleted.";}
};
int main()
{
    Pixel obj;
    return 0;
}
```

4.2
```cpp
#include <iostream>
using namespace std;
class Rectangle {
    float width, length;
public:
    Rectangle(){ width = 3; length = 8; }
    float area(){ return width*length; }
};
int main()
{
    Rectangle r;
    cout<<"Area of rectangle is: "<<r.area();
    return 0;
}
```

Identify and correct the errors in the programs or class definitions in Exercises 4.3 through 4.7.

4.3
```
#include <iostream>
using namespace std;
class Circuit {
    float res, vol;
    void set(float r, float v){ res=r, vol=v; }
public:
    float current();
};
float current()
{
    return vol/res;
}
int main()
{
    float r,v;
    Circuit crc;
    cout<<"Enter resistance => ";
    cin>>r;
    cout<<"\nEnter voltage => ";
    cin>>v;
    crc.set();
    cout<<"\n\nThe current is => "<<current()<<" A";
    return 0;
}
```

4.4
```
class Text{
    char *st;
    int n;
public:
    void Text(int x, char *t)
    {
        st=new int[x];
        strcpy(st,t);
```

```
            n=x;
            delete st;
        }
        void display()
        {
            cout<<st;
        }
};
```

4.5
```
class NumsHex {
    int n1, n2;
public:
    NumsHex(int a, int b) {n1=a; n2=b;}
    NumsHex(int x, int y) {n1=x; n2=y;}
    void showHex(){ cout<<hex<<x<<y;}
};
```

4.6
```
#include <iostream>
using namespace std;
class Nums {
    int x, y;
public:
    Nums(int a, int b){ a=x; b=y;}
    int product() { return x*y; }
};
int main()
{
    Nums n1(3,8);
    Nums n2;
    n2=n1;
    cout<<"Result ="<<n2.product();
    return 0;
}
```

4.7
```
#include <iostream>
using namespace std;
class Nums {
    int x, y;
public:
    void set(int a){ x=a; y=x*2; }
    void display(){ cout<<x<<y; }
};
int main()
{
    Nums *nptr;
    int x=10;
    nptr = new int[x];
    if(nptr==0)
        cout<<"Memory allocation error.";
    for(int i=0; i<x; i++)
    {
        nptr[i].set(i);
        nptr[i].display();
    }
    return 0;
}
```

PROGRAMMING PROJECTS

4.1 Design a class named LC_Circuit with two data members (L and C) that are used to store a circuit's inductance and capacitance, respectively. The class also uses two member functions as follows:

        a. a *non-inline* get_values() function which gets the values of L and C from the user

        b. an ***inline*** res_freq() function which computes and displays an f resonance frequency

Design the ***main( )*** function that will instantiate an object of the LC_Circuit class and then use the object to call class member functions.

NOTE: $f = \dfrac{1}{2\pi\sqrt{LC}}$

4.2 Design a class named `Court` that contains all data members needed to store the following data for a tennis court:

- Length and width of a clay area
- Length and width of a concrete area
- Cost of fencing per ft.
- Cost of clay per square ft.
- Cost of concrete per square ft.

The class should have two constructor functions—a first constructor that initializes class data members to default values (a standard court), and a second constructor that initializes class data members to the values that the user will enter (a customized court). The class should also have all member functions needed to get the input from the user and to compute the total cost of building the tennis court.

Assume that a fence surrounds the clay area (see Figure 4.19). The total cost of building the court should include the cost of fencing around the clay area, the cost of installing clay, and the cost of concrete. Notice that the functions that compute costs should call the utility member functions to compute both the area and circumference of the clay portion and the area of concrete. The user should have the option to choose either the standard court or a customized court. After the user enters the data for a court, the program will compute and display all of the costs of building the court—including the total cost.

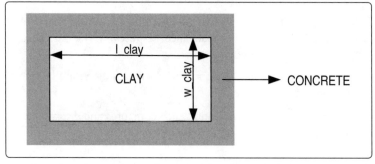

Figure 4.19 *Representation of a tennis court to be built.*

4.3 Design a program that will prompt the user to enter a string, get the string, capitalize each character, and then display the string after capitalization.

The program should use a class with two data members—a character pointer to point to the string entered by the user, and an integer variable to store the size of the string. The class should use a constructor to dynamically allocate a memory block that is the same size as the string entered by the user. The constructor should also initialize that memory block to the entered string. The class destructor should free memory allocated by the constructor. The class should also have member functions that capitalize and display the string.

4.4 Design a `Box` class that uses its data members to store three sides and the volume of a box. The class should also use member functions to set the values of the box's sides, as well as to compute its volume. Design a non-member `totVolume()` function that will dynamically instantiate as many objects (boxes) of the `Box` class as requested by the user and get the values of their sides. The function will compute and return the total volume of all boxes.

The **main( )** function will call `totVolume()`.

 NOTE: `volume=side1*side2*side3`

4.5 Design a program that uses the `Spacecraft` class. This class should store and process the data of a moving spacecraft, such as displacement, velocity, and acceleration in the x and y direction—as well as the time interval in which the spacecraft's motion was processed. The program should obtain the values of the initial velocity and acceleration in the x and y direction from the user, as well as the time interval. It will then compute and display the craft's displacement and velocity in the x and y direction every second within the time interval specified by the user. All input, output, and data processing operations should be done by the `Spacecraft` class member functions.

 NOTE:
$$x = v_{0x}t + \frac{1}{2}a_x t^2 \qquad v_x = v_{0x} + a_x t$$

where x, v_x, v_{0x}, a_x, and t are displacement, velocity, initial velocity, and acceleration in the x direction, and a moment of time within the time interval specified by the user, respectively. The same equations are used to compute y and v_y, using the values of initial velocity and acceleration in the y direction.

CHAPTER 5

Classes:
Advanced Topics

OBJECTIVES

- To understand the mechanisms of passing objects to functions and returning objects from functions

- To understand the need for a copy constructor

- To be able to use *friend* functions and *friend* classes

- To be able to use *static* class members

- To understand the *this* pointer

CHAPTER CONTENTS

INTRODUCTION

The fundamentals of C++ classes have now been introduced, and this chapter will cover the more advanced class concepts. It begins with a discussion of the procedures of passing and returning objects to or from functions. If not performed properly, these operations can be a source of serious errors. A **copy constructor**, which is discussed next, is a solution to the common problems that may occur when passing or returning objects. Friend functions and *friend* classes will be introduced and the reasons for their use will be reviewed. This chapter also discusses a special kind of class members, called *static* members. In addition, the chapter introduces the *this* pointer, which is used when calling member functions. The final topic in this chapter discusses the benefits of using *const* member functions.

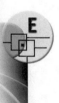

5.1 PASSING TO AND RETURNING OBJECTS FROM FUNCTIONS

Objects can be passed to functions in a similar way to the passing of any other value or variable. Both C and C++ compilers create copies of the values passed to functions in memory and destroy them when the functions are terminated. These copies are not created if the values are passed by pointer or by reference; instead, the addresses of memory locations that store the original values are passed.

When creating an object, a class constructor is automatically invoked. The objects' destruction, on the other hand, invokes the class destructor. The question of whether or not the constructor and destructor functions are also invoked when creating and destroying the object's copies is raised. The answer to this question is very important because knowing it may prevent some serious logic errors.

When passing an object to a function, its copy is created in memory. *It does not, however, invoke a class constructor.* The primary purpose of a constructor function is to initialize a newly created object. When this object is passed to a function, it is necessary to create a copy of the *current* value stored in the object, not the *initial* value. For this reason, the C++ compiler does not invoke the object's constructor when creating its copies.

When a function that has class objects as parameters terminates, the copies of the objects that are passed to the function are destroyed at that point. *The class destructor is called* as many times as there are copies to destroy.

PROG5_1, shown in Program Example 5.1, demonstrates the process of passing objects to functions. It uses a regular, non-member function with two objects as arguments.

PROGRAM EXAMPLE 5.1: PROG5_1

```
1   //PROG5_1: Program demonstrates the process of passing objects
2   //          to functions.
3   #include <iostream>
```

```
4   using namespace std;
5
6   int bcount=0;                    //counter that counts objects
7
8   class Box {
9      float side1, side2, side3;       //three sides of a box
10  public:
11     Box(float s1, float s2, float s3)        //constructor
12     {
13         side1=s1; side2=s2; side3=s3;  //Initializes sides
14         bcount++;                  //Increments counter
15     }
16     ~Box()                     //destructor
17     {
18         bcount--;                  //Decrements counter
19         cout<<"\t\tBox destroyed!\n";
20     }
21     float getVolume()          //Returns volume
22     {
23         return  side1 * side2 * side3;
24     }
25  };
26  float addBoxes(Box, Box);    //objects as function parameters
27
28  int main()
29  {
30     Box a(1,2,3), b(2,3,4);
31     cout<<bcount<<" boxes built so far.\n";
32     cout<<"\t\tTotal volume = "<<addBoxes(a, b)<<endl;
33     cout<<bcount<<" boxes built so far.\n";
34     return 0;
35  }
36
```

```
37 float addBoxes(Box b1, Box b2)    //Returns the total volume of
38 {                                  //the two objects passed
39    cout<<"\t\tAdding boxes:\n";
40    cout<<"\t\t"<<bcount<<" boxes built so far.\n";
41    return b1.getVolume()+b2.getVolume();
42 }
```

The output produced by PROG5_1 is shown in Figure 5.1.

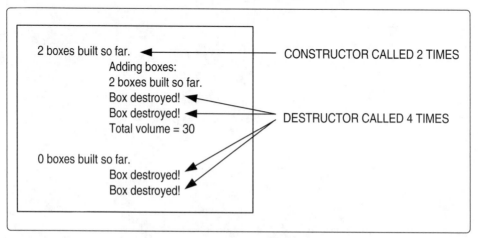

Figure 5.1 *Output produced by PROG5_1.*

PROG5_1 uses a variable bcount to store a number of objects created during the execution of the program. Please note that bcount is declared globally and initialized to 0 (line 6). It must be accessible to member and non-member functions in this program. As it is well known, declaring variables globally is not good programming practice. Section 5.5 will discuss a tool that can be used to avoid this global declaration.

The Box class constructor increments bcount, while its destructor decrements bcount (lines 14 and 18). This might be a way of keeping track of a number of existing objects during the execution of the program. PROG5_1, however, does not count objects correctly and produces incorrect results. This is caused by the process of passing objects to the function addBoxes(). The *main()* function first instantiates two objects, a and b, of the Box class (line 30). The Box constructor increments bcount twice, and the *main()* outputs 2 boxes built so far. (line 31). It then calls the addBoxes() function, and copies b1 and b2 of the objects a and b are created when passed to the function. Note that the *constructor is not called* when creating copies b1 and b2. For this reason, addBoxes() also displays 2 boxes built so far. Before addBoxes() returns the total volume of the two boxes passed to it, the *destructor is called* twice to destroy copies b1 and b2. The destructor is again called twice when *main()* terminates to destroy the original objects a and b. The number of destructor calls (4 calls) does not match the number of constructor calls (2 calls). This may cause some serious problems.

The process of passing objects to functions may become a source of various logic errors, such as incorrect results, which is demonstrated in PROG5_1. Parts of the original objects passed to the function may also be destroyed as a result of this process. Assume, for example, that the destructor frees memory dynamically allocated for an object, which is passed to a function. When the object's copy is destroyed, the destructor will free memory allocated for the original object, which will damage the original object.

One way to prevent destructor calls when passing objects to functions is passing references or addresses of the objects rather than their values. Copies of the objects passed to the function will not be created in this case, and the destructor will not be called when the function terminates. Program Example 5.2 exhibits PROG5_2 as a modified version of PROG5_1 that applies this solution.

PROGRAM EXAMPLE 5.2: PROG5_2

```
1   //PROG5_2: Program demonstrates passing objects' references
2   //          to functions.
3   #include <iostream>
4   using namespace std;
5
6   int bcount = 0;
7   class Box{
8     float side1, side2, side3;
9   public:
10    Box(float s1, float s2, float s3)
11    {
12        side1 = s1; side2 = s2; side3 = s3;
13        bcount++;
14    }
15    ~Box()
16    {
17        bcount--;
18        cout<<"\t\tBox destroyed!\n";
```

```
19    }
20    float getVolume()
21    {
22        return  side1 * side2 * side3;
23    }
24 };
25
26 float addBoxes(Box &, Box &);        //references to objects as
27                                      //function parameters
28 int main()
29 {
30    Box a(1,2,3), b(2,3,4);
31    cout<<bcount<<" boxes built so far.\n";
32    cout<<"\t\tTotal volume = "<<addBoxes(a,b)<<endl;
33    cout<<bcount<<" boxes built so far.\n";
34    return 0;
35 }
36
37 float addBoxes(Box &b1, Box &b2)
38 {
39    cout<<"\t\tAdding boxes:\n";
40    cout<<"\t\t"<<bcount<<" boxes built so far.\n";
41    return b1.getVolume()+b2.getVolume();
42 }
```

Unlike PROG5_1, PROG5_2 produces the desired output that is shown in Figure 5.2. The number of constructor and destructor calls is evenly matched in this example.

A function may return an object by using the **return** statement. The function return type, in this case, must be the class type of that object. The process of returning objects from functions is similar to the process of returning any other *non-object* value.

In Program Example 5.3, PROG5_3 demonstrates the process of returning objects from functions. It uses a member function and a regular, non-member function, both returning a class object.

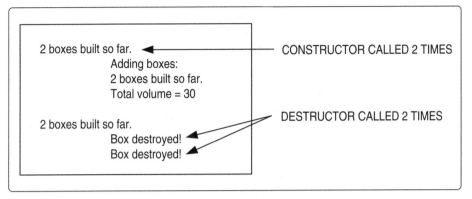

Figure 5.2 *Output produced by PROG5_2.*

PROGRAM EXAMPLE 5.3: PROG5_3

```
1   //PROG5_3: Program demonstrates functions returning objects.
2   #include <iostream>
3   using namespace std;
4
5   class Pixel {
6      int x, y;     //x and y coordinates of a pixel
7   public:
8      Pixel(){ x=0; y=0; }              //default constructor
9      ~Pixel(){cout<<"\t\tPixel destroyed!"<<endl;}  //destructor
10     void setXY(int x1, int y1) { x=x1; y=y1; }
11     void getCoord(){
12        cout<<"Pixel's coordinates:"<<endl;
13        cout<<"X="<<x<<" Y="<<y<<endl;
14     }
15     Pixel move_10(Pixel t){ //Changes x and y values of an object
16        t.x = t.x + 10; //passed and then returns the object.
17        t.y = t.y + 10;
18        return t;
19     }
20  };
21  Pixel setCoord()  //Gets x and y values from the user
```

```
22 {                        //and then instantiates, initializes
23    int x1, y1;                      //and returns an object.
24    cout<<"Enter x and y coordinates =>";
25    cin>>x1>>y1;
26    Pixel temp;
27    temp.setXY(x1,y1);
28    return temp;
29 }
30
31 int main()
32 {
33    Pixel p1, p2;
34    p1=setCoord();   //a non-member function returning an object
35    p1.getCoord();
36    p2 = p1.move_10(p1); //a member function returning an object
37    p2.getCoord();
38    p1.getCoord();
39    return 0;
40 }
```

The Pixel class uses the default constructor to initialize the x and y coordinates of a pixel to 0 (line 8). It also contains the destructor function (line 9), which displays the message Pixel destroyed! The only purpose of the destructor function in this program is to demonstrate the destructor calls. The class contains a member function named move_10() with a Pixel object as a parameter (lines 15–19). Calling the move_10() function creates a copy named t of the object passed to it and changes t's x and y coordinates by adding 10 to their current values (lines 16, 17). It then returns the t object with the new values of x and y (line 18).

The program uses a non-member function named setCoord() (lines 21–29), which gets the values of x and y from the user. It instantiates an object named temp (line 26), initializes temp to the x and y values entered by the user (line 27), and then returns the temp object (line 28).

The *main()* function instantiates two objects, named p1 and p2 (line 33). It then calls the setCoord() function and assigns the object returned by the function to p1 (line 34). *main()* first displays the values of x and y stored in p1 after setCoord() is called (line 35), and then displays the values of x and y in p2 set by the function move_10() (lines 36 and 37). It again displays the values stored in p1 at the end (line 38). It should be noted that p1 is passed first to move_10() and that the object returned by move_10() is then copied into p2 (line 36).

A sample run of PROG5_3 is shown in Figure 5.3.

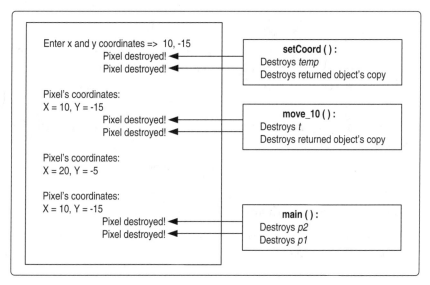

Figure 5.3 *Output produced by PROG5_3.*

It is important to know that a function, which returns an object, first creates a temporary object in memory to store the return value and then returns that value to the program statement that calls the function. *The class destructor is automatically called* to destroy this temporary object after its value is returned. The process of returning objects from functions, therefore, automatically invokes the object's destructor, which may cause similar side effects to those discussed when passing objects to functions.

PROG5_3 calls the class default constructor twice to initialize p1 and p2, while the class destructor is called six times to destroy the following:

1. The local temp object of the function setCoord()

2. A temporary object returned by setCoord()

3. A copy t of the object p1 which was passed to the function move_10()

4. A temporary object returned by move_10()

5. The p2 object instantiated by *main()*

6. The p1 object instantiated by *main()*

Examples PROG5_1 and PROG5_3 demonstrate that the total number of constructor and destructor calls in a program may not be matched, as the result of the operations performed when passing objects to functions or returning objects from functions. This mismatch may cause side effects, if the destructor function performs actions that should reverse the constructor's actions, such as freeing memory dynamically allocated by the constructor or decrementing a counter incremented by the constructor. A C++ tool—discussed in the next section—can prevent these side effects.

5.2 COPY CONSTRUCTOR

C++ provides a special type of constructor function called the **copy constructor**. This constructor overloads a regular class constructor. Unlike the regular constructor, which is called when a new object is instantiated, the copy constructor is called when an object is copied.

The copy constructor is automatically called to initialize an object if one of the following three situations occurs:

1. An object is used to initialize another object in a declaration statement
2. An object is passed to a function
3. An object is returned from a function

Assume the `Pixel` class declaration is given. The following code example demonstrates all three situations when the copy constructor is called:

```
Pixel p1; //Calls the default constructor to initialize p1
Pixel p2=p1;  //p1 initializes p2; Calls the copy constructor (1)
Pixel p3(p2); //p2 initializes p3; Calls the copy constructor (1)
fun1(p1);//p1 is passed to fun1(); Calls the copy constructor (2)
p2=fun2();          //fun2() returns an object to p2;
                //Calls the copy  constructor (3)
p3=p2;              //The copy constructor is not called here.
```

 NOTE: The copy constructor is not called when assigning an object to another object if it is not a declaration statement.

The general format for defining a copy constructor is shown in Figure 5.4.

```
class_name (const class_name & object_name)
{
//Body of the copy constructor
}
```

Figure 5.4 *General format of a copy constructor definition.*

A copy constructor has one parameter, which is a reference to the object to be copied. The *const* keyword precedes the reference because the original object should not be changed. In Program Example 5.4, PROG5_4 demonstrates all three situations when the copy constructor is called.

PROGRAM EXAMPLE 5.4: PROG5_4

```
1   //PROG5_4: Program demonstrates the copy constructor calls.
2   #include <iostream>
3   using namespace std;
4
5   class Pixel{
6       int x, y;
7   public:
8       Pixel(int a, int b)        //regular constructor
9       {
10          x=a; y=b;
11          cout<<"\tNormal Constructor"<<endl;
12      }
13      Pixel(const Pixel &p)      //copy constructor
14      {
15          x=p.x; y=p.y;
16          cout<<"\tCopy Constructor"<<endl;
17      }
18      ~Pixel( ){ cout<<"\tDestructor"<<endl; }
19      void setX(int x1) { x=x1; }
20      void setY(int y1) { y=y1; }
21      void showXY(){ cout<<"X="<<x<<" Y="<<y<<endl; }
22  };
23
24  Pixel center(Pixel tp)        //Sets x and y coordinates to 512
25  { //and returns the object
26      tp.setX(512);
27      tp.setY(512);
```

```
28    return tp;
29  }
30
31  int main()
32  {
33    Pixel p1(10, 20);        //Calls regular constructor
34    p1.showXY();
35    Pixel p2=p1;             //Calls the copy constructor
36    p2.showXY();
37    p2=center(p1);           //Calls the copy constructor twice
38    p2.showXY();
39    return 0;
40  }
```

PROG5_4 produces the output shown in Figure 5.5.

```
              Normal Constructor
      X=10  Y=20
              Copy Constructor
      X=10  Y=20
              Copy Constructor
              Copy Constructor
              Destructor
              Destructor
      X=512  Y=512
              Destructor
              Destructor
```

Figure 5.5 *Output produced by PROG5_4.*

Please note that the purpose of the copy constructor and the destructor functions in this example is to demonstrate the situations when they are called. The copy constructor (lines 13–17) initializes an object to the value of the object passed to it and displays the message Copy Constructor to identify when it is called. The program uses a function named center(), which has an object of the Pixel class as a parameter (lines 24–29). The center() function returns an object where x and y coordinates are set to 512. The copy constructor is called three times in this program, as follows:

1. p2 is declared and initialized to p1 (line 35)

2 p1 is passed to center() (line 37)

3. center() is returning an object to p2 (line 37)

The destructor is called four times in the following order:

1. To destroy a copy of p1 passed to center()

2. To destroy a temporary object that center() uses to store the value to be returned

3. To destroy p2

4. To destroy p1

It should be noted that the number of destructor calls is equal to the total number of all constructor calls (copy constructor calls plus regular constructor calls).

If a class does not have an explicit copy constructor definition, the C++ compiler will create the **default copy constructor**, which will simply make an identical (bit-by-bit) copy of an object. Programmers would have more control over their programs if they defined copy constructors explicitly, although a bit-by-bit copy of an object that is provided by the default copy constructor might be what they need.

In some cases, such as those discussed in Section 5.1, an explicit copy constructor is needed to prevent errors. Assume, for example, that an object contains a pointer that is used to dynamically allocate memory for that object. If a bit-by-bit copy of the object is created, it will contain the pointer pointing to the same memory location as the pointer in the original object. When the object's copy is destroyed, the destructor will free the memory that is still being used by the original object. The original object will therefore be damaged, resulting in an error. To prevent this type of error, a copy constructor should be designed.

PROG5_5 demonstrates a practical use of the copy constructor in Program Example 5.5.

PROGRAM EXAMPLE 5.5: PROG5_5

```
1  //PROG5_5: Program demonstrates a practical use of the copy
2  //         constructor.
3  #include <iostream>
4  using namespace std;
5
6  class Message {
```

EXAMPLE

```
7    char *mes;
8  public:
9    Message(char *m);  //regular constructor
10   Message(const Message &cm);  //copy constructor
11   ~Message();         //destructor
12   void printMes(){ cout<<"\tMessage: "<<mes<<endl; }
13   char * getMes(){ return mes; }
14 };
15
16 Message::Message(char *m)    //regular constructor definition
17 {
18   cout<<"Normal Constructor Called!"<<"  ";
19   mes = new char[strlen(m)+1];
20   cout<<"mes ==> "<<(int)mes<<endl;
21   if(!mes) {
22      cout<<"Allocation Error!";
23      exit(1);
24   }
25   strcpy(mes, m);
26 }
27                               //copy constructor definition
28 Message::Message(const Message &cm)
29 {
30   cout<<"Copy Constructor Called!"<<"    ";
31   mes = new char[strlen(cm.mes)+1];
32   cout<<"mes ==> "<<(int)mes<<endl;
33   if(!mes) {
34      cout<<"Allocation Error!";
35      exit(1);
36   }
37   strcpy(mes, cm.mes);
38 }
39 Message::~Message()          //destructor definition
```

```
40 {
41    cout<<"Destructor Called!"<<"        ";
42    cout<<"mes ==> "<<(int)mes<<"   "<<endl;
43    delete []mes;
44 }
45 void upperMes(Message m)      //Modifies a message to uppercase
46 {                            //and then prints the message
47    int n = strlen(m.getMes());
48    char * t = m.getMes();
49    for(int i=0; i<n; i++)
50       t[i] = toupper(t[i]);
51    t[n] = '\0';
52    Message temp(t);
53    temp.printMes();
54 }
55
56 int main()
57 {
58    Message m1("PROG5_5");
59    m1.printMes( );
60    Message m2("Demonstrates copy constructor!");
61    Message m3 = m2;            //Calls the copy constructor
62    m3.printMes();
63    upperMes(m3);              //Calls the copy constructor
64    return 0;
65 }
```

The Message class in PROG5_5 contains a regular class constructor (lines 16–26). This constructor dynamically allocates memory to store a string accessed through the mes pointer. The class uses the destructor (lines 39–44) to free memory allocated by the constructor. The Message class also contains the copy constructor (lines 28–38), which allocates memory for an object's copy when it is made. The copy constructor is called twice in this program—first when the m3 object is instantiated (line 61), and then when m3 is passed to the upperMes() function (line 63). The copy constructor makes a copy of m3, which contains a pointer cm.mes that is used to access dynamically allocated memory. This pointer does not point to the same memory location as the pointer in the original m3 object; therefore, an error will not occur when its copy is destroyed. Note that the normal constructor, copy constructor, and destructor also print a memory address that the mes pointer points to at the moment of each function call (lines 20, 32, and 42) to indicate which memory location is allocated or destroyed.

The output produced by PROG5_5 is shown in Figure 5.6.

```
Normal Constructor Called!    mes = => 8195760
   Message: PROG5_5
Normal Constructor Called!    mes = => 8195120
Copy Constructor Called!      mes = => 8193536
   Message: Demonstrates copy constructor!
Copy Constructor Called!      mes = => 8195392
Normal Constructor Called!    mes = => 8195312
   Message: DEMONSTRATES COPY CONSTRUCTOR!
Destructor Called!            mes = => 8195312
Destructor Called!            mes = => 8195392
Destructor Called!            mes = => 8193536
Destructor Called!            mes = => 8195120
Destructor Called!            mes = => 8195760
```

Figure 5.6 *Output produced by PROG5_5.*

 TIP: The copy constructor should be explicitly defined when the destructor frees memory dynamically allocated by the constructor.

5.3 FRIEND FUNCTIONS AND CLASSES

5.3.1 FRIEND FUNCTIONS

Hiding data inside a class and letting only class member functions have direct access to *private* data is a very important OOP concept. C++ also provides another kind of function called the *friend* function. A *friend* function is not a member function but can still access class *private* members.

There are several reasons for using *friend* functions and the most important are the following:

- To have one function that can access *private* members of two or more different classes

- To create some types of I/O functions

- To design some types of **operator** functions (covered in Chapter 6)

Consider the following real-life situation. Two families, designated in this example as A and B, are dealing with the same problem. Each family has its private and public *stuff.* The information that is kept private within each family is needed to solve the problem. Assuming that there is no relationship between these two families and their members have never met, how do we solve their problem? A miracle solution to this problem situation is a mutual friend who has access to the private stuff of both families and knows how to solve their problem.

C++ classes are similar to families in real life. They have their private and public stuff, constructive and destructive members, and they could also have family friends. There could be as many constructive members (constructors) within a family as necessary to make the family functional and successful, while only one destructor is sufficient to destroy the family. Other *family-type* relationships will be discussed in Chapters 7 and 8.

A *friend* function takes on the following properties:

- Its prototype is placed inside the class definition and preceded by the **friend** keyword.

- It is defined outside the class as a normal, non-member function.

- It is called just like a normal non-member function. An object and the dot (.) separator do not precede a **friend** function name when it is called.

If a function is a *friend* of two or more different classes, each class must contain the *friend* function prototype within its body.

In Program Example 5.6, PROG5_6 uses two different *friend* functions and both functions have access to the *private* members of two classes. It is used to solve the problem shown in Figure 5.7.

The circuit shown below is a series inductor, capacitor circuit supplied by an ac (alternating current) voltage source. The resonant frequency of this circuit is the natural frequency that the circuit would alternately store and release energy associated with the inductor and capacitor if there was no ac voltage source in the circuit.

PROBLEM: Given the frequency f=200 Hz of the ac source, the inductance L=0.01 H and the capacitance C=0.005 F compute:

A) the reactance of the inductor and capacitor
B) the resonant frequency of the circuit

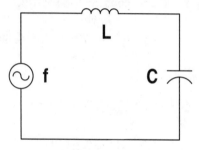

SOLUTION: A) Inductive reactance $X_L=2\pi fL$
$X_L=2*\pi*200*0.01=12.567\ \Omega$

Capacitive reactance $X_c=1/(2\pi fC)$
$X_c=1/(2*\pi*200*0.005)=0.159\ \Omega$

Inductive reactance is greater than capacitive reactance.

B) Resonant frequency $f = 1/(2\pi\sqrt{LC})$
$f = 1/(2*\pi*\sqrt{0.001*0.005}) =22.5079$ Hz

Figure 5.7 *The problem for PROG5_6.*

PROGRAM EXAMPLE 5.6: PROG5_6

```
1  //PROG5_6: Program demonstrates friend functions.
2  #include <iostream>
3  #include <iomanip>
4  #include <cmath>
```

```
5   using namespace std;
6   const double PI=3.14159265;
7
8   class Capacitor;        //forward class declaration, Capacitor
9                           //used in Inductor before its definition
10  class Inductor {
11     double inductance;
12     double frequency;
13     double reactance;
14  public:
15     Inductor(double i, double f) {
16         inductance=i;
17         frequency=f;
18         reactance=2*PI*frequency*inductance;
19     }
20     friend void compReactance(Inductor, Capacitor);
21     friend double resFrequency(Inductor, Capacitor);
22  };
23  class Capacitor {
24     double capacitance;
25     double frequency;
26     double reactance;
27  public:
28     Capacitor(double c, double f)
29     {
30         capacitance=c;
31         frequency=f;
32     reactance=1/(2*PI*frequency*capacitance);
33     }
34     friend void compReactance(Inductor, Capacitor);
35     friend double resFrequency(Inductor, Capacitor);
36  };
37  //friend function definition
```

```
38 void compReactance(Inductor in, Capacitor cp)
39 {
40   if(in.reactance>cp.reactance)
41   {
42       cout<<"Inductive reactance is greater than capacitive ";
43       cout<<"reactance."<<endl;
44   }
45   else if(in.reactance<cp.reactance)
46   {
47       cout<<"Capacitive reactance is greater than inductive ";
48       cout<<"reactance."<<endl;
49   }
50   else
51       cout<<"Inductive and capacitive reactances are equal.\n";
52 }
53 //friend function definition
54 double resFrequency(Inductor in, Capacitor cp)
55 {
56   return 1/(2*PI*sqrt(in.inductance*cp.capacitance));
57 }
58
59 int main()
60 {
61   Inductor ind(0.01,200);
62   Capacitor cap(0.005,200);
63   compReactance(ind, cap);          //friend function call
64   cout<<setiosflags(ios::fixed)<<setprecision(4);
65   cout<<"\n\nResonant Frequency = "<<resFrequency(ind, cap);
66   cout<<" Hz\n\n";
67   return 0;
68 }
```

```
friend function call
```

The Inductor and Capacitor classes in PROG5_6 have two mutual *friend* functions: compReactance() and resFrequency(). Their prototypes are placed within the class bodies (lines 20, 21, 34, and 35). It should be noted that the *friend* function prototypes are placed in the *public* sections of both classes. They could be placed in the *private* section as well and it would not change the outcome because *private/public* access specifiers only affect the class members.

A forward declaration of the Capacitor class (line 8) is necessary in order to use a parameter of this type in the *friend* function prototypes within the Inductor class. This forward reference informs the compiler that Capacitor is a class whose definition follows.

The *friend* functions are defined outside the classes (lines 38–52 and 54–57) just like normal non-member functions. The compReactance() function compares the reactance of an inductor and a capacitor and displays which one is greater. The resFrequency() function computes and returns the resonant frequency. Both functions have an object of the Inductor class and the Capacitor class as parameters. These objects must be passed to *friend* functions to give them access to the *private* class members. For example, a copy of the cap object (named cp) is used by the resFrequency() *friend* function to access capacitance (line 56), which is the Capacitor class *private* data member.

The *main()* function calls *friend* functions just like normal non-member functions, and passes the two ind and cap objects to both functions (lines 63 and 65).

The output produced by PROG5_6 is shown in Figure 5.8.

```
Inductive reactance is greater than capacitive reactance.

Resonant Frequency = 22.5079 Hz
```

Figure 5.8 *Output produced by PROG5_6.*

A *friend* function *cannot be inherited*. Each parent or child class in the inheritance chain should have its own friends. Inheritance issues will be discussed in Chapter 7.

A *friend* function *may be a member* of one class and a *friend* of another. This means that friends are not necessarily *orphans*—they might have their own families as well.

Assume that the resFrequency() function in PROG5_6 is a *public* member function of the Inductor class, and a *friend* of the Capacitor class. The following lines in PROG5_6 would have to be changed:

- **line 21:**   //within the Inductor class

        friend double resFrequency(Inductor, Capacitor);

would have to be changed to:

```
double resFrequency(Capacitor);
//Inductor is removed from the parameter list.
```

- line 35:   //within the Capacitor class

```
friend double resFrequency(Inductor, Capacitor);
```

would have to be changed to:

```
friend double Inductor::resFrequency(Capacitor);
//Inductor and '::' precedes the function name.
```

- lines 54–57:   //function definition

```
double resFrequency(Inductor in, Capacitor cp)
{
        return 1/(2*PI*sqrt(in.inductance*cp.capacitance));
}
```

would have to be changed to:

```
double Inductor::resFrequency(Capacitor cp)
{
        return 1/(2*PI*sqrt(inductance*cp.capacitance));
}
//A member of Inductor has direct access to inductance.
```

- line 65:   //in main()

```
cout<<"\n\nResonant Frequency = "<<resFrequency(ind, cap);
```

would have to be changed to:

```
cout<<"\n\nResonant Frequency = "<<ind.resFrequency(cap);
//Calling function as a member of Inductor (not friend)
```

A summary of all the changes that should be done in PROG5_6 when changing resFrequency() from the *friend* function to the Inductor member function is as follows:

1. The *friend* keyword before the resFrequency() function return type must be deleted from the function prototype within the Inductor class.

2. The Inductor object should be deleted from the function's list of arguments.

This argument is not necessary because with the function being a member now, it has direct access to the Inductor's **private** members.

3. The Inductor class name and the scope resolution operator (::) must precede the function name in the function prototype within the Capacitor class, as well as in the function definition, to identify that the function is a member of Inductor.

4. An object of the Inductor class and the dot separator (.) must precede the function name in the function call.

Although the *friend* functions may be needed and are very important in some cases (see Chapter 6), *they should not be overused.* Note that in programming, as in real life, it is better to have a few *really good* friends rather than too many friends.

 NOTE: While the **friend** function is not a member of a class, it has access to the class **private** members through an object of that class passed as a parameter to the function.

5.3.2 FRIEND CLASSES

An entire class can be a *friend* of another class. This approach can be used when all member functions of one class should access the data of another class.

Designing functions as *friend* functions requires that their prototypes be placed within each class individually. An entire class, on the other hand, can be designed as a *friend* class and all its member functions automatically granted a friendship by the class to which it is a *friend*.

This is the same kind of relationship as a real-life relationship in which family A grants a friendship to family B. As a result of that relationship, the members of family B can access the *private* data of family A. It is not true in reverse, unless specified explicitly—i.e., the members of family A cannot access the *private* data of family B unless B grants its friendship to A.

To make the A class a *friend* of the B class, the *friend* keyword must precede the A class name and be placed within the body of the B class. The A class should be defined prior to the B class or its forward reference must be placed before the B class definition as follows:

```
class A;                //forward class declaration
class B {
    //private members of B
public:
    friend A;           //A is a friend of B
    //public members of B
};
```

The statement `friend A;` can also be placed in the ***private*** section of the B class; however, it would make no difference.

PROG5_7 (shown in Program Example 5.7) is a modified version of PROG5_6, in which the `Capacitor` class is created as a ***friend*** of the `Inductor` class.

PROGRAM EXAMPLE 5.7: PROG5_7

```
1   //PROG5_7: Program demonstrates friend classes.
2   #include <iostream>
3   #include <iomanip>
4   #include <cmath>
5   using namespace std;
6   const double PI=3.14159265;
7   class Capacitor;                //forward class declaration
8
9   class Inductor {
10     double inductance;
11     double frequency;
12     double reactance;
13  public:
14     Inductor(double i, double f)
15     {
16         inductance=i;
17         frequency=f;
18         reactance=2*PI*frequency*inductance;
19     }
20     friend Capacitor;           //Capacitor is a friend of Inductor
21  };
22
23  class Capacitor {
24     double capacitance;
25     double frequency;
26     double reactance;
27  public:
```

```
28    Capacitor(double c, double f)
29    {
30        capacitance=c;
31        frequency=f;
32        reactance=1/(2*PI*frequency*capacitance);
33    }
34    void compReactance(Inductor);
35    double resFrequency(Inductor);
36 };
37
38 void Capacitor::compReactance(Inductor in)
39 {
40    if(in.reactance>reactance)
41    {
42        cout<<"Inductive reactance is greater than capacitive ";
43        cout<<"reactance."<<endl;
44    }
45    else if(in.reactance<reactance)
46    {
47        cout<<"Capacitive reactance is greater than inductive ";
48        cout<<"reactance."<<endl;
49    }
50    else
51        cout<<"Inductive and capacitive reactances are equal.\n";
52 }
53 double Capacitor::resFrequency(Inductor in)
54 {
55    return 1/(2*PI*sqrt(in.inductance*capacitance));
56 }
57
58 int main()
59 {
60    Inductor ind(0.01, 200);
```

```
61    Capacitor cap(0.005, 200);
62    cap.compReactance(ind);
63    cout<<setiosflags(ios::fixed)<<setprecision(4);
64    cout<<"\n\nResonant Frequency = "<<cap.resFrequency(ind);
65    cout<<" Hz\n\n";
66    return 0;
67  }
```

Please note that the compReactance() and resFrequency() functions in PROG5_7 are member functions of the Capacitor class (lines 34 and 35), which is a *friend* class of the Inductor class (line 20). Being members of the *friend* class automatically gives these functions access to the *private* data of the Inductor class (granted the friendship). These two functions have exactly the same access privileges as they have in PROG5_6, in which they are individually designed as *friend* functions.

Using *friend* classes provides a means of establishing relationships between classes. C++, however, provides some other more common and more efficient tools to establish these relationships (see Chapters 7–9).

NOTE: A friendship is NOT:

- Reverse — If A is a *friend* of B, it does not mean that B is a *friend* of A, unless specified explicitly.

- Transitive — If A is a *friend* of B and B is a *friend* of C, it does not mean that A is a *friend* of C.

- Inherited — If A is a *friend* of B, it does not mean that A is a *friend* of a child of B as well (Chapter 7).

5.4 STATIC MEMBERS

A *static* class member is a new kind of a class member. When members of a class—either data members or member functions—are declared *static,* they take on a different meaning than if they are regular, *non-static* members. Class members can be declared *static* simply by placing the *static* keyword at the beginning of their declaration statements inside the class.

5.4.1 STATIC DATA MEMBERS

Unlike regular data members, *static* data members do not belong to any particular object of a class. They belong, instead, to the class itself. C++ creates one copy of each *static* data member in memory, *no matter how many class objects are instantiated.* All objects of the class therefore share the same copy of a *static* member. To make a data member *static,* the *static* keyword must precede the data member name when it is declared inside the class.

The following class example contains a *static* data member:

```
class Amplifier {
    float gain, voltage;
public:
    static int acount;
    void calc();
};
```

If it is assumed that 10 objects of the `Amplifier` class are instantiated, then there will be 10 copies of values of the *non-static* data members `gain` and `voltage` in memory and only one copy of the *static* member `acount`.

To allocate memory for regular *non-static* data members, objects must be instantiated. Each object will have its own copies of all *non-static* data members. Because *static* data members do not belong to objects, they have to be defined individually outside the class in order to allocate memory for their values.

To define a *static* data member outside the class, the general format shown in Figure 5.9 is used.

```
data_type class_name::stvar_name = initial_value;
```

Figure 5.9 *General format of a* **static** *data member definition statement outside the class.*

An example of this statement for the `Amplifier` class could be as follows:

```
int Amplifier::acount=1;
```

Remember that the class name and the :: operator must precede the *static* data member name when declared outside the class, or the compiler will process it as a non-member variable. All *static* data members are initialized to 0 by default. The programmer can also initialize a *static* data member to a value of his or her choice.

A *static* data member is similar to a global variable because all functions—member or non-member—have access to its value. It is, however, safer than a global variable because its scope is restricted to the class to which it belongs. For this reason, each time a *static* member is used or accessed by a non-member function, the class name and the :: operator must precede the *static* member name. This is demonstrated in the following example, which uses the `acount` *static* member of the `Amplifier` class:

```
void fun()
{
    Amplifier::acount++;
}
```

```
int main()
{
    //…
    cout<<Amplifier::acount;
    //…
}
```

The `fun()` and ***main( )*** functions in this example are non-member functions; therefore, the `Amplifier` class name and the **::** operator must precede `acount` in order to access its value. Note that the class name and **::** do not have to precede the ***static*** member name if accessed by a member function.

All ***static*** data members exist in memory before any object of their class is instantiated. Being independent from objects, they are good candidates for the following:

- Counters that count the number of objects instantiated or destroyed
- Totals that accumulate values stored in objects
- Variables that control access to the devices shared by all objects, such as servers, printers, and disk drives

In Program Example 5.8, PROG5_8 demonstrates a practical use of ***static*** data members.

PROGRAM EXAMPLE 5.8: PROG5_8

```
1   //PROG5_8: Program demonstrates static data members.
2   #include <iostream>
3   using namespace std;
4
5   class Node {
6       int num;                //node number
7   public:
8       static int ncount;      //counts nodes
9       static int pcount;      //counts how many nodes used printer
10      Node(){ num=1; ncount++; }          //constructor #1
11      Node(int x){ num=x; ncount++; }     //constructor #2
12      ~Node(){ ncount--; }                //destructor
13      void printer();
14  };
```

```
15 void Node::printer()
16 {
17    pcount++;
18    cout<<"\nThere are "<<ncount<<" nodes."<<endl;
19    cout<<"\t\t\tNode #"<<num<<" uses printer now!"<<endl;
20    cout<<pcount<<" node(s) used printer so far."<<endl;
21 }
22 int Node::ncount=0;   //Allocates memory for static data members
23 int Node::pcount=0;   //and explicitly initializes to 0 (clearer)
24 int main()
25 {
26    cout<<"\nThere are "<<Node::ncount<<" nodes."<<endl;
27    Node n1, n2(2), n3(3);        //n1 invokes constructor #1
28    n2.printer();
29    {
30       Node n4(4), n5(5);
31       n5.printer();
32    }
33    cout<<"\nThere are "<<Node::ncount<<" nodes."<<endl;
34    return 0;
35 }
```

PROG5_8 uses the Node class, which has two *static* data members (ncount and pcount) used to track the number of nodes instantiated and the number of nodes that used the printer, respectively. Class constructors increment ncount while the class destructor decrements it. The *main()* function accesses ncount before any object of the Node class is instantiated (line 26). It then instantiates three objects, n1, n2, and n3 (line 27), and uses n2 to call the printer() function (line 28). Figure 5.10 shows the memory contents after the execution of line 28.

178

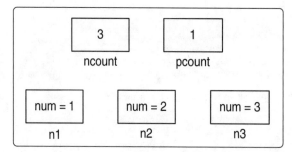

Figure 5.10 *Memory contents after the execution of the line 28 in PROG5_8.*

There are three objects in memory at this point, and one copy each of ncount and pcount. A block of code between lines 29 and 32 instantiates two new objects, n4 and n5, and then uses n5 to call the printer() function. These two objects are destroyed when the block ends (line 32).

The output of PROG5_8 is shown in Figure 5.11.

PROG5_8 simulates a real-life situation in which several nodes or computers share the same printer. Static data members are used in this example to track the statistics of a number of active nodes and the printer's usage.

Static data members can be processed by *static* member functions that are discussed in the next section.

```
There are 0 nodes.

There are 3 nodes.
             Node #2 uses printer now!
1 node(s) used printer so far.

There are 5 nodes.
             Node #5 uses printer now!
2 node(s) used printer so far.

There are 3 nodes.
```

Figure 5.11 *Output produced by PROG5_8.*

5.4.2 STATIC MEMBER FUNCTIONS

A member function can be declared *static* simply by preceding the function return type with the *static* keyword in a class definition. It is important to know that *static* member functions can be called from across different programs that are linked together. Static member functions are used and processed in a different way than *non-static* functions. The most important differences between *static* and *non-static* member functions are the following:

- A *static* member function is not attached to any object.

- An object is not needed when calling *static* member functions. Instead, a class name followed by the scope resolution (::) operator should precede the *static* function name when called.

- A *static* member function does not have direct access to the *private* class data members. A pointer or a reference to an object should be passed to the function to enable access to the object's *private* data.

- A *static* member function does not have a *this* pointer (the *this* pointer will be discussed in the next section).

PROG5_9 (see Program Example 5.9) is a modified version of PROG5_8, in which the printer() function is changed to a *static* member function. Both programs produce the same output.

PROGRAM EXAMPLE 5.9: PROG5_9

```
1  //PROG5_9: Program demonstrates static member functions.
2  #include <iostream>
3  using namespace std;
4
5  class Node {
6      int num; //node number
7  public:
8      static int ncount; //counts nodes
9      static int pcount; //counts printer's usage
10     Node(){ num=1; ncount++; }
11     Node(int x){ num=x; ncount++; }
12     ~Node() { ncount--; }
13     static void printer(Node &n);       //static function prototype
14  };                    //pass a reference to access private data
15  void Node::printer(Node &n)   //static function definition
16  {
```

```
17    pcount++;
18    cout<<"\nThere are "<<ncount<<" nodes."<<endl;
19    cout<<"\t\t\tNode #"<<n.num<<" uses printer now!"<<endl;
20    cout<<pcount<<" node(s) used printer so far."<<endl;
21 }
22 int Node::ncount=0;
23 int Node::pcount=0;
24 int main()
25 {
26    cout<<"\nThere are "<<Node::ncount<<" nodes."<<endl;
27    Node n1, n2(2), n3(3);
28    Node::printer(n2);                  //static function call
29    {
30        Node n4(4), n5(5);
31        Node::printer(n5);              //static function call
32    }
33    cout<<"\nThere are "<<Node::ncount<<" nodes."<<endl;
34    return 0;
35 }
```

Note that the printer() function, defined as *static* in this program, takes on different properties as compared to the same function designed as *non-static* in PROG5_8. The *static* printer() function uses a reference to a Node object, named n, in order to access the object's *private* data member num (line 19). This reference is not needed in the printer() function, designed as *non-static* in PROG5_8, because it can access num directly. Notice also that a specific object is not used when calling the *static* printer() function in PROG5_9; instead, the Node class name and :: precede the function name (lines 28 and 31).

Static member functions are used to manipulate *static* data members. They can also be used for **external linkage** (used in different programs that are linked together). There are few practical reasons for their use other than those mentioned, and they are rarely used.

 TIP: Avoid global variables and use *static* data members instead for counters, totals, and other variables that are shared between objects of a specific class.

5.5 THE *this* POINTER

The C++ compiler creates and uses a special kind of pointer called the ***this*** pointer. The ***this*** pointer stores the address of an object used to call a *non-static* member function.

It should be noted that each *non-static* member function name must be preceded with an object name when calling the function. The address of that object is passed to the function and stored in ***this***. In order to access the data stored in the object, the function uses the object's address stored in ***this***. Most of the time the ***this*** pointer is hidden from programmers and is handled and processed implicitly by the compiler. Programmers, however, can use the pointer explicitly as well. It is also important to be aware of the existence of the ***this*** pointer *behind the scenes* in order to properly use some advanced OOP tools.

Assume the following definition of the `Pixel` class:

```
class Pixel {
    int x, y;
public:
    void set(int a, int b) { x=a; y=b; }    //the this pointer is
    void get() { cout<<x<<y; }   //hidden here
}
```

The `Pixel` class can be redefined by using the ***this*** pointer explicitly, as follows:

```
class Pixel {
    int x, y;
public:                //the this pointer is used explicitly
    void set(int a, int b) { this->x=a; this->y=b; }
    void get() { cout<<this->x<<this->y; }
}
```

When calling `set()` or `get()`—*non-static* member functions of the `Pixel` class—the address of the object for which the function is called is stored in ***this***. Values of the object's data members can be explicitly accessed through the ***this*** pointer by using one of the two general formats shown in Figure 5.12.

Note that the syntax shown in Figure 5.12 is the same syntax that is used to access structure members by using a pointer that points to a structure variable.

```
        this->member_name

        or

        (*this).member_name
```

Figure 5.12 *Accessing class members through the **this** pointer.*

The type of ***this*** pointer is the type of a class whose object's address is stored in ***this***. For example, the ***this*** type in member functions set() and get() of the Pixel class is Pixel *. If a member function is declared ***const***, the ***this*** type is const Pixel *.

In the example shown, and in most other cases, it is not necessary to use the ***this*** pointer explicitly. It even adds unnecessary complexity to a program. There are, however, cases when it is necessary to return an object that is used to call the function. Because the object is passed implicitly by ***this***, it is necessary to use ***this*** explicitly in order to return the object, as follows:

```
return  * this;
```

Note that ***this*** must be dereferenced in the same way as any other pointer, in order to get the value stored at the pointed address.

In Program Example 5.10, PROG5_10 demonstrates an explicit use of the ***this*** pointer.

PROGRAM EXAMPLE 5.10: PROG5_10

```
1   //PROG5_10: Program demonstrates an explicit use of the this
2   //          pointer.
3   #include <iostream>
4   using namespace std;
5
6   class Pixel{
7       int x, y;
8   public:
9       Pixel() { cout<<"\t\tPixel created!"<<endl; x=0; y=0; }
10      ~Pixel() { cout<<"\t\tPixel destroyed!"<<endl; }
11      void setCoord(int x1, int y1) { x=x1; y=y1; }
12      void getCoord()
```

```
13    {
14        cout<<"Pixel's coordinates:"<<endl;
15        cout<<"X="<<x<<" Y="<<y<<endl;
16    }
17    Pixel move_10()
18    {
19        x = x + 10;
20        y = y + 10;
21        return * this;      //the this pointer is used explicitly
22    }
23 };
24 int main()
25 {
26    Pixel p1, p2;
27    int x1, y1;
28    cout<<"Enter X and Y coordinates =>";
29    cin>>x1>>y1;
30    p1.setCoord(x1,y1);
31    p1.getCoord();
32    p2 = p1.move_10();
33    p2.getCoord();
34    p1.getCoord();
35    return 0;
36 }
```

A sample run of PROG5_10 is shown in Figure 5.13.

```
                    Pixel created!
                    Pixel created!
          Enter X and Y coordinates =>3 95
          Pixel's coordinates:
          X=3 Y=95
                        Pixel destroyed!
          Pixel's coordinates:
          X=13 Y=105
          Pixel's coordinates:
          X=13 Y=105
                        Pixel destroyed!
                        Pixel destroyed!
```

Figure 5.13 *Sample run of PROG510.*

The move_10() function is called by using the p1 object (line 32). This means that the address of p1 is passed to move_10() and stored in **this**. The x and y coordinates of p1 are accessed through **this** in move_10() and changed by adding the number 10 to each. The function uses **this** explicitly to return the value of p1 (line 21) after changing its x and y values. The new value of p1 is then copied by the assignment operator into p2 (line 32).

To conclude this section, it is important to remember that every *non-static* member function has an implicit parameter which is created by the C++ compiler. That parameter is the **this** pointer. Although the **this** pointer is not created explicitly by programmers, it is important that they understand its operation in order to properly design the operator functions discussed in the next chapter.

 NOTE: Friend and *static* functions *do not* have the **this** pointer.

 TIP: Use **this** explicitly when returning an object that is used to call a *non-static* member function.

5.6 CONSTANT MEMBER FUNCTIONS

A *const* member function is a special type of a member function. Unlike regular *non-const* member functions, a *const* member function cannot modify the object that is used to invoke the function. The object, on which the member function is invoked, is passed by the **this** pointer to the function.

To declare a member function as **const**, the **const** keyword must be inserted after the closing bracket of the parameter list, in both the function prototype and function definition (see Figure 5.14).

```
//const member function prototype
return_type function_name(parameter list) const;


    //const member function definition
return_type class_name::function_name(parameter list)const
{
    //body of the function
}
```

Figure 5.14 *General format of a* **const** *member function.*

The advantage of **const** member functions over *non-const* member functions is that any inadvertent attempt to modify the object on which the function is invoked will be detected at compile time, preventing some types of run-time errors. Constant member functions must be used when working with **constant objects**. Any object whose data members need to be protected against any change at run-time should be declared as a constant object. To declare an object as a constant object, the **const** keyword must precede the object type as follows:

```
const Power source(110, 60);
```

The `source` object of the `Power` class in this example is declared as a constant object. Any attempt, therefore, to modify the values stored in the `source` object will be detected by the compiler and result in a syntax error.

Assume the following definition of the `Power` class:

```
class Power {
    float voltage;
    float frequency;
public:
    Power(float v, float f) { voltage = v; frequency = f; }
    void display(){ cout<<voltage<<frequency; }
    float getVolt() { return voltage; }
};
```

This class uses two regular *non-const* member functions—display() and getVolt()—as well as a constructor function.

Given the previously defined Power class, the following code fragment contains some syntax errors:

```
const Power source(110, 60);    //CORRECT; a const object is
                                            //instantiated

Power bat1(12, 0);              //CORRECT; a non-const object is
                                            //instantiated

float v1, v2;
v1=source.getVolt();     //ERROR; non-const function cannot
                                    //process const object
v2=bat1.getVolt();              //CORRECT
source.display();        //ERROR; non-const function cannot
                                    //process const object
bat1.display();                 //CORRECT
```

Syntax errors in this example are caused by an attempt to process the **const** source object by the display() and getVolt() *non-const* functions. To eliminate these errors, the display() and getVolt() functions must be changed to **const** functions as follows:

```
class Power {
    float voltage;
    float frequency;
public:
    Power(float v, float f) { voltage = v; frequency = f; }
    void display() const { cout<<voltage<<frequency; }
    float getVolt() const { return voltage;}
};
```

Notice that the Power constructor is used to initialize the **const** source object, although the constructor is not specified as **const**. Destructor and constructor functions cannot be declared as **const** functions. An object declared as **const** gains its **const** status after being initialized by a constructor and remains **const** until the destructor is invoked to *clean up* the object.

A **const** member function can be overloaded with a *non-const* function. The compiler will chose the **const** version of the overloaded function if a **const** object is used to invoke the function, and will choose the *non-const* version if a *non-const* object is used.

When using *const* member functions and *const* objects, each of the following actions will cause a syntax error:

- Attempting to modify a **const** object
- Using a **const** object to invoke a *non-const* member function
- Using a **const** member function to modify class data members
- Declaring a constructor or destructor as **const**
- Attempting to modify a **const** object by using the assignment operator
- Calling a *non-const* member function from the body of a **const** function

Declaring non-modifiable objects as *const* is good programming practice because the compiler will detect any attempt to modify these objects and prevent run-time errors. Constant member functions are required to work with *const* objects.

Remember that member functions, which modify the initial values of class data members, cannot be declared as *const*. Declaring the following two functions as *const* member functions of the Power class, therefore, results in a syntax error:

```
void set(float v, float f ) const
{                    //ERROR; this function cannot be const
    voltage = v; frequency = f;
}

void setVolt() const    //ERROR; this function cannot be const
{
    cout<<"Enter voltage:";
    cin>>voltage;
}
```

 TIP: It is good programming practice to declare all member functions that do not modify objects that are used to invoke the functions as **const** because these functions can be used to work with *non-const* objects as well as **const** objects.

SUMMARY

1. Passing an object to a function does not invoke a class constructor when creating a copy of the object. The class destructor is called to individually destroy the copies of all objects passed to the function. To prevent destructor calls, objects should be passed to functions by reference or by address.

2. Functions returning objects create a temporary copy of an object to be returned. After the object's value is returned, the destructor is called to destroy the temporary object.

3. The total number of constructor and destructor calls may not be matched in a program as a result of the operations performed when passing to or returning objects from functions. This may become a source of errors in cases when destructors are designed to reverse the constructor's actions.

4. A copy constructor is automatically invoked when an object's copy is created in declaration statements or when passing to or returning objects from functions. An explicit copy constructor should be designed to prevent some types of errors that may occur when copying objects.

5. A *friend* function is not a member function but it still has access to the class *private* members through an object passed as a parameter to the function.

6. A class can be a *friend* of another class. All member functions of the *friend* class have the same access privileges as individual *friend* functions.

7. A friendship is neither reverse, transitive, nor inherited in nature.

8. A *static* data member does not belong to any specific object of its class. All objects share the same copy of the *static* data member.

9. Static member functions are not attached to any object and are usually used to manipulate *static* data members.

10. The C++ compiler creates the *this* pointer for all *non-static* member functions and uses it to store the address of the object used when calling a function. Friend and *static* functions do not have the *this* pointer.

11. Const member functions must be used when working with *const* objects.

EXERCISES

Identify and correct the errors in the code fragments in Exercises 5.1 through 5.5.

5.1
```
class Point {
    int a, b;
    static int c = 1;
public:
    Point(Point &x) { a = x.a; b = x.b; }
    Point(int x) { a = b = x; }
    int calc(int c) { return (a * c + b); }
    friend void display();
};
void display()
{
    cout<<a<<b;
}
```

5.2
```
class Stat {
    static float total;
    float x;
public:
    Stat(float y) { x = y; }
    static void add();
};
static void Stat::add()
{
    total += x;
}
```

5.3
```
class Nums {
    int x, y;
public:
    Nums(){ x = 3; y = 5; }
    void inc()
```

```
        {
            this->x++;
            this->y++;
            return this;
        }
    };
```

5.4
```
class Resistor {
    float r, v;
public:
    Resistor() { r = 100; v = 110; }
    friend float current(Resistor res);
};
float Resistor::current(Resistor res)
{
    return res.v / res.r;
}
```

5.5
```
class Power {
    float voltage;
    float frequency;
public:
    Power() const { voltage = 110; frequency = 60; }
    void display() const { cout<<voltage<<frequency; }
    float getVolt() const { return voltage; }
    void setVolt() const {
        cout<<"Enter voltage:";
        cin>>voltage;
    }
};
```

5.6 Given the following Pixel class definition, write a definition of the display() **friend** function that will display the values of x and y. Give an example of the function call.

```
class Pixel {
```

```
        int x, y;
    public:
        Pixel(int a, int b){ x = a; y = b; }
        friend void display(Pixel obj);
    };
```

5.7 Code the missing fragments in the following program. The `area()` *friend* function will return the area of a circle when it is called.

```
#include <iostream>
using namespace std;
class Circle {
    float radius;
public:
    Circle(float r) { radius = r; }
    friend float area(Circle c);
};
    //definition of the area() function

int main()
{
    float r;
    cout<<"Enter radius ==> ";
    cin>>r;
    Circle c1(r);
    cout<<"\nThe area is: ";
    cout<< _____    //function call is missing here
    return 0;
}
```

State the output produced by programs in Exercises 5.8 and 5.9.

5.8
```
#include <iostream>
using namespace std;
class Pixel {
    int x, y;
```

```cpp
public:
    static int count;
    Pixel(){ count++; }
    ~Pixel(){count--; }
};
int Pixel::count = 0;
int main()
{
    Pixel p[5];
    Pixel p1 = p[0];
    cout<<Pixel::count<<endl;
    {
        Pixel p2[3];
        cout<<Pixel::count<<endl;
    }
    cout<<Pixel::count;
    return 0;
}
```

5.9
```cpp
#include <iostream>
using namespace std;
class Pixel{
    int x,y;
public:
    static int count;
    Pixel(){ count++; }
    ~Pixel(){count--; }
    Pixel(const Pixel &obj)
    {
        x=obj.x;  y=obj.y;   count++;
    }
};
int Pixel::count = 0;
int main()
```

```
{
    Pixel p[10];
    Pixel pg1 = p[1];
    Pixel pg2 = p[2];
    cout<<Pixel::count<<endl;
    return 0;
}
```

PROGRAMMING PROJECTS

5.1 Modify PROG5_I (See Program Example 5.I) and change the global bcount variable to a *static* data member of the Box class. Design a copy constructor for the Box class to enable bcount to correctly count the number of active objects during program execution. Note that the total number of all constructor calls must match the number of destructor calls.

5.2 Design Amplifier and Speaker classes that can be used to store and process the data of an amplifier and a speaker. Both classes should have two mutual *friend* functions as follows:

        I. display() *friend* function that displays data of the amplifier and the speaker

        2. compare() *friend* function that compares the impedances of the amplifier and the speaker and displays whichever is greater. If the impedances are equal, it should display the message Impedances are matched!

Design the *main( )* function to call both *friend* functions.

5.3 Modify the previous program and make the Speaker class a *friend* of the Amplifier class. The display() and compare() *friend* functions should be changed to member functions of the Speaker class.

5.4 Create a class named Temperature that contains the following members:

- A temp data member used to store a temperature
- A totTemp *static* data member used to store the total of all temperatures entered by the user
- A member function that obtains a value of the temperature (temp) from the user and accumulates totTemp—i.e., adds temp to the current value of totTemp
- A *static* member function that computes and returns the weekly average temperature

Design the *main( )* function to create an array of objects of the `Temperature` class and call class member functions to obtain temperatures for a week from the user and compute and display the average temperature.

5.5 Design a class that uses an `iptr` integer pointer to access a dynamically allocated array. The class constructor should dynamically allocate memory to store as many integer values as requested by the user and use `iptr` to access that memory block. The class destructor should free memory allocated by the constructor. A copy constructor should be designed to prevent unwanted destructor calls. The class should also use two member functions to assign values to the array elements and display them, respectively.

Design the *main( )* function to instantiate two objects of this class. The first object will contain an integer array, the elements of which are sorted in ascending order, while in the second object they are in descending order. When instantiating the second object, it should be initialized by the first object, which will invoke the copy constructor.

5.6 Design a class that simulates an output buffer. The class should use a *static* string as a buffer to store the messages sent by class objects. Each object should have its own string data member named `message`. The class should have a `putMessage()` member function that puts the object's message into the buffer.

Design two *static* functions for this class as follows:

      1. a `clearBuf()` *static* function that clears the buffer

      2. a `display()` *static* function that displays the content of the buffer

Design the *main( )* function to first instantiate three objects of the class as shown in Figure 5.15. It should then call `putMessage()` with each object to put their messages into the buffer. The content of the buffer will be displayed by calling `display()` before and after clearing the buffer with `clearBuf()`.

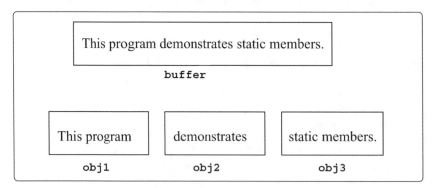

Figure 5.15 *Sample of memory contents during the execution of the program in Programming Project 5.6.*

CHAPTER 6

Operator Overloading

OBJECTIVES

- To understand the fundamentals of operator overloading
- To be able to design member operator functions and *friend* operator functions
- To understand the differences between overloading binary and unary operators
- To be able to overload the stream insertion and stream extraction operators

CHAPTER CONTENTS

INTRODUCTION

Both C and C++ contain a rich collection of operators. The use of operators enables programmers to write concise expressions and produce clearer code. Operators defined in the C/C++ library perform operations on variables or objects of built-in data types. C++ is a more extensible language than C. It provides, for example, a tool called **operator overloading** that enables programmers to use existing operators to manipulate objects of their own classes. This chapter will address all aspects of operator overloading and demonstrate some practical examples of programs that implement operator overloading.

6.1 FUNDAMENTALS OF OPERATOR OVERLOADING

Operator overloading is a special type of function overloading. It is a process in which programmers instruct the C++ compiler to apply existing operators in an effort to manipulate objects of their own abstract data types.

An operator is overloaded if it can be used to perform multiple operations. Some operators are already overloaded in the C++ library. The * operator, for example, can be used to multiply two values of built-in types such as *int, float,* or *double,* to declare or dereference a pointer. It can be further overloaded to multiply two objects of user-defined types, such as two ac currents or two vectors, or to perform any other operation defined by the programmer. The following example demonstrates some operations that can be performed using the * operator:

```
int x=3, y=5, z;
z=x*y;              //* is used to perform integer multiplication
float f=3.4;
float *fpt=&f;      //* is used to declare a pointer
*fpt=5.6;           //* is used to dereference the pointer
Current c1(1,45), c2(2,0), c3;
c3=c1*c2;           //* is used to perform a user-defined operation
                    //relative to the Current class
```

The * operator in this example is used to perform four different operations, three of which (integer multiplication, pointer designation, and pointer dereferencing) are defined in the C++ library. The fourth operation is defined by the programmer and it is relative to the Current class. This operation is performed on two objects of the Current class, named c1 and c2. The * operator is, therefore, overloaded in a binary form because it requires two operands (objects). The * operator can be overloaded in its unary form as well. Please note that there are four operators that can be overloaded in both unary and binary forms (see Figure 6.3).

Most of the operators in C++ can be overloaded, with an exception of the five operators shown in Figure 6.1.

```
    .        .*       ::       ?:       sizeof
```

Figure 6.1 *Non-overloadable operators.*

The operators that can be overloaded are shown in Figure 6.2. When an operator is overloaded, it keeps its original meaning(s) and gains an additional meaning through the overloading process that is relative to the class for which it is defined.

new	delete	new[]	delete[]	()
+	-	*	/	%
^	&	|	~	!
=	<	>	+=	-=
*=	/=	%=	^=	&=
|=	<<	>>	>>=	<<=
==	!=	<=	>=	&&
||	++	--	,	->*
→	[]			

Figure 6.2 *Overloadable operators.*

Most of the operators in C++ can have only one form—either unary or binary—and they can only be overloaded in that form. An attempt to create a binary version of a unary operator such as **++** through operator overloading will produce a syntax error. Some operators, however, can have both versions and can be separately overloaded in both unary and binary forms. These operators are shown in Figure 6.3. Note that the only ternary operator in C++ (**?:**) cannot be overloaded.

Figure 6.3 *Operators that can be overloaded in unary and binary forms.*

When overloading operators, the following cannot be changed:

- Operator precedence
- Grouping (which symbols can be grouped together to create a new operator)
- Number of operands
- Original meaning (an operation that is performed on objects of built-in types)

Attempting to overload an operator that cannot be overloaded, or change any of the four properties of an operator listed above, will result in a syntax error.

The **=** **(assignment)** operator and the **&** **(address of)** operator can be used with objects of every user-defined type without explicitly overloading these two operators relative to any specific class. The **=** operator, by default, creates a *bit-by-bit* copy of an object, while the **&** operator returns a memory address of the object.

When necessary, these two operators can also be overloaded relative to a specific class. It is particularly important to overload the **=** operator relative to a class containing pointers as members, to avoid having the same pointer in two or more different objects. Destroying one object in this case would damage another objects. To prevent this type of error, it is necessary to overload the = operator relative to the class from which these objects are instantiated. See Section 6.3 for a demonstration of this concept.

An excessive use of operator overloading in a program can decrease program readability. It is highly recommended that a new operation designed for an operator performing on user-defined types be similar to the operation that the operator performs on built-in types. For example, the = = operator should be overloaded to compare two objects of a user-defined type by equality rather than, for example, adding or subtracting the objects. It should be noted that C++ would not prevent overloading = = for an addition or subtraction operation, but this type of poor programming practice may cause difficulties in source code comprehension.

NOTE: C++ enables programmers to overload only existing operators. Programmers cannot design new symbols or group existing symbols together to create new operators

TIP: Operators should be overloaded to perform operations on user-defined objects similar to the operations they perform on built-in objects.

To overload an operator, an **operator function** must be defined. The next section discusses this special type of C++ function.

6.2 OPERATOR FUNCTIONS

An operator function defines an operation that is performed on objects of specific types. To define an operator function, the general format shown in Figure 6.4 is used.

```
return_type operator@( parameter list )
{
        //operation to be performed
}
```

Figure 6.4 *General format of an operator function.*

An operator function is similar to any other C++ function, with the exception that the name of the function must be the *operator* keyword followed by the symbol (operator) to be overloaded. Note that the symbol **@** in Figure 6.4 represents one of the operators that can be overloaded (see Figure 6.2). The return type of the operator function can be any built-in or user-defined type—including *void*. It is often the type of class for which the operator function is defined.

Operator functions can be designed as

- *non-static* member functions
- non-member functions, including **friend** functions

Member operator functions must be *non-static* in order to access *non-static* data members of the class. When using non-member functions to overload operators, **friend** functions are preferred over *non-friend* functions. The reason for this is that, unlike *non-friend*, non-member functions, **friend** functions have direct access to a class's **private** and **protected** data members. The only way for *non-friend*, non-member functions to access the class's **private** and **protected** data is through **public** member interface functions. This process involves unnecessary function calls and may decrease the speed of a program.

To call an operator function, its symbol (operator) should be used in an expression with objects of the class for which the function is defined. An operator function can also be invoked in the same way as any other regular, non-operator function by using the function name followed by brackets that enclose the function arguments (`operator@( )`). It is not common, however, to use this method of calling operator functions because the main reason for using operators is to write concise expressions that use symbols rather than lengthy words. The following code fragment demonstrates some examples of the operator functions' calls:

```
Amplifier a1, a2, a3;    //Instantiates class objects
Speaker s1, s2;
//Calling operator functions:
a3=a1+a2;      //Calls operator+() in the Amplifier class
//Same as (friend): a3=operator+(a1,a2);
//or (member): a3=a1.operator+(a2);
~a1;           //Calls operator~() in the Amplifier class
//Same as (friend): operator~(a1);
//or (member): a1.operator~();
if(s1==s2)     //Calls operator==() in the Speaker class
    cout<<"Speakers are identical";
//Same as (friend): if(operator==(s1,s2))
//or (member): if(s1.operator==(s2))
//cout<<"Speakers are identical";
```

The + and ~ operators are used with the a1 and a2 objects of the Amplifier class. This invokes the operator+() and operator~() functions, the definitions of which are relative to the Amplifier class. Note that the + operator is overloaded in its

binary form while the ~ operator is overloaded as a unary operator. The ==
operator is overloaded relative to the Speaker class because it performs an operation on the s1 and s2 objects of this class. Note that the three operator functions
demonstrated in this example can be designed as either member functions or *friend*
functions of Amplifier and Speaker, respectively. An expression that uses an
operator (not a function name) to invoke the function is the same in both member
and *friend* cases.

The operators shown in Figure 6.5 must be overloaded using member operator
functions.

$$= \qquad\qquad () \qquad\qquad [] \qquad\qquad ->$$

Figure 6.5 *Operators that must be overloaded using member operator functions.*

Most of the *overloadable operators* (except the operators shown in Figure 6.5) can be
overloaded by either *non-static* member functions or *friend* functions. A question
arises as to which of these two types of operator functions should be used.
Remember that *non-friend*, non-member functions are not considered because of
their performance.

The most important difference between member and *friend* functions when overloading operators is that member functions, unlike *friend* functions, use the *this*
pointer. As a result, when overloading operators through member functions, one
object (operand) is always passed implicitly by *this* to the function. This limits the
use of member operator functions to the following two cases:

1. An object on the *left side* of a binary operator must be instantiated from the
   same class to which the operator function belongs.

2. The object on which a unary operator operates on must be instantiated from
   the operator's function class.

Assume the following two expressions that call member operator functions:

```
x*y        //Calls operator*()
x++        //Calls operator++()
```

The first expression calls the operator*() function that is a member of the same
class of which the x object is an instance. The x object is passed implicitly by *this* to
the operator*() function. The y object can be of any type and is passed explicitly
to the operator function. The operator*() member function has one explicit parameter in this example that is the same type as y.

The second expression calls the operator++() function, which must be a member
of x's class. The x object is passed implicitly by *this* to the operator++() function.

The operator function in this example has no explicit parameters.

The `operator*()` and `operator++()` functions in the previous example could be designed as *friend* functions as well. The `operator*()` would have two explicit parameters in that case, while the `operator++()` would have one explicit parameter. There are two cases when a *friend* operator function is commonly used:

1. When an object on the left side of a binary operator is not instantiated from the operator's function class.

2. To design commutative operators where types of objects (operands) are different. An operator is commutative if its operands can switch positions.

Member operator functions cannot be used in either of the two cases above because the *this* pointer cannot pass an object that is not of the same type as itself.

 TIP: Use *friend* functions rather than *non-friend* functions when overloading operators through non-member functions.

6.3 OVERLOADING BINARY OPERATORS

When overloading binary operators using member functions, an operator function has one explicit argument. The other argument is the implicit *this* pointer. Remember that the object on the left side of the operator is passed by *this*, while the object on the right side is passed explicitly.

In Program Example 6.1, PROG6_1 demonstrates a practical use of a member operator function to solve the problem shown in Figure 6.6.

PROGRAM EXAMPLE 6.1: PROG6_1

```
1  //PROG6_1: Program demonstrates a use of a member operator
2  //         function that overloads the binary operator + to
3  //         add two ac currents.
4  #include <iostream>
5  #include <iomanip>
6  #include <cmath>
7  using namespace std;
8  const double D2R=2*3.141592/360;   //Converts deg to rad
9  const double R2D=360/(2*3.141592); //Converts rad to deg
10
11 class ACcurrent {
12 private:
```

```
13    float mag, phase; //magnitude and phase shift of an ac current
14 public:
15    ACcurrent(float m=0, float p=0) { mag=m; phase=p; }
16    ACcurrent operator+(ACcurrent);   //operator function prototype
17    void print()
18    {
19       cout<<setiosflags(ios::fixed)<<setprecision(2);
20       cout<<"("<<setw(6)<<mag;
21       cout<<","<<setw(6)<<phase<<(char)248<<" ) [A]";
22    }
23 };
24 ACcurrent ACcurrent::operator+(ACcurrent c) //operator function
25 {                                            //definition
26    //Adds two AC currents and returns the total current
27    ACcurrent temp;            //total current
28    float real, imag;         //real and imaginary part
29    real = mag*cos(phase*D2R) + c.mag*cos(c.phase*D2R);
30    imag = mag*sin(phase*D2R) + c.mag*sin(c.phase*D2R);
31    temp.mag = sqrt(real*real + imag*imag);
32    temp.phase = atan(imag/real)*R2D;
33    return temp;
34 }
35 int main()
36 {
37    ACcurrent c1(2,0), c2(2,90), c3;
38    c3=c1+c2;     //Calls operator+() function in ACcurrent
39    cout<<"c1 = ";
40    c1.print();
41    cout<<"\nc2 = ";
42    c2.print();
43    cout<<"\n\nc3 = c1+c2 = ";
44    c3.print();
45    return 0;
46 }
```

An alternating current (ac current) is a current that varies with time. A common form of ac current is a sine waveform, the characteristics of which are magnitude, phase angle, and frequency. When performing arithmetic operations such as addition, subtraction, division, or multiplication on ac currents, a phasor (complex number) form of an ac current is used. The phasor form of an ac current can be expressed in the following two ways:

$$i = I_M \angle \varphi \qquad \text{(polar form)}$$
$$i = i_x + j\, i_y \qquad \text{(rectangular form)}$$

where:

I_M is the magnitude (effective value) of an ac current

φ is the phase angle of an ac current

i_x is the real part of an ac current

i_y is the imaginary part of an ac current

PROBLEM: Given magnitudes (I_{1M}, I_{2M}) and phase angles (φ_1, φ_2) of two ac currents i_1 and i_2, find the magnitude I_M and phase shift φ of the current that is the sum of i_1 and i_2.

Assume: 1. $I_{1M} = I_{2M} = 2A$, $\varphi_1 = 0°$, $\varphi_2 = 90°$
2. i_1 and i_2 have the same frequency

SOLUTION: Adding currents in rectangular form =>

$$i = i_1 + i_2 = (i_{1x} + i_{2x}) + j(i_{1y} + i_{2y}) = i_x + j\, i_y$$
$$i_x = I_{1M} \cos\varphi_1 + I_{2M} \cos\varphi_2 = 2(\cos 0° + \cos 90°) = 2$$
$$i_y = I_{1M} \sin\varphi_1 + I_{2M} \sin\varphi_2 = 2(\sin 0° + \sin 90°) = 2$$

Total current: $i = 2 + j2$

Using rectangular to polar transformation =>

$$i = I_M \angle \varphi = 2.828 \angle 45°$$

$$\boxed{I_M = 2.828 \text{ A}, \quad \varphi = 45°}$$

Figure 6.6 *The problem for Program Example 6.1.*

The `operator+()` function (lines 24–34) is a member of the `ACcurrent` class and the function return type is `ACcurrent` because the function returns an object of the same class. This function takes two arguments when called (line 38). The `c1` object is passed by **this**, while the `c2` object is passed explicitly and copied into the explicit argument of `operator+()` named `c`. The operator function first adds the real and imaginary parts of the two objects (ac currents) passed to the function (lines 29 and 30). The function then computes the total magnitude and the total phase shift of the two currents and stores them in an object called `temp` (lines 31 and 32), which represents the total current. A value of the `temp` object is returned by the `operator+()` function and copied into the `c3` object that is instantiated by **main()**. The program displays values of the magnitude and phase shift of the two currents `c1` and `c2`, as well as the total current `c3` (lines 40, 42, and 44). The output produced by PROG6_1 is shown in Figure 6.7.

```
                c1 = (   2.00,   0.00° ) [A]
                c2 = (   2.00, 90.00° ) [A]


          c3 = c1+c2 = (   2.83, 45.00° ) [A]
```

Figure 6.7 *The output produced by the program PROG6_1.*

The performance of the `operator+()` function in PROG6_1 can be improved if objects (arguments) are passed by reference rather than by values to the function. This reduces function call overhead because copies of arguments are not created when calling the function. To protect the original objects against any inadvertent modification, their references should be specified as **const** in the parameter list of the operator function. The function should also be specified **const**, thus allowing it to be used to process both **const** and **non-const** objects.

PROG6_2, in Program Example 6.2, uses two member operator functions specified as **const**, with arguments that are passed by **const** references. The operator functions in PROG6_2 are used to subtract and compare two ac currents (see Figure 6.6).

PROGRAM EXAMPLE 6.2: PROG6_2

```
1  //PROG6_2: Program uses operator-() to subtract two ac currents
2  //         and operator==() to compare two ac currents by
3  //         equality.
4  #include <iostream>
```

```
5   #include <iomanip>
6   #include <cmath>
7   using namespace std;
8   const double D2R=2*3.141592/360;    //Converts deg to rad
9   const double R2D=360/(2*3.141592);  //Converts rad to deg
10
11  class ACcurrent {
12  private:
13     float mag, phase;
14  public:
15     ACcurrent(float m=0, float p=0) { mag=m; phase=p; }
16     ACcurrent operator-(const ACcurrent &) const;    //const operator
17     bool operator==(const ACcurrent &) const; //function
18     void print() const
19     {
20        cout<<setiosflags(ios::fixed)<<setprecision(2);
21        cout<<"("<<setw(6)<<mag;
22        cout<<","<<setw(6)<<phase<<(char)248<<" ) [A]";
23     }
24  };
25  ACcurrent ACcurrent::operator-(const ACcurrent & c) const
26  {
27     ACcurrent temp;
28     float real, imag;
29     real = mag*cos(phase*D2R)-c.mag*cos(c.phase*D2R);
30     imag = mag*sin(phase*D2R)-c.mag*sin(c.phase*D2R);
31     temp.mag = sqrt(real*real+imag*imag);
32     if(!((real==0)&&(imag==0)))
33        temp.phase=atan(imag/real)*R2D;
34     else
35        temp.phase=0;
36     return temp;
37  }
```

```
38 bool ACcurrent::operator==(const ACcurrent & c) const
39 {
40    if((mag==c.mag)&&(phase==c.phase))
41       return true;
42    else
43       return false;
44 }
45 int main()
46 {
47    const ACcurrent c1(1,0);            //constant object
48    ACcurrent c2(1,45), c3;
49    c3=c1-c2;                           //Calls operator-()
50    cout<<"c1 = ";
51    c1.print();
52    cout<<"\nc2 = ";
53    c2.print();
54    cout<<"\n\nc3 = c1-c2 = ";
55    c3.print();
56    if(c1==c2)                          //Calls operator==()
57       cout<<"\nc1 and c2 are equal.";
58    else
59    {
60       cout<<"\nc1 and c2 have different either magnitude, ";
61       cout<<"or phase shift, or both.";
62    }
63    return 0;
64 }
```

This program uses the operator-() function (lines 25–37) to subtract two ac currents. The function receives two arguments (objects of the ACcurrent class). It returns an object, the magnitude and phase shift of which is computed by subtracting two ac currents passed to the function. The program also uses the operator==() function (lines 38–44) to compare two ac currents by equality. The function returns *true* only if both magnitude and phase shift of the two currents passed are equal. It returns *false* if either magnitude or phase shift, or both, are different.

The **main()** function instantiates a c1 **const** object (line 47) and two *non-const* objects—c2 and c3 (line 48). It then calls the operator-() function to subtract c1 and c2 (line 49). The object returned by operator-() is assigned to c3. Please note that the c1 **const** object is passed by **this**, while c2 is explicitly passed to the operator function. **main()** next invokes the print() member function on c1, c2, and c3, respectively (lines 51, 53, 55), to display their values. It then calls the operator==() function from an *if* statement and passes c1 and c2 to the function (line 56). Based on the **true/false** value returned by operator==(), **main()** will display an appropriate message (lines 57, 60, and 61).

Both operator functions in PROG6_2 are specified as **const**, therefore they can process the c1 **const** object as well as the c2 *non-const* object. This program produces the output shown in Figure 6.8.

```
        c1 = (   1.00,   0.00° ) [A]
        c2 = (   1.00,  45.00°) [A]

  c3 = c1-c2 = (   0.77,-67.50° ) [A]
  c1 and c2 have different either magnitude, or phase shift, or both.
```

Figure 6.8 *Output produced by PROG6_2.*

A binary operator (except the four operators shown in Figure 6.5) can be overloaded by using a *friend* function rather than a member function. Remember that *friend* functions do not have the *this* pointer; therefore, both operands (arguments) are passed explicitly to the *friend* operator function. Friend operator functions provide one very important feature. Unlike member functions, they can be used to overload binary operators where the operand on the left side of the operator is of a built-in type.

PROG6_3 demonstrates the practical use of a *friend* operator function that overloads a binary operator in Program Example 6.3. The *friend* operator function in PROG6_3 is used to *shift* the phase angle of an ac current—that is, to add a positive/negative value to the phase angle.

PROGRAM EXAMPLE 6.3: PROG6_3

```
1  //PROG6_3: Program demonstrates a friend operator<<() that is
2  //         used to shift the phase angle of an ac current.
3  #include <iostream>
4  #include <iomanip>
```

```
 5  using namespace std;
 6
 7  class ACcurrent {
 8  private:
 9     float mag, phase;
10  public:
11     ACcurrent(float m=0, float p=0) { mag=m; phase=p; }
12     //friend operator function
13     friend void operator<<(float p, ACcurrent & c)
14     {
15         c.phase = c.phase + p;
16     }
17     void print() const
18     {
19         cout<<setiosflags(ios::fixed)<<setprecision(2);
20         cout<<"("<<setw(6)<<mag;
21         cout<<","<<setw(6)<<phase<<(char)248<<" ) [A]";
22     }
23  };
24  int main()
25  {
26     ACcurrent c1(1,60);
27     cout<<"c1 = ";
28     c1.print();
29     45.0<<c1;                //Calls operator<<()
30     cout<<"\n\nAfter shifting phase for 45"<<(char)248<<endl;
31     cout<<"\nc1 = ";
32     c1.print();
33     return 0;
34  }
```

This program uses the operator<<() function to overload the << operator in order to shift the phase of an ac current (lines 13–16). Remember that this operator is already overloaded in C++ to perform the binary left shift and stream insertion operations. The operator<<() has two explicit arguments—a floating point value named p that is the value of the phase shift, and an object of the ACcurrent class whose phase is to be shifted. The *main()* function calls operator<<() to shift the phase of the c1 object by 45.0° (line 29). The c1 object is passed by reference to the operator function, which modifies c1's phase by adding the value of the argument p (45.0°, in this example). There is no need for a *return* statement in operator<<() because the function modifies the phase of the original object through the object's reference. The return type of the operator function, therefore, is *void*. The *main()* function displays the value of c1 before and after shifting its phase (lines 26 and 30). PROG6_3 produces the output shown in Figure 6.9.

```
c1 = (   1.00,  60.00° ) [A]
After shifting phase for 45°
c1 = (   1.00,105.00° ) [A]
```

Figure 6.9 *Output produced by PROG6_3.*

The operator<<() *friend* function in PROG6_3 cannot be changed to a member operator function, because the left-side operand is a built-in type and therefore cannot be passed by *this*.

 NOTE: A *friend* operator function can have both arguments (operands) of any type. It can operate on *non-const* and **const** objects.

 TIP: A *friend* operator function should be used to overload a binary operator, where the left-side operand is a built-in type.

Remember that the = operator can only be overloaded by a member operator function. C++ automatically creates the default assignment operator function for every class for which a user-defined = operator function is not supplied. The default = operator creates an identical (bit-by-bit) copy of an object on the right side of the operator and copies it into the object on the left side. If the object to be assigned (copied) dynamically allocates memory, the = operator should be explicitly overloaded to avoid the same side effects that were discussed when the copy constructor was introduced. The most serious problem occurs due to the destruction of one of the two objects that were used with the = operator. This results in damage to the other object as well, as both objects use the same dynamically allocated memory.

Assume the following class definition:

```
1   class Numbers {
2   private:
3       float *fptr;        //points to a float array
```

```
4     int num;                    //size of the array
5   public:
6     Numbers(int=6);                   //regular constructor
7     Numbers(const Numbers &);         //copy constructor
8     ~Numbers() { delete [] fptr; }   //destructor
9     const Numbers &operator=(const Numbers &);
10    //other functions
11  };
12  Numbers::Numbers(int x)      //regular constructor definition
13  {
14    num=x;
15    fptr=new float[num];       //Allocates memory dynamically
16    if(!fptr)
17    {
18       cout<<"Memory allocation error!";
19       exit(1);
20    }
21    for(int i=0; i<num; i++)   //Initializes array
22       fptr[i]=0;
23  }
24  Numbers::Numbers(const Numbers &f)  //copy constructor definition
25  {
26    num = f.num;
27    fptr=new float[num];             //Allocates memory dynamically
28    if(!fptr)
29    {
30       cout<<"Memory allocation error!";
31       exit(1);
32    }
33    for(int i=0; i<num; i++)
34       fptr[i]=f.fptr[i];            //Copies arrays
35  }
```

The Numbers class contains a regular constructor function (lines 12–23) that dynamically allocates memory for an array of floating point values. The array is accessed through the fptr pointer, and its size is stored in the num data member. This constructor also initializes all array elements to 0s (line 22).

The class also contains a copy constructor (lines 24–35) that is similar to its regular constructor. The copy constructor uses the array values of its argument (an object passed by reference) to initialize the object that is being constructed. The class also uses the destructor function to free dynamically allocated memory when an object is destroyed (line 8).

The Numbers class should have an operator function that overloads the = operator relative to this class to prevent the default bit-by-bit copy of an object. The operator=() function should be defined as follows:

```
1   const Numbers & Numbers::operator=(const Numbers &f)
2   {
3     if(&f!=this)      //Prevents self-assignment
4     {
5         delete [] fptr;   //Frees memory allocated by constructor
6         num=f.num;
7         fptr=new float[num];
8         if(!fptr)
9         {
10              cout<<" Memory allocation error.";
11              exit(1);
12         }
13         for(int i=0; i<num; i++)
14              fptr[i]=f.fptr[i];
15     }
16     return *this;
17  }
```

The function first tests whether the address of the f object to be copied is different from the address of the receiving object passed by *this* (line 3). This test is necessary to prevent a self-assignment that can be dangerous. The following code fragment demonstrates an example of a self-assignment:

```
Numbers x, y;
x=y=x;                 //x is assigned to itself
```

If the addresses are not the same, the `operator=()` frees memory allocated by the constructor for the receiving object (line 5). The operator function then allocates a new memory block for the receiving object (line 7) and copies the array stored in the source object into the receiving object (line 14). The function returns the receiving object that is accessed through *this* (line 16).

The format of the `operator=()` function illustrated in this example enables the assignment operation to be performed as a multiple assignment. The following code segment illustrates the concept:

```
Numbers x, y, z;

x = y = z;                  //multiple assignment
```

If the `operator=()` function return type is changed to *void,* the multiple assignments shown above cannot be done.

 TIP: The **=** operator should be explicitly overloaded for every class that contains pointers as data members for dynamically allocating memory.

6.4 OVERLOADING UNARY OPERATORS

Like binary operators, unary operators can be overloaded by using either *non-static* member functions or non-member functions (preferably *friend* functions). It is good programming practice to use member functions rather than non-member functions whenever possible. This practice is recommended in order to obey the fundamental encapsulation (data hiding) rule—that is, only class member functions should have access to the class data members.

When using a *non-static* member function to overload a unary operator, the function has no explicit arguments. The only argument of the function is the implicit *this* pointer. If using a *friend* function to overload a unary operator, the function has one argument—either an object of the class or a reference to the object.

In Program Example 6.4, PROG6_4 demonstrates the practical use of both *non-static* member functions and *friend* functions to overload unary operators. The operator functions in PROG6_4 are used to perform the following operations on ac currents (see Figure 6.6):

1. Increment the real and imaginary parts of an ac current (`operator++()`)

2. Decrement the real and imaginary parts of an ac current (`operator--()`)

3. Shift the phase angle of an ac current by −180° (`operator~()`)

PROGRAM EXAMPLE 6.4: PROG6_4

```
1   //PROG6_4: Program demonstrates overloaded unary operators.
2   #include <iostream>
```

```
3   #include <iomanip>
4   #include <cmath>
5   using namespace std;
6   const double D2R = 2 * 3.141592 / 360;
7   const double R2D = 360 / (2 * 3.141592);
8
9   class ACcurrent {
10  private:
11      float mag, phase;
12  public:
13      ACcurrent(float m=0, float p=0) { mag=m; phase=p; }
14      ACcurrent operator++();         //member operator function
15      ACcurrent operator--();         //member operator function
16      friend void operator~(ACcurrent &c)  //friend operator function
17      {                       //Shifts the phase angle by -180
18          c.phase=c.phase-180;
19      }
20      void print() const
21      {
22          cout<<setiosflags(ios::fixed)<<setprecision(2);
23          cout<<"("<<setw(6)<<mag;
24          cout<<","<<setw(6)<<phase<<(char)248<<" ) [A]";
25      }
26  };
27  ACcurrent ACcurrent::operator++()  //Increments the real and
28  {                   //imaginary parts of an ac current
29      float real, imag;
30      real=mag*cos(phase*D2R);   //Computes the real part
31      imag=mag*sin(phase*D2R);   //Computes the imaginary part
32      ++real;
33      ++imag;
34      mag=sqrt(real*real+imag*imag);      //Computes the magnitude
35      phase=atan(imag/real)*R2D;          //Computes the phase angle
```

```
36     return *this;
37 }
38 ACcurrent ACcurrent::operator--()   //Decrements the real and
39 {      //imaginary parts of an ac current
40    float real, imag;
41    real=mag*cos(phase*D2R);
42    imag=mag*sin(phase*D2R);
43    --real;
44    --imag;
45    mag=sqrt(real*real+imag*imag);
46    phase=atan(imag/real)*R2D;
47    return *this;
48 }
49 int main()
50 {
51    ACcurrent c1(1,60);
52    cout<<"c1 = ";
53    c1.print();
54    ++c1;                           //Calls operator++()
55    cout<<"\n\nAfter incrementing:"<<endl;
56    cout<<"c1 = ";
57    c1.print();
58    --c1;                           //Calls operator--()
59    cout<<"\n\nAfter decrementing:"<<endl;
60    cout<<"c1 = ";
61    c1.print();
62    ~c1;                            //Calls operator~()
63     cout<<"\n\nAfter shifting phase for -180";
64     cout<<(char)248<<": "<<endl;
65     cout<<"c1 = ";
66    c1.print();
67     return 0;
68 }
```

This program uses two *non-static* member operator functions to overload the **pre-increment** operator (**++**) and the **pre-decrement** operator (**- -**). The operator++() function first computes the real and imaginary parts of an ac current passed by *this*, and then increments their values (lines 30–33). It then computes the current's magnitude and phase shift by using incremented values of the real and imaginary parts (lines 34 and 35). The function returns a new value of the ac current (line 36). The operator--() function (lines 38–48) is similar to operator++(). The only difference between these two functions is that operator--() decrements the current's real and imaginary parts prior to computing its magnitude and phase shift. Both functions are invoked from *main()* (lines 54 and 58) by using the operator symbol with the c1 object, which is passed implicitly by *this* to the operator functions. The *main()* function outputs the values of c1's magnitude and phase shift prior to and after calling the operator functions (lines 57, 61, and 66).

PROG6_4 also uses a *friend* function to overload the **bitwise complement** operator (**~**). The operator~() function (lines 16–19) shifts the phase of an ac current by −180°. The current is passed explicitly to the function by its c reference. The operator~() is called in *main()* (line 62) to operate on the c1 object. The *main()* function displays the values stored in c1 after c1's phase is shifted by operator~(). PROG6_4 produces the output shown in Figure 6.10.

```
c1 = (  1.00, 60.00° ) [A]

After incrementing:
c1 = (  2.39, 51.21° ) [A]

After decrementing:
c1 = (  1.00, 60.00° ) [A]

After shifting phase for -180°:
c1 = (  1.00,-120.00° ) [A]
```

Figure 6.10 *Output produced by PROG6_4.*

Both the **++** operator and the **- -** operator have two forms: **prefix** and **postfix**. When overloading these two unary operators, it is important to overload them in both forms. Each form requires a separate operator function. Both operator functions in this case have the same name—operator++() or operator--()—and the same parameter lists. Remember that overloaded functions must have different parameter lists to prevent **ambiguity** (*compiler's confusion*). C++ adds a *dummy argument* to the parameter list of the **postfix** form in order to distinguish between the two forms when overloading **++** and **- -**. This *useless argument* is an unnamed *int* and its only purpose is to eliminate ambiguity.

PROG6_5 demonstrates an example of the overloaded increment operator in both forms in Program Example 6.5.

PROGRAM EXAMPLE 6.5: PROG6_5

```
1   //PROG6_5: Program demonstrates the overloaded increment operator
2   // in the prefix and postfix forms.
3   #include <iostream>
4   using namespace std;
5
6   class Pixel {
7   private:
8      int x, y;
9   public:
10     Pixel(int a=0, int b=0) { x=a; y=b;}
11     Pixel operator++();        //prefix form of operator++()
12     Pixel operator++(int);     //postfix form of operator++()
13     void print() const { cout<<"X="<<x<<", Y="<<y<<endl; }
14  };
15  Pixel Pixel::operator++()     //pre-increment definition
16  {
17     ++x;
18     ++y;
19     return *this;
20  }
21  Pixel Pixel::operator++(int)   //post-increment definition
22  {
23     Pixel temp=*this;
24     ++x;
25     ++y;
26     return temp;
27  }
28  int main()
29  {
```

```
30    Pixel p1(3,8), p2;
31    cout<<"p1: ";
32    p1.print();
33    p2=++p1;              //Calls pre-increment
34    cout<<"\nAfter pre-increment:"<<endl;
35    cout<<"p1: ";
36    p1.print();
37    cout<<"p2: ";
38    p2.print();
39    p2=p1++;              //Calls post-increment
40    cout<<"\nAfter post-increment:"<<endl;
41    cout<<"p1: ";
42    p1.print();
43    cout<<"p2: ";
44    p2.print();
45    return 0;
46 }
```

The increment operator is overloaded by using a *non-static* member function for each form (lines 15–27). Each version of the operator++() function in this program increments the x and y coordinates of the p1 object passed by ***this*** to the function (lines 17, 18, 24, and 25). The prefix form of the operator++() returns a new value of p1 after its x and y values are incremented (line 19). The postfix form first assigns a value of p1 accessed through ***this*** to a temporary object (line 23). It then increments the x and y values stored in p1 and returns the value of the temporary object at the end—that is, the original value of p1 before incrementing (line 26).

The ***main()*** function is designed to test the operator functions. It instantiates two objects of the Pixel class, named p1 and p2 (line 30). ***main()*** then calls both forms of the operator++() function on the p1 object (lines 33 and 39). Values returned by the operator functions are assigned to the p2 object. The ***main()*** function displays the values of p1 and p2 after calling each form of operator++() (lines 36, 38, 42, and 44). The output of PROG6_5 is shown in Figure 6.11.

```
p1: X=3, Y=8

After pre-increment:
p1: X=4, Y=9
p2: X=4, Y=9

After post-increment:
p1: X=5, Y=10
p2: X=4, Y=9
```

Figure 6.11 *Output produced by PROG6_5.*

6.5 OVERLOADING THE STREAM OPERATORS

One of the most important features of operator overloading in C++ is its capability to overload the **stream insertion** (<<) and **stream extraction** (>>) operators in order to perform user-defined I/O operations. These two operators are already overloaded in the C++ library to perform the bitwise left-shift and right-shift operations, respectively.

The C++ *iostream* library contains a large number of classes that define a wide range of I/O operations. The two classes called *istream* and *ostream* from the *iostream* library are used when overloading the << and >> operators. The *istream* class defines stream-input operations, while the *ostream* class defines stream-output operations. The predefined objects *cin* and *cout* are instances of these two classes as follows:

- **cin** is an instance of the **istream** class and is connected to the standard input device, most commonly a keyboard.

- **cout** is an instance of the **ostream** class and is connected to the standard output device, most commonly a display screen.

To overload the stream insertion operator, a *friend* operator function (the general format of which is shown in Figure 6.12) should be used.

The operator<<() function returns a reference to an object of the *ostream* type. This reference is identified as str in the general format shown in Figure 6.12. Any other valid C++ identifier can be used instead of str. The keywords and required identifiers are highlighted in Figure 6.12. Because the << operator is a binary operator, a *friend* function that overloads this operator must have two explicit parameters.

```
friend ostream &operator <<(ostream &str, class_name obj)
{
        //body of the insertion operator
     return str;
}
```

Figure 6.12 *General format of a* **friend** *operator function that overloads the* << *operator.*

These parameters are

- A reference to an object of the **ostream** type
- An object of a class for which the operator function is defined

Within the body of the function, the programmer defines the format of the output as well as the values that will be inserted into the output stream when the function is called. The following code fragment illustrates some examples of the operator<<() function calls:

```
ACcurrent c1(1,45), c2;
cout<<c1;                  //Calls user-defined operator<<()
cout<<"Current c2 ="<<c2; //Calls built-in and user-defined
                                        //operator<<()
cout<<c1<<c2;              //Calls user-defined operator<<() twice
```

The cout<<c1 expression invokes the user-defined operator<<() function relative to the ACcurrent class. The operand on the left side of the << operator is the built-in *cout* object, which is passed by reference (str in Figure 6.12) to the operator function. The operand on the right side is the c1 object of the ACcurrent class and is passed explicitly. It is good programming practice to pass this argument by a *const* reference to the operator function, although it is not specified in Figure 6.12. The operator function uses the reference to *cout* (str in Figure 6.12) to manipulate the output, and returns this reference to the calling statement when finished. This enables multiple calls of the operator<<() function in one expression as given in the example of the cout<<c1<<c2 expression. When inserting built-in types into the output stream such as the string Current c2 =, the built-in operator<<() is invoked.

To overload the >> operator, a *friend* operator function (the general format of which is shown in Figure 6.13) should be used. The format of the operator>>() function shown in Figure 6.13 is similar to the format of the operator<<() function shown in Figure 6.12. There are two primary differences between these two functions:

- A reference to an object of the **istream** class must be passed to and returned from `operator>>()`

- An object of a user-defined class must be passed by reference to `operator>>()`

```
friend istream &operator>>(istream &str, class_name &obj)
{
        //body of the extraction operator
     return str;
}
```

Figure 6.13 *General format of a* **friend** *operator function that overloads the* >> *operator.*

The body of `operator>>()` defines stream-input operations to be performed on an object of the user-defined class, for which the operator function is defined. The following is an example of the statements that call `operator>>()`:

```
ACcurrent c1, c2, c3;
cin>>c1;                    //Calls user-defined operator>>()
cin>>c2>>c3;                //calls user-defined operator>>() twice
```

Program Example 6.6 demonstrates the practical use of the overloaded << and >> operators. The overloaded stream operators are used in PROG6_6 to input and output an ac current.

PROGRAM EXAMPLE 6.6: PROG6_6

```
1  //PROG6_6: Program demonstrates the overloaded stream operators.
2  #include <iostream>
3  #include <iomanip>
4  using namespace std;
5
6  class ACcurrent {
7  private:
8     float mag, phase;
9  public:
10     ACcurrent(float m=0, float p=0){mag=m; phase=p;} //constructor
11
```

```
12    //overloads operator>>() to input an object of ACcurrent
13    friend istream &operator>>(istream &inst, ACcurrent &c);
14
15    //overloads operator<<() to output an object of ACcurrent
16    friend ostream &operator<<(ostream &outst, const ACcurrent &c);
17
18    //overloads operator<<() to shift the phase angle
19    friend  void operator<<(float p, ACcurrent &c)
20    {
21        c.phase = c.phase+p;
22    }
23 };
24
25 istream &operator>>(istream &inst, ACcurrent &c)
26 {
27    cout<<"Enter magnitude: ";
28    inst>>c.mag;
29    cout<<"Enter phase shift: ";
30    inst>>c.phase;
31    return inst;
32 }
33 ostream &operator<<(ostream &outst, const ACcurrent &c)
34 {
35    outst<<setiosflags(ios::fixed)<<setprecision(2);
36    outst<<"("<<setw(6)<<c.mag;
37    outst<<","<<setw(6)<<c.phase<<(char)248<<" ) [A]";
38    return outst;
39 }
40
41 int main()
42 {
43    ACcurrent c1;
44    cin>>c1;          //Calls operator>>()
```

```
45   cout<<"\nc1 = "<<c1;        //Calls ostream operator<<()
46   45.0<<c1;                   //Calls void operator<<()
47   cout<<"\n\nAfter shifting phase for 45"<<(char)248<<endl;
48   cout<<"\nc1 = "<<c1;        //Calls ostream operator<<()
49   return 0;
50 }
```

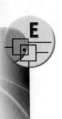

This program uses the operator>>() function to obtain values of the magnitude and phase shift for an object of the ACcurrent class (lines 25–32) from the user. This function is called in **main()** on the c1 object (line 44). The program also uses the operator<<() function, which defines output operations when an object of the ACcurrent class is inserted into the output stream (lines 33–39). The function is called in **main()** to output the c1 object before and after its phase is shifted (lines 45 and 48). It should be noted that c1 is passed by a reference named c to operator<<() to reduce the function call overhead. The reference is specified as **const** to prevent inadvertent changes of the c1 object. inst also serves as a reference to **cin** in operator>>(), while outst serves as a reference to **cout** in operator<<(). A sample run of PROG6_6 is shown in Figure 6.14.

```
Enter magnitude: 10
Enter phase shift: 90


c1 = ( 10.00, 90.00°) [A]


After shifting phase for 45°


c1 = ( 10.00,135.00°) [A]
```

Figure 6.14 *Sample run of PROG6_6.*

This chapter has demonstrated some standard operator overloading techniques. Not every technique has been utilized in the program examples. C++ contains a large number of operators and there are many different ways to overload them. Programmers should overload C++ operators by using standard operator functions similar to those in the C++ library. Using a nonstandard way to overload operators can make programs difficult to read.

TIP: Avoid nonstandard and excessive use of operator overloading. Use overloaded operators rather then explicit function calls when it makes the code clearer.

6.6 CASE STUDY: AC CURRENT CALCULATOR

This case study demonstrates several operator overloading techniques. Operator functions are designed to overload the arithmetic operators **+, -,** and ***** relative to a class that describes the attributes and behavior of an ac current. These operator functions are used to perform common operations on ac currents, such as adding or subtracting two ac currents or multiplying a current by a resistance. In addition, two operator functions are designed to overload the **<<** and **>>** operators in an effort to input or output an ac current.

PROBLEM DESCRIPTION

The program should obtain values of two ac currents from the user. The user should be offered options to enter the currents' values in either polar or rectangular coordinates. After the values have been entered, the user should chose to either add or subtract the two currents, or multiply a current by the value of a resistor. The result of each operation that is performed on ac currents should be displayed in polar coordinates.

INPUT/OUTPUT

Requested **input** from the user:

1. A selection of either polar or rectangular coordinates

2. The values of two ac currents (the magnitude and phase shift if polar form is selected, or the real and imaginary parts if rectangular form is selected)

3. A selection of an operation (adding currents, subtracting currents, multiplying a current by a resistance, or exiting the program)

Requested **output**: The results of the operation selected by the user (displayed in polar form)

PSEUDOCODE

Design the `ACcurrent` class with the following skeleton:

- **Data members (*private*):**

    1. `double mag;`   `//magnitude of an ac current`

    2. `double phase;`   `//phase angle of an ac current`

    3. `double real;`   `//real part of an ac current`

    4. `double imag;`   `//imaginary part of an ac current`

- **Member functions (*private*):**

    1. `void setRect();`

       `//COMPUTES AND SETS REAL AND IMAGINARY PARTS`

```
                        START
                        REAL=MAG*COS(PHASE*D2R)
                        IMAG=MAG*SIN(PHASE*D2R)
                        STOP
```

2. `void setPolar();`

```
                        //COMPUTES AND SETS MAGNITUDE AND PHASE ANGLE
                        START
                        MAG=SQRT(REAL*REAL+IMAG*IMAG)
                        IF NOT(REAL==0 AND IMAG==0) THEN
                                PHASE=ATAN(IMAG/REAL)*R2D
                        ELSE
                                PHASE=0
                        END IF
                        STOP
```

- **Member functions (*public*):**

  1. `ACcurrent(double m=0, double p=0);`

  ```
                        //INITIALIZES DATA MEMBERS
                        START
                        MAG=M
                        PHASE=P
                        EXECUTE SETREC()
                        STOP
  ```

  2. `ACcurrent operator-(const ACcurrent &c) const;`

  ```
                        //SUBTRACTS TWO AC CURRENTS
                        START
                        TREAL=MAG*COS(PHASE*D2R)-C.MAG*COS(C.PHASE*D2R)
                        TIMAG=MAG*SIN(PHASE*D2R)-C.MAG*SIN(C.PHASE*D2R)
                        TEMP.MAG=SQRT(TREAL*TREAL+TIMAG*TIMAG)
                        IF NOT(TREAL==0 AND TIMAG==0) THEN
                            TEMP.PHASE=ATAN(TIMAG/TREAL)*R2D
                        ELSE
                            TEMP.PHASE=0
                        END IF
  ```

```
        RETURN TEMP
        STOP
```

3. `ACcurrent operator+(const ACcurrent &c) const;`

```
        //ADDS TWO AC CURRENTS
        START
        TREAL=MAG*COS(PHASE*D2R)+C.MAG*COS(C.PHASE*D2R)
        TIMAG=MAG*SIN(PHASE*D2R)+C.MAG*SIN(C.PHASE*D2R)
        TEMP.MAG=SQRT(TREAL*TREAL+TIMAG*TIMAG)
        IF NOT(TREAL==0 AND TIMAG==0) THEN
          TEMP.PHASE=ATAN(TIMAG/TREAL)*R2D
        ELSE
          TEMP.PHASE=0
        END IF
        RETURN TEMP
        STOP
```

4. `ACcurrent operator*(double r) const;`

```
        //MULTIPLIES AN AC CURRENT BY A RESISTANCE
        START
        TEMP.MAG=MAG*R
        TEMP.PHASE=PHASE
        EXECUTE TEMP.SETRECT()
        RETURN TEMP
        STOP
```

5. `int getCoord();`

```
        //GETS A CHOICE OF COORDINATES FROM THE USER
        START
        DO WHILE SELECTION !=1 AND SELECTION !=2
          PRINT "SELECT:"
          PRINT "1) AC CURRENT IN POLAR COORDINATES"
          PRINT "2) AC CURRENT IN RECTANGULAR COORDINATES"
          PRINT "ENTER SELECTION"
          READ SELECTION
        END DO
```

```
RETURN SELECTION
STOP
```

- **Friend functions:**

    1. istream & operator>>(istream &inst, ACcurrent &c);

    ```
    //GETS AN AC CURRENT EITHER IN POLAR OR RECTANGULAR
    //COORDINATES BASED ON THE USER'S SELECTION
    START
    CHOICE=C.GETCOORD()
    IF CHOICE==1 THEN
        PRINT "ENTER MAGNITUDE"
        READ C.MAG
        PRINT "ENTER PHASE SHIFT"
        READ C.PHASE
        EXECUTE C.SETRECT()
    ELSE IF CHOICE==2 THEN
            PRINT "ENTER REAL PART"
            READ C.REAL
            PRINT "ENTER IMAGINARY PART"
            READ C.IMAG
            EXECUTE C.SETPOLAR()
        END IF
    END IF
    RETURN INST
    STOP
    ```

    2. ostream & operator<<(ostream &outst, ACcurrent &c);

    ```
    //DISPLAYS AN AC CURRENT
    START
    PRINT C.MAG
    PRINT C.PHASE
    RETURN OUTST
    STOP
    ```

- **Non-member functions:**

    I. `int menu();`

    ```
    //DISPLAYS MENU OPTIONS AND GETS A SELECTION FROM USER
    START
    DO WHILE SELECTION<1 OR SELECTION>4
            PRINT "SELECT OPERATION"
            PRINT "1) ADD CURRENTS"
            PRINT "2) SUBTRACT CURRENTS"
            PRINT "3) MULTIPLY CURRENT BY RESISTANCE"
            PRINT "4) EXIT"
            PRINT "ENTER SELECTION (1-4)"
            READ SELECTION
    END DO
    RETURN SELECTION
    STOP
    ```

FLOWCHARTS

Figure 6.15 shows the flowchart of the *main( )* function.

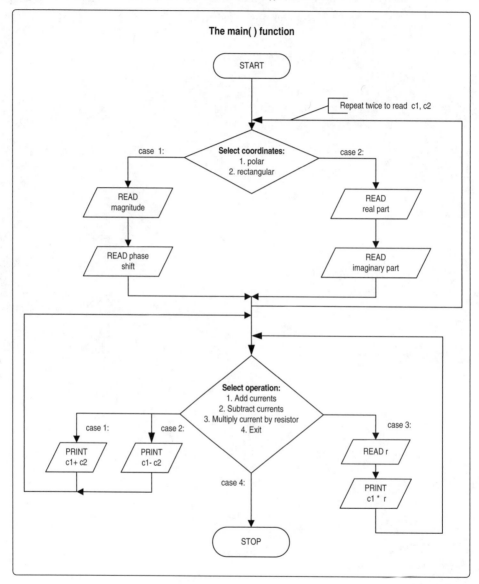

Figure 6.15 *Flowchart of the* **main( )** *function of CASEST6.*

SOURCE CODE
PROGRAM EXAMPLE 6.7: SOURCE CODE FOR CASEST6

```
1   //CASEST6: Program demonstrates an ACcurrent class.
2   #include <iostream>
3   #include <iomanip>
4   #include <cmath>
5   using namespace std;
6   const double D2R=2*3.141592/360;   //Converts degrees to radians
7   const double R2D=360/(2*3.141592); //Converts radians to degrees
8
9   class ACcurrent {
10  private:
11    double mag, phase;
12    double real, imag;
13    void setRect();    //Sets rectangular coordinates
14    void setPolar();   //Sets polar coordinates
15  public:
16    ACcurrent(double m=0, double p=0)   //constructor
17    {
18       mag=m; phase=p; setRect();
19    }
20    ACcurrent operator-(const ACcurrent & c) const;
21    ACcurrent operator+(const ACcurrent & c) const;
22    ACcurrent operator*(double) const;
23    int getCoord();
24    friend istream &operator>>(istream &inst, ACcurrent &c);
25    friend ostream &operator<<(ostream &outst, const ACcurrent &c);
26  };
27  int ACcurrent::getCoord()
28  {
29    int selection;
30    do {
```

```
31        cout<<"\nSelect:\n\t1) AC current in polar coordinates ";
32        cout<<"\n\t2) AC current in rectangular coordinates ";
33        cout<<"\n\tEnter selection: ";
34        cin>>selection;
35     }while((selection!=1)&&(selection!=2));
36     return selection;
37 }
38 void ACcurrent::setRect()
39 {
40     real=mag*cos(phase*D2R);
41     imag=mag*sin(phase*D2R);
42 }
43 void ACcurrent::setPolar()
44 {
45     mag=sqrt(real*real+imag*imag);
46     if(!((real==0)&&(imag==0)))
47         phase=atan(imag/real)*R2D;
48     else
49         phase=0;
50 }
51 ACcurrent ACcurrent::operator-(const ACcurrent & c) const
52 {
53     ACcurrent temp;
54     double treal, timag;
55     treal = mag*cos(phase*D2R)-c.mag*cos(c.phase*D2R);
56     timag = mag*sin(phase*D2R)-c.mag*sin(c.phase*D2R);
57     temp.mag = sqrt(treal*treal+timag*timag);
58     if(!((treal==0)&&(timag==0)))
59         temp.phase = atan(timag/treal)*R2D;
60     else
61         temp.phase=0;
62     return temp;
63 }
```

```
64 ACcurrent ACcurrent::operator+(const ACcurrent & c) const
65 {
66    ACcurrent temp;
67    double treal, timag;
68    treal = mag*cos(phase*D2R)+c.mag*cos(c.phase*D2R);
69    timag = mag*sin(phase*D2R)+c.mag*sin(c.phase*D2R);
70    temp.mag = sqrt(treal*treal+timag*timag);
71    if(!((treal==0)&&(timag==0)))
72       temp.phase = atan(timag/treal)*R2D;
73    else
74       temp.phase=0;
75    return temp;
76 }
77 ACcurrent ACcurrent::operator *(double r) const
78 {
79    ACcurrent temp;
80    temp.mag = mag*r;
81    temp.phase = phase;
82    temp.setRect();
83    return temp;
84 }
85 istream &operator>>(istream &inst, ACcurrent &c)
86 {
87    int choice=c.getCoord();
88    if(choice==1)
89    {
90       cout<<"\nEnter magnitude: ";
91       inst>>c.mag;
92       cout<<"Enter phase shift: ";
93       inst>>c.phase;
94       c.setRect();
95    }
96    else if(choice==2)
```

```
97      {
98          cout<<"\nEnter real part: ";
99          inst>>c.real;
100     cout<<"Enter imaginary part: ";
101     inst>>c.imag;
102     c.setPolar();
103 }
104      return inst;
105 }
106 ostream &operator<<(ostream &outst, const ACcurrent &c)
107 {
108     outst<<setiosflags(ios::fixed)<<setprecision(2);
109     outst<<"("<<setw(6)<<c.mag;
110     outst<<","<<setw(6)<<c.phase<<(char)248<<" ) [A]";
111     return outst;
112 }
113 int menu()
114 {
115     int selection;
116     do {
117         cout<<"\n\n\tSelect operation:"<<endl;
118         cout<<"\t\t 1) Add currents"<<endl;
119         cout<<"\t\t 2) Subtract currents"<<endl;
120         cout<<"\t\t 3) Multiply current by resistance"<<endl;
121         cout<<"\t\t 4) Exit"<<endl;
122         cout<<"\t\tEnter selection (1-4): ";
123         cin>>selection;
124     }while (selection<1||selection>4);
125     return selection;
126 }
127
128 int main()
129 {
```

```
130     ACcurrent c1, c2;
131     int operation;
132     cin>>c1>>c2;
133     do {
134         operation=menu();
135         switch(operation)
136         {
137             case 1:
138                 cout<<"\n\tc1+c2 = "<<(c1+c2);
139                 break;
140             case 2:
141                 cout<<"\n\tc1-c2 = "<<(c1-c2);
142                 break;
143             case 3:
144                 double r;
145                 cout<<"\nEnter resistance: ";
146                 cin>>r;
147                 cout<<"\n\tc1*R = "<<(c1*r);
148                 break;
149             case 4:
150                 break;
151         }
152     }while (operation!=4);
153     return 0;
154 }
```

OUTPUT

A sample run of CASEST6 is shown in Figure 6.16.

```
Select:
        1) AC current in polar coordinates
        2) AC current in rectangular coordinates
        Enter selection: 1


Enter magnitude: 0.5
Enter phase shift: 90

Select:
        1) AC current in polar coordinates
        2) AC current in rectangular coordinates
        Enter selection: 2


Enter real part: 0.7
Enter imaginary part: -1.2


Select operation:
        1) Add currents
        2) Subtract currents
        3) Multiply current by resistance
        4) Exit
        Enter your selection (1-4): 2


c1 - c2 = ( 1.84, -67.62°) [A]


Select operation:
        1) Add currents
        2) Subtract currents
        3) Multiply current by resistance
        4) Exit
        Enter your selection (1-4): 4
```

Figure 6.16 *A sample run of CASEST6.*

E
X
E
R
C
I
S
E

SUMMARY

1. Operator overloading enables programmers to use existing operators to perform operations on objects of their own classes.

2. When an operator is overloaded, it keeps its original meaning(s) and gains an additional meaning relative to the class for which it is defined.

3. The number of operands of an operator and its precedence cannot be changed through the overloading process.

4. To overload an operator, an operator function must be defined relative to a specific class.

5. Operator functions can be designed as *non-static* member functions or non-member functions (preferably **friend** functions).

6. When overloading binary operators using member functions, the object on the left side of the operator is passed by the **this** pointer. The left-side operand (object), therefore, must be instantiated from the class of the operator function.

7. The assignment operator can only be overloaded by a member operator function. It should be explicitly overloaded for every class, where objects contain pointers to dynamically allocate memory.

8. When using a *non-static* member function to overload a unary operator, the function will have no explicit arguments.

9. The **<<** and **>>** operators can be overloaded to perform user-defined I/O operations.

EXERCISES

Identify the errors in the operator functions in Exercises 6.1 through 6.9.

6.1
```
void Pixel::operator+(Pixel &p1, Pixel &p2, int a)
{
        p1.x = p1.x + a;
        p1.y = p1.y + a;
        p2.x = p2.x + a;
        p2.y = p2.y + a;
}
```

6.2
```
Pixel Pixel::operator++(Pixel &p1, Pixel &p2)
{
```

```
              p1.x++;
              p1.y++;
              p2.x++;
              p2.y++;
        }
```

6.3
```
//function prototype
   friend void &operator=(Impedance &v1, Impedance &v2);
```

6.4
```
//function prototype
   friend int operator?:(Resistor &r1, Resistor &r2)  const;
```

6.5
```
Pixel Pixel::operator-(int a, Pixel &p)
   {
         p.x = a - p.x;
         p.y = a - p.y;
         return *this;
   }
```

6.6
```
istream &operator<<(istream &ist, Impedance imp)
   {
         cout<<"Enter resistance";
         ist>>imp.r;
         cout<<"Enter reactance";
         ist>>imp.x;
   }
```

6.7
```
Pixel Pixel::operator--(int)
   {
         x--;
         y--;
         return *this;
   }
```

6.8 `ACcurrent ACcurrent::operator*(double r)  const`

```
    {
            real = real * r;
            imag = imag * r;
            return *this;
    }
```

6.9 `//function prototype`
`friend void operator/(ACcurrent &c);`

Change member operator functions in Exercises 6.10 through 6.12 to *friend* functions.

6.10 `bool ACcurrent::operator==(const ACcurrent & c)  const`

```
    {
            if((mag == c.mag) && (phase == c.phase))
                return true;
            else
                return false;
    }
```

6.11 `ACcurrent ACcurrent::operator-(const ACcurrent & c)`

```
    {
            ACcurrent temp;
            float real, imag;
            real=mag*cos(phase*D2R)-c.mag*cos(c.phase*D2R);
            imag=mag*sin(phase*D2R)-c.mag*sin(c.phase*D2R);
            temp.mag=sqrt(real*real+imag*imag);
            if(!((real==0)&&(imag==0)))
                temp.phase=atan(imag/real)*R2D;
            else
                temp.phase = 0;
            return temp;
    }
```

6.12
```
ACcurrent ACcurrent::operator++( )
{
        float real, imag;
        real=mag*cos(phase*D2R);
        imag=mag*sin(phase*D2R);
        ++real;
        ++imag;
        mag=sqrt(real*real+imag*imag);
        phase=atan(imag/real)*R2D;
        return *this;
}
```

Change *friend* operator functions in Exercises 6.13 through 6.15 to member functions.

6.13
```
//function prototype
friend  void operator<<(ACcurrent &, float);

//function definition
void operator<<(ACcurrent &c, float p)
{
        c.phase=c.phase+p;
}
```

6.14
```
//function prototype
friend void operator~(ACcurrent &);

//function definition
void operator~(ACcurrent &c)
{
        c.phase = c.phase - 180;
}
```

6.15   `//function prototype`
`friend Pixel operator+(const Pixel &, const Pixel &);`

`//function definition`
`Pixel operator+(const Pixel &p1, const Pixel &p2)`
`{`
`        Pixel temp;`
`        temp.x = p1.x + p2.x;`
`        temp.y = p1.y + p2.y;`
`        return temp;`
`}`

PROGRAMMING PROJECTS

6.1   Design an `Impedance` class that contains two data members: an active resistance R and reactive resistance (reactance) X. Note that $Z = R + i*X$, where R is a real part, and X an imaginary part, of the impedance Z. The class should use a constructor function to initialize the data members.

The class should also contain operator functions to perform the following operations:

1. Add impedances connected in series and return equivalent impedance (`Zs=Z1+Z2+Z3`)

2. Compute and return equivalent impedance of the impedances connected in parallel (`Zp=Z1||Z2||Z3`)

3. Change the sign of the reactance (`X = -X`)

4. Input an impedance (`cin>>Z`)

5. Output an impedance (`cout<<Z`)

Design the *main( )* function to test the `Impedance` class and all of its operator functions.

6.2   Design a `Vector` class that stores the vector's data in polar and rectangular coordinates (magnitude, angle, real part, and imaginary part). The class should use utility functions that convert rectangular coordinates into polar coordinates and vice versa. Operator functions should be designed to perform the following operations on vectors:

• Add vectors

• Subtract vectors

• Multiply vectors

- Divide vectors

- Input a vector in polar or rectangular coordinates (chosen by the user)

- Output a vector in polar and rectangular coordinates

Design the **main( )** function to prompt the user to enter two vectors in either polar or rectangular coordinates (user's choice). It should then display a menu with the options to add, subtract, multiply, or divide vectors and prompt the user to choose an option. After the user has chosen an operation to be performed, **main( )** should call appropriate operator functions to compute and output the result of the operation.

6.3 Design a class that contains the sine and cosine values of a floating point number as data members. The class should use operator functions to add, subtract, multiply, and divide **sin** and **cos** values. Design the **main( )** function to prompt the user to enter a value of an angle in degrees. After the user has entered the angle, **main( )** should then prompt the user to choose an operation to be performed on the **cos** and **sin** values of the entered angle (addition, subtraction, multiplication, or division). The program should display the result of the operation chosen as well as the **sin** and **cos** values of the entered angle.

6.4 Design a class that contains the numerator and denominator of a ratio as data members. The class should use operator functions to add, subtract, divide, multiply, increment, and decrement ratios. Design a program that prompts the user to enter two ratios and choose an operation to be performed on these numbers. The program should use operator functions to perform required operations, as well as to display the result of the chosen operation in the form of a ratio.

6.5 Design a class that uses a pointer to dynamically allocate and access an array of integer numbers. The class should have a default constructor and a copy constructor, each of which dynamically allocates and initializes the array. The destructor function that frees dynamically allocated memory will be necessary. The class should also have an operator function that overloads the assignment operator relative to this class. Design **main( )** so that three objects of the class are instantiated. A first object should contain an array of randomly generated integer numbers. Two other objects should contain the same array sorted in descending and ascending order, respectively. The = operator should be used to copy objects before sorting.

CHAPTER 7

INHERITANCE

INTRODUCTION

Code reusability is a very important programming concept, and C++ facilitates this concept more efficiently than C. **Inheritance** is one of the most powerful OOP tools in the implementation of code reusability in C++. When using inheritance, a new class can be created by establishing *parent-child* relationships with existing classes. This chapter will address the most important aspects of the implementation of inheritance, such as: constructing and destroying derived classes, using multiple-direct and multiple-indirect inheritance, as well as overriding and dominating inherited class members.

7.1 FUNDAMENTALS OF INHERITANCE

Inheritance is a relationship between classes in which one class inherits the properties (attributes and behaviors) of another class. Implementing inheritance promotes code reusability because new classes are created from existing classes.

Inheritance is also called **derivation** or an **is-a** relationship. It enables a hierarchy of classes to be designed. The hierarchy begins with the most general class and moves to more specific classes. There are many examples of this relationship in real life and in engineering. For example, an inverting operational amplifier *is a* type of operational amplifier (OPAMP) and an OPAMP *is a* type of amplifier. A hierarchy of classes in this example can be designed as shown in Figure 7.1.

Whenever an object is a type or subgroup of another object, it is appropriate to use inheritance. By implementing inheritance, data members and member functions from one class (higher in hierarchy) can become properties (members) of another class (lower in hierarchy) without coding them explicitly within this class.

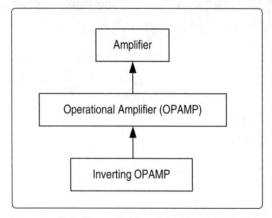

Figure 7.1 *Example of an inheritance hierarchy.*

The following terms are used when describing a relationship between classes that is established through inheritance:

- base (or parent) class
- derived (or child) class

A class that is inherited (higher in hierarchy) is called a **base class** or a **parent class**. A class (lower in hierarchy) that inherits properties of another class (base class) is called a **derived class** or **child class**. For example, an OPAMP class is derived from an amplifier class that serves as a base class. On the other hand, the OPAMP class is a base class of an inverting OPAMP class, which is the lowest-level derived class in this example of inheritance hierarchy (see Figure 7.1).

The implementation of inheritance begins with the definition of a base class. The base class defines all properties that can be inherited by any derived class, as well as some non-inheritable *private* properties of its own. Inheritance continues with the definition of a derived class that contains the properties inherited from the base class and some other properties that are specific to the derived class.

The general format of a derived-class definition is shown in Figure 7.2.

```
class derived_class_name:access_specifier base_class_name
{

    //specific properties of the derived-class


};
```

Figure 7.2 *General format of a derived class.*

The following is an example of a base-class and a derived-class definition:

```
class Amplifier {             //base class
public:
    float gain;               //gain
    float involt, outvolt;    //input and output voltage
    void setGain();           //Sets gain
    void setInvolt();         //Sets input voltage
    void getOutvolt();        //Computes and displays output voltage
};


class OPAMP : public Amplifier {        //derived class
private:
    float rin;                //input resistor
    float rout;               //feedback resistor
public:
    void setRes();            //Sets resistors
```

```
    float getGain();           //Computes and returns gain
};
```

The `Amplifier` class contains six ***public*** properties, three of which are the data members `gain`, `involt`, and `outvolt`, and three member functions `setGain()`, `setInvolt()`, and `getOutvolt()`. All six ***public*** members of the `Amplifier` class are inherited by the `OPAMP` class that is derived from `Amplifier`. In addition to the six inherited members, the `OPAMP` class also contains four other members—`rin`, `rout`, `setRes()`, and `getGain()`—that are specific to this class. Notice that the definition of the derived `OPAMP` class contains only `rin`, `rout`, `setRes()`, and `getGain()`, although the class actually has 10 properties (members). By establishing a relationship between the `Amplifier` and `OPAMP` classes, redundant coding is eliminated—i.e., code reusability is promoted.

There are two types of inheritance:

- Single inheritance
- Multiple inheritance

Single inheritance is the simplest type of inheritance, in which a class is derived from only one base class (a child class has only one parent class). A parent class, however, can have many child classes. The relationship between the `Amplifier` and `OPAMP` classes in the previous example is an example of single inheritance. Figure 7.3 graphically illustrates two examples of single inheritance, assuming that A, B, C, and D represent classes. With **multiple inheritance,** a class can have more than one parent class. Multiple inheritance is discussed in Section 7.4.

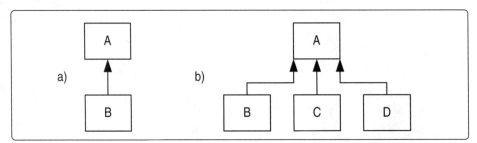

Figure 7.3 *Two examples of single inheritance: a) ONE parent class, ONE child class; and b) ONE parent class, THREE child classes.*

When defining a derived class, an access specifier that precedes a base-class name defines the status of the members inherited from the base class within the derived class. The ***private*** access specifier before the base-class name means that all members inherited from the base-class will be ***private*** in the derived class. If the access specifier is ***public***, all inherited members will have the **same status** in the derived class as the status these members have in the base-class. The meaning of same status will be discussed in more detail in the following section. In the previous example of the OPAMP derived class, the ***public*** access is specified prior to the Amplifier base-class name. This means that all six members inherited from Amplifier will be ***public*** in OPAMP, which is the same status these members have in the Amplifier class.

When inheriting from a base-class, the default access is ***private***. It can therefore be omitted in the header of a derived-class definition as follows:

```
class OPAMP : Amplifier {
        //members specific to OPAMP
};
```

The members that are inherited from the Amplifier class are ***private*** to the OPAMP class in this example. Any class that is derived from OPAMP cannot inherit these members.

The following data members and functions *cannot be inherited* from a base-class:

- ***private*** members (***private*** data members and ***private*** member functions)
- Constructor and destructor functions
- ***friend*** functions
- ***static*** functions
- Operator functions that overload the assignment operator

Note that all members, including data members, were specified ***public*** in the previous example of the Amplifier class. This was done to make the Amplifier class members inheritable by the OPAMP class because ***private*** members cannot be inherited. Making data ***public*** violates the fundamental encapsulation rule. To provide some level of data protection and to make these members inheritable at the same time, C++ provides a new access specifier called ***protected***.

7.2 THE *protected* ACCESS SPECIFIER

The ***protected*** access specifier is used only when implementing inheritance. Its purpose is to enable a derived class to access members of a base-class while keeping these members hidden from the rest of the program.

Members of a base-class that are specified as ***protected*** can be accessed directly by

- Any *non-static* member function of a base-class
- Any ***friend*** function of a base-class
- Any *non-static* member function of a class derived from the base-class
- Any ***friend*** function of a class derived from the base-class

In terms of *level of protection* of class members, the **protected** access specifier falls between **private** and **public**. Remember that the **private** access specifier provides the highest level of protection. The following is a redefined Amplifier/OPAMP example that uses the **protected** access specifier:

```
class Amplifier {            //base-class
private:
    float involt, outvolt;   //input and output voltage
protected:
    float gain;              //gain
public:
    void setGain();          //Sets gain
    void setInvolt();        //Sets input voltage
    float getOutvolt();      //Computes and displays output voltage
};

class OPAMP : public Amplifier {      //derived class
private:
    float rin;               //input resistor
    float rout;              //feedback resistor
public:
    void setResist();        //Sets resistors
    float getGain();         //Computes and returns gain
};
```

The OPAMP class inherits a **protected** data member gain and three **public** member functions setGain(), setInvolt(), and getOutvolt() from the Amplifier class. The **public** access specifier precedes the Amplifier base-class name in the header of the OPAMP definition. The members inherited from Amplifier, therefore, will have the same status in OPAMP as the status these members have in Amplifier (**protected** or **public**). Table 7.1 lists all of the members of the OPAMP class with the status they have in OPAMP.

When defining a derived class, **protected** can also be used to specify a type of inheritance. The type of inheritance is specified by the access specifier (**private**, **protected**, or **public**), which precedes a base-class name in the header of a derived class. All **public** and **protected** members inherited from the base-class with the **protected** access specifier will be **protected** in the derived class. Table 7.2 shows the three types of inheritance and how each type affects the status of inherited members within a derived class.

Table 7.1 Members of the OPAMP Class

Member	Access Status
rin	*private*
rout	*private*
gain	*protected*
setResist()	*public*
getGain()	*public*
setGain()	*public*
setInvolt()	*public*
getOutvolt()	*public*

Table 7.2 Access Status of Derived Class's Members*

Type of Inheritance	Access Status within Base-Class	
	protected	*public*
	Access Status within Derived-Class	
private	*private*	*private*
protected	*protected*	*protected*
public	*protected*	*public*

* based on the type of inheritance and the status within the base-class

The ***protected*** status violates the fundamental encapsulation rule to a lesser extent than ***public***. This type of access, however, should not be overused because it does not protect data as well as the ***private*** access specifier does.

 TIP: The ***protected*** access specifier should not be overused because it violates encapsulation to a certain extent.

7.3 CONSTRUCTING AND DESTROYING DERIVED CLASSES

Every base and derived class in an inheritance hierarchy should have its own constructor and destructor functions. Constructors and destructors *cannot be inherited*. If an explicit constructor or destructor is not created, C++ will use the default constructor and destructor.

Assume that each class in an inheritance hierarchy has its own constructor and destructor functions. When instantiating an object of a derived class, constructors of all of its parent classes are executed prior to the derived-class constructor. This is understandable because when *creating a child*, all of its parents have to be created before the child can be created. The constructor functions, therefore, are executed in the order of derivation within the inheritance hierarchy.

Consider the following example. If C inherits B and B inherits A (Figure 7.4), the order of constructor calls when instantiating an object of C is A-B-C. Destructor functions are always executed in the *reverse order*. When C's object goes out of scope, therefore, the destructors are called in C-B-A order.

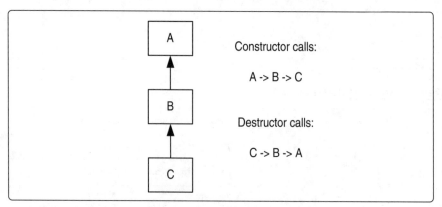

Figure 7.4 *Order of the constructor and destructor calls in an inheritance hierarchy.*

If a base-class constructor has arguments, these arguments also have to be added to the argument list of any class derived from this base class. When instantiating an object of the derived class, all of the arguments required by the base constructor and derived constructor are first passed to the derived constructor. The derived constructor then passes appropriate arguments along to the base-class constructor.

To pass arguments from a derived class to a base class, a **constructor initialization list** must be created when defining the derived-class constructor. The general format is shown in Figure 7.5.

It should be noted that arg_list1 contains all of the arguments required by both the base-class and derived-class constructors. Each argument in arg_list1 must have a data type specified, as well as an identifier (name). The arg_list2 argument list, which follows the base-class name, contains only the identifiers (*not data types*) of the arguments that are passed to the base-class constructor.

 TIP: Specifying a data type for an argument that is passed to a base-class constructor in a constructor initialization list is a syntax error.

```
derived_class(arg_list1):base_class(arg_list2)
{
        //body of derived-class constructor
}
```

Figure 7.5 *General format of a derived class' constructor with a constructor initialization list.*

Note that both the base-class and derived-class constructors can use the same argument(s). It is also possible for the derived-class constructor to use no arguments and just pass all arguments along to the base-class constructor.

In Program Example 7.1, PROG7_1 uses a derived-class constructor with a constructor initialization list and demonstrates the order of the constructor and destructor calls in an inheritance hierarchy. PROG7_1 is designed to solve the problem shown in Figure 7.6.

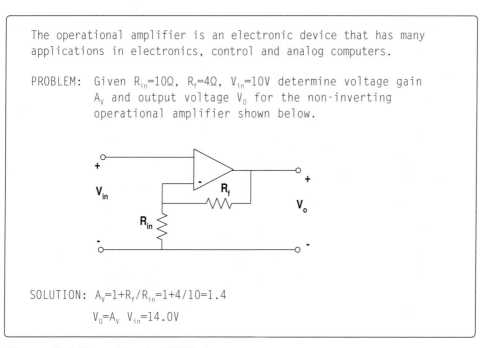

```
The operational amplifier is an electronic device that has many
applications in electronics, control and analog computers.

PROBLEM:  Given R_in=10Ω, R_f=4Ω, V_in=10V determine voltage gain
          A_V and output voltage V_0 for the non-inverting
          operational amplifier shown below.
```

$$A_V = 1 + R_f/R_{in} = 1 + 4/10 = 1.4$$
$$V_0 = A_V \, V_{in} = 14.0V$$

SOLUTION:

Figure 7.6 *The problem for PROG7_1.*

PROGRAM EXAMPLE 7.1: PROG7_1

```
1  //PROG7_1: Program demonstrates the mechanisms of constructing
2  //          and destroying objects of derived classes.
3  #include <iostream>
4  #include <iomanip>
5  using namespace std;
6
7  class Amplifier {      //base-class
8     float involt;       //input voltage
9     float outvolt;      //output voltage
10 protected:
11    float gain;
12 public:
13    Amplifier(float=0, float=1);              //constructor
14    ~Amplifier(){cout<<"Destroying amplifier!"<<endl;} //destructor
15    void setInvolt(float inv) { involt=inv; }
16    float getOutvolt(){outvolt=involt*gain;  return outvolt;}
17 };
18 Amplifier::Amplifier(float inv, float g)   //base constructor
19 {
20    cout<<"Constructing amplifier!"<<endl;
21    involt=inv; gain=g;
22    outvolt=involt*gain;
23 }
24 class OPAMP_NI:public Amplifier {    //derived class
25    float rin;    //input resistor
26    float rf;     //feedback resistor
27 public:
28    OPAMP_NI(float=0, float=1, float=0, float=0);    //constructor
29    ~OPAMP_NI(){cout<<"\nDestroying OPAMP!"<<endl;}  //destructor
30    void setRes(float r1, float r2){rin=r1; rf=r2;}
31    float getGain(){gain=1+rf/rin;   return gain;}
```

```
32 };
33 OPAMP_NI::OPAMP_NI(float v, float a, float r1, float r2):
34                 Amplifier(v, a)
35 {                              //derived constructor
36    cout<<"Constructing OPAMP!"<<endl;
37    rin=r1;  rf=r2;
38 }
39
40 int main()
41 {
42    OPAMP_NI amp1;          //derived class's object
43    float r1, r2, volt;
44    cout<<"\n\tEnter input and feedback resistor => ";
45    cin>>r1>>r2;
46    amp1.setRes(r1,r2);
47    cout<<"\tEnter input voltage => ";
48    cin>>volt;
49    amp1.setInvolt(volt);
50    cout<<setiosflags(ios::fixed)<<setprecision(2);
51    cout<<"\n\t\tGain = "<<amp1.getGain()<<endl;
52    cout<<"\t\tOutput Voltage = "<<amp1.getOutvolt()<<" [V]\n";
53    return 0;
54 }
```

This program uses the Amplifier class (lines 7–17) as a base-class where inheritance begins. The Amplifier constructor (lines 18–23) uses two default arguments to initialize the involt and gain data members (line 21). This constructor function also initializes outvolt by multiplying values of involt and gain and assigning the result to outvolt. The OPAMP_NI class (lines 24–32) is derived from the Amplifier class by using *public* inheritance (line 24). As a result, members inherited from Amplifier: gain (*protected*), setInvolt() (*public*), and getOutvolt() (*public*), will have the same access status in OPAMP_NI. The OPAMP_NI class uses its constructor (lines 33–38) to initialize the rin and rf data members. Notice that this constructor function has 4 arguments, two of which (v, a) are passed along to the Amplifier class' constructor (line 34). The OPAMP_NI's constructor uses two other arguments (r1, r2) to initialize rin and rf (line 37). Both classes contain destructor functions (lines 14 and 29), the purpose of which is to output a message that indicates when destructors are executed. Constructors also display appropriate messages (lines 20 and 36).

The **main( )** function instantiates an amp1 object of the OPAMP_NI class (line 42). When instantiating amp1, the Amplifier constructor is executed first; followed by the OPAMP_NI constructor, and both constructors use the default values of their arguments. Destructor calls are made in the reverse order of constructor calls. The OPAMP_NI destructor is executed first, followed by the Amplifier destructor, with the resultant destruction of amp1 at the end of **main()**. A sample run of PROG7_1 is shown in Figure 7.7.

```
Constructing amplifier!
Constructing OPAMP!
    Enter input and feedback resistor => 10 4
    Enter input voltage => 10
        Gain = 1.40
        Output Voltage = 14.00 [V]
Destroying OPAMP!
Destroying amplifier!
```

Figure 7.7 *Sample run of PROG7_1.*

PROG7_1 demonstrates an example of **single inheritance**—that is, the derived class OPAMP_NI has only one parent class (Amplifier). The following section will introduce two types of **multiple inheritance**, in which a derived class has more than one parent.

7.4 MULTIPLE INHERITANCE

When implementing multiple inheritance, a class can be derived directly or indirectly from as many parent classes as necessary. There are two types of multiple inheritance:

- **Direct** multiple inheritance
- **Indirect** multiple inheritance

If A, B, and C represent three classes, the two types of multiple inheritance can be graphically represented, as shown in Figure 7.8.

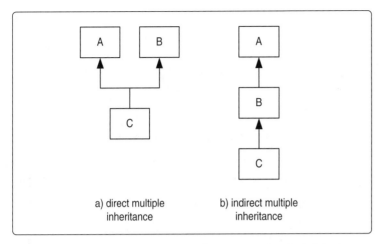

a) direct multiple inheritance

b) indirect multiple inheritance

Figure 7.8 *Graphic representation of two types of multiple inheritance.*

7.4.1 DIRECT MULTIPLE INHERITANCE

When implementing **direct multiple inheritance**, a derived class can *directly* inherit more than one base-class. In the example in Figure 7.8a, the C class directly inherits the A and B classes (C has two direct parents). To define a class that directly inherits multiple base classes, the general format shown in Figure 7.9 is used.

```
class Derived_class: access_specifier Base1_class,
                     access_specifier Base2_class, ...,
                     access_specifier BaseN_class
{
    //body of derived-class
};
```

Figure 7.9 *General format of a derived-class definition that directly inherits multiple base classes.*

Access specifiers that precede base classes Base1_class, Base2_class,..., BaseN_class can be either *private*, *protected*, or *public*. The derived class can inherit each base-class with a different access specifier. When multiple base classes are directly inherited, constructors are executed in the order (from left to right) in which the base classes are listed in the header of a derived class' definition (Base1_class, Base2_class,..., BaseN_class). Destructors are executed in the reverse order (BaseN_class, BaseN-1_class,..., Base1_class).

Program Example 7.2 demonstrates an example of direct multiple inheritance with PROG7_2. This program designs the low-pass filter shown in Figure 7.10.

A **low-pass** filter is a circuit that is designed to pass signals with low frequences and reject signals with high frequences. A typical low-pass filter is designed from an RC circuit, where the output is taken off the capacitor. The main characteristic of this filter is the **cutoff frequency** that is expressed as follows:

$$\omega_c = 1/RC$$

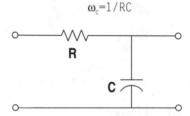

PROBLEM: Given R=1000Ω, C=4.7 10^{-7}F determines ω_c.

SOLUTION: $\omega_c = 1/RC = 2127.66$ rad/s

Figure 7.10 *The problem for PROG7_2.*

PROGRAM EXAMPLE 7.2: PROG7_2

```
1   //PROG7_2: Program demonstrates direct multiple inheritance.
2   #include <iostream>
3   using namespace std;
4
5   class Resistor {              //base-class # 1
6   protected:
7       double res;               //resistance
8   public:
9       Resistor(double r) { res=r; }
10      void setRes() { cout<<"\tEnter R = "; cin>>res; }
11      double getRes() { return res; }
12  };
13
```

```
14 class Capacitor {              //base-class # 2
15 protected:
16     double cap;               //capacitance
17 public:
18     Capacitor(double c) { cap=c; }
19     void setCap() { cout<<"\tEnter C = "; cin>>cap; }
20     double getCap() { return cap; }
21 };
22
23 class Low_Pass:public Resistor,public Capacitor{   //derived class
24     double frq_cut;     //cutoff frequency
25 public:
26     Low_Pass (double, double);        //derived constructor
27     void setFreq() { frq_cut=1/(res*cap); }
28     double getFreq() { return frq_cut; }
29 };
30 Low_Pass::Low_Pass(double r, double c):Resistor(r),Capacitor(c)
31 {               //derived constructor with initialization list
32   setFreq();
33 }
34
35 int main()
36 {
37   Low_Pass filter(1000, 0.00000047);
38   cout<<"Low-Pass Filter:"<<endl;
39   cout<<"\tR = "<<filter.getRes()<<" ohms"<<endl;
40   cout<<"\tC = "<<filter.getCap()<<" F"<<endl;
41   cout<<"\tCutoff Frequency = "<<filter.getFreq()<<" rad/s";
42   cout<<"\n\nAfter changing R and C:"<<endl;
43   filter.setRes();
44   filter.setCap();
45   filter.setFreq();
46   cout<<"\tCutoff Frequency = "<<filter.getFreq()<<" rad/s";
```

```
47    return 0;
48 }
```

The relationship between classes in this program is graphically illustrated in Figure 7.11.

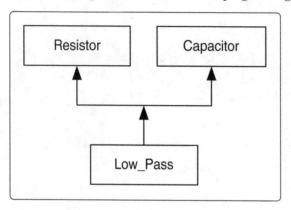

Figure 7.11 *Inheritance hierarchy in PROG7_2.*

The Low_Pass class (lines 23–29) describes some attributes and behaviors of a passive low-pass filter. This class directly inherits the Resistor and Capacitor classes with the ***public*** access specifier (line 23). The Resistor's constructor uses one argument to initialize its class' data member, res (line 9), representing the resistance of a low-pass filter. The Capacitor's constructor has one argument that is used to initialize the filter's capacitance, cap (line 18). Table 7.3 shows all members of the Low_Pass class, along with their access status.

While no derived-class variables are used as arguments of the derived-class constructor (lines 30–33), two arguments are required. These two arguments must be added to the argument list of the Low_Pass constructor because they are required by the parent classes Resistor and Capacitor when instantiating a Low_Pass object. The Low_Pass constructor just passes these two arguments along to the Resistor's and Capacitor's constructor to initialize res (line 9) and cap (line 18), respectively. To pass the arguments from Low_Pass to Resistor and Capacitor, a constructor initialization list is required for the Low_Pass constructor (line 30).

Table 7.3 Members of the Low-Pass Class

Member	Access Status
frq_cut	*private*
res	*protected* *
cap	*protected* **
Low_Pass()	*public*
setFreq()	*public*
getFreq()	*public*
setRes()	*public* *
getRes()	*public* *
setCap()	*public* **
getCap()	*public* **

* member is inherited from Resistor
** member is inherited from Capacitor

The **main()** function instantiates a filter object of the derived Low_Pass class (line 37). **main()** then uses this object to invoke all of the member functions of the derived-class including the functions inherited from Resistor and Capacitor (lines 39–41 and 43–46). A sample run of PROG7_2 is shown in Figure 7.12.

7.4.2 INDIRECT MULTIPLE INHERITANCE

A class can **indirectly** inherit members of another class through its base-class. The original base-class in this case is derived from another base/parent class, creating a multilevel inheritance hierarchy.

This type of inheritance is graphically represented in the example shown in Figure 7.8b. The C class has two parent classes in this example: A (indirect parent) and B (direct parent). The A class is an indirect parent of C because C inherits A indirectly through B.

```
Low-Pass Filter:
        R = 1000 ohms
        C =   4.7e-007 F
        Cutoff Frequency = 2127.66 rad/s
After changing R and C:
        Enter R = 200
        Enter C = 0.000001
        Cutoff Frequency = 5000 rad/s
```

Figure 7.12 *Sample run of PROG7_2.*

PROG7_3 is a modified version of PROG7_2 that is used to demonstrate indirect multiple inheritance, in Program Example 7.3. Both programs produce low-pass filter designs.

PROGRAM EXAMPLE 7.3: PROG 7_3

```
1   //PROG7_3: Program demonstrates indirect multiple inheritance.
2   #include <iostream>
3   using namespace std;
4   class RC_Circuit {                    /base-class
5   protected:
6       double res;                       //resistance
7       double cap;                       //capacitance
8   public:
9       RC_Circuit(double r, double c) { res=r; cap=c; }
10      void setRes() { cout<<"\tEnter R = "; cin>>res; }
11      double getRes() { return res; }
12      void setCap() { cout<<"\tEnter C = "; cin>>cap; }
13      double getCap() { return cap; }
14  };
15  class Filter:public RC_Circuit {      //derived classs #1
16  protected:
17      double frq;    //frequency
18  public:
19      Filter(double r, double c, double f):RC_Circuit(r,c){frq=f;}
20      double getFreq() { return frq; }
21  };
22  class Low_Pass:public Filter {        //derived-class #2
23      double frq_cut;      //cutoff frequency
24  public:
25      Low_Pass (double, double, double);
26      void setCutoff() { frq_cut=1/(res*cap); }
27      double getCutoff() { return frq_cut; }
28      bool isPreserved();
```

```
29 };
30 Low_Pass::Low_Pass(double r, double c, double f):Filter(r,c,f)
31 {
32     setCutoff();
33 }
34 bool Low_Pass::isPreserved()
35 {
36     return ((frq<=frq_cut)? true : false);
37 }
38 int main()
39 {
40     Low_Pass filter(1000, 0.00000047, 2500);
41     cout<<"Low-Pass Filter:"<<endl;
42     cout<<"\tR = "<<filter.getRes()<<" ohms"<<endl;
43     cout<<"\tC = "<<filter.getCap()<<" F"<<endl;
44     cout<<"\tCutoff Frequency = "<<filter.getCutoff()<<" rad/s";
45     if(filter.isPreserved()) {
46         cout<<"\n\tFrequency = "<<filter.getFreq();
47         cout<<" rad/s is preserved."<<endl;
48     }
49     else {
50         cout<<"\n\tFrequency = "<<filter.getFreq();
51         cout<<" rad/s is attenuated."<<endl;
52     }
53     cout<<"\n\nAfter changing R and C:"<<endl;
54     filter.setRes();
55     filter.setCap();
56     filter.setCutoff();
57     cout<<"\tCutoff Frequency = "<<filter.getCutoff()<<" rad/s";
58     if(filter.isPreserved()) {
59         cout<<"\n\tFrequency = "<<filter.getFreq();
60         cout<<" rad/s is preserved."<<endl;
61     }
```

```
62    else {
63        cout<<"\n\tFrequency = "<<filter.getFreq();
64        cout<<" rad/s is attenuated."<<endl;
65    }
66    return 0;
67 }
```

The Low_Pass class in PROG7_3 is derived from the Filter class, while the Filter class is derived from the RC_Circuit class (Figure 7.13). The Low_Pass class, therefore, inherits directly from Filter and indirectly from RC_Circuit through Filter. This inheritance hierarchy is logical because a low-pass filter is a subtype of a filter circuit and a filter circuit can be designed from an RC circuit.

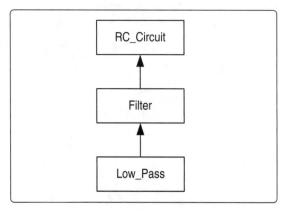

Figure 7.13 *Inheritance hierarchy in PROG7_3.*

The RC_Circuit class (lines 4–14) serves as a base-class where the inheritance hierarchy begins. This class has two **protected** data members—res (resistance) and cap (capacitance)—as well as **public** interface functions to manipulate these two data members. The RC-Circuit constructor (line 9) uses two arguments to initialize res and cap. The Filter class is derived from RC_Circuit by using **public** inheritance (line 15), and as a result, all inherited members from RC_Circuit retain the same access status (**protected** or **public**) as in Filter. In addition to the members inherited from RC_Circuit, Filter has a **protected** data member, frq, representing the frequency of a signal to be filtered and a **public** function, getFreq(), that returns frq (line 20). The constructor function of Filter has three arguments, two of which are passed to RC_Circuit while a third argument is used to initialize frq (line 19).

The Low_Pass class is derived from Filter by using **public** inheritance (line 22). Low_Pass, therefore, inherits all **protected** and **public** members from Filter, excluding the constructor function. The members inherited by Low_Pass from Filter include all members that `Filter` inherited from `RC_Circuit`. The access status of these members in `Low_Pass` is the same as in `Filter` (*public* inheritance). The `Low_Pass` class in this example is the lowest-level derived-class in the inheritance hierarchy. In addition to the members inherited from `Filter`, `Low_Pass` has some other specific members:

- A *private* data member, frq_cut, representing the cutoff frequency of a low-pass filter (line 23)

- A *public* constructor function (line 25)

- A *public* function, `setCutoff()`, that computes the cutoff frequency (line 26)

- A *public* function, `getCutoff()`, that returns the cutoff frequency (line 27)

- A *public* function, `isPreserved()`, that returns *true* if `frq` is less then or equal to `frq_cut`, or *false* if not (line 28)

The `Low_Pass` constructor has three arguments and passes all three of them to `Filter` (line 30). It also calls `setCutoff()` to compute and initialize `frq_cut` (line 32). The *main()* function instantiates a `Low_Pass` object named `filter` (line 40). Notice that three values are passed to `Low_Pass`'s constructor when instantiating `filter`. `Low_Pass`'s constructor passes all three values to `Filter`'s constructor, two of which are then passed to `RC_Circuit`'s constructor. The order of constructor function execution when instantiating `filter` is:

1. `RC_Circuit`'s constructor

2. `Filter`'s constructor

3. `Low_Pass`'s constructor

The *main()* function uses the `filter` object to invoke member functions of `Low_Pass`, including those functions directly inherited from `Filter` and indirectly inherited from `RC_Circuit`. A sample run of PROG7_3 is shown in Figure 7.14.

```
Low-Pass Filter:
        R = 1000 ohms
        C =  4.7e-007 F
        Cutoff Frequency = 2127.66 rad/s
        Frequency = 2500 rad/s is attenuated.

After changing R and C:
        Enter R = 200
        Enter C = 0.000001
        Cutoff Frequency = 5000 rad/s
        Frequency = 2500 rad/s is preserved.
```

Figure 7.14 *Sample run of PROG7_3.*

The selection of either direct or indirect multiple inheritance should be based on the logic of a problem to be solved. A class should be derived from a class or classes that is a logical supergroup of the class to be derived. It is not a good, logical plan to derive a filter circuit class from a low-pass filter class, for example, because low-pass filters are a subgroup of filter circuits. When using multiple inheritance, programmers should use a simple logical approach and avoid complex inheritance hierarchy trees.

 TIP: When designing an inheritance hierarchy, it should be kept simple to prevent logic errors.

7.5 DOMINATING AND OVERRIDING BASE-CLASS MEMBERS

When inheriting from a base-class, some inherited members can be overridden and the others dominated by members of a derived-class. In either case, members inherited from the base-class have the same name (identifier) as members of the derived-class that override or dominate the inherited members.

PROG7_4 uses two simple classes—Resistor and Circuit—to demonstrate C++ principles of dominating and overriding inherited members. This program, shown in Program Example 7.4, does not illustrate common programming practices. The only purpose of PROG7_4 is to demonstrate some important aspects of inheritance.

PROGRAM EXAMPLE 7.4: PROG7_4

```
1   //PROG7_4: Program demonstrates the principles of dominating and
2   //         overriding inherited members.
```

```
3   #include <iostream>
4   using namespace std;
5   class Resistor {                      //base-class
6   public:
7       float r;          //resistance
8       Resistor(float x = 0) { r=x; }
9       void getVal() { cout<<"R = "<<r<<endl; }
10  };
11  class Circuit:public Resistor {       //derived-class
12  public:
13      float r;          //resistance
14      double c;         //capacitance
15      Circuit(float x, double y):Resistor(330) { r=x; c=y; }
16      void getVal() { cout<<"R = "<<r<<"   C = "<<c<<endl; }
17  };
18  int main()
19  {
20      Resistor res1(470);
21      Circuit cir1(200, 0.0001), cir2(1000, 0.0005);
22      cout<<"\t\tAccessing data members:\n\n";
23      cout<<"res1.r = "<<res1.r<<endl;
24      cout<<"cir1.r = "<<cir1.r<<endl;
25      cout<<"cir2.r = "<<cir2.r<<endl;
26      cout<<"cir1.Resistor::r = "<<cir1.Resistor::r<<endl;
27      cout<<"cir2.Resistor::r = "<<cir2.Resistor::r<<endl;
28      Resistor res2=cir2;
29      cout<<"res2.r = "<<res2.r<<endl;
30      cout<<"\n\t\tExecuting member functions:\n\n";
31      res1.getVal();
32      cir1.getVal();
33      cir1.Resistor::getVal();
34      cout<<"\n\t\tUsing a base-class pointer:\n\n";
35      Resistor *rptr;
```

```
36      rptr=&res1;
37      rptr->getVal();
38      rptr=&cir1;
39      rptr->getVal();
40      return 0;
41  }
```

Both classes—the `Resistor` base class as well as the `Circuit` derived class, have an `r` data member representing the resistance of a resistor and circuit, respectively. When `Circuit` inherits `Resistor` (line 11), `r` from `Resistor` becomes a member of `Circuit` as well. The `Circuit` class, therefore, has two data members with the same name and of the same type. The question is raised: which of these two members is accessed when using the syntax such as `cir1.r` (line 24), where `cir1` represents an object of the `Circuit` class? C++ applies the following principle in this case: *a data member of a derived class dominates a data member inherited from a base class that uses the same identifier*. `cir1.r`, therefore, will access `r` declared in `Circuit`.

To access members inherited from a base class by using a derived-class object, the general format as shown in Figure 7.15 can be used.

```
derived_object.base_class_name::inherited_member
```

Figure 7.15 *Accessing members inherited from a base-class by using a derived-class object.*

Notice that to access `r`, which is inherited from `Resistor` within the `cir1` object (derived-class object), the syntax `cir1.Resistor::r` must be used. The statements that use the syntax in PROG7_4, as shown in Figure 7.15, are in lines 26, 27, and 33.

The ***main()*** function instantiates two objects of `Resistor` named `res1` and `res2` (lines 20 and 28), as well as two objects of `Circuit` named `cir1` and `cir2` (line 21). Note that `res2` is initialized in line 28 by using `cir2` and the = operator (a derived-class' object is assigned to a base-class' object). In this case, the value of `Resistor::r` stored in `cir2` is copied into `res2`. Values stored in all four objects that ***main()*** instantiates are shown in Figure 7.16.

The base-class name followed by the scope resolution operator (::) is used only in cases in which it is necessary to distinguish inherited members from the members with the same name declared within the derived-class.

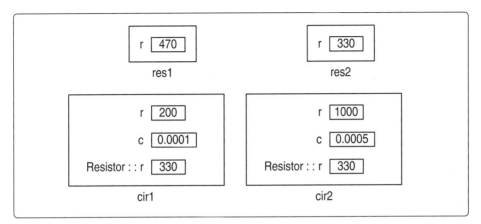

Figure 7.16 *Memory contents when executing line 28 of PROG7_4.*

Both classes also use a member function, getVal(), with no parameters that has the same name and return type in each class—i.e., the same signature (lines 9 and 16). The getVal() function in Resistor displays r, while getVal() in Circuit displays r and c. Because Circuit class inherits getVal() from Resistor, there are two getVal() functions in Circuit that are performing different operations.

To determine which of these two functions will be invoked when using cir1.getVal() (line 32), C++ uses the following principle: *a function defined within a derived-class overrides a function with the same signature that is inherited from a base-class.* The format shown in Figure 7.15 must be used to invoke the inherited function by using a derived object. cir1.getVal() therefore invokes the getVal() function defined in Circuit, while cir1.Resistor::getVal() invokes the getVal() function defined in Resistor. The output produced by PROG7_4 is shown in Figure 7.17.

PROG7_4 also demonstrates how to use pointers of a base-class type to invoke functions that are members of a derived-class. The ***main()*** function declares a rptr pointer of the Resistor type (line 35). The rptr pointer first points to the res1 object of Resistor (line 36). While pointing to res1, the pointer is used to invoke the getVal() function by using the syntax rptr->getVal() (line 37). The getVal() function defined in Resistor is executed because rptr points to the Resistor class object. The pointer is then changed to point to the cir1 object of Circuit (line 38). While pointing to cir1, the pointer is used again to invoke getVal(). Based on the previously discussed overriding rule, one would probably expect that rptr->getVal() would invoke the getVal() function defined in Circuit because rptr points to the Circuit object. This is not the case, however. Instead, getVal() defined in Resistor is executed because the pointer is the Resistor type.

```
        Accessing data members:

res1.r = 470

cir1.r = 200

cir2.r = 1000

cir1.Resistor::r = 330

cir2.Resistor::r = 330

res2.r = 330


        Executing member functions:

R = 470

R = 200   C = 0.0001

R = 330


        Using a base-class pointer:

R = 470

R = 330
```

Figure 7.17 *Output produced by PROG7_4.*

Using pointers that point to class objects to invoke member functions is common but powerful programming practice. When designing an inheritance hierarchy, a pointer, which is a base-class type where inheritance hierarchy begins, can also be used to point to objects of any derived class. The opposite is not true, however, because a derived-class pointer cannot point to objects of a base class unless type casting is used. If a base-class pointer is explicitly cast to be a derived-class pointer, it can only point to derived-class objects. Table 7.4 summarizes the use of pointers within an inheritance hierarchy, based on the pointer type as well as the object type.

Table 7.4 Using Pointers within an Inheritance Hierarchy

Pointer type	Object type	
	Base-class	Derived-class
Base-class	NO PROBLEM	NO PROBLEM, if referring to inherited members
Derived-class	ERROR!	NO PROBLEM

A problem may occur when using a base-class pointer to invoke a function defined within a derived-class that has the same signature as the function inherited from the base-class. This case is illustrated in PROG7_4.

C++ offers a tool that enables resolving problem situations such as the one demonstrated in PROG7_4. This tool (***virtual*** functions) is discussed in Chapter 9.

 NOTE: A base-class pointer can point to an object of any class that is derived from the base-class without using type cast.

SUMMARY

1. Inheritance (derivation) promotes code reusability. It enables a new class to be created by inheriting properties from existing classes.

2. An inheritance hierarchy begins with a definition of a base or parent class.

3. A class that inherits properties of a base-class is called a derived or child class.

4. A new access specifier called ***protected*** is introduced when implementing inheritance. Class members specified as ***protected*** can be passed between classes that form an inheritance chain and cannot be accessed outside of this family of classes.

5. The access specifier (***private***, ***protected***, or ***public***) that precedes a base-class name in the header of a derived-class defines the access status of inherited members within the derived-class.

6. When implementing single inheritance a class is derived from only one base-class, while with multiple inheritance a class can be derived from as many base classes as necessary.

7. There are two types of multiple inheritance: multiple-direct and multiple-indirect inheritance.

8. Constructors and destructors cannot be inherited.

9. When instantiating a derived-class object, constructors of all its base classes (direct and indirect) are executed prior to the derived-class' constructor. Destructors are executed in the reverse order of that in which constructors are executed.

10. To pass arguments from a derived-class to a base-class, a constructor initialization list must be created.

11. A data member of a derived-class dominates a data member inherited from a base-class that has the same name.

12. A function defined within a derived-class overrides an inherited function with the same signature.

13. A base-class pointer can point to a derived-class object without any problem if referring to members inherited from the base-class.

14. A base-class/derived-class pointer can be converted to a derived-class/base-class pointer by using an explicit cast.

15. A derived-class object can be assigned to a base-class object, while assigning a base-class object to a derived-class object causes an error.

EXERCISES

State the members and their access status in each of the classes that form the inheritance hierarchies in Exercises 7.1 through 7.3. Identify the type of inheritance in each case.

7.1

```
class A {
    static int count;
    protected:
    int x;
public:
    A();
    ~A();
    void display();
    friend float calc(A obj);
};
class B : public A {
private:
    int y;
public:
    B();
    void get();
};
```

7.2

```
class First {
private:
```

```
   int x;
protected:
  float y;
public:
  int get();
};
class Second: protected First {
private:
  int z;
protected:
  float y;
public:
  Second();
  int get_z();
};
class Third: public Second {
private:
  char *st;
public:
  Third();
  void display();
};
```

7.3
```
class Base1  {
protected:
  float x, y;
public:
  Base1();
  void get();
};
class Base2  {
private:
  int z;
```

```
protected:
  float w;
public:
  Base2();
  float  compute();
};
class Derived: public Base1, Base2 {
private:
  float v;
public:
  Derived();
  void display();
};
```

7.4. Assume that the `Amplifier` and `Speaker` classes have been defined. Code a statement that declares a `Stereo` class that directly inherits `Amplifier` and `Speaker`. The members inherited from `Amplifier` should be private in `Stereo`, while the members inherited from `Speaker` should have the same access status in `Stereo` as the status they have in `Speaker`.

Given the following `Resistor` class definition, identify and correct the errors in the code fragments in Exercises 7.5 through 7.7.

```
class Resistor {
private:
    float r;          //resistance
protected:
    float get_r() { return r; }
public:
    Resistor(float x) { r=x; }
    float get_current(float volt) { return volt/r; }
};
```

7.5
```
class Circuit : public Resistor {
private:
  float ind;          //inductance
  float frq;          //frequency
```

```
public:
   Circuit(float i, float f) { ind=i;  frq=f; }
   float getImpedance();
};
float Circuit::getImpedance()
{
   float r=get_r();
   float x=2*3.14*frq*ind;
   return  sqrt( r*r + x*x );
}
```

7.6
```
int main()
{
   Resistor  res1,
   cout<<"Resistance = "<<res1.get_r();
   return 0;
}
```

7.7
```
class Circuit : private Resistor {
   // Body of the Circuit class
};
int main()
{
   Circuit c(100, 0.001, 60);
   cout<<"Current  = "<<c.get_current(20);
   Resistor res(100);
   Circuit *cptr=&res;
   cout<<"Impedance = "<<cptr->getImpedance();
   return 0;
}
```

Determine the output produced by the programs in Exercises 7.8 and 7.9.

7.8
```
#include <iostream>
using namespace std;
class A {
private:
   int i;
public:
   A(int x) {   cout<<"Constructing A"<<endl;   i=x;   }
   ~A() { cout<<"Destroying A"<<endl; }
   void get_i()   { cout<<i<<endl; }
};
class B : public A {
private:
   int j;
public:
   B(int n, int m) : A(m)   {
      cout<<"Constructing B"<<endl;
      j=n;
   }
   ~B() { cout<<"Destroying B"<<endl; }
   void get_j() {   cout<<j<<endl;   }
};
int main()
{
   B   obj(6, 49);
   obj.get_i();
   obj.get_j();
   return 0;
}
```

7.9
```
#include <iostream>
using namespace std;
```

```
class A {
private:
   int a;
public:
   A (int x) { a=x;  }
   void getA() { cout<<a; }
};
class B : public A {
private:
   int b, c;
public:
   B (int x, int y, int z) : A(z) { b=x; c=y; }
   void getValues() { cout<<' '<<b<<' '<<c;  }
};
class C : public B {
private:
   int d;
public:
   C(int x, int y, int z, int q) : B(y, z, q) { d=x; }
   void show(){ getA(); getValues(); cout<<' '<<d<<endl; }
};
int main()
{
   C obj1(1,2,3,4); A obj2(5);
   A *ptr=&obj1;
   obj1.show();
   ptr->getA();
   ptr=&obj2;
   ptr->getA();
   return 0;
}
```

274

PROGRAMMING PROJECTS

7.1 Create a `Circle` class with the following members:

- A data member that stores the radius of a circle

- A constructor function with an argument that initializes the radius

- A function that computes and returns the area of a circle

Create two derived classes (`Sector` and `Segment`) that inherit the `Circle` class. Both classes inherit radius and the function that returns the circle's area from `Circle`. In addition to the members inherited from `Circle`, `Sector`, and `Segment` have some specific members as follows:

`Sector`
- A data member that stores the central angle of a sector (in radians)

- A constructor function with arguments that initialize radius and angle

- A function that computes and returns the area of a sector

`Segment`
- A data member that stores the length of a segment in a circle

- A constructor function with arguments that initialize radius and length

- A function that computes and returns the area of a segment

Create the **main()** function to instantiate an object of each class and then call appropriate member functions to compute and return the area of a circle, sector, and segment.

NOTE: Area_of_Circle = πr^2

Area_of_Sector = $r^2\theta/2$

Area_of_Segment=r^2 arccos((r-h)/r)-(r-h)(2rh-h^2)$^{1/2}$

where r is the radius of a circle, θ is the central angle of a sector in radians, h is the length of a segment, and `arccos((r-h)/r)` is in radians (Figure 7.18).

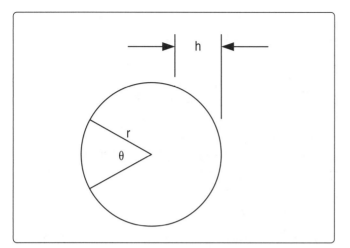

Figure 7.18 *Sector and segment of a circle.*

7.2 Create a `Circuit` class that uses three data members to store the resistance, input voltage, and current of a circuit. The `Circuit` class also has the following member functions:

- A constructor with arguments to initialize data members

- A function that computes and returns current (input voltage divided by resistance)

- A function that displays values of resistance, input voltage and current

Create an `Amplifier` class that inherits all members from `Circuit` except constructor (cannot be inherited). In addition to the inherited members, the `Amplifier` class has some specific members:

- A data member `gain`

- A constructor with arguments to initialize data members

- A function that computes and returns an output voltage (input voltage multiplied by `gain`)

- a function that returns `gain`

Design the ***main( )*** function to instantiate an object of the `Amplifier` class and then use this object to call all member functions.

7.3   Design a program that uses a hierarchy of classes shown in Figure 7.19.

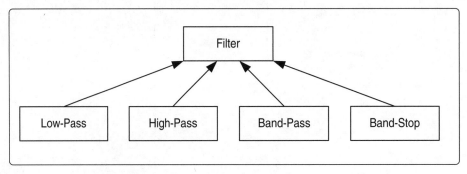

Figure 7.19 *An inheritance hierarchy (Project 7.3).*

The `Filter` class should define the general properties (attributes and behaviors) that are common to all four types of filter circuits. Four derived classes should inherit the general properties from `Filter` and each class should also define some properties that are specific to a particular type of a filter circuit.

7.4   Design a program that can be used to process the calibration data of a device. The program should use a `Device` class that stores and processes data such as a device description, serial number, and date of the most recent test. A second `Test` class should be used to store and process a description of measurements to be done on a device when doing a test, as well as a number of tests per year. A third `Calibration` class should inherit `Device` and `Test` (Figure 7.20). In addition to the members inherited from `Device` and `Test`, the `Calibration` class should have member function(s) that notify the user when a specific device is due for a calibration.

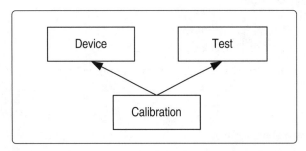

Figure 7.20 *An inheritance hierarchy (Project 7.4).*

CHAPTER 8

Composition

OBJECTIVES

- To understand the differences between inheritance and composition
- To be able to create composed classes
- To be able to construct and destroy composed objects
- To be able to design programs that combine inheritance and composition

CHAPTER CONTENTS

INTRODUCTION

Code reusability can be promoted in C++ by establishing relationships between classes. Implementing inheritance is one way to establish these relationships. This chapter will discuss a new kind of relationship between classes called **composition**. The differences between the approaches used when implementing inheritance and composition will be introduced first and then all aspects of the implementation of composition will be discussed. This chapter will demonstrate some practical examples of composition, as well as how to combine composition and inheritance.

8.1 COMPOSITION VERSUS INHERITANCE

One of the most important features of C++ is the manner in which it reuses code. C++ provides two kinds of relationships between classes to promote **code reusability**. By establishing a relationship between new and existing classes, a new class can inherit and/or embed the code from one or more existing classes.

One approach to the implementation of code reusability is **inheritance**, which was discussed in the previous chapter. It results in an **is-a** relationship. For cxamplc, an AND gate *is a* type of gate, and a gate *is a* type of logic circuit. Therefore, an AND gate class is derived from a gate class and the gate class is derived from a logic circuit class, as shown in Figure 8.1. Although inheritance offers many advantages, it is not always appropriate to use this approach because sometimes an object is not a type or subgroup of another object.

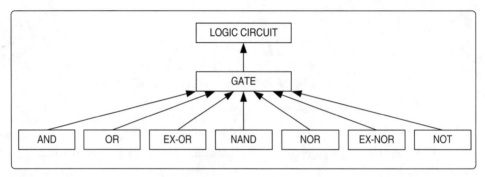

Figure 8.1 *Example of an **is-a** relationship.*

C++ provides another relationship between classes called **composition**, which is also known as a **has-a** relationship. For example, a CPU is not a type of PC, however, a PC *has a* CPU as well as many other components. Therefore, a PC class could be **composed** of a CPU class and some other classes, as shown in Figure 8.2. A new class can be composed from as many existing classes and built-in types as an application requires.

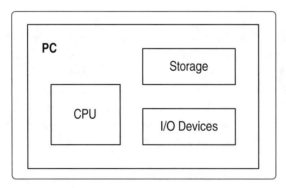

Figure 8.2 *Example of a **has-a** relationship.*

To compose a class from existing classes, an object of each class should be declared as a member of the new class. Consider the following example of a `Storage` class, which is composed of the three classes `Hard_Disk`, `RAM`, and `Floppy`:

```
class Storage                    //composed class
{
    float capacity;
    Hard_Disk hdst;              //an object of the Hard_Disk class
    RAM ramst;                   //an object of the RAM class
    Floppy fpst;                 //an object of the Floppy class
public:
    Storage();
    ~Storage();
};
```

It is assumed that the `Hard_Disk`, `RAM`, and `Floppy` classes have been previously defined and tested. Classes that are used to build a composed class can be referred to as **subclasses** and their objects as **embedded objects**, or **subobjects**. In addition to the three embedded objects, `hdst`, `ramst`, and `fpst`, the `Storage` class contains a built-in type as well. The embedded objects are *private* members of the `Storage` class. They can be designed as *public* members as well. The differences between these two solutions are discussed in the program examples that follow.

 NOTE: A new class can be composed of objects from previously built and tested classes.

8.2 USING COMPOSITION

Consider Program Example 8.1, which exhibits PROG8_1 using a composed class and embedded objects as *public* members of the composed class.

PROGRAM EXAMPLE 8.1: PROG8_1

```
1   //PROG8_1: Program demonstrates a composed class
2   //         with embedded objects as public members.
3   #include <iostream>
4   using namespace std;
5
```

```
6   class Pixel{              //subclass
7     int x, y;               //x and y coordinates of a pixel
8   public:
9     Pixel(){ x=0; y=0; }
10    void set(int a, int b) { x=a; y=b; }
11    int getx() const { return x; }
12    int gety() const { return y; }
13  };
14
15  class Rectangle{          //composed class
16    int perimeter;
17  public:
18    Pixel p1, p2;           //embedded objects as public members
19    Rectangle(){ perimeter=0; }
20    void getperim();
21  };
22  void Rectangle::getperim()
23  {
24    int x1 = p1.getx();     //Calls the embedded objects'
25    int x2 = p2.getx();     //member functions
26    int y1 = p1.gety();
27    int y2 = p2.gety();
28    cout<<"Top-left corner coordinates :[";
29    cout<<x1<<','<<y1<<']'<<endl;
30    cout<<"Bottom-right corner coordinates: [";
31    cout<<x2<<','<<y2<<']'<<endl;
32    cout<<"Perimeter = "<<(2*(x2-x1)+2*(y2-y1));
33  }
34
35  int main()
36  {
37    Rectangle r;            //composed object
38    r.p1.set(5,5);          //Using composed object to access
```

```
39    r.p2.set(10,10);          //members of the embedded objects.
40    r.getperim();
41    return 0;
42 }
```

The x and y data members of the `Pixel` subclass are *private* members. It is therefore completely safe to embed the p1 and p2 objects of the `Pixel` type as *public* members in the `Rectangle` class (line 18). The security of the subclass's *private* members is maintained, even if the embedded objects have *public* access in the composed class.

To access *public* members of the subobjects in *main()* or any other non-member function, a composed object or an object of its subclass should be created. The general format shown in Figure 8.3 is used when accessing a member of a subclass through a composed object. Each level of objects or subobjects is separated by a dot (.) separator.

```
composed_object.subobject.subobject_member
```

Figure 8.3 *Using a composed object to access a member of its embedded object.*

The statements of that format in PROG8_1 are the following (lines 38 and 39):

```
r.p1.set(5, 5);
r.p2.set(10, 10);
```

The interface between the *main()* function and the `Rectangle` and `Pixel` classes is established through the *public* interface functions of both classes, as shown in Figure 8.4.

282

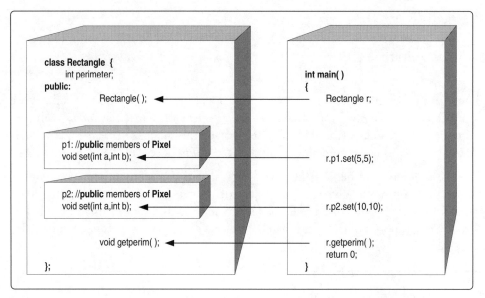

Figure 8.4 *Interface between **main( )** and the* Rectangle *and* Pixel *classes in PROG8_1.*

 NOTE: Both subobjects, as well as their members, should be *public* in order to access them outside the composed class.

The composed class can only access *public* members of its subclass. Access to the *private* members of the subclass is limited to the members of that subclass.

The output produced by PROG8_1 is shown in Figure 8.5.

```
Top-left corner coordinates: [5,5]
Bottom-right corner coordinates: [10,10]
Perimeter = 20
```

Figure 8.5 *Output produced by PROG8_1.*

While the previous example used *public* embedded objects, it is good programming practice to make the embedded objects *private* in the composed class. The *public* interface functions of the composed class can then use the embedded objects and their interface functions. The *public* members of the subclass, in this case, cannot be accessed outside of the composed class through the objects of the composed class.

PROG8_2, which is a modified version of PROG8_1, creates the embedded objects as *private* members of the composed Rectangle class, as shown in Program Example 8.2.

PROGRAM EXAMPLE 8.2: PROG8_2

```cpp
1   //PROG8_2: Program demonstrates composition with embedded
2   //          objects as private members.
3   #include <iostream>
4   using namespace std;
5
6   class Pixel {
7      int x, y;
8   public:
9      Pixel(){ x = 0; y = 0; }
10     void set(int a, int b) { x = a; y = b; }
11     int getx() const { return x; }
12     int gety() const { return y; }
13  };
14
15  class Rectangle {
16     int perimeter;
17     Pixel p1, p2;          //embedded objects as private members
18  public:
19     Rectangle(){ perimeter = 0; }
20     void getperim();
21  };
22  void Rectangle::getperim()
23  {
24     p1.set(5,5);  //Calls the embedded objects'
25     p2.set(10,10);    //interface functions
26     int x1 = p1.getx();
27     int x2 = p2.getx();
28     int y1 = p1.gety();
29     int y2 = p2.gety();
30     cout<<"Top-left corner coordinates : [";
31     cout<<x1<<','<<y1<<']'<<endl;
```

```
32    cout<<"Bottom-right corner coordinates : [";
33    cout<<x2<<','<<y2<<']'<<endl;
34    cout<<"Perimeter = "<<(2*(x2-x1)+2*(y2-y1));
35 }
36
37 int main()
38 {
39    Rectangle r;        //Instantiates a composed object and
40    r.getperim();       //calls its interface function
41    return 0;
42 }
```

The embedded p1 and p2 objects are *private* members in the composed Rectangle class (line 17). The composed object r, therefore, cannot be used in *main( )* to call their *public* interface functions. These functions are called in the getperim( ) function (lines 22–35), which is a *public* interface function of the composed Rectangle class. The interface between the *main( )* function and the Rectangle and Pixel classes is established through the getperim( ) function, as shown in Figure 8.6.

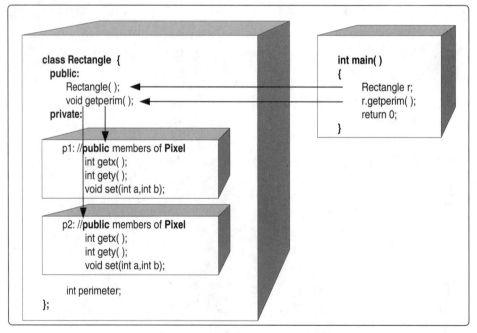

Figure 8.6 *Interface between main( ) and the classes in PROG8_2.*

Note that the arrows in Figures 8.4 and 8.6 show directions of the function calls. PROG8_2 produces the same output as PROG8_1, which is shown in Figure 8.5.

If the embedded objects are created as ***private*** members of the composed class, their ***public*** interface functions are used to communicate with the composed class. The interface between the classes and the rest of the program in this case is established through the ***public*** interface functions of the composed class. It makes the program more maintainable, simplifies its logic, and provides a *safer interface*. Safer, in this context, means that the embedded objects are hidden from the rest of the program and can only be accessed by the members of its composed class.

 TIP: It is good programming practice to make the embedded objects ***private*** in the composed class.

8.3 CONSTRUCTING AND DESTROYING COMPOSED CLASSES

If a class is composed from one or more subclasses, the subclass embedded objects will be constructed first when the composed class is instantiated. For example, when object r in PROG8_2 is instantiated in ***main( )***, the `Pixel` constructor is called twice to construct embedded `p1` and `p2` objects, and then the `Rectangle` constructor is called. Notice that the classes designed in the previous program examples with composition use default constructor functions.

If a subclass uses a non-default constructor function with arguments, the programmer must define a composed class constructor with a **constructor initialization list** (this will be demonstrated in PROG8_3). If this is not done, the compiler may not be able to construct composed objects.

A constructor initialization list should be designed if the subclasses have constructors with arguments. To design the initialization list, a solution similar to the one discussed in Chapter 7 is used. The only difference is that the names of the embedded objects are used instead of the names of the base classes to pass values between constructors. The general format of a composed class constructor with the initialization list is shown in Figure 8.7. A parameter list of the composed class constructor should include all of the arguments needed to initialize the data members of the composed class, as well as the arguments needed to initialize its embedded objects.

```
composed_constructor( parameter list ):
subobj1(values1),subobj2(values2),…,subobjn(valuesn)
{
    //body of the composed constructor
}
```

Figure 8.7 *General format of a composed class constructor with the initialization list.*

The identifiers `values1`, `values2`, … , `valuesn` in Figure 8.7 represent the sets of values passed to the constructors of the subclasses to initialize the embedded objects `subobj1`, `subobj2`, … , `subobjn`. The values passed to an individual subclass's constructor are placed inside the brackets following the object of that class and separated by commas. A number of values and their order should match the number and order of arguments in the constructor function of the subclass. It should be noted that a colon (:) separator is used between the composed class parameter list and the list of embedded objects. Spacing after the colon (:) separator is optional. In PROG8_2 it might resemble the following:

```
Rectangle(int a, int b, int c, int d) : p1(a, b), p2(c, d)
{
    perimeter = 0;
}
```

The idea behind the syntax used in the example above is that the constructors needed to initialize the p1 and p2 subobjects are called before the execution of the body of the composed class constructor. It is logical because it is necessary to build the subobjects first in order to build an overall composed class object. The same syntax can also be used if a class is composed of built-in types, as shown in the following example:

```
class Circuit {
    char * type;
    int quantity;
    float price;
public:
    Circuit(char *t, int q, float p):
            type(t), quantity(q), price(p) { }
};
```

This example demonstrates an often-used, good coding style. Some programmers, however, prefer the *old coding style* with the = operator... (i.e., `quantity=q;`) within the body of the constructor, instead of `quantity(q)` prior to the constructor's body. In either case, the assignment operation is performed.

When constructing a composed object, the constructors are called starting with the constructors of the subclasses followed by the constructor of the composed class. The order of instantiating the embedded objects in the composed class determines the order in which the constructors are called. *The order of the constructor calls is not affected by the order of the embedded objects in the constructor initialization list.*

As with inheritance, programmers need not be concerned with calling destructors for the composed objects and their embedded objects. The C++ compiler calls the proper destructors automatically when a composed object goes out of scope. The order of the destructor calls is exactly reverse of the order of the constructor calls.

Program Example 8.3 demonstrates the order of the constructor and destructor calls when constructing and destroying composed objects. In this example, PROG8_3 simulates the process of constructing/destroying a stereo that is made up of two components—an amplifier and speakers. Note that the impedance is a characteristic of both speakers and amplifier and should ideally be equal or matched.

PROGRAM EXAMPLE 8.3: PROG8_3

```
1   //PROG8_3:  Program demonstrates the order of the constructor and
2   //          destructor calls when constructing and destroying a
3   //          composed object.
4   #include <iostream>
5   using namespace std;
6
7   class Speaker {                              //subclass #1
8      float impedance;
9   public:
10     Speaker(float imp)                        //constructor #1
11     {
12         impedance = imp;
13         cout<<"Constructing speaker."<<endl;
14     }
15     float getimp()const { return impedance; }
```

```
16   ~Speaker()                                  //destructor #1
17   {
18       cout<<"Destroying speaker."<<endl;
19   }
20 };
21
22 class Amplifier {                              //subclass #2
23   float impedance;
24 public:
25   Amplifier(float imp )                        //constructor #2
26   {
27       impedance = imp;
28       cout<<"Constructing amplifier."<<endl;
29   }
30   float getimp()const { return impedance;}
31   ~Amplifier()                                 //destructor #2
32   {
33       cout<<"Destroying amplifier."<<endl;
34   }
35 };
36
37 class Stereo {                                 //composed class
38   Speaker sp;        //embedded object #1
39   Amplifier amp;     //embedded object #2
40 public:
41   Stereo(float x, float y):sp(x), amp(y)
42   {                      //composed constructor
43       cout<<"Constructing stereo."<<endl;
44   }
45   void matching()    //Compares the impedances
46   {
47       if(sp.getimp()==amp.getimp())
48           cout<<"Impedances are matched."<<endl;
```

```
49      else
50              cout<<"Impedances are not matcheed."<<endl;
51      }
52   ~Stereo()                    //composed destructor
53      {
54        cout<<"Destroying stereo."<<endl;
55      }
56 };
57
58 int main()
59 {
60   Stereo st(8, 8);             //composed object
61   st.matching();
62   return 0;
63 }
```

The output produced by PROG8_3 is shown in Figure 8.8.

```
Constructing speaker.
Constructing amplifier.
Constructing stereo.
Impedances are matched.
Destroying stereo.
Destroying amplifier.
Destroying speaker.
```

Figure 8.8 *Output produced by PROG8_3.*

Please note that the output of PROG8_3 will not change even if the order of the embedded objects is changed in the constructor initialization list as follows:

```
Stereo(float x, float y): amp(x), sp(y)
{
    cout<<"Constructing stereo."<<endl;
}
```

A constructor of a composed class can also take **objects as arguments**. Doing this results in a much shorter list of arguments, whereas the constructors of the embedded objects require many individual arguments. Applying this method to PROG8_3, an additional constructor of the Stereo class can be designed as follows:

```
Stereo(Speaker s, Amplifier a): sp(s), amp(a) { }
```

The s and a objects passed to the composed Stereo constructor are assigned to the embedded sp and amp objects, respectively.

A composed class can contain **pointers to subobjects** as members. This class may use its constructor function to dynamically allocate subobjects and store their addresses in the member pointers. Note that the composed class destructor must free memory dynamically allocated by the constructor. In Program Example 8.4, PROG8_4 (a modified version of PROG8_3) creates pointers to subobjects as *private* members of the composed Stereo class.

PROGRAM EXAMPLE 8.4: PROG8_4

```
1  //PROG8_4: Program demonstrates a composed class containing
2  //         pointers to subobjects as members.
3  #include <iostream>
4  using namespace std;
5
6  class Speaker { //subclass #1
7     float impedance;
8  public:
9     Speaker()      //constructor #1
10    {
11       cout<<"Constructing speaker."<<endl;
12    }
13    void setimp(float imp) { impedance=imp; }
14    float getimp()const { return impedance; }
15    ~Speaker()     //destructor #1
16    {
17       cout<<"Destroying speaker."<<endl;
18    }
19 };
```

```
20 class Amplifier {        //subclass #2
21    float impedance;
22 public:
23    Amplifier()           //constructor #2
24    {
25        cout<<"Constructing amplifier."<<endl;
26    }
27    void setimp(float imp) { impedance=imp; }
28    float getimp()const { return impedance; }
29    ~Amplifier()          //destructor #2
30    {
31        cout<<"Destroying amplifier."<<endl;
32    }
33 };
34 class Stereo {           //composed class
35    Speaker *ptsp;        //pointer to subobject #1
36    Amplifier *ptamp;     //pointer to subobject #2
37 public:
38    Stereo(Speaker &s, Amplifier &a)
39    {   //composed constructor
40        ptsp=new Speaker;
41        ptamp=new Amplifier;
42        *ptsp=s;
43        *ptamp=a;
44        cout<<"\tConstructing stereo."<<endl;
45    }
46    void matching()     //Compares the impedances
47    {
48        if(ptsp->getimp()==ptamp->getimp())
49            cout<<"Impedances are matched."<<endl;
50        else
51            cout<<"Impedances are not matcheed."<<endl;
52    }
```

```
53   ~Stereo()            //composed destructor
54   {
55       delete ptsp;
56       delete ptamp;
57       cout<<"\tDestroying stereo."<<endl;
58   }
59 };
60 int main()
61 {
62   Amplifier a;
63   a.setimp(8);
64   Speaker s;
65   s.setimp(8);
66   Stereo st(s, a);   //composed object
67   st.matching();
68   return 0;
69 }
```

The *main()* function instantiates an Amplifier object named a (line 62) and a Speaker object named s (line 64). It then uses a and s to call their member functions to initialize these objects (lines 63 and 65). The objects are then passed by reference to the Stereo constructor to construct a composed object named st (line 66). The Stereo constructor dynamically allocates two embedded objects (lines 40 and 41) using the *new* operator. Note that this operation invokes the Speaker and Amplifier constructors. The Stereo constructor then uses member pointers to access dynamically-allocated memory and initialize embedded objects to s and a, respectively (lines 42 and 43). The destructor function of the Stereo class frees memory allocated dynamically in the heap by the constructor to store embedded objects (lines 55 and 56). The output produced by this program is shown in Figure 8.9.

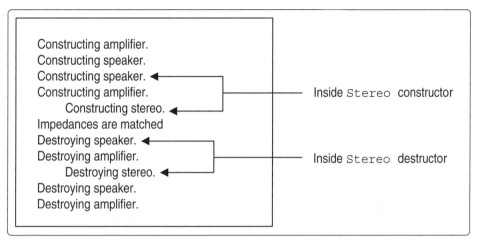

Figure 8.9 *Output produced by PROG8_4.*

Creating pointers to subobjects as members of a composed class (demonstrated in PROG8_4) may be a solution if the subobjects are to persist after their composed object is destroyed. From output shown in Figure 8.9, the composed object of the Stereo class is destroyed before the Amplifier and Speaker subobjects are destroyed.

 NOTE: A composed class can contain pointers to its subobjects as members. Pointers to composed objects can be used to dynamically allocate and destroy composed objects.

8.4 COMBINING INHERITANCE AND COMPOSITION

Inheritance and composition can be combined to build more complex classes. In Program Example 8.5, PROG8_5 demonstrates a use of these two tools combined together in the same class.

PROGRAM EXAMPLE 8.5: PROG8_5

```
1   //PROG8_5: Program demonstrates a use of inheritance and
2   //composition combined together to build a complex class.
3   #include <iostream>
4   using namespace std;
5
6   class Pixel {            //subclass
7      int x, y;
8   public:
9      Pixel(int a, int b)           //constructor
```

```
10    {
11        x = a;
12        y = b;
13        cout<<"SubConstructor"<<" x="<<x<<" y="<<y<<endl;
14    }
15    ~Pixel(){cout<<"SubDestructor"<<endl;}   //destructor
16 };
17 class RecShape {        //base class
18 protected:
19    int lg, wd;
20 public:
21    RecShape(int l, int w)           //constructor
22    {
23        lg = l;
24        wd = w;
25        cout<<"BaseConstructor"<<" lg="<<lg<<" wd="<<wd<<endl;
26    }
27    ~RecShape(){cout<<"BaseDestructor"<<endl;}        //destructor
28 };
29
30 class Rectangle:public RecShape {       //derived & composed class
31    int perimeter;
32    Pixel p1, p2;       //subobjects
33 public:
34    Rectangle(int x1,int y1,int x2,int y2):        //constructor
35    RecShape(x2-x1,y2-y1),p1(x1,y1),p2(x2,y2)
36    {
37        perimeter = 0;
38        cout<<"CombConstructor"<<" x1="<<x1<<" y1="<<y1;
39        cout<<" x2="<<x2<<" y2="<<y2<<endl;
40 }
41 void getperim()
42 {
```

```
43          cout<<"Perimeter = "<<(2*lg + 2*wd)<<endl;
44      }
45      ~Rectangle(){cout<<"CombDestructor"<<endl;}   //destructor
46 };
47
48 int main()
49 {
50     Rectangle r(5,5,10,10);
51     r.getperim();
5      return 0;
53 }
```

The relationship between classes in this program is shown in Figure 8.10. The
Rectangle class is derived from the RecShape class and composed of the Pixel class.

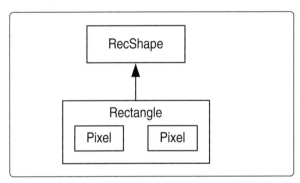

Figure 8.10 *Relationship between classes in PROG8_5.*

The constructor initialization list of the Rectangle class calls the RecShape and Pixel
constructors as shown in Figure 8.11.

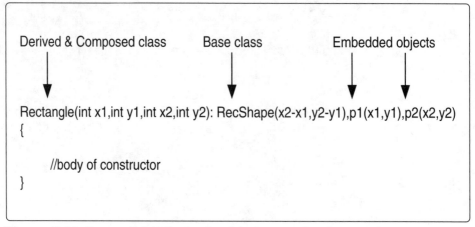

Figure 8.11 *Constructor initialization list of the* Rectangle *class.*

When constructing an object of the Rectangle class (line 50), the base class constructor, RecShape, is called first. The Pixel subclass constructor is then called twice to build the p1 and p2 embedded objects. The Rectangle class constructor is the last called. The order of the destructor calls is the exact reverse of the order of the constructor calls, as shown in the output of PROG8_5 (Figure 8.12).

```
BaseConstructor      lg=5  wd=5
SubConstructor       x=10  y=10
SubConstructor       x=15  y=15
CombConstructor      x1=10  y1=10  x2=15  y2=15


                     Perimeter = 20
CombDestructor
SubDestructor
SubDestructor
BaseDestructor
```

Figure 8.12 *Output produced by PROG8_5.*

Consider a more complex example, which combines multiple inheritance and composition as shown in Figure 8.13. The Derived1 class is derived from the Base1 and Base2 parent classes. It also has the two embedded objects of the Sub1 and Sub2 classes. The Derived2 class is derived from the Derived1 class and composed of the Sub3 and Sub4 classes.

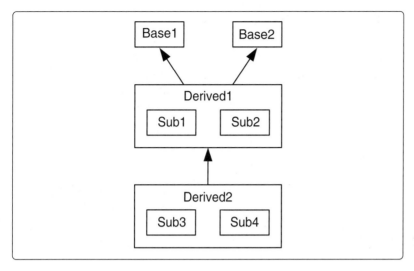

Figure 8.13. *Multiple inheritance and composition combined together.*

When constructing and destroying an object of the `Derived2` class, the order of the constructor and destructor calls is shown in Figure 8.14.

The construction always starts with each level of the base classes first and is followed by the embedded objects' constructors. The last constructor called is the composed class constructor that is the lowest-level constructor within the inheritance chain. The order stated above cannot be changed by swapping the calls in the constructor initialization list.

```
Constructor calls:          Destructor calls:
    Base1                        Derived2
    Base2                        Sub4
    Sub1                         Sub3
    Sub2                         Derived1
    Derived1                     Sub2
    Sub3                         Sub1
    Sub4                         Base2
    Derived2                     Base1
```

Figure 8.14 *Order of the constructor and destructor calls for the example in Figure 8.13.*

8.5 CASE STUDY: COMPUTER SYSTEM CONFIGURATOR

This case study demonstrates the use of composition to build a new class from existing classes. It also demonstrates a method of constructing a composed object and its embedded objects. In addition, an inserter operator function is designed for each class. The embedded objects are created as *private* members of the composed class. The interface with *main( )* is established through the *public* interface functions of the composed class.

PROBLEM DESCRIPTION

The program should allow the user to choose from a list of computer parts to make up a computer system. The list should include basic components such as a CPU, RAM, and a hard disk. There should be several options for each component. The program should display a list of the parts selected by the user and the cost of the system. It should also allow the user to 1) change any of the parts if the total cost does not meet a budget, or 2) to design another system.

INPUT/OUTPUT

Requested **input** from the user:

     1. A selection of parts from the menu options offered

     2. A choice of one of the following options:

         • Display the current system configuration

         • Change a part

         • Exit the program

Requested **output**: A list of all the parts selected, including the cost of each part and the total cost.

PSEUDOCODE

Use the following skeleton to design the `CPU`, `RAM`, and `Hard_Drive` subclasses.

Note that the function prototypes use a type placeholder named `Part`. The `CPU`, `RAM`, and `Hard_Drive` class types should replace the type placeholder `Part` when defining specific subclasses.

- **Data members (*private*):**

     1. `char * bPart[3];`   `//stores 3 options for a part`

     2. `float cPart[3];`   `//stores a cost of each part option`

- **Member functions (*public*):**

     1. `Part( );`

```
//INITIALIZES bpart AND cpart
START
BPART[0]="OPTION1"
BPART[1]="OPTION2"
BPART[2]="OPTION3"
CPART[0]=VALUE1
CPART[1]=VALUE2
CPART[2]=VALUE3
STOP
```

2. void select_PART(char *temp[1], float &cost);

```
//Gets and returns a selection from the user.
START
DO WHILE SELECT<1 OR SELECT>3
        PRINT "SELECT A PART FROM THE ABOVE ==>"
        READ SELECT
END DO
TEMP[0]=BPART[SELECT-1]
COST=CPART[SELECT-1]
STOP
```

- **Friend functions:**

1. ostream & operator<<(ostream &out, PART &a);

```
//Displays menu options for a part.
START
PRINT "      PART     COST      "
I=0
FOR I<3
    PRINT I+1
    PRINT A.BPART[I]
    PRINT A.CPART[I]
    I=I+1
END FOR
```

```
RETURN OUT
STOP
```

Design the PC class with the following skeleton:

- **Data members *(private)*:**

    1. `char * parts[3];`   `//stores parts selected by the user`
    2. `float pcost[3];`   `//stores costs of the selected parts`
    3. `float total;`   `//total cost of the system`
    4. `CPU cpu;`   `//a CPU object`
    5. `RAM ram;`   `//a RAM object`
    6. `Hard_Drive hd;`   `//a Hard_Drive object`

- **Member functions *(public)*:**

    1. `PC();`

        `//INITIALIZES parts TO "NOT SELECTED" AND pcost TO 0.`
        ```
        START
        TOTAL=0
        I=0
        FOR I<3
            PARTS[I]="NOT SELECTED"
            PCOST[I]=0
            I=I+1
        END FOR
        STOP
        ```

    2. `void display_cpu();`

        `//DISPLAYS CPU OPTIONS AND GETS A SELECTION FROM THE USER.`
        ```
        START
        PRINT CPU
        EXECUTE CPU.SELECT_CPU()
        STOP
        ```

    3. `void display_mem();`

        `//DISPLAYS RAM OPTIONS AND GETS A SELECTION FROM THE USER.`
        ```
        START
        ```

```
PRINT RAM

EXECUTE RAM.SELECT_RAM()

STOP
```

4. `void display_hdrive();`

```
//DISPLAYS HARD DISK OPTIONS AND GETS A SELECTION FROM THE
//USER.

START

PRINT HD

EXECUTE HD.SELECT_HDRIVE()

STOP
```

- **Friend functions:**

  1. `ostream & operator<<(ostream &out,PC a);`

```
//DISPLAYS THE SYSTEM SELECTED BY THE USER AND THE TOTAL
//COST.

START

I=0

FOR I<3

    A.TOTAL=A.TOTAL+A.PCOST[I]

    I=I+1

END FOR

PRINT "PART    TYPE    COST"

PRINT "CPU"

PRINT A.PARTS[0]

PRINT A.PCOST[0]

PRINT "RAM"

PRINT A.PARTS[1]

PRINT A.PCOST[1]

PRINT "HARD DRIVE"

PRINT A.PARTS[2]

PRINT A.PCOST[2]

PRINT "THE TOTAL COST OF THE SYSTEM"
```

```
PRINT A.TOTAL
STOP
```

- **Non-member functions:**

    1. char menu();

        ```
        //DISPLAYS MENU OPTIONS AND GETS SELECTION FROM THE USER.
        START
        PRINT "COMPUTER SYSTEM"
        PRINT "A) SELECT CPU"
        PRINT "B) SELECT RAM"
        PRINT "C) SELECT HARD DRIVE"
        PRINT "D) DISPLAY THE SYSTEM AND TOTAL COST"
        PRINT "X) EXIT"
        PRINT "ENTER YOUR CHOICE"
        READ SELECTION
        RETURN SELECTION
        STOP
        ```

- **The *main()* function:**

    ```
    START
    INSTANTIATE COMPUTER FROM PC
    DO WHILE SELECTION != 'X'
        READ SELECTION (EXECUTE MENU())
        SWITCH SELECTION
            CASE 'A': EXECUTE COMPUTER.DISPLAY_CPU(), BREAK
            CASE 'B': EXECUTE COMPUTER.DISPLAY_MEM(), BREAK
            CASE 'C': EXECUTE COMPUTER.DISPLAY_HDRIVE(), BREAK
            CASE 'D': PRINT COMPUTER, BREAK
            CASE 'X': BREAK
            DEFAULT:  PRINT "INCORRECT INPUT"
        END SWITCH
    END DO
    STOP
    ```

SOURCE CODE

PROGRAM EXAMPLE 8.6: SOURCE CODE FOR CASEST8

```cpp
1  //CASEST8:      The program demonstrates a practical use of
2  //             composition to configure a computer system.
3  #include<iostream>
4  #include<iomanip>
5  using namespace std;
6
7  class CPU        //Subclass CPU
8  {
9     char *bcpu[3];       //CPU options
10    float pcpu[3];       //costs of CPU options
11 public:
12    CPU() {              //CPU constructor
13       bcpu[0]="Pentium III 866 MHz ";
14       bcpu[1]="Pentium IV 1.4 GHz ";
15       bcpu[2]="Pentium IV 2.0 GHz ";
16       pcpu[0]=150; pcpu[1]=270; pcpu[2]=450;
17    }
18    friend ostream &operator <<(ostream &out, CPU &a);
19    void select_cpu(char *temp[1], float &cost);
20 };
21 ostream &operator <<(ostream &out, CPU &a)
22 {
23    out<<"\n\n      CPU                         \t\t\t\tCOST\n" ;
24    out<<"————————————-\t\t\t—- \n";
25    for(int i = 0; i<3; i++)
26    {
27       out<<setiosflags(ios::left | ios::fixed)<<setprecision(2);
28       out<<(i+1)<<") "<<setw(64)<<a.bcpu[i];
29       out<<"\t$"<<a.pcpu[i]<<endl;
30       out<<'\n';
```

```
31    }
32    return out;
33 }
34 void CPU::select_cpu(char *temp[1], float &cost) //Selects a CPU
35 {
36    int select;
37    cout<<'\n';
38    do{
39       cout<<"Select a CPU from the above  ==> ";
40       cin>>select;
41    }while((select<1) ||( select>3));
42    temp[0] = bcpu[select-1];
43    cost = pcpu[select-1];
44 }
45
46 class RAM {              //Subclass RAM
47    char *bmem[3];        //RAM options
48    float pmem[3];        //costs of RAM options
49 public:
50    RAM() { //RAM constructor
51       bmem[0]="64 MB ";
52       bmem[1]="128 MB ";
53       bmem[2]="256 MB ";
54       pmem[0]=39.99; pmem[1]=68; pmem[2]=152;
55    }
56    friend ostream &operator <<(ostream &out, RAM b);
57    void select_ram(char *temp[1], float &cost);
58 };
59 ostream &operator <<(ostream &out, RAM b) //Displays RAM options
60 {
61    out<<"\n\n    RAM        \t\t\t\tCOST\n" ;
62    out<<"———————————————\t\t\t—- \n";
63    for(int i=0; i<3; i++)
```

```
64    {
65        out<<setiosflags(ios::left | ios::fixed)<<setprecision(2);
66        out<<(i+1)<<")"<<setw(62)<<b.bmem[i];
67        out<<"\t$"<<b.pmem[i]<<endl;
68        out<<'\n';
69    }
70    return out;
71 }
72 void RAM::select_ram(char *temp[1], float &cost) //Selects a RAM
73 {
74    int select;
75    cout<<"\n";
76    do{
77        cout<<"Select RAM from the above  ==> ";
78        cin>>select;
79    }while((select<1)||( select>3));
80    temp[0] = bmem[select-1];
81    cost = pmem[select-1];
82 }
83
84 class Hard_Drive {          //Subclass Hard_Drive
85        char *bhd[4];
86        float phd[4];
87 public:
88    Hard_Drive() {
89        bhd[0]="10.0 GB ";
90        bhd[1]="15.3 GB";
91        bhd[2]="30.0 GB";
92        bhd[3]="40.0 GB";
93        phd[0]=110; phd[1]=124; phd[2]=174; phd[3]=220;
94    }
95    friend ostream &operator <<(ostream &out, Hard_Drive &c);
96    void select_hdrive(char *temp[1], float &cost);
```

```
97 };
98 ostream &operator <<(ostream &out, Hard_Drive &c)
99 {
100   out<<"\n\n   HARD DRIVE        \t\t\t\tCOST\n" ;
101   out<<"————————————-\t\t\t——- \n";
102   for(int i=0; i<4; i++)
103   {
104      out<<setiosflags(ios::left | ios::fixed)<<setprecision(2);
105      out<<(i+1)<<") "<<setw(62)<<c.bhd[i];
106      out<<"\t$"<<c.phd[i]<<endl;
107      out<<'\n';
10    }
109   return out;
110 }
111 void Hard_Drive::select_hdrive(char *temp[1], float &cost)
112 {
113   int select;
114   cout<<'\n';
115   do{
116      cout<<"Select a hard drive from the above ==> ";
117      cin>>select;
118   }while((select<1)||( select>4));
119   temp[0] = bhd[select-1];
120   cost = phd[select-1];
121 }
122
123 class PC {      //Composed class
124   char *parts[3];    //parts selected by the user
125   float pcost[3];    //costs of the selected parts
126   float total; //total cost of the system
127   CPU cpu; //subobjects
128   RAM ram;
129   Hard_Drive hd;
```

```
130 public:
131  PC();
132  void display_cpu()
133  {
134     cout<<cpu;
135     cpu.select_cpu(& parts[0], pcost[0]);
136  }
137  void display_mem()
138  {
139     cout<<ram;
140     ram.select_ram(& parts[1], pcost[1]);
141  }
142  void display_hdrive()
143  {
144     cout<<hd;
145     hd.select_hdrive(& parts[2], pcost[2]);
146  }
147  friend ostream &operator <<(ostream &out, PC a);
148 };
149 PC::PC()        //PC constructor
150 {
151  total=0;
152  for(int i=0;i<3;i++)
153  {
154     parts[i] = "Not Selected";
155     pcost[i] = 0;
156  }
157 }
158 ostream &operator <<(ostream &out, PC a)
159 {         //Displays the system chosen and total cost
160  for(int i=0;i<3;i++)
161     a.total = a.total + a.pcost[i];
162  out<<setiosflags(ios::left | ios::fixed)<<setprecision(2);
```

```
163    out<<" PART           TYPE               \t\t\tCOST\n ";
164    out<<"————————————-\t\t\t——"<<endl;
165    out<<'\n'<<setw(15)<<"CPU:"<<setw(54)<<a. parts[0];
166    out<<"\t$"<<a.pcost[0]<<endl;
167    out<<'\n'<<setw(15)<< "RAM:"<<setw(54)<<a. parts[1];
168    out<<"\t$"<<a.pcost[1]<<endl;
169    out<<'\n'<<setw(15)<<"Hard drive:"<<setw(54)<<a. parts[2];
170    out<<"\t$"<<a.pcost[2]<<endl;
171    out<<"\n\n\t\t\t\t\tThe total cost of the system===>$";
172    out<<a.total<<endl;
173    return out ;
174  }
175  char menu()
176  {
177    char selection;
178    cout<<"\n\n\n \t\t\t         Computer System       "<<endl;
179    cout<<"\t\t———————————————————-\n\n";
180    cout<<"\t\ta) Select CPU \n";
181    cout<<"\t\tb) Select RAM \n";
182    cout<<"\t\tc) Select Hard Drive\n";
183    cout<<"\t\td) Display the system and total cost\n";
184    cout<<"\t\tx) Exit\n\n";
185    cout<<"\t\t Enter your choice here ===> ";
186    cin>> selection;
187    return selection;
188  }
189
190  int main()
191  {
192  char selection;
193  PC computer;              //Composed object
194  do {
195    selection=menu();
```

```
196     switch(selection)
197     {
198         case 'a': computer.display_cpu(); break;
199         case 'b': computer.display_mem(); break;
200         case 'c': computer.display_hdrive(); break;
201         case 'd':
202             cout<<" The system chosen : \n\n";
203             cout<<computer;
204             break;
205         case 'x': cout<<"\n\n\n\t\tEnd of program."; break;
206         default: cout<<"\n\t Incorrect input! ";
207     }
208 } while(selection!='x');
209 return 0;
210 }
```

OUTPUT

A sample run of CASEST8 is shown in Figures 8.15 and 8.16.

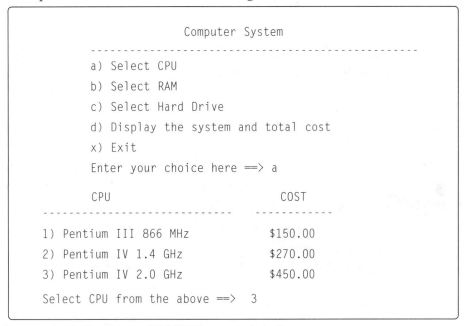

```
                         Computer System
            ------------------------------------------------
            a) Select CPU
            b) Select RAM
            c) Select Hard Drive
            d) Display the system and total cost
            x) Exit
            Enter your choice here ==> a

            CPU                          COST
            ------------------------------  ------------
          1) Pentium III 866 MHz         $150.00
          2) Pentium IV 1.4 GHz          $270.00
          3) Pentium IV 2.0 GHz          $450.00
          Select CPU from the above ==>  3
```

Figure 8.15 *Sample run of CASEST8—a selection of a part.*

```
                      Computer System
           -------------------------------------------
           a) Select CPU

           b) Select RAM

           c) Select Hard Drive

           d) Display the system and total cost

           x) Exit

           Enter your choice here ==> d
    The system chosen:
        PART                   TYPE                  COST
    -----------             ----------            -----------

      CPU:               Pentium IV 2.0 GHz        $450.00

      Memory:            256 MB                    $152.00

      Hard drive:        40.0 GB                   $220.00

           The total cost of the system ==>   $822.00
```

Figure 8.16 *Sample run of CASEST8—a system selection.*

CONCLUSION

The interface between subclasses and the composed class in CASEST8 is straight-forward. Because of this simplicity, it is relatively easy to make program modifications. These changes may be required to add new components or modify existing components. Please note that the program could be improved by using some of the tools that will be discussed in the following chapters. It is common programming practice to use the I/O file (see Chapter 12) when solving problems similar to those in this case study.

SUMMARY

1. Inheritance and composition are used to promote code reusability.

2. Composition, which is also known as a **has-a** relationship, is used to build new classes by embedding the code from the existing classes.

3. To compose a class from existing classes, an object of each class should be declared as a member of the new class.

4. The embedded objects can be **private** as well as **public** members of the composed class.

5. The **public** members of a subclass can be accessed outside of the composed class through a composed object, if its embedded object has **public** access in the composed class. The **private** members of the subclass remain inaccessible outside the composed class.

6. If the embedded objects are **private** members of the composed class, their **public** interface functions cannot be called outside of the composed class by using a composed object. The interface between the classes and the rest of the program in this case is usually established through the **public** interface functions of the composed class.

7. If the subclasses have constructors with arguments, a constructor initialization list must be created. The initialization list uses the embedded objects' identifiers to pass values to the constructors of the subclasses.

8. When constructing a composed object, the constructors of the subclasses are called first, following the order of their objects' declarations in the composed class. The order of the constructor calls is not affected by the order of the embedded objects in the constructor initialization list.

9. The destructors are automatically called when a composed object goes out of scope.

10. Inheritance and composition can be combined together to build more complex classes. The construction, in that case, always starts with each level of the base classes. The embedded objects' constructors are called next. The last constructor called is the constructor of the composed class that is the lowest-level derived class in the inheritance chain.

EXERCISES

State the order of the constructor and destructor calls in Exercises 8.1 through 8.4.

NOTE: A, B, C, D, E, and F are class identifiers.

8.1

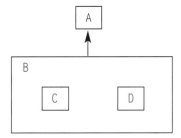

8.2
```
class A: public B, C {
    D dobj;
    E eobj;
public:
    A();
    ~A();
};
```

8.3

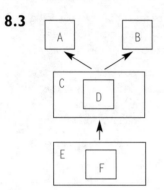

8.4
```
class B: A {
public:
    C cobj;
    D dobj;
    B();
    ~B();
};
class E: public B {
    F fobj;
public:
    E();
    ~E();
};
```

8.5 Identify and correct the errors in the following program:
```
#include <iostream>
using namespace std;
```

```
class Point {
public:
  int x, y;
  Point(int a, int b) {x=a; y=b;}
};
class Rectangle {
  int perimeter;
  Point p1, p2;
public:
  Rectangle(int a, int b, int c, int d):p1(), p2()
  {
        perimeter=2*((p2.y-p1.y)+(p2.x-p2.x));
  }
  void display(){ cout<<"Perimeter: "<<perimeter; }
};
int main()
{
  Rectangle r;
  r.display();
  return 0;
}
```

8.6 State the output produced by the following program:

```
#include <iostream>
using namespace std;
class Floppy {
  float capacity;
public:
  Floppy(float c) { capacity=c;}
  friend ostream & operator<<(ostream & out, Floppy obj);
};
ostream & operator<<(ostream & out, Floppy obj)
{
```

```
        out<<"Capacity = "<<obj.capacity<<" M";
        return out;
    }
    class Disk {
        float price;
        Floppy fd;
    public:
        Disk(float x, float y): fd(y) { price = x; }
        friend ostream & operator<<(ostream & out, Disk obj);
    };
    ostream & operator<<(ostream & out, Disk obj)
    {
        out<<"Floppy disk: "<<endl;
        out<<obj.fd<<endl;
        out<<"Price = "<<"$"<<obj.price;
        return out;
    }
    int main()
    {
        Disk d(0.99,1.4);
        cout<<d;
        return 0;
    }
```

PROGRAMMING PROJECTS

8.1   Modify PROG8_4 and use a pointer to an object of the Stereo composed class to dynamically allocate as many composed objects as requested by the user at run-time. Use the pointer to call the matching( ) member function for each composed object.

8.2   Design a Resistor class with the following members:

     1. A data member used to store a resistance

     2. A constructor function with an argument that is used to initialize resistance

3. An `operator<<()` function that displays a resistor's value and uses the following format:

    `Resistance = 40.7 kΩ`

4. A destructor function that displays the message:

    `Resistor is destroyed.`

Design a Circuit composed class with the following members:

1. Data members used to store a current and a voltage

2. An object of the `Resistor` class

3. A constructor function with arguments that calls the `Resistor`'s constructor, initializes voltage, and computes and initializes current

4. An `operator<<()` function that displays values of the voltage and current, and calls the `operator<<()` function of the `Resistor` class

5. A destructor function that displays the message:

    `Circuit is destroyed.`

Design the **main()** function that creates a composed object. The two values should be passed to the constructor function of the `Circuit` class. The **main()** should then call the `operator<<()` function of the `Circuit` class to display the values stored in the composed object.

8.3 Design a `Coil` class that is used to store and process data for a coil, such as current, voltage, and the number of turns. The member functions should include a constructor with arguments and functions that are used to get, store, and output values of a coil. Design another class called `Transformer` that is composed of the two objects of the `Coil` class—i.e., the primary and secondary coils as shown in Figure 8.17. The `Transformer` class should have the following member functions:

1. A constructor function with arguments

2. A function that computes and displays the turns ratio N

3. A function that computes and returns the secondary current if given the turns ratio and primary current

4. A function that computes and returns the secondary voltage if given the turns ratio and primary voltage

Design the **main()** function that is used to test the `Transformer` class. It should create a composed object first and then call the appropriate member functions to process the data of a transformer.

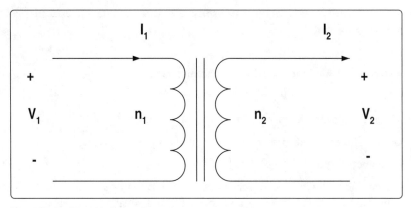

Figure 8.17 *Ideal transformer.*

The relationships between primary and secondary quantities in an ideal transformer are as follows:

$$N = n_2/n_1, \quad V_2 = NV_1, \quad I_2 = I_1/N,$$

where V_1 and I_1 are primary voltage and primary current; V_2 and I_2 are secondary voltage and secondary current; and n_1 and n_2 are numbers of turns of the primary and secondary coil, respectively.

8.4 Design a class composed of the three classes—Amplifier, Transformer and Speaker. Each class should have a constructor function with arguments to initialize its data members. The Amplifier class should process the following data members—input power P_{in}, output power P_{out}, power gain G_p, and impedance R_a. The Transformer class stores and processes the turns ratio N that is needed to provide a maximum power transfer from amplifier to speaker. The Speaker class should have the two data members—an integer nSp representing a number of speakers connected in parallel, and a speaker's impedance R_s.

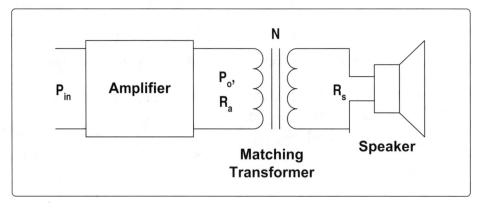

Figure 8.18 *Speaker(s) matched to an amplifier by transformer for maximum power transfer.*

The program should obtain the following values from the user: P_{in}, P_{out}, R_a, R_s, and nSp. It should compute and display the amplifier's power gain G_P, turns ratio N, and the equivalent impedance of speakers connected in parallel R_{ST}.

$$G_P = P_{out} / P_{in}$$

$$N = \sqrt{\frac{R_{ST}}{R_a}}$$

8.5 Design a program that can be used to estimate the cost of building a house. The program should use a House class composed of the classes representing different elements of a house, such as walls, ceilings, floors, roof, etc.

EXERCISE

CHAPTER 9

Polymorphism and Virtual Functions

OBJECTIVES

- To understand the differences between dynamic and static binding

- To understand the need for *virtual* functions when applying run-time polymorphism

- To be able to use abstract base classes

- To understand the importance of *virtual* destructors

CHAPTER CONTENTS

INTRODUCTION

Polymorphism is one of the three most important concepts in object-oriented programming (OOP). It is supported at compile time through function overloading and operator overloading. Run-time polymorphism enables programmers to design a common interface that can be used on different but related objects, thus reducing the complexity of a program as well as its development time. This chapter begins with a discussion of the differences between static and dynamic binding. It also addresses the importance of *virtual* functions when applying run-time polymorphism—a form of dynamic binding in OOP. Abstract base classes and *virtual* destructors are also discussed.

9.1 DYNAMIC VERSUS STATIC BINDING

Dynamic binding occurs at run-time, while **static binding** is implemented when the code is compiled. When compiling a program, the compiler reserves a space in memory for all user-defined functions and keeps track of the addresses of memory locations allocated to store each of the functions. *A function's name is bound with the function's address*, which is the starting address of the storage space in memory reserved for the function's code.

Consider PROG9_1 in Program Example 9.1, which uses two *non-inline* functions to simulate an AND and OR logic gate, respectively (Figure 9.1).

A logic gate is a circuit that implements the logical AND, OR, NAND, NOR, XOR, X-NOR, or NOT functions. Logic gates are used as building blocks of digital devices.

An AND gate is a logic circuit whose output is high (Y=1) only when all of its inputs are high (A=1 and B=1).

An OR gate is a logic circuit whose output is high (Y=1) when any or all of its inputs is/are high (A=1 or B=1, or both).

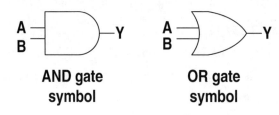

Figure 9.1 *An AND and OR logic gate demonstrated in PROG9_1.*

PROGRAM EXAMPLE 9.1: PROG9_1

```
1   //PROG9_1: Program demonstrates static binding.
2   #include <iostream>
3   using namespace std;
4   void and_gate(int,int);      //Simulates an AND gate
5   void or_gate(int,int);       //Simulates an OR gate
6   int main()
7   {
8       int a = 0, b = 1;        //input signals of a gate
```

```
9    cout<<"Address of and_gate(): "<<and_gate<<endl;
10   cout<<"Address of  or_gate(): "<<or_gate<<endl;
11   and_gate(a, b);
12   or_gate(a, b);
13   return 0;
14 }
15 void and_gate(int x, int y)
16 {
17   cout<<x<<" AND "<<y<<" = "<<(x && y)<<endl;
18 }
19 void or_gate(int x, int y)
20 {
21   cout<<x<<" OR  "<<y<<" = "<<(x || y)<<endl;
22 }
```

An example of the output produced by PROG9_1 is shown in Figure 9.2.

```
Address of and_gate(): 004011A9
Address of  or_gate(): 004010AF
0 AND 1 = 0
0 OR  1 = 1
```

Figure 9.2 *Output produced by PROG9_1.*

This program uses the and_gate() and or_gate() *non-inline* functions (lines 15–18 and 19–22, respectively). The functions' names are bound with the starting addresses of the memory storage that the compiler reserves for the functions' code (004011A9 and 004010AF in the example in Figure 9.2). Lines 9 and 10 print the addresses of and_gate() and or_gate() by inserting the functions' names into the output stream. Remember that a function's name, without the brackets and arguments, represents the address of the function.

The type of binding that is used in PROG9_1 is called **static binding**, or **early binding,** because the compiler binds all function calls (lines 11 and 12) to the addresses of the code that implement each of the functions (lines 17 and 21) *at compile time.* The compiler substitutes a function's name in each statement that calls the function with the function's address if the function is not an ***inline*** function. Note that in the case of ***inline*** functions, the function's name is substituted with the actual function's code (not its address).

When applying static binding in programs, the order of function calls is determined at compile time and cannot be changed at run-time. For example, the order of the function calls in PROG9_1 is as follows:

1. *main()*
2. and_gate()
3. or_gate()

Static binding is not appropriate when solving some real-life programming problems, particularly when using an OOP approach. In addition to compile-time static binding, function calls can also be resolved at run-time. This concept is called **dynamic binding**, or **late binding**. The order of the function calls in programs that use dynamic binding depends on an action taken by the user. Such programs can be described as user driven, as opposed to programs in which the programmer dictates the order of the function calls.

C language implements dynamic binding through function pointers. In addition to dynamic binding that uses function pointers, C++ provides additional enhanced tools (Section 9.2) to implement dynamic binding.

Note that a function pointer is a pointer that stores the starting address of a function's code. The function, therefore, can be called either by using the function's name, or by using the pointer that stores the function's address.

Consider the following code:

```
void (*fpt)(int, int)=and_gate;    //fpt points to and_gate()
fpt(1,0);             //Using the fpt pointer to call and_gate()
fpt=or_gate;                       //fpt points to or_gate()
fpt(1,1);             //Using the fpt pointer to call or_gate()
```

It is assumed that the and_gate() and or_gate() functions have been defined. These functions may be the same functions that are used in PROG9_1. The fpt function pointer is declared and initialized to the address of the and_gate() function. Note that fpt, according to its declaration, can point to any function that has two integer arguments and a *void* return type. The pointer is first used to call the and_gate() function to which it points. It is then changed to point to the or_gate() function and next used to call this function. In each case, two integer values are passed to functions.

An array of function pointers can be created as follows:

```
void (*ptar[])(int,int)={ and_gate, or_gate, nand_gate,
                          nor_gate, xor_gate };
```

The `ptar` array of function pointers has five elements, each of which is initialized to an address of a different function, as shown in Figure 9.3. Notice that the size of the array is not specified because the array is initialized when declared.

Pointer	points to	Function
ptar [0]	———▶	and_gate ( )
ptar [1]	———▶	or_gate ( )
ptar [2]	———▶	nand_gate ( )
ptar [3]	———▶	nor_gate ( )
ptar [4]	———▶	xor_gate ( )

Figure 9.3 *Function pointers as array elements.*

Any of the function pointers that are stored in this array can be changed to point to another function, as follows:

```
ptar[2]=xor_gate; //ptar[2] points to xor_gate() as does ptar[4]
```

Assume the following code:

```
int x;
cout<<"Chose an option 0-4: ";
cin>>x;
ptar[x](1, 1);  //Calling a function based on the user's input
```

In this example, the `ptar[x](1,1)` syntax is used to call a function, where a value of x entered by the user determines which of the five functions is called. The function calls, therefore, are resolved at run-time.

In Program Example 9.2, PROG9_2 demonstrates the use of function pointers to implement dynamic binding.

PROGRAM EXAMPLE 9.2: PROG9_2

```
1   //PROG9_2: Program demonstrates dynamic binding.
2   #include <iostream>
3   using namespace std;
4   void and_gate(int,int);
5   void or_gate(int,int);
```

```
6
7   int main()
8   {
9       int a=0, b=1, selection;
10      //array of function pointers
11      void (*ptr[])(int,int)={and_gate, or_gate};
12      do {
13          cout<<"\nOptions: \n\t1) AND gate\n\t2) OR gate";
14          cout<<"\n\t3) EXIT\n\n";
15          cout<<"Select an option (1, 2 or 3) >> ";
16          cin>>selection;
17          if((selection==1)||(selection==2))
18              ptr[selection-1](a, b);      //Calling a function
19      } while (selection!= 3);
20      return 0;
21  }
22  void and_gate(int x, int y)
23  {
24      cout<<"\n\t\t"<<x<<" AND "<<y<<" = "<<(x && y)<<endl;
25  }
26  void or_gate(int x, int y)
27  {
28      cout<<"\n\t\t"<<x<<" OR  "<<y<<" = "<<(x || y)<<endl;
29  }
```

PROG9_2 is a modified version of PROG9_1, which demonstrated static binding. The ptr array of two pointers is declared and initialized to the addresses of and_gate() and or_gate() (line 11). The program obtains a selection of a gate from the user (line 16) and then uses the pointer to call an appropriate function based on the user's selection (line 18). Unlike PROG9_1, in which the function calls were resolved at compile time, in PROG9_2 they are resolved at run-time. The user dictates the order of the function calls. A sample run of this program is shown in Figure 9.4.

```
Options:
    1) AND gate
    2) OR gate
    3) EXIT
Select an option (1, 2, or 3) >> 2
            0 OR 1 = 1
Options:
    1) AND gate
    2) OR gate
    3) EXIT
Select an option (1,2 or 3) >> 3
```

Figure 9.4 *A sample run of the program PROG9_2.*

Programs that offer a menu with multiple options for the user commonly use the *switch* statement, or multiple *if* statements, to switch between the options and execute those selected by the user. The function-pointer technique, used to implement dynamic binding in PROG9_2, eliminates the need for the *switch* or *if* statements. A single statement (line 18) can replace multiple lines of code when applying this technique.

 TIP: Use an array of function pointers pointing to functions that perform different menu options to eliminate the *switch* or multiple *if* statements.

Dynamic binding involves more function overhead than static binding, and therefore may reduce the speed of a program. On the other hand, dynamic binding is much more flexible than static binding and can respond to the *user's events* at run-time. In most of the practical examples in which run-time flexibility is a priority, the programmer would not consider the tradeoff of speed over flexibility.

9.2 VIRTUAL FUNCTIONS

C++ provides a tool called *virtual* functions to support dynamic binding and run-time polymorphism in object-oriented programs. Virtual functions are used with inheritance to resolve conflicts when both base and derived classes declare member functions with *the same signature* (the same name and parameter list).

Consider the inheritance hierarchy shown in Figure 9.5.

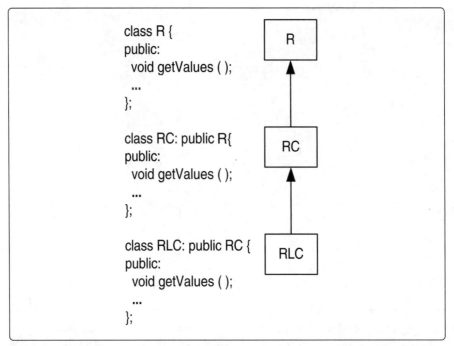

Figure 9.5 *Inheritance hierarchy in which each class declares a function with the same signature.*

The hierarchy in this example uses indirect multiple inheritance. The RLC class inherits RC, and the RC class inherits R. The R class, therefore, is a direct parent of RC and an indirect parent of RLC through RC. Note that the code in Figure 9.5 does not provide complete definitions of the three classes that form the hierarchy. It only defines the relationship between the classes and specifies that each class declares the getValues() function with the same signature.

Assume the following code fragment that uses the inheritance hierarchy in Figure 9.5:

```
1 R obj1;
2 RC obj2;
3 RLC obj3;
4 R *ptr=&obj1;      //Instantiates a pointer of the base class
5 ptr->getValues();  //Invokes getValues() in the base class
6 ptr=&obj2;         //The pointer points to a first derived object
7 ptr->getValues();  //Invokes getValues() in the base class
8 ptr=&obj3;         //The pointer points to a second derived object
9 ptr->getValues();  //Invokes getValues() in the base class
```

Lines 1, 2, and 3 instantiate an object of each class. The `ptr` pointer of the `R` type (base class) is instantiated and initialized to the address of the base class object, `obj1` (line 4). While pointing to `obj1`, the pointer is used to invoke the `getValues()` function (line 5). It is then changed to point first to the `obj2` object of `RC` and then to `obj3` of `RLC` (lines 6 and 8). After each change, the pointer is used to invoke `getValues()` (lines 7 and 9). Although each of the classes defines its own version of the `getValues()` function and the pointer points to objects of different classes, in all of these cases `getValues()` as defined in the `R` base class is invoked.

`R::getValues()` overrides `RC::getValues()` and `RLC::getValues()` in `RC` and `RLC`, respectively. Remember that the `ptr` pointer is type `R`; therefore, `R::getValues()` is always invoked through `ptr` whether it points to an object of `R`, `RC`, or `RLC`. This problem can be resolved, without creating a pointer for each class individually, by changing the `getValues()` function to a ***virtual*** function.

To declare a member function as ***virtual***, the ***virtual*** keyword must precede the function's declaration within a class, as shown in the general format in Figure 9.6. If a member function is declared as ***virtual*** within a base class, a member function with the same signature (the same name and parameter list) declared within a class derived directly or indirectly from the base class overrides the ***virtual*** function inherited from the base class. This means that if a pointer of the base-class type points to a derived-class object, the ***virtual*** function declared within the derived class will be invoked by using the pointer.

```
virtual return_type function_name(list of parameters);
```

Figure 9.6 *General format of a **virtual** function declaration.*

Note that the function declared within the derived class, which has the same signature as the ***virtual*** function in the base class, is also ***virtual*** whether or not it is explicitly declared as ***virtual***. The function declared in the derived class can, therefore, also be overridden by another version of that function declared within any class that directly or indirectly inherits the derived class.

In Program Example 9.3, PROG9_3 demonstrates the use of ***virtual*** functions in the previously discussed inheritance hierarchy (Figure 9.5). `R`, `L`, and `C` represent the resistance, inductance, and capacitance of an electric circuit, respectively.

PROGRAM EXAMPLE 9.3: PROG9_3

```
1   //PROG9_3: Program demonstrates virtual functions.
2   #include <iostream>
```

```
3   using namespace std;
4
5   class R {         //base class
6   protected:
7     double res;      //resistance
8   public:
9     R(double r) { res=r; }
10    virtual void getValues()  //virtual function
11    {
12        cout<<"R = "<<res<<endl;
13    }
14  };
15  class RC:public R {                      //derived class #1
16  protected:
17    double cap;      //capacitance
18  public:
19    RC(double r, double c):R(r) { cap=c; }
20    void getValues(){cout<<"R = "<<res<<" C = "<<cap<<endl;}
21  };
22  class RLC: public RC {                    //derived class #2
23    double ind;      //inductance
24  public:
25    RLC(double r, double c, double i):RC(r,c) { ind=i; }
26    void getValues()
27    {
28        cout<<"R = "<<res<<" C = "<<cap<<" L = "<<ind<<endl;
29    }
30  };
31
32  int main()
33  {
34    R obr(100), *ptr;
35    RC obrc(200, 0.001);
```

```
36    RLC obrlc(300, 0.005, 0.001);
37    ptr = &obr;              //ptr points to an object of R
38    ptr->getValues();  //Using ptr to call virtual function
39    ptr = &obrc;             //ptr points to an object of RC
40    ptr->getValues();  //Using ptr to call virtual function
41    ptr = &obrlc;            //ptr points to an object of RLC
42    ptr->getValues();  //Using ptr to call virtual function
43    return 0;
44 }
```

The `getValues()` function is declared as a ***virtual*** function within the R class (lines10–13). The function is then redefined by the RC class that is derived from R (line 20). The `RC::getValues()` function overrides `R::getValues()`, which is inherited from R. It should be noted that `RC::getValues()` is also ***virtual***, although it is not declared as such. The RLC class redefines `getValues()` as well (lines 26–29); therefore, `RC::getValues()` is overridden by `RLC::getValues()`. When using the `ptr` base-class pointer to invoke `getValues()` (lines 38, 40, and 42), an appropriate version of this function is invoked—`R::getValues()`, `RC::getValues()`, or `RLC::getValues()`—depending on the type of the object whose address is stored in `ptr`. The output of PROG9_3 is shown in Figure 9.7.

```
R = 100
R = 200    C = 0.001
R = 300    C = 0.005    L = 0.001
```

Figure 9.7 *Output produced by PROG9_3.*

If the `getValues()` function is changed to a *non-virtual* member function in R by deleting the ***virtual*** keyword before the function's declaration in line 10, PROG9_3 would produce the output shown in Figure 9.8.

```
                    R = 100
                    R = 200
                    R = 300
```

Figure 9.8 *Output produced by PROG9_3 if the keyword* **virtual** *is deleted.*

The `R::getValues()` *non-virtual* function is inherited first by `RC`, and then by `RLC` through `RC`. This function overrides `RC::getValues()` and `RLC::getValues()` within the `RC` and `RLC` classes, respectively. When using the `ptr` pointer to invoke `getValues()`, the `R::getValues()` function is invoked in each case to display the `res` value in `obj1`, `obj2`, and `obj3` (lines 38, 40, and 42).

When using *virtual* functions within inheritance hierarchies of classes, an object of each class has its own version of a *virtual* function. The version of the *virtual* function that will be invoked is determined at run-time (dynamic binding) based on the type of the object which is used. This is also a true polymorphism because one interface is used with different types of objects.

Virtual functions serve as placeholders for different versions of these functions defined within classes that form an inheritance hierarchy. A *virtual* function can also be seen as a function that overrides itself.

A class that declares or inherits a *virtual* function is called a **polymorphic class**. The `R`, `RC`, and `RLC` classes in PROG9_3 are examples of polymorphic classes.

 NOTE: It is not necessary to use the *virtual* keyword within a derived class to explicitly specify that a member function is *virtual*, as long as it is declared as *virtual* within a base class.

 TIP: Use a *virtual* function whenever it is anticipated that a derived class may define its own version of the function.

9.3 ABSTRACT BASE CLASSES

When designing an inheritance hierarchy, *virtual* functions should be used to define common behavior(s) (actions) of the classes that form the hierarchy. The definition of a common behavior, in the form of a *virtual* function, begins with a base class at the top of the hierarchy. The *virtual* function is then redefined (overridden) at every level of derived classes to describe a specific behavior of each class. If a derived class does not redefine the *virtual* function, then the behavior (function) of its base class is inherited.

In some cases, a base class may be used only as a framework from which other classes will be derived, while the individual objects of this class will never be instantiated. When designing such base classes, **pure *virtual* functions** should be used whenever there is no need to define these functions within the base class. A pure *virtual* function is a *virtual* function that does not have a definition (code) in its class.

A base class that has one or more pure *virtual* member functions is called an **abstract base class**.

To declare a pure *virtual* function, the **=0;** initializer must substitute the body of the function as shown in Figure 9.9. This initializer specifies that the function has no body (definition).

```
virtual return_type function_name(list of parameters)=0;
```

Figure 9.9 *General format of a pure* **virtual** *member function.*

Note that the braces { } that enclose a body of a *virtual* function can be left empty if there is no meaningful operation to be performed within a base class. Instead of using empty braces, the syntax shown in Figure 9.9 should be used to specify that the *virtual* function has no body (definition) within the base class. The class becomes an abstract base class in this case.

The syntax in Figure 9.9, with the =0; initializer, instructs the compiler that each class derived from the abstract class must override (redefine) the *virtual* function. Using a pure *virtual* function, therefore, is a secure way to force each class derived from an abstract class to supply its own definition of the *virtual* function.

 NOTE: It is a syntax error not to redefine a pure *virtual* function within a class derived from an abstract base class.

An object cannot be instantiated from an abstract class due to the incomplete class definition resulting from the missing code in the pure *virtual* function(s). Unlike objects, *pointers and references to abstract classes can be instantiated.* To implement run-time polymorphism (dynamic binding), it is common to use a pointer of an abstract base-class type. The opposite of an abstract class is a **concrete class**, from which objects can be instantiated. A concrete class does not contain any member function declared as a pure *virtual* function.

In Program Example 9.4, PROG9_4 is a modified version of PROG9_3, in which the R class is changed to an abstract base class.

PROGRAM EXAMPLE 9.4: PROG9_4

```
1  //PROG9_4: Program demonstrates an abstract base class.
2  #include <iostream>
3  using namespace std;
4  const double PI=3.14159265;
5  const double f=60;
6
7  class R {        //abstract base class
```

```
8   protected:
9     double res;      //resistance
10  public:
11    virtual void getValues(){cout<<"R = "<<res<<endl;}
12    virtual double reactance()=0;    //pure virtual function
13  };
14  class RC : public R {
15  protected:
16    double cap;      //capacitance
17  public:
18    RC(double r, double c) { res=r; cap=c; }
19    void getValues(){cout<<"R = "<<res<<" C = "<<cap<<endl;}
20    double reactance(){ return (-1/(2*PI*f*cap)); }
21  };
22  class RLC :  public RC {
23    double ind;      //inductance
24  public:
25    RLC(double r, double c, double i):RC(r,c) { ind=i; }
26    void getValues()
27    {
28        cout<<"\nR = "<<res<<" C = "<<cap<<" L = "<<ind<<endl;
29    }
30    double reactance(){ return (2*PI*f*ind-1/(2*PI*f*cap)); }
31  };
32
33  int main()
34  {
35    R *ptr;
36    RC obrc(200, 0.001);
37    RLC obrlc(300, 0.005, 0.001);
38    ptr=&obrc;          //ptr points to an object of RC
39    ptr->getValues();
40    cout<<"Reactance = ";
```

```
41    cout<<ptr->reactance()<<endl; //Calling pure virtual function
42    ptr=&obrlc;          //ptr points to an object of RLC
43    ptr->getValues();
44    cout<<"Reactance = ";
45    cout<<ptr->reactance()<<endl; //Calling pure virtual function
46    return 0;
47 }
```

The R class is an abstract base class because it contains the reactance() function declared as a pure *virtual* function (line 12). This function is first overridden by the RC derived class (line 20) and then by the final RLC derived class (line 30). The reactance() function is intended to compute and return the circuit's reactance. Assuming that the R, RC, and RLC classes represent R (resistor), RC (resistor-capacitor), and RLC (resistor-inductor-capacitor) circuits, respectively, there is no need to define the reactance() function in the R class. The RC class redefines this function to compute the capacitive reactance ($X=-1/2\pi fC$), while the RLC class redefines the reactance() function to compute the inductive and capacitive reactance in series ($X=2\pi fL-1/2\pi fC$).

The *main()* function instantiates a ptr pointer of the R-type abstract class (line 35), as well as an obrc object of RC (line 36) and an obrlc object of RLC (line 37). Notice that unlike PROG9_3, this program does not instantiate an object of R (R is an abstract class). The ptr pointer points first to obrc (line 38), and then to obrlc (line 42). While pointing to each object, the pointer is used to invoke the getValues() regular *virtual* function (lines 39 and 43) as well as the reactance() pure *virtual* function (lines 41 and 45). This program produces the output shown in Figure 9.10.

```
R = 200      C = 0.001
Reactance = -2.65258


R = 300      C = 0.005      L = 0.001
Reactance = -0.153525
```

Figure 9.10 *Output produced by PROG9_3.*

PROG9_4 demonstrates the following common OOP techniques and good programming practices:

- Inheritance is used to promote code reusability.

- Virtual functions are used to describe common behavior within a family of classes.
- A pure **virtual** function is used in the base class where the hierarchy begins, in order to force the function to be redefined in each derived class.
- A pointer to an abstract base class is used to invoke **virtual** functions, thus implementing run-time polymorphism and dynamic binding.

9.4 VIRTUAL DESTRUCTORS

A **virtual** function can be inherited by a derived class and is overridden by a member function of this class that has the same name and parameter list as the inherited **virtual** function. It would seem that constructors and destructors could not be declared as **virtual** functions because of the following reasons:

- Constructors and destructors cannot be inherited.
- Constructors' and destructors' names have to match the names of their corresponding classes.

Even though destructors are not inherited and each destructor within an inheritance hierarchy of classes has a different name, *destructors can be declared* **virtual**. It is sometimes necessary to create **virtual** destructors in order to prevent some problems that occur when objects of polymorphic classes (classes that have **virtual** functions) are dynamically allocated.

 NOTE: Unlike destructors, constructors cannot be **virtual**.

To create a **virtual** destructor, the general format shown in Figure 9.11 must be used.

```
virtual ~class_name()
{
      //body of destructor
}
```

Figure 9.11 *General format of a* **virtual** *destructor.*

If a base-class destructor is declared **virtual**, then destructors of all classes directly or indirectly derived from the base class are also **virtual**. Creating **virtual** destructors for polymorphic classes ensures that an appropriate destructor is called when using the **delete** operator to destroy dynamically allocated objects of these classes.

Assume that a base-class pointer is used to access dynamically allocated objects of polymorphic classes that form an inheritance hierarchy. The base-class destructor is invoked each time when using the base-class pointer and **delete** to destroy an object of any class within the hierarchy. The pointer could point to a derived-class object; however, the base-class destructor is invoked when destroying this object.

C++ decides which class destructor to invoke by checking a pointer type, not the type of an object to which the pointer points. This can cause a variety of problems, the most serious of which is a difficult to detect *memory leak*. To prevent these problems, a polymorphic class should have a ***virtual*** destructor, even if the class does not require an explicit destructor.

PROG9_5 demonstrates ***virtual*** destructors in Program Example 9.5. Note that the only purpose of the inheritance hierarchy of classes used in this example is to demonstrate the mechanism of calling destructors when destroying dynamically allocated objects of polymorphic classes.

PROGRAM EXAMPLE 9.5: PROG9_5

```
1   //PROG9_5: Program demonstrates virtual destructors.
2   #include <iostream>
3   using namespace std;
4
5   class A {                  //base class
6      int x;
7   public:
8      A(){ x=1; cout<<"A is constructed."<<endl; }
9      virtual ~A(){ cout<<"\tA is destroyed."<<endl; }  //virtual
10  };                                                    //destructor
11
12  class B : public A {       //derived class #1
13     int y;
14  public:
15     B(){ y=2; cout<<"B is constructed."<<endl; }
16     ~B(){ cout<<"\tB is destroyed."<<endl; } //virtual destructor
17  };
18
19  class C : public B {       //derived class #2
20     int z;
21  public:
22     C(){ z=3; cout<<"C is constructed."<<endl; }
```

```
23    ~C(){ cout<<"\tC is destroyed."<<endl; } //virtual destructor
24 };
25
26 int main()
27 {
28    A *ptr;        //a base-class pointer
29    ptr=new B;     //pointer points to a derived-class (#1) object
30    delete ptr;    //destroying the derived-class object
31    ptr=new C;     //pointer points to a derived-class (#2) object
32    delete ptr;    //destroying the derived-class object
33    return 0;
34 }
```

The A class is a base class in which inheritance begins in PROG9_5. The B class inherits A, and the C class inherits B. Each class has its own explicit destructor (lines 9, 16, and 23, respectively). The A class destructor is declared *virtual* (line 9), thus forcing the B and C destructors to be *virtual*, although not explicitly specified as such. In addition to the destructor, each class has a constructor function (lines 8, 15, and 22).

The *main( )* function instantiates the ptr base-class pointer (line 28). It then uses ptr and the *new* operator to dynamically allocate an object of B (line 29). This object is then destroyed by using ptr and *delete* (line 30). The same sequence is repeated for an object of the C class (lines 31 and 32). This program produces the output shown in Figure 9.12.

```
A is constructed.
B is constructed.
        B is destroyed.
        A is destroyed.
A is constructed.
B is constructed.
C is constructed.
        C is destroyed.
        B is destroyed.
        A is destroyed.
```

Figure 9.12 *Output produced by PROG9_5, if the **virtual** destructor is used.*

Note that the B destructor invokes the A destructor and the C destructor invokes the B and A destructors. Declaring the A destructor *virtual* provides that this destructor is overridden by the B and C destructors within the B and C classes, respectively.

Assume that the A destructor was not declared *virtual* in PROG9_5—i.e., the *virtual* keyword is deleted in line 9. This would result in the A destructor not being overridden by the B and C destructors within their respective classes. This, in turn, would cause incorrect destructor calls when destroying dynamically allocated objects of the B and C classes. PROG9_5, in this case, would produce the output shown in Figure 9.13.

```
A is constructed.
B is constructed.
        A is destroyed.
A is constructed.
B is constructed.
C is constructed.
        A is destroyed.
```

Figure 9.13 *Output produced by PROG9_5, without the* **virtual** *destructor.*

Note that in the previously discussed case, the A destructor is invoked when intending to destroy dynamically allocated objects of the B and C classes.

As inherited classes may require their own explicit destructors, provide *virtual* destructors for all classes that have *virtual* member functions to avoid possible errors.

 NOTE: A destructor in a derived class overrides a base-class destructor that is declared *virtual*.

 TIP: Always provide *virtual* destructors for classes that have *virtual* member functions.

9.5 USING POLYMORPHISM

Virtual functions (including *virtual* destructors) and abstract base classes are fundamental tools in the implementation of run-time polymorphism (dynamic binding in OOP). Polymorphism enables programmers to use the same interface (functions) on different types of objects, thus reducing program development time. It is the essence of the true object-oriented approach to programming.

Polymorphism is applied all the time in real life. For example, the same word can be used to describe similar actions (operations) on different types of objects such as: `start` the motor, `start` the race, `start` studying programming, and `start` the movie. There is a similarity between all of these actions, yet each action is implemented in a different way depending on the object type. A specific action is described through polymorphism for each object's type on which the `start` operation is performed. A programming language can be compared to a spoken language in many aspects. Using the same word for similar actions simplifies the language and makes communication easier.

Polymorphism is applied in engineering, as well. For example, the same PID regulator can control different processes in control systems, or the same remote controller can be used to control different types of devices.

The following code fragment illustrates a practical example of polymorphism:

```
class TV {
public:
    virtual ~TV() = 0;
    virtual void powerOn() = 0;
    virtual void powerOff() = 0;
    virtual void changeVolume(int) = 0;
    virtual void changeChanel(int) = 0;
};
class BrandX : public TV {
public:
    ~BrandX();
    void powerOn();
    void powerOff();
    void changeVolume(int);
    void changeChanel(int);
};
class BrandY : public TV {
public:
    ~BrandY();
    void powerOn();
    void powerOff();
```

```
    void changeVolume(int);
    void changeChanel(int);
};
```

The TV abstract base class defines some common properties and behaviors of all TV sets. A class that defines a specific type/brand of a TV set can be derived from the TV class (BrandX and BrandY in this example). It is easy to add a new type of a TV set to the existing family when applying this approach.

Applying polymorphism as demonstrated in this example provides one more advantage in addition to the advantages that have been discussed so far. A family of classes (inheritance hierarchy) can be easily extended by adding new classes, without modifying the existing structure of the family.

9.6 CASE STUDY: LOGIC CIRCUIT CALCULATOR

This case study demonstrates a use of *virtual* functions and abstract base classes in designing the three-layer digital circuit shown in Figure 9.14. An abstract base class that contains the general properties and methods of a logic gate circuit is designed. Four classes are derived from the abstract base class, each of which contains methods (functions) that are specifically designed for an AND, NAND, OR, and NOR logic gate, respectively. The base class contains a pure *virtual* function, which is redefined in each derived class to compute the output of a specific type of logic gate. In addition to classes that process data of specific types of logic gates, a class is also designed to process data for a three-layer logic circuit that is built of seven logic gates.

PROBLEM DESCRIPTION

The program should obtain a selection of logic gates (AND, NAND, OR, or NOR) from the user for seven gates, as well as eight logic inputs (0 or 1) for the first layer of four gates. It should then compute and display the output of each gate (gates 1–7 in Figure 9.14). Note that the output of gate 7 is the output of the entire three-layer logic circuit.

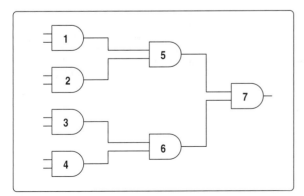

Figure 9.14 *Three-layer logic circuit.*

INPUT/OUTPUT

Requested **input** from the user:

    1. A selection of logic gates (AND, NAND, OR, or NOR) for seven gates.

    2. Eight logic inputs (0 or 1) for the first layer of four gates.

Requested **output**: The output signal (logic 0 or logic 1) for each gate.

PSEUDOCODE

Design the `Gate` abstract base class with the following skeleton:

- Data members (***protected***):

    1. `int input1;`   `//a logic gate input #1`

    2. `int input2;`   `//a logic gate input #2`

- Member functions (***public***):

    1. `virtual int calc()=0;`

        `//PURE VIRTUAL FUNCTION`

        `//COMPUTES THE OUTPUT LOGIC OF A LOGIC GATE`

- **Friend** functions:

    1. `friend istream & operator>>(istream &in, Gate &obj);`

        `//GETS TWO INPUTS FOR A LOGIC GATE.`

        `START`

        `PRINT "ENTER INPUTS (1 OR 0)"`

        `PRINT "FIRST =>"`

        `READ OBJ.INPUT1`

        `PRINT "SECOND =>"`

        `READ OBJ.INPUT2`

        `RETURN IN`

        `STOP`

Derive the `And` class from `Gate` with the following skeleton:

- Member functions (***public***):

    1. `And(int a, int b);`

        `//INITIALIZES TWO INPUTS`

        `START`

        `INPUT1=A`

        `INPUT2=B`

```
STOP
```

2. `int calc();`

```
//COMPUTES AND RETURNS THE OUTPUT OF AN AND GATE
START
RETURN INPUT1 & INPUT2
STOP
```

Derive the `Nand` class from `Gate` with the following skeleton:

- Member functions (***public***):

   1. `Nand(int a, int b);`

```
//INITIALIZES TWO INPUTS
START
INPUT1=A
INPUT2=B
STOP
```

   2. `int calc();`

```
//COMPUTES AND RETURNS THE OUTPUT OF A NAND GATE
START
RETURN !(INPUT1 & INPUT2)
STOP
```

Derive the `Or` class from `Gate` with the following skeleton:

- Member functions (***public***):

   1. `Or(int a, int b);`

```
//INITIALIZES TWO INPUTS
START
INPUT1=A
INPUT2=B
STOP
```

   2. `int calc();`

```
//COMPUTES AND RETURNS THE OUTPUT OF AN OR GATE
START
RETURN INPUT1 | INPUT2
STOP
```

Derive the `Nor` class from `Gate` with the following skeleton:

- Member functions (**public**):

    I. `Nor(int a, int b);`

        ```
        //INITIALIZES TWO INPUTS
        START
        INPUT1=A
        INPUT2=B
        STOP
        ```

    2. `int calc();`

        ```
        //COMPUTES AND RETURNS THE OUTPUT OF A NOR GATE
        START
        RETURN !(INPUT1 | INPUT2)
        STOP
        ```

Design the `Circuit` class with the following skeleton:

- Data members (**private**):

    I. `int output;`   //the output of a three-layer logic circuit
    2. `int choice;`   //a selection of a logic gate
    3. `int layer2[4];` //four inputs of the second layer
    4. `int layer3[2];` //two inputs of the third layer

- Member functions (**public**):

    I. `void menu();`

        ```
        //DISPLAYS TYPES OF LOGIC GATES AND GETS A SELECTION
        //FROM THE USER
        START
        COUNT=1
        PRINT "LIST OF GATES: 1)AND 2)NAND 3)OR 4)NOR"
        DO WHILE CHOICE<1 OR CHOICE>4
            PRINT "CHOOSE GATE #"
            PRINT COUNT
            READ CHOICE
        END DO
        COUNT=COUNT+1
        STOP
        ```

2. `void layer1_out()`

   ```
   //SETS UP THE FIRST LAYER AND COMPUTES INPUTS FOR THE
   //SECOND LAYER
   START
   A=0
   FOR A<4
        EXECUTE MENU()
        IF CHOICE==1 THEN
             INSTANTIATE AND OBJ
             READ OBJ
             LAYER2[A]=OBJ.CALC()
        END IF
        IF CHOICE==2 THEN
             INSTANTIATE NAND OBJ
             READ OBJ
             LAYER2[A]=OBJ.CALC()
        END IF
        IF CHOICE==3 THEN
             INSTANTIATE OR OBJ
             READ OBJ
             LAYER2[A]=OBJ.CALC()
        END IF
        IF CHOICE==4
             INSTANTIATE NOR OBJ
             READ OBJ
             LAYER2[A]=OBJ.CALC()
        END IF
        A=A+1
   END FOR
   STOP
   ```

3. `void layer2_out();`

   ```
   //SETS UP THE SECOND LAYER AND COMPUTES INPUTS FOR THE
   //THIRD LAYER
   ```

```
START
I=0
J=0
FOR J<2
    EXECUTE MENU()
    IF CHOICE==1 THEN
        INSTANTIATE AND OBJ
        INITILAIZE OBJ TO LAYER2[I], LAYER2[I+1]
        I=I+2
        LAYER3[J]=OBJ.CALC()
    END IF
    IF CHOICE==2 THEN
        INSTANTIATE NAND OBJ
        INITILAIZE OBJ TO LAYER2[I], LAYER2[I+1]
        I=I+2
        LAYER3[J]=OBJ.CALC()
    END IF
    IF CHOICE==3 THEN
        INSTANTIATE OR OBJ
        INITILAIZE OBJ TO LAYER2[I], LAYER2[I+1]
        I=I+2
        LAYER3[J]=OBJ.CALC()
    END IF
    IF CHOICE==4
        INSTANTIATE NOR OBJ
        INITILAIZE OBJ TO LAYER2[I], LAYER2[I+1]
        I=I+2
        LAYER3[J]=OBJ.CALC()
    END IF
    J=J+1
END FOR
STOP
```

4. ` void layer3_out();`

```
//SETS UP THE THIRD LAYER AND COMPUTES THE OUTPUT
START
EXECUTE MENU()
J=0
IF CHOICE==1 THEN
    INSTANTIATE AND OBJ
    INITIALIZE OBJ TO LAYER3[J], LAYER3[J+1]
    J=J+2
    OUTPUT=OBJ.CALC()
END IF
IF CHOICE==2 THEN
    INSTANTIATE NAND OBJ
    INITIALIZE OBJ TO LAYER3[J], LAYER3[J+1]
    J=J+2
    OUTPUT=OBJ.CALC()
END IF
IF CHOICE==3 THEN
    INSTANTIATE OR OBJ
    INITIALIZE OBJ TO LAYER3[J], LAYER3[J+1]
    J=J+2
    OUTPUT=OBJ.CALC()
END IF
IF CHOICE==4 THEN
    INSTANTIATE NOR OBJ
    INITIALIZE OBJ TO LAYER3[J], LAYER3[J+1]
    J=J+2
    OUTPUT=OBJ.CALC()
END IF
EXECUTE DISPLAY()
STOP
```

5. `void display();`

```
//DISPLAYS OUTPUTS
START
PRINT "OUTPUTS:"
PRINT "GATE #1"
PRINT LAYER2[0]
PRINT "GATE #5"
PRINT LAYER3[0]
PRINT "GATE #2"
PRINT LAYER2[1]
PRINT "GATE #7"
PRINT OUTPUT
PRINT "GATE #3"
PRINT LAYER2[2]
PRINT "GATE #6"
PRINT LAYER3[1]
PRINT "GATE #4"
PRINT LAYER2[3]
STOP
```

- The **main()** function:

```
START
INSTANTIATE CIRCUIT OBJ
EXECUTE LAYER1_OUT()
EXECUTE LAYER2_OUT()
EXECUTE LAYER3_OUT()
STOP
```

SOURCE CODE
PROGRAM EXAMPLE 9.6: CASEST9 SOURCE CODE

```
1   #include <iostream>
2   using namespace std;
3
4   //*************** ABSTRACT BASE CLASS ***************
```

```
5   class Gate

6   {

7      protected:

8          int input1, input2;    //gate inputs

9      public:

10         virtual int calc()=0; //pure virtual function

11         friend istream & operator>>(istream &in, Gate &obj);

12  };

13  istream & operator>>(istream &in, Gate &obj)

14  {

15     cout<<"\nEnter inputs ( 1 or 0 ):\n\n";

16     cout<< "First => ";

17     in>> obj.input1;

18     cout<< "Second => ";

19     in>> obj.input2;

20     return in;

21     }

22  //*************** DERIVED CLASSES ***************

23

24  class And : public Gate      //AND gate

25  {

26     public:

27         And(int a, int b){ input1=a; input2=b; }

28         int calc(){ return input1&input2; }

29  };

30

31  class Nand : public Gate      //NAND gate

32  {

33     public:

34         Nand(int a, int b){ input1=a; input2=b;}

35         int calc(){ return !(input1&input2); }

36  };

37
```

```
38 class Or : public Gate        //OR gate
39 {
40   public:
41       Or(int a, int b){ input1=a; input2=b;}
42       int calc(){ return input1|input2; }
43 };
44
45 class Nor : public Gate       //NOR gate
46 {
47   public:
48       Nor(int a, int b){ input1=a; input2=b;}
49       int calc() { return !(input1|input2); }
50 };
51 //*************** DIGITAL CIRCUIT CLASS ***************
52 class Circuit
53 {
54   private:
55       int output;        //circuit's output
56       int choice;        //gate's selection
57       int layer2[4];     //2nd layer inputs
58       int layer3[2];     //3rd layer inputs
59   public:
60       void menu();        //Gets the user's selection of gates
61       void layer1_out();  //Sets up the first layer
62   void layer2_out();  //Sets up the second layer
63   void layer3_out();  //Sets up the third layer
64   void display();     //Displays outputs
65 };
66 //~~~~~~~~~~ Gets the user's selection of gates ~~~~~~~~~~
67 void Circuit :: menu ()
68 {
69   static int count=1;      //gate counter
70   cout<<"List of gates:\n\n1. And \n2. Nand \n";
```

```
71      cout<<"3. Or \n4. Nor \n\n";
72      do {
73          cout<<"Choose gate #" << count << " => ";
74          cin>>choice;
75      }while((choice<1)||(choice>4));
76      count++;
77  }
78  //~~~~~~~~~~ Sets up the first layer ~~~~~~~~~~
79  void Circuit :: layer1_out()
80  {
81      for(int a=0; a<4; a++)
82      {
83          menu();
84          if(choice==1)
85      {
86          And obj(0,0);           //Instantiates an AND gate
87          cin>>obj;               //Gets input signals
88          layer2[a]=obj.calc();      //Computes output
89      }
90      else if(choice==2)
91      {
92          Nand obj(0,0);          //Instantiates a NAND gate
93          cin>>obj;
94          layer2[a]=obj.calc();
95      }
96      else if(choice==3)
97          {
98          Or obj(0,0);            //Instantiates an OR gate
99          cin>>obj;
100         layer2[a]=obj.calc();
101     }
102     else if(choice==4)
103         {
```

```
104            Nor obj(0,0);              //Instantiates a NOR gate
105            cin>>obj;
106            layer2[a]=obj.calc();
107          }
108       }
109  }
110  //~~~~~~~~~~~~~ Sets up the second layer ~~~~~~~~~~~~~
111  void Circuit :: layer2_out()
112  {
113     int i=0;
114     for(int j=0; j<2; j++ )
115     {
116        menu();
117        if(choice==1)
118        {
119            And obj(layer2[i],layer2[i+1]);
120            i=i+2;
121            layer3[j]=obj.calc();
122        }
123        else if(choice==2)
124        {
125            Nand obj(layer2[i],layer2[i+1]);
126            i=i+2;
127            layer3[j]=obj.calc();
128        }
129        else if(choice==3)
130        {
131            Or obj(layer2[i],layer2[i+1]);
132            i=i+2;
133            layer3[j]=obj.calc();
134        }
135        else if(choice==4)
136        {
```

```
137              Nor obj(layer2[i],layer2[i+1]);
138              i=i+2;
139              layer3[j]=obj.calc();
140          }
141      }
142 }
143 //~~~~~~~~~~~~~ Sets up the third layer ~~~~~~~~~~~~~~
144 void Circuit :: layer3_out()
145 {
146     menu();
147     int j=0;
148     if(choice==1)
149     {
150         And obj(layer3[j],layer3[j+1]);
151         j=j+2;
152         output=obj.calc();
153     }
154     else if (choice==2)
155     {
156         Nand obj(layer3[j],layer3[j+1]);
157         j=j+2;
158         output=obj.calc();
159     }
160     else if (choice==3)
161     {
162         Or obj(layer3[j],layer3[j+1]);
163         j=j+2;
164         output=obj.calc();
165     }
166     else if(choice==4)
167     {
168         Nor obj(layer3[j],layer3[j+1]);
169         j=j+2;
```

```
170        output=obj.calc();
171    }
172    display();
173 }
174 //~~~~~~~~~~~~ Displays outputs ~~~~~~~~~~~~
175 void Circuit :: display()
176 {
177    cout << "\n\nOutputs:\n========\n";
178
179    cout<<"\nGate #1 = "<<layer2[0]<<endl;
180    cout<<"\t\t Gate #5 = "<<layer3[0];
181    cout<<"\nGate #2 = "<<layer2[1]<<endl;
182    cout<<"\t\t\t\t  Gate #7 = "<<output;
183    cout<<"\nGate #3 = "<<layer2[2]<<endl;
184    cout<<"\t\t Gate #6 = "<<layer3[1];
185    cout<<"\nGate #4 = "<<layer2[3]<<endl;
186 }
187 //=======================================================
188 int main ()
189 {
190    Circuit dgcir;           //Instantiates an object of Circuit
191    dgcir.layer1_out();      //Sets up the first layer
192    dgcir.layer2_out();      //Sets up the second layer
193    dgcir.layer3_out();      //Sets up the third layer
194    return 0;
195 }
196 //=======================================================
```

OUTPUT

A sample run of CASEST9 is shown in Figures 9.15 and 9.16.

```
        List of gates:

        1. And
        2. Nand
        3. Or
        4. Nor

        Choose gate #1 => 1

        Enter inputs (1 or 0):
        First => 1
        Second => 1
```

Figure 9.15 *Sample run of CASEST9 (an input screen for gates 1–4).*

 NOTE: For gates 5–7, only a gate type is requested.

```
    Outputs:
    ========

    Gate #1 = 1
                        Gate #5 = 0

    Gate #2 = 0
                                    Gate #7 = 1

    Gate #3 = 1
                        Gate #6 = 1

    Gate #4 = 0
```

Figure 9.16 *Sample run of CASEST9 (an output screen).*

CONCLUSION

This case study applies polymorphism in designing a three-layer digital circuit consisting of seven logic gates. A family of classes is designed for different types of logic gates. This inheritance hierarchy can be easily extended by adding classes for new logic gates (X-OR and X-NOR, for example) without modifying the existing structure of the family. The interface between member functions of the Circuit class is

354

straightforward. Because of this simplicity, it is relatively easy to make program modifications to design digital circuits with different structures (different number of layers and/or different number of logic gates in each layer).

SUMMARY

1. A function's name is bound with an address of the storage space in memory reserved for the function's code.

2. When using static binding (early binding), function calls are resolved at compile time.

3. Dynamic binding (late binding) is a technique of resolving function calls at run-time, thus increasing flexibility of a program. It can be implemented through the use of function pointers.

4. Polymorphism enables the use of one interface with different types of objects.

5. Virtual functions are used to implement dynamic binding and run-time polymorphism in object-oriented programs. A class that declares or inherits a *virtual* function is called a polymorphic class.

6. A *virtual* function that is not defined in its class is called a pure *virtual* function.

7. An abstract base class is a class that contains one or more pure *virtual* functions. Unlike concrete classes, objects cannot be instantiated from abstract classes.

8. Virtual destructors are needed when dynamically allocating objects from polymorphic classes.

EXERCISES

Determine the output produced by the programs in Exercises 9.1 and 9.2.

9.1
```
#include <iostream>
using namespace std;
class First {
protected:
      int x;
public:
      First(int a){x=a;}
```

```
        virtual void display(){cout<<x<<endl;}
};
class Second:public First {
public:
        Second(int a):First(a){}
        void display(){cout<<hex<<x<<endl;}
};
int main()
{
        First *pt, obj1(13);
        Second obj2(15);
        pt=&obj1;
        pt->display();
        pt=&obj2;
        pt->display();
        return 0;
}
```

9.2
```
#include <iostream>
using namespace std;
class Base {
        int a;
public:
        Base(int x){a=x;}
        virtual void display(){cout<<a<<endl;}
};
class D1:public Base {
        int b,c;
public:
        D1(int x,int y,int z):Base(z){b=x;c=y;}
        void display(){cout<<b<<''<<c<<endl;}
};
class D2:public D1 {
```

```
        int d;
public:
        D2(int x,int y,int z,int q):D1(y,z,q){d=x;}
        void display(){cout<<d<<endl;}
};
int main()
{
        Base obj1(1),*ptr;
        D1 obj2(1,2,3);
        D2 obj3(1,2,3,4);
        ptr=&obj1;
        ptr->display();
        ptr=&obj2;
        ptr->display();
        ptr=&obj3;
        ptr->display();
        return 0;
}
```

9.3 Determine the output produced by the programs in Exercises 9.1 and 9.2, if the display( ) function is changed to a *non-virtual* function.

Given the following Device class definition, identify the errors (if any) in the code segments in Exercises 9.4 through 9.7.

```
class Device {
protected:
    float power, voltage;
    char *description;
public:
    virtual void getValues()=0;
    virtual void print()=0;
};
```

9.4
```
int main()
{
```

```
        Device obj;
        obj.getValues();
        return 0;
    }
```

9.5
```
class Dryer : public Device {
public:
        virtual Dryer();
        virtual ~Dryer();
    void print()
    {
        cout<<"Description: "<<description<<endl;
        cout<<power<<" W "<<voltage<<" V";
    }
};
```

9.6
```
class Amplifier : public Device {
public:
    virtual void compute()=0;
//other member functions
};
```

9.7
```
int main()
{
    Device *ptr;
    Washer w;     //Assume Washer is derived from Device
    ptr=&w;
    ptr->getValues();
    ptr->print();
    return 0;
}
```

PROGRAMMING PROJECTS

9.1 Design a Vehicle class that contains the following properties of motor vehicles: fuel tank capacity, average fuel consumption per 100 km, and the distance a vehicle can travel on a full tank. The Vehicle class should be designed as an abstract base class from which the Car and Truck classes are derived. The derived classes should have the following member functions:

- A function that obtains data for a vehicle from the user (the fuel tank capacity and average fuel consumption)

- A function that computes and returns the distance a vehicle can travel on a full tank

- A function that computes and returns how many times a vehicle has to be refueled to travel a given distance

These functions should be defined as pure *virtual* functions in the Vehicle class and redefined by the derived classes. Design the *main( )* function that instantiates a pointer of Vehicle type, and a Car and Truck object, respectively. The pointer should be used to invoke appropriate member functions to get and process data for a car and truck. The program should output how many times each vehicle has to be refueled to travel the distance entered by the user, as well as the distance each vehicle can travel on a full tank.

9.2 Design a program that uses the hierarchy of classes shown in Figure 9.17.

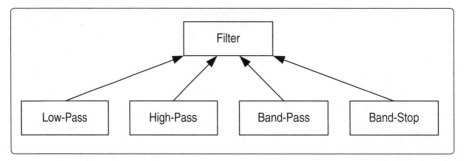

Figure 9.17 *Inheritance hierarchy of filter circuits.*

The Filter class should define the general properties (attributes and behaviors) that are common to all four types of filter circuits. This class should be defined as an abstract base class with pure *virtual* functions. Four derived classes should inherit the general properties from Filter and each class should also define some properties that are specific to a particular type of a filter circuit. The derived classes should also redefine *virtual* functions to process data for a specific type of filter.

9.3   Design a hierarchy of classes in which each class contains a *virtual* destructor. Design the *main()* function that dynamically allocates and destroys an object(s) of each class. A base class pointer should be used when allocating the derived class object(s). The output produced by the program should indicate which destructor is invoked when a specific object is deleted (destroyed).

CHAPTER 10

Templates

INTRODUCTION

Templates (**function templates** and **class templates**) promote code reusability because one function or class template can be used to generate many functions or classes. This chapter will discuss class templates and their relationship with inheritance. In addition, container and iterator classes will be discussed. The chapter will introduce the Standard Template Library (STL) and demonstrate practical examples that use this library.

10.1 CLASS TEMPLATES

A **class template** defines a family of classes. It serves as a class outline, from which specific classes are generated at compile time. Class templates promote code reusability and reduce a program's development time. One template can be used to generate many classes.

To define a class template, the *template* keyword followed by a **template parameter list** must precede a class declaration. The template parameter list is enclosed in angle brackets (< >), as shown in Figure 10.1.

```
template <template_parameter_list>
class class_template_name {
        //body of the class template
};
```

Figure 10.1 *General format of a class template.*

The following example defines a class template named `Array` that has one template type parameter named `Tarr`:

```
template<class Tarr>
class Array {
    Tarr * ptarr;  //pointer to an array
    int n;         //number of array elements
public:
    Array();
    ~Array();
    void getValues();
    void print();
};
```

The `ptarr` data member of the `Array` class template represents a pointer to an array. This pointer is specified as a `Tarr` type (**template type parameter**). The actual type of `Tarr` will be determined at compile time.

To generate a specific class from a class template, an object must be instantiated using the template name followed by the actual template arguments enclosed in angle brackets. For example, three different classes can be generated from the `Array` class template using the following declarations:

```
Array<double> a1;        //instances of the Array class template
Array<int> a2;
Array<Circuit> a3;
```

The `a1`, `a2`, and `a3` objects are instantiated from three different classes. These classes are generated at compile time from the same `Array` class template. When generating these classes, the compiler substitutes the `Tarr` template type parameter in each class with the ***double***, ***int***, and `Circuit` types, respectively. Note that `Circuit` represents a user-defined type.

10.1.1 Template Parameters

There are three forms of template parameters:

- Type parameters
- Non-type parameters
- Template parameters

A **type parameter** defines a type identifier. When instantiating a template class, a specific data type listed in the template argument list will substitute for the type identifier. Note that either the ***class*** keyword, or the ***typename*** keyword must precede a template type parameter in a template parameter list. There is no difference between these two keywords when declaring template type parameters. The following example demonstrates declarations of two class templates with type parameters:

```
template<class T1, class T2, class T3> class X ;
template<typename A, typename B> class Y ;
```

When instantiating objects from the X and Y class templates, type identifiers (`T1`, `T2`, `T3`, A, and B) will be substituted with specific data types. For example,

```
X<int, float, int> x1;      //T1=int, T2=float, T3=int
Y<char, int> y1;            //A=char, B=int
Y<int, double*> y2;         //A=int, B=double*
```

instantiates three objects named `x1`, `y1`, and `y2` from the X and Y class templates.

A **non-type parameter** can be one of the following types:

- Integral type (***char***, ***int***, ***bool***)
- Enumeration type

- Reference to object or function
- Pointer to object, function, or member

A **non-type parameter** *cannot* be one of the following types:

- Floating point type (*float, double*)
- Class type
- *void*

Some examples of correct and incorrect declarations of class templates with non-type parameters are demonstrated in the following code segment:

```
template<int i, char c, bool b> class X;        //CORRECT
template<float *fp, double &dr> class Y;        //CORRECT
template<Circuit cr> class Z; //ERROR; cannot be a class type
template<double d> class Q;    //ERROR; cannot be floating point type
```

A non-type parameter is treated and processed as a constant. A non-type template argument must therefore be a constant expression, as shown in the following example:

```
const int a = 4;
X<a,'C',true> obj; //Non-type template arguments are constants.
```

A template parameter may have a **default argument**. The default template argument is specified after the = operator in the template parameter declaration. Any form of template parameters (type or non-type) can have default arguments. The following is an example of the Array class template, in which template parameters have default arguments:

```
template<class Tarr=float, int n=10> class Array { /* Body */ };
```

The Tarr type template parameter and n non-type template parameter have default arguments—*float* and 10 respectively. When using this template to generate specific classes, therefore, one or both arguments can be optional. The following code segment demonstrates valid and invalid statements used to instantiate objects of the previously defined Array class template:

```
Array< > ar1;          //Valid; same as: Array<float, 10> ar1;
Array ar2;             //Syntax Error; missing < >
Array<int, 50> ar3;    //Valid
Array<char> ar4;       //Valid; same as: Array<char,10> ar4;
Array<20> ar5;         //Invalid; missing type template argument
```

The default template arguments may be specified in a declaration or definition of a class template. These arguments, however, cannot be specified in the parameter list of a class template's member definition.

 TIP: It is good programming practice to use a non-type template parameter with a default argument (whenever possible) to specify the size of an array class template. This eliminates the run-time overhead when using **new** to dynamically allocate memory, and protects against a fatal run-time error when **new** fails to allocate memory.

10.1.2 Member Functions of Class Templates

The member function of a class template is treated as a function template. This function can be defined inside or outside the body of the class template. When defining a member function outside the body of the class template, the template header must precede the definition of the member function. In Program Example 10.1, PROG10_1 demonstrates a class template with member functions defined inside, as well as outside, the body of the class template.

PROGRAM EXAMPLE 10.1: PROG10_1

```
1   //PROG10_1: Program demonstrates a class template.
2   #include <iostream>
3   using namespace std;
4
5   template<class Tarr>          //template header
6   class Array {                 //class template definition
7   private:
8     Tarr *ptarr;        //pointer to array
9     int n;              //number of array elements
10  public:
11    Array(int x=20);
12    ~Array() { delete [] ptarr; }
13    void getValues();
14    void print();
15  };
16  template<class Tarr>                //template header
17  Array<Tarr>::Array(int x)           //constructor
18  {
```

```
19    n=x>0?x:20;              //Initializes size of the array
20    ptarr=new Tarr[n];       //Allocates memory dynamically
21    if(!ptarr)
22    {
23        cout<<"Memory Allocation Error!";
24        exit(1);
25    }
26    for(int i=0;i<n;i++)      //Initializes array
27        ptarr[i]=0;
28 }
29 template<class Tarr>        //template header
30 void Array<Tarr>::getValues()    //Obtains values from the user
31 {                               //and stores into the array
32    for(int i=0;i<n;i++)
33    {
34        cout<<"\tEnter value "<<(i+1)<<": ";
35        cin>>ptarr[i];
36    }
37 }
38 template<class Tarr>        //template header
39 void Array<Tarr>::print()   //Displays values of the
40 {                               //array elements
41    cout<<"\nArray elements =>"<<endl;
42    for(int i=0;i<n;i++)
43    {
44        cout<<"\tArray["<<i<<"]="<<ptarr[i]<<endl;
45    }
46 }
47
48 int main()
49 {
50    Array<int> intArr(4);
51    Array<char> chArr(5);
```

```
52    cout<<"Integer values =>\n";
53    intArr.getValues();
54    intArr.print();
55    cout<<"\nCharacter values =>\n";
56    chArr.getValues();
57    chArr.print();
58    return 0;
59 }
```

The `Array` class template uses a generic `Tarr` type (type template parameter) to specify the type of array that is accessed through a `ptarr` pointer (line 8). This class template contains four member functions: a constructor, a destructor, and the `getValues()` and `print()` functions. Note that the constructor, and the `getValues()` and `print()` functions have definitions outside the class template; therefore, the template header precedes each function (lines 16, 29, and 38). The destructor function is defined inside the class template (line 12) and is not preceded by the template header. The constructor function first dynamically allocates an array based on the user's input and assigns the address of the dynamic array to `ptarr` (line 20). It then uses `ptarr` to initialize the array to 0s (line 27). The destructor function frees dynamically allocated memory—i.e., deletes the array from the heap (line 12). The `getValues()` template function obtains values from the user and stores them in the array (lines 29–37), while `print()` displays these values (lines 38–46) .

The ***main()*** function creates two instances of the `Array` class template (lines 50 and 51). When instantiating from the class template, the compiler first generates two template classes and replaces `Tarr` in each class with ***int*** and ***char***, respectively. It then automatically invokes constructor functions of both template classes to construct objects named `intArr` and `chArr`. These objects are used to invoke member template functions `getValues()` (lines 53 and 56) and `print()` (lines 54 and 57). A sample run of PROG10_1 is shown in Figure 10.2.

```
                    Integer values =>
                            Enter value 1: 43
                            Enter value 2: 16
                            Enter value 3: 101
                            Enter value 4: 7

                    Array elements =>
                            Array[0]=43
                            Array[1]=16
                            Array[2]=101
                            Array[3]=7

                    Character values =>
                            Enter value 1: T
                            Enter value 2: E
                            Enter value 3: M
                            Enter value 4: P
                            Enter value 5: L

                    Array elements =>
                            Array[0]=T
                            Array[1]=E
                            Array[2]=M
                            Array[3]=P
                            Array[4]=L
```

Figure 10.2 *Sample run of PROG10_1.*

One class template is used in PROG10_1 to generate two classes for an integer and character array, respectively (code reusability is promoted). Note that the Array class template can be used to process any type of array. When instantiating objects from the Array class template, the compiler (not programmer) automatically generates code (a class definition) for a specific array type.

NOTE: Every member function of a class template is treated as a function template and must be preceded by the template header when defined outside its class template.

10.1.3 Using Friends and Static Members with Class Templates

A class template can have friends (*friend* functions and *friend* classes) as well as *static* members (*static* data members and *static* member functions).

There are several types of relationships between class templates and friends. The following functions/classes can be used as friends of a template class:

- Global function
- Member function of a non-template class
- Member function of a template class
- Non-template class
- Template class

Consider the following example of a class template declaration:

```
template<class Tf>
class Probe {
    friend void fun1();                        //friendship #1
    friend void Test1::fun2();                 //friendship #2
    friend void fun3(Probe<Tf> &);             //friendship #3
    friend void Test2<Tf>::fun4(Probe<Tf> &);  //friendship #4
    friend class Test3;                        //friendship #5
    friend class Test4<Tf>;                    //friendship #6
    //members of the Probe class template
};
```

The Probe class template has four *friend* functions and two *friend* classes with the following relationships according to their declarations:

1. fun1() is a *friend* function of every template class that is instantiated from the Probe class template.

2. fun2() is a member function of the Test1 class and also a *friend* function of every template class that is instantiated from Probe.

3. fun3() is a *friend* function of a template class that is instantiated from Probe for a particular type. For example, fun3(Probe<int> &) is a *friend* of Probe<int> and is not a *friend* of Probe<float>, Probe<double>, or Probe<char>.

4. `fun4()` is a member function of the `Test2` template class and also a *friend* function of a template class that is instantiated from `Probe` for a particular type. For example, `Test2<int>::fun4(Probe<int>&)` is a member function of the `Test2<int>` template class and a *friend* function of `Probe<int>`.

5. `Test3` is a *friend* class of every template class generated from `Probe`. Every member function of `Test3`, therefore, is also a *friend* function of every template class instantiated from `Probe`.

6. A template class instantiated from the `Test4` class template for a particular type is a *friend* class of a template class generated from `Probe` for this type. For example, `Test4<double>` is a *friend* class of `Probe<double>`.

A class template can contain *static* data members and *static* member functions, as shown in the following example:

```
template<class Ttype>
class Test {
public:
        static Ttype tot;
        static void fun();
        //non-static members
};
        //static data member definition
template<class Ttype> Ttype Test<Ttype>::tot=0;
        //static member function definition
template<class Ttype>
void Test<Ttype>::fun()
{
        cout<<tot<<endl;
}
```

Every template class instantiated from a class template that contains *static* members will have its own copy of all *static* members. Each template class instantiated from `Test`, therefore, will have its own copies of `tot` and `fun()`. Note that when defining *static* members that use generic types, the template header with a list of all type parameters must precede the *static* member's definition. The following code segment demonstrates a use of *static* members of the `Test` class template outside the class template's definition—i.e., in *main()*, or any other non-member function of `Test`.

```
Test<int>::tot=13;
```

```
Test<float>::tot=7.9;
Test<int>::fun();              //prints 13
Test<float>::fun();            //prints 7.9
```

Note that when using a *static* member outside of its class template definition, the class template name, followed by the actual data type(s) and the scope resolution operator (::), must precede the *static* member's name.

10.1.4 Using the *void* Pointer

Note that a *void* pointer is a generic pointer type. It can point to an object of any type. This type of a pointer, therefore, can be used as an alternative to a generic type parameter and eliminate the need for function templates or class templates. In Program Example 10.2, PROG10_2 is a modified version of PROG10_1, which uses a generic *void* pointer as an alternative to the Tarr type template parameter.

PROGRAM EXAMPLE 10.2: PROG10_2

```
1   //PROG10_2: Program demonstrates a void pointer as an
2   //          alternative to templates.
3   #include <iostream>
4   using namespace std;
5   const int size1=4;
6   const int size2=5;
7
8   typedef void *vptr;    //defines vptr as a void pointer
9
10  class Array {
11  private:
12     vptr *ptarr;        //ptarr can point to an array of any type
13     int n;              //number of array elements
14  public:
15     Array(int x=20);
16     ~Array() { delete [] ptarr; }
17     void getValues(vptr val, int i);
18     vptr print(int i);
19  };
```

```
20  Array::Array(int x)            //constructor
21  {
22      n=x>0?x:20;                //Initializes size of the array
23      ptarr=new vptr[n];         //Allocates memory dynamically
24      if(!ptarr)
25      {
26          cout<<"Memory Allocation Error!";
27          exit(1);
28      }
29      for(int i=0;i<n;i++)       //Initializes array
30          ptarr[i]=0;
31  }
32  void Array::getValues(vptr val, int i)//Obtains values from
33  {                              //the user and stores into the array
34      ptarr[i]=val;
35  }
36  vptr Array::print(int i)             //Displays values of the
37  {                                    //array elements
38      return ptarr[i];
39  }
40
41  int main()
42  {
43      Array intArr(size1);
44      Array chArr(size2);
45      int x, i;
46      char c;
47
48      cout<<"Integer values =>\n";
49      for(i=0; i<size1; i++)
50      {
51          cout<<"Enter value "<<(i+1)<<" : ";
52          cin>>x;
```

```
53        intArr.getValues((int*)x, i);   //cast void pointer as int*
54      }
55      cout<<"\nArray elements =>"<<endl;
56      for(i=0;i<size1;i++)
57      {
58          cout<<"\tArray["<<i<<"]="<<(int)intArr.print(i)<<endl;
59      }
60
61      cout<<"\nCharacter values =>\n";
62      for(i=0; i<size2; i++)
63      {
64          cout<<"Enter value "<<(i+1)<<" : ";
65          cin>>c;
66          chArr.getValues((char*)c, i); //cast void pointer as char*
67      }
68      cout<<"\nArray elements =>"<<endl;
69      for(i=0;i<size2;i++)
70      {
71          cout<<"\tArray["<<i<<"]="<<(char)chArr.print(i)<<endl;
72      }
73      return 0;
74 }
```

This program first uses the *typedef* statement to define vptr as a *void ** pointer type (line 8). The program then uses vptr within the Array class to specify:

- The type of the ptarr data member (line 12)
- The type of the val parameter of the getValues() function (line 17)
- The return type of the print() function (line 18)

 NOTE: Array is a regular class in PROG10_2 (not a class template as it is in PROG10_1). Its member functions, therefore, are regular non-template functions.

The *main()* function in PROG10_2 is similar to the *main()* function in PROG10_1 with the following exceptions:

- intArr and chArr are instantiated as regular class objects (lines 43 and 44)

- Type cast *void* pointer as *int** and *char** when calling getValues() in lines 53 and 66

- Type cast the value returned by print() as *int* and *char* (lines 58 and 71)

PROG10_2 produces the same output as PROG10_1, as shown in Figure 10.2. PROG10_2 demonstrates that classes with generic *void* pointers can substitute class templates in certain cases. Class templates, however, are more powerful and can be used in a much wider range of programming problems.

NOTE: • A *void* pointer cannot be dereferenced in order to access the current value that is referenced by the pointer.

• A *void* pointer can be assigned to a *non-void* pointer, but first its type has to be changed by using an explicit type cast to match the type of the pointer to which it will be assigned.

10.2 TEMPLATES AND INHERITANCE

Inheritance can be implemented with class templates in the same way as with regular non-template classes. Class templates can be organized into an inheritance hierarchy of classes, as follows:

- A class template can be derived from a template or non-template class.

- A class template can serve as a base class from which a template or non-template class can be derived.

In Program Example 10.3, PROG10_3 demonstrates class templates and inheritance.

PROGRAM EXAMPLE 10.3: PROG10_3

```
1   //PROG10_3: Program demonstrates templates and inheritance.
2   #include <iostream>
3   using namespace std;
4
5   //********** CLASS TEMPLATE AS A BASE CLASS **********
6   template<class Tarr>
7   class Array {
8   protected:
9     Tarr * ptarr;        //pointer to array
10    int n;               //number of array elements
11  public:
12    Array(int x=20);                    //base constructor
```

```
13    ~Array() { delete [] ptarr; }      //base destructor
14    void getValues();
15    void print();
16  };
17  template<class Tarr>
18  Array<Tarr>::Array(int x)             //base constructor definition
19  {
20    n=x>0?x:20;
21    ptarr=new Tarr[n];
22    if(!ptarr)
23    {
24       cout<<"Memory Allocation Error!";
25       exit(1);
26    }
27    for(int i=0; i<n; i++)
28       ptarr[i]=0;
29  }
30  template<class Tarr>
31  void Array<Tarr>::getValues()        //Gets values from the user
32  {
33    for(int i=0;i<n;i++)
34    {
35       cout<<"\tEnter value "<<(i+1)<<": ";
36       cin>>ptarr[i];
37    }
38  }
39  template<class Tarr>
40  void Array<Tarr>::print()            //Displays values
41  {
42    cout<<"\nArray elements =>"<<endl;
43    for(int i=0;i<n;i++)
44    {
45       cout<<"\tArray["<<i<<"]="<<ptarr[i]<<endl;
```

```
46     }
47 }
48 //********** CLASS TEMPLATE AS A DERIVED CLASS **********
49 template<class Tarr>
50 class Sorting:public Array<Tarr> {
51 public:
52    Sorting(int a):Array<Tarr>(a){}      //derived constructor
53    void sort();
54 };
55 template<class Tarr>
56 void Sorting<Tarr>::sort()       //Sorts array in ascending order
57 {
58    Tarr temp;
59    for(int i=1;i<n;i++)
60       for(int j=0;j<n-1;j++)
61          if(ptarr[j]>ptarr[j+1])
62          {
63             temp=ptarr[j];
64             ptarr[j]=ptarr[j+1];
65             ptarr[j+1]=temp;
66          }
67 }
68 int main()
69 {
70    Sorting<int> intArr(4);
71    Sorting<char> chArr(5);
72    cout<<"Integer values =>\n";
73    intArr.getValues();
74    intArr.sort();
75    intArr.print();
76    cout<<"\nCharacter values =>\n";
77    chArr.getValues();
78    chArr.sort();
```

```
79    chArr.print();
80    return 0;
81 }
```

This program uses the Array class template from PROG10_1 as a base class in which inheritance begins. The only modification made in Array is that its data members are changed to **protected** to make these members inheritable. A second class template named Sorting is derived from Array (line 50). The Sorting derived class template inherits all data members and member functions from Array and also defines its own member function named sort() (lines 55–67). The sort() function template from Sorting can be used to sort an array of any type. Notice that Sorting also has a constructor (line 52), the only purpose of which is to pass an argument to the Array base constructor when constructing derived objects.

The **main()** function instantiates two objects of the Sorting derived class template for **int** and **char** types, respectively (lines 70 and 71). It then uses these objects to invoke getValues(), sort(), and print() member template functions (lines 73–75 and 77–79).

A sample run of PROG10_3 is shown in Figure 10.3.

```
            Integer values =>
                    Enter value 1: 89
                    Enter value 2: 15
                    Enter value 3: 3
                    Enter value 4: 56


        Array elements =>
                Array[0]=3
                Array[1]=15
                Array[2]=56
                Array[3]=89


        Character values =>
                    Enter value 1: S
                    Enter value 2: G
                    Enter value 3: A
                    Enter value 4: D
                    Enter value 5: J


        Array elements =>
                Array[0]=A
                Array[1]=D
                Array[2]=G
                Array[3]=J
                Array[4]=S
```

Figure 10.3 *Sample run of PROG10_3.*

10.3 CONTAINERS AND ITERATORS

A **container** is an object (data structure) that stores other objects. Containers are instances of **container classes**. C++ uses class templates to generate container classes. Template type parameters can be used to specify types of objects contained in a container.

C++ provides the following types of containers:

- Sequence containers (**vector, list, deque, ...**)
- Associative containers (**set, multiset, map, multimap**)
- Special containers (**basic_string, valarray, bitset, ...**)

10.3.1 Sequence Containers

A **sequence container** is a container that organizes a finite set of objects of the same type into an ordinal sequence. C++ provides three basic types of sequence containers named **vector, list**, and **deque.** Sequence containers are similar to arrays, in which each element has a specific position (a location within an array or container) that is independent of its value.

One of the most commonly used sequence containers is **vector** (defined in the **vector** header file). The **vector** class template defines a data structure in which objects (container's elements) are stored in contiguous memory locations. Each element of a **vector** container has a unique index (subscript) that is used to access the element. The subscript operator ([ ]) is overloaded relative to **vector**, therefore the same array notation that is used to access elements of a regular C/C++ array can be used to access elements of a **vector** container. Program Example 10.4 demonstrates **vector** containers.

PROGRAM EXAMPLE 10.4: PROG10_4

```
1   //PROG10_4: Program demonstrates vector containers.
2   #include <iostream>
3   #include <vector>
4   using namespace std;
5
6   int main()
7   {
8       vector<int> vint;    //Instantiates a vector container
9       cout<<"Number of objects in container vint = "<<vint.size();
```

```
10    cout<<"\n***Pushing integers into vint***"<<endl;
11    for(int i=0; i<9; i++)
12        vint.push_back(i+1);        //Pushes an integer into container
13    cout<<"Number of objects in container vint = "<<vint.size();
14    cout<<"\n***Deleting an object from vint***"<<endl;
15    vint.erase(vint.begin()+3);
16    cout<<"Objects stored in vint =>"<<endl;
17    for(int j=0; j<vint.size();j++)
18        cout<<vint[j]<<' ';
19
20    vector<char *> vstr; //Instantiates a vector container
21    char *prog[4]={"FORTRAN","PASCAL","C++","JAVA"};
22    char *c="C LANGUAGE";
23    cout<<"\n\n***Pushing strings into container vstr***"<<endl;
24    for(int k=0; k<4; k++)
25        vstr.push_back(prog[k]);    //Pushes strings into container
26    cout<<"Number of objects in container vstr = "<<vstr.size();
27    cout<<"\n***Inserting an object into vstr***"<<endl;
28    vstr.insert(vstr.end()-2,c);
29    cout<<"Objects stored in vstr =>"<<endl;
30    for(int l=0; l<vstr.size();l++)
31        cout<<vstr[l]<<", ";
32    return 0;
33 }
```

PROG10_4 instantiates two containers of the *vector* class template (lines 8 and 20). These vint and vstr containers are used to store integer numbers and strings, respectively. The *main()* function uses vint and vstr to invoke the following member functions (function templates) of *vector*:

- **size()** — To get the number of elements stored in a container (lines 9, 13, 17, 26, and 30)

- **push_back()** — To insert an object to the end of a container (lines 12 and 25)

- **erase()** — To remove an object from a container (line 15)

- **insert()** — To insert an object into a container (line 28)

Integer numbers from 1 to 9 are first pushed into `vint` (line 12). The fourth element of `vint` (number 4) is then removed from this container (line 15), and all objects (integer numbers) contained in `vint` are displayed (line 18). Notice that the expression in line 15—`vint.begin()+3`—specifies the fourth element of `vint` (same as `vint[3]`). The `vstr` container first stores four strings (line 25). A new string is then inserted into `vstr` at the location specified as `vstr.end()-2`—that is, before the second-to-last element in `vstr` (line 28). At the end, the content of the `vstr` container is displayed (line 31).

The output produced by PROG10_4 is shown in Figure 10.4.

```
          Number of objects in container vint = 0
          ***Pushing integers into vint***
          Number of objects in container vint = 9
          ***Deleting an object from vint***
          Objects stored in vint =>
          1 2 3 5 6 7 8 9


          ***Pushing strings into container vstr***
          Number of objects in container vstr = 4
          ***Inserting an object into vstr***
          Objects stored in vstr =>
          FORTRAN, PASCAL, C LANGUAGE, C++, JAVA,
```

Figure 10.4 *Output produced by PROG10_4.*

The *vector* class template contains member functions (some of them are demonstrated in PROG10_4) that have equivalent member functions in most of other container classes, such as *list, queue, set, map*, etc. Commonly used member functions of the *vector* class template are shown in Table 10.1.

Please note that the *vector* class template also contains constructors, a destructor, operator functions, and iterators (discussed in Section 10.3.3), in addition to the member functions shown in Table 10.1. Sequence containers control allocation and deallocation of objects stored in these containers through constructor and destructor functions, as well as member functions that perform insert and delete operations.

Table 10.1 Member Functions of the vector Class Template

Function	Description
assign()	Erases all elements and then inserts new elements (2 versions)
at()	Checks the range (0 to *size* -1)
back()	Returns a reference to the last element
capacity()	Returns the size of the allocated storage
empty()	Returns *true* if the *size* is zero
erase()	Removes element(s) from the container (2 versions)
front()	Returns a reference to the first element
insert()	Inserts new element(s) (2 versions)
max_size()	Returns the size of the largest possible vector
pop_back()	Removes the last element
push_back()	Inserts a new element at the end
reserve()	Increases the capacity of the storage
resize()	Changes the size of the container
size()	Returns the number of elements
swap()	Swaps elements

When using the three basic sequence containers (*vector*, *list*, and *deque*), different complexity and efficiency tradeoffs are considered. These containers should be used as follows:

- *Vector* should be used by default.
- *List* should be used when insertions or deletions frequently occur in the middle of the sequence.
- *Deque* should be used when insertions or deletions frequently take place at the beginning or at the end of the sequence.

 NOTE: A container of *vector* type can dynamically change its size.

10.3.2 Associative Containers

An **associative container** is a container that provides means for fast storage and retrieval of data based on **keys** (also called *search keys*). C++ provides four basic types of associative containers named *set, multiset, map,* and *multimap.*

Keys are values of a specific type that are maintained in sorted order within an associative container. The *map* and *multimap* class templates are used to instantiate containers that provide methods for storing and manipulating values associated with keys. Unlike *map* and *multimap* containers that store and manipulate pairs of values (keys and values associated with keys), *set* and *multiset* containers store and manipulate keys only. A summary of the main characteristics of four basic types of associative containers is shown in Table 10.2

The four basic types of associative containers are defined in the *map, multimap, set,* and *multiset* header file, respectively. It is beyond the scope of this text to discuss and demonstrate all types of containers that C++ provides, as well as operations that can be performed with objects/data stored in these containers. Please note that the next section will demonstrate a *map* container and some methods that this type of associative container provides. A list of commonly used types of containers is provided in Appendix D.

Table 10.2 Four Basic Types of Associative Containers

Container type	Description
map	• Used for fast storage and retrieval of values based on keys • A single value can only be associated with each key • Supports unique keys (duplicate keys are not allowed)
multimap	• Used for fast storage and retrieval of values based on keys • Multiple values can be associated with a single key • Duplicate keys are allowed
set	• Used for fast storage and retrieval of keys • Supports unique keys (duplicate keys are not allowed)
multiset	• Used for fast storage and retrieval of keys • Duplicate keys are allowed

10.3.3 Iterators

An *iterator* is an object that moves through a container that contains other objects. Iterators are used to access objects stored in a container (one at a time), whether or not the container provides methods of accessing its objects directly. Iterators are also called *smart* and *safe pointers*. They usually perform operations similar to the operations that pointers perform. Iterators can use the same operators and notation that pointers use.

Iterators are instances of **iterator class templates**. C++ provides different types of iterators and a variety of classes that can be used to instantiate iterators. Basic operations that can be performed using iterators include

- Positioning the iterator at a specific location within the container
- Checking whether an object exists at the current location
- Getting a value of the object stored at the current location
- Changing the value of the object at the current location
- Deleting the current object
- Inserting a new object before the current object
- Moving the iterator to the next location within the container

In Program Example 10.5, PROG10_5 demonstrates iterators that are used to access objects stored in an associative *map* container. The container stores pairs of values representing colors of resistor color bands and their corresponding codes (integer numbers). Each color has a unique code. Color codes serve as **keys** (key values) in PROG10_5. Remember that duplicate keys are not allowed in *map* containers.

PROGRAM EXAMPLE 10.5: PROG10_5

```
1   //PROG10_5: Program demonstrates iterators and associative
2   //          containers of map type.
3   #include <iostream>
4   #include <map>
5   using namespace std;
6
7   typedef map<int,char *> Rband;    //map container type definition
8   void cbLoad(Rband &);             //Loads the container
9   void cbDisplay(Rband &);      //Displays the container's contents
10  void cbSearch(Rband &);       //Searches for an object in the container
11
12  int main()
13  {
14      Rband res;
15      cbLoad(res);
16      cout<<res.size()<<" objects in container\n\n";
```

```
17    cbDisplay(res);
18    cbSearch(res);
19    return 0;
20 }
21
22 void cbLoad(Rband & r)   //Loads colors and color codes of resistor
23 {                                   //color bands
24    r[0]="BLACK";
25    r[1]="BROWN";
26    r[2]="RED";
27    r[3]="ORANGE";
28    r[4]="YELLOW";
29    r[5]="GREEN";
30    r[6]="BLUE";
31    r[7]="VIOLET";
32    r[8]="GRAY";
33    r[9]="WHITE";
34 }
35 void cbDisplay(Rband & r)     //Displays colors and their codes
36 {
37    Rband::iterator cit;      //Instantiates an iterator
38    cout<<"  ***Resistor color bands***"<<endl;
39    cout<<"\tCode    Color"<<endl;
40    //Uses the iterator to access objects in the container
41    for(cit=r.begin(); cit!=r.end(); cit++)
42       cout<<'\t'<<cit->first<<"   => "<<cit->second<<endl;
43 }
44 void cbSearch(Rband & r)     //Searches for a color code
45 {
46    int x;
47    Rband::iterator cit;         //Instantiates an iterator
48    cout<<"\n   ***Searching for a band***"<<endl;
49    cout<<"Enter a color code => ";
```

```
50    cin>>x;
51    //Uses the iterator to access objects in the container
52    for(cit=r.begin(); cit!=r.end(); cit++)
53        if(cit->first==x)
54            cout<<"The color is "<<cit->second<<endl;
55 }
```

This program defines a ***map*** container type named `Rband` (line 7). `Rband`-type containers can store pairs of integer values and their corresponding string values, where integer values represent color codes and strings represent colors. The ***main()*** function first instantiates an `Rband` container named `res` (line 14). It then invokes the `cbLoad()` function to load values into the `res` container (line 15). ***main()*** next invokes `cbDisplay()` and `cbSearch()` functions (lines 17 and 18) to display the colors and their codes, as well as to search for a specific color code based on the user's input.

The `cbLoad()` function (lines 22–34) uses array notation to access elements of a container passed to the function. Values enclosed in square brackets ([ ]) are keys, while the values associated with keys are assigned by using the = operator. Notice that in this program example, keys are integer values 0 through 9 representing color codes. Keys, however, can be values of another data type as well. Strings representing colors of resistor color bands in PROG10_5, for example, can serve as keys. In this case, the expression `r[0]="BLACK"` should be changed to `r["BLACK"]=0`, `r[1]= "BROWN"` should be changed to `r["BROWN"]=1` and so forth. When loading a ***map*** container (in addition to using array notation), the ***insert()*** member function can also be used.

The `cbDisplay()` and `cbSearch()` functions instantiate an iterator named `cit` that can work on `Rband`-type containers (lines 37 and 47). The `cit` iterator serves as a loop control variable in both functions (lines 41 and 52). It is initially positioned at the location of the first object in the `r` container by using the expression `cit=r.begin()`. The iterator is then moved through a container—i.e., `cit++`—locating one object at a time until the last object is reached (`cit!=r.end()`). While pointing to each object, the `cit` iterator is used to access values stored in the object (lines 42, 53, and 54). Note that the `cit->first` expression is used to access a key value (a color code), while the `cit->second` expression is used to access the value associated with the key value (a color). The output produced by PROG10_5 is shown in Figure 10.5.

The mechanism of accessing values stored in containers through iterators is similar to the mechanism of accessing members of data structures via pointers. In both cases, the *member selection via pointer* operator (->) can be used.

The ***map*** class template demonstrated in PROG10_5 has member functions equivalent to the member functions of the ***vector*** class template shown in Table 10.1. ***map*** containers can be used to simulate functions in math ($y=f(x)$), where each x value has a corresponding y value. The x values can be used as keys. Remember that keys are maintained in sorted order within a container.

```
10 objects in container

     ***Resistor color bands***
        Code          Color
         0            BLACK
         1            BROWN
         2            RED
         3            ORANGE
         4            YELLOW
         5            GREEN
         6            BLUE
         7            VIOLET
         8            GRAY
         9            WHITE

    ***Searching for a color band***
Enter a color code => 3
The color is ORANGE
```

Figure 10.5 *Output produced by PROG10_5.*

10.4 STANDARD TEMPLATE LIBRARY (STL)

The **Standard Template Library (STL)** is a collection of class templates and function templates that is supported by the C++ standard. The STL is part of the C++ language; therefore, every standard C++ compiler must support this library.

The STL promotes code reusability and also provides a powerful tool for programmers. They can find numerous data structures and algorithms in the STL that can be used when solving a broad variety of programming problems. These data structures and algorithms are accurate and efficient. When designing their own templates and algorithms, programmers have to spend a significant amount of time on a program's testing, to ensure that their algorithms are correct and efficient. By using the STL components, the time spent on testing is significantly reduced.

C++ supports **generic programming** by providing both the template mechanism and the STL that contains generic algorithms and data structures that can be used as containers for data of any type.

The STL components can be categorized in the following five groups:

- Containers
- Iterators
- Function objects
- Adaptors
- Algorithms

Function objects provide a mechanism of passing functions as parameters to other functions (algorithms).

An **adaptor** is an instance of an **adaptor class**. The STL provides a variety of adaptor classes that can be used with containers, iterators, and function objects. Adaptors provide an interface for containers. Different types of adaptors applied to a specific container allow the objects contained in the container to be organized into different data structures. The three standard types of container adaptors are the following:

1. The **stack** adaptor class (defined in the **stack** header file) enables insertions in and deletions of objects from a container at one end only (also known as a **last-in-first-out** data structure).

2. The **queue** adaptor class (defined in the **queue** header file) enables insertions at the back end of a container and deletions of objects from the front end of the container (also known as a **first-in-first-out** data structure).

3. The **priority-queue** adaptor class (defined in the **queue** header file) enables insertions of data in sorted order into a container and deletions of data from the front end of the container (first-in-order-first-out).

Program Example 10.6 demonstrates the **stack** and **queue** container adaptors that are used with the **vector**, **deque**, and **list** containers.

PROGRAM EXAMPLE 10.6: PROG10_6

```
1   //PROG10_6: Program demonstrates container adaptors.
2   #include <iostream>
3   #include <vector>
4   #include <stack>
5   #include <list>
6   #include <queue>
```

```
7   using namespace std;
8
9   int main()
10  {
11     typedef vector<char> vchar; //vector container type
12     stack<int> dqStack;    //stack adaptor with a deque container
13     stack<char,vchar> vecStack;  //stack adaptor with a vector
14     char ad[]="CONTAINER ADAPTOR";
15     cout<<"*Using stack adaptor with deque and vector containers*";
16     cout<<"\nPushing values into containers ..."<<endl;
17     for(int i=0; i<10; i++)
18     {
19        dqStack.push((i+1)*2);
20        vecStack.push(ad[i]);
21     }
22     cout<<"Removing values from containers ..."<<endl;
23     cout<<"\ndeque container => ";
24     while(!dqStack.empty())
25     {
26        cout<<dqStack.top()<<' ';
27        dqStack.pop();
28     }
29     cout<<"\n\nvector container => ";
30     while(!vecStack.empty())
31     {
32        cout<<vecStack.top()<<' ';
33        vecStack.pop();
34     }
35     typedef list<double> lstf;      //list container type
36     queue <double,lstf> lstQueue;  //queue adaptor with a list
37     double values[5]={1.1,2.2,3.3,4.4,5.5};
38     cout<<"\n\n*Using queue adaptor with list container*"<<endl;
39     cout<<"Pushing values into container ..."<<endl;
```

```
40      for(int j=0;j<5;j++)
41      {
42          lstQueue.push(values[j]);
43      }
44      cout<<"Removing values from container ..."<<endl;
45      cout<<"\nlist container => ";
46      while(!lstQueue.empty())
47      {
48          cout<<lstQueue.front()<<' ';
49          lstQueue.pop();
50      }
51      return 0;
52 }
```

PROG10_6 instantiates three container adaptors as follows:

1. A **stack** adaptor named dqStack, used with a **deque** container (line 12)

2. A **stack** adaptor named vecStack, used with a **vector** container (line 13)

3. A **queue** adaptor named lstQueue, used with a **list** container (line 36)

Notice that, by default, a **stack** adaptor is implemented with a **deque** container; therefore, it is not necessary to specify the **deque** container type in the declaration of the dqStack adaptor in line 12. The program uses these adaptors to insert into (using **push()**) and remove (using **pop()**) values from the three containers (lines 19, 20, 27, 33, 42, and 49). The dqStack and vecStack **stack** adaptors use the **top()** member function to get a reference to the top object stored in the container, with which the adaptor is implemented. The top object is removed from the container using **pop()** (lines 26 and 32). Remember that a **stack** adaptor can insert or delete objects from one end of a container only. An object deleted from a container by using a **stack** adaptor is always the last object inserted into the container—i.e., values are removed from the container in the reverse order in which they were inserted into the container. For example, values inserted into a container using dqStack are even integer numbers from 2 to 20 (line 19). These values are removed from the container in the reverse order (20, 18, 16, ... , 4, 2).

Unlike a **stack** adaptor, a **queue** adaptor enables insertions at the back end of a container and deletions from the front end of the container. The lstQueue adaptor in PROG10_6 uses the **front()** member function to get a reference to the first object entered into its container (line 48). It then uses **pop()** to remove this object from the container (line 49). This process continues until all objects are removed from the container. The ***while*** loop condition (`!1stQueue.empty()`) in line 46 is ***false*** when the container is empty. The objects are removed from the container in the same order in which they were inserted into the container. PROG10_6 produces the output shown in Figure 10.6.

```
*Using stack adaptor with deque and vector containers *
Pushing values into containers …
Removing values from containers …

deque container => 20 18 16 14 12 10 8 6 4 2
vector container => R E N I A T N O C


*Using queue adaptor with list container*
Pushing values into container …
Removing values from container …

 list container => 1.1 2.2 3.3 4.4 5.5
```

Figure 10.6 *Output produced by PROG10_6.*

In addition to containers, iterators, function objects, and adaptors, the STL library also contains approximately 70 algorithms that are designed as non-member function templates. These function templates (algorithms) can be used with containers or regular C++ arrays.

An **algorithm** is a finite sequence of logical programming steps (program instructions) that are used to solve a specific programming problem. The STL provides numerous accurate and efficient algorithms to solve problems such as: sorting or merging values, searching, finding the largest or smallest value, performing numeric operations, and many others.

It is not possible to discuss and demonstrate all of the algorithms that the STL provides within the scope of this text. Some commonly used STL algorithms are demonstrated in Program Example 10.7. Please note that Appendix D contains a list of almost all of the STL algorithms, with a brief description of each algorithm.

PROGRAM EXAMPLE 10.7: PROG10_7

```
1  //PROG10_7: Program demonstrates generic STL algorithms
2  #include <iostream>
```

```
3   #include <algorithm>
4   #include <numeric>
5   using namespace std;
6
7   const int SIZE=10;
8   template <class T>
9   void print(T *p, int x)
10  {
11      for(int i=0;i<x;i++)
12          cout<<p[i]<<' ';
13  }
14  int main()
15  {
16      int x[SIZE]={9,8,7,6,5,4,3,2,1,0};
17      int y[SIZE]={23,25,21,26,24,29,20,27,28,22};
18      int z[SIZE];
19      char str[]="QAZJSKEDC";
20      int n=strlen(str);
21      sort(str,str+n);
22      cout<<"str after sorting =>\n\t";
23      print(str,n);
24      sort(x,x+5);
25      cout<<"\n\nx after sorting first 5 elements =>\n\t";
26      print(x,SIZE);
27      sort(y,y+SIZE);
28      cout<<"\n\ny after sorting =>\n\t";
29      print(y,SIZE);
30      merge(x,x+5,y,y+5,z);
31      cout<<"\n\nz after merging first 5 elements from x and y";
32      cout<<" =>\n\t";
33      print(z,SIZE);
34      int sum=accumulate(x,x+3,0);
35      cout<<"\n\nSum of first 3 numbers in x = "<<sum;
```

```
36    iter_swap(x+3,y+5);
37    cout<<"\n\ny after swapping y[5] and x[3] =>\n\t";
38    print(y,SIZE);
39    cout<<"\n\nx after swapping y[5] and x[3] =>\n\t";
40    print(x,SIZE);
41    const int *pm=max_element(z,z+SIZE);
42    cout<<"\n\nLargest number in z = "<<*pm;
43    cout<<"\n\n***SEARCHING***";
44    if(binary_search(str,str+n,'S'))
45       cout<<"\n\tLetter S is found in str";
46    else
47       cout<<"\n\tLetter S is NOT found in str";
48    if(binary_search(y,y+SIZE,0))
49       cout<<"\n\tNumber 0 is found in x";
50    else
51       cout<<"\n\tNumber 0 is NOT found in x";
52    return 0;
53 }
```

This program uses a user-defined *print()* function template (lines 8–13) to print values stored in an array, the type of which is defined as the T template type parameter. PROG10_7 also uses the following STL generic algorithms:

- *sort()* — (lines 21, 24, and 27) To sort elements of the str, x, and y arrays, respectively. The *sort( )* function template takes two arguments that specify the first and the last value of the segment of values to be sorted.

- *merge()* — (line 30) To merge two specified segments of elements of the x and y array and insert into the z array.

- *accumulate()* — (line 34) To compute the sum of all values within the specified segment of x and add the sum to the initial value passed as the last argument.

- *iter_swap()* — (line 36) To swap the elements of the x and y array.

- *max_element()* — (line 41) To get the largest value within the specified segment of the z array.

- *binary_search()* — (lines 44 and 48) To search for a specific value within the specified segment of the str and y array, respectively.

PROG10_7 produces the output shown in Figure 10.7.

```
str after sorting =>
          A C D E J K Q S Z
x after sorting first 5 elements =>
          5 6 7 8 9 4 3 2 1 0
y after sorting =>
          20 21 22 23 24 25 26 27 28 29
z after merging first 5 elements from x and y =>
          5 6 7 8 9 20 21 22 23 24
Sum of first 3 numbers in x = 18


y after swapping y[5] and x[3] =>
          20 21 22 23 24 8 26 27 28 29
x after swapping y[5] and x[3] =>
          5 6 7 25 9 4 3 2 1 0
Largest number in z = 24


***SEARCHING***
          Letter S is found in str
          Number 0 is not found in x
```

Figure 10.7 *Output produced by PROG10_7.*

Notice that PROG10_7 uses the STL generic algorithms (function templates) on *char* and *int* arrays. These algorithms can also be used to manipulate container objects. Iterators should be used with containers, in this case, to specify locations of the objects within a container to be processed by a specific algorithm.

SUMMARY

1. A class template serves as a class outline, from which specific classes are generated at compile time. Class templates promote code reusability.

2. There are three forms of template parameters: type parameters, non-type parameters, and template parameters. Every template parameter may have a default argument.

3. A type parameter defines a type identifier, which will be substituted with the actual data type when instantiating objects from a class template.

4. A non-type parameter is treated and processed as a constant.

5. A member function of a class template is treated as a function template and can be defined inside or outside the body of the class template.

6. A class template can have *friend* functions and classes. A global function, as well as a member function of a non-template or template class, can be a *friend* function of a class template. Template and non-template classes can be *friend* classes of a class template.

7. A class template can contain *static* data members and *static* member functions. Every template class instantiated from a class template will have its own copy of all *static* members.

8. Classes with generic *void* pointers can substitute class templates in certain cases. A *void* pointer cannot be dereferenced in order to access the current value that is referenced by the pointer.

9. Inheritance can be implemented with class templates in the same way as regular non-template classes. A class template can be a base class for a template or non-template class, or it can be derived from a template or non-template class.

10. A container is an object that stores other objects. C++ provides sequence, associative, and special-type containers.

11. A sequence container organizes a finite set of objects of the same type into an ordinal sequence (similar to arrays). C++ provides three basic types of sequence containers, named *vector*, *list*, and *deque*. A *vector* container (a default sequence container) can change its size dynamically.

12. An associative container provides means for fast storage and retrieval of data based on search keys. C++ provides four basic types of associative containers named *set*, *multiset*, *map*, and *multimap*.

13. An iterator is an object that moves through a container that contains other objects. Iterators (*smart* and *safe* pointers) usually perform operations similar to the operations that pointers perform. An iterator is an instance of an iterator class template.

14. The Standard Template Library (STL) is a collection of class templates and function templates that is supported by the C++ standard. The STL components are containers, iterators, function objects, adaptors, and algorithms.

15. An adaptor provides an interface for a container. The three standard types of adaptors are **stack** (last-object-in-first-object-out), **queue** (first-object-in-first-object-out), and **priority_queue** (first-object-in-order-first-object-out).

16. The STL provides numerous built-in algorithms (function templates) that can be used to sort, search, and merge objects stored in containers and regular arrays.

EXERCISES

Identify and correct the errors in the code segments in Exercises 10.1 through 10.10.

10.1
```
template<Tc, int n=10>
class Circuit {
    //body of the template
};
```

10.2
```
template<class T=int>
class Array {
        //body of the template
};
//Instantiating objects from the Array class template
    Array a;
    Array<double> b;
    Array<> c;
    Array<int,float> d;
    Array<float*> e;
```

10.3
```
template<float, char>
class X {
   //body of the template
};
```

10.4 `template<X, void> class Y;`

10.5
```
template<class T>
class X {
   friend int fun1(int);
   friend class Y;
   friend void Z<T1>fun2();
};
```

10.6
```
template<class T>
class X {
public:
   static void fun();
   //non-static members;
};
void X::fun()
{
   //body of the function
}
```

10.7
```
template<class Ttype>
class X {
   static Ttype num;
   //non-static members
};
Ttype X::num=0;
```

10.8
```
template<class T> class Base;
template<class T>
```

```
class Derived : public Base {
  //body of the derived class template
};
```

10.9
```
vector v;
v.push_back();
cout<<v.size()<<" objects in container";
```

10.10
```
typedef map<int,float> XY;
XY values;
values[0]=1.1;
values[1]=2.2;
XY::iterator ptr;
ptr->first=ptr->second;
```

Determine the output produced by the code segments in Exercises 10.11 through 10.14. Assume default settings if not otherwise specified.

10.11
```
vector<char> vch;
char tool[]="TEMPLATES";
for(int i=0; i<9; i++)
  vch.push_back(tool[i]);
vch.erase(vch.begin()+3);
vch.insert(vch.end()-2,'C');
for(int j=0;j<9;j++)
  cout<<vch[j];
```

10.12
```
typedef map<int, int> X;
X val;
for(int i=0; i<10; i++)
  val[i]=i*2;
X::iterator it;
it=val.begin();
it=it+3;
cout<<it->first<<' '<<it->second;
```

10.13
```
typedef vector<int> v;
stack<int,v> vst;
for(int j=0; j<5; j++)
    vst.push(j);
while(!vst.empty())
{
    cout<<vst.top()<<' ';
    vst.pop();
}
```

10.14
```
int a[]={1,3,5,7,9}, b[]={2,4,6,8,10}; c[6];
iter_swap(a+1,b+2);
merge(a,a+3,b,b+3,c);
for(int j=0; j<6; j++)
    cout<<c[j]<<endl;
```

PROGRAMMING PROJECTS

10.1 Design a class template that can be used to process an ac current. The class template should have data members of a generic type that are used to store the magnitude and phase shift of an ac current. It should also have member functions that are used to get values of the magnitude and phase shift from the user, as well as to compute and display the current in rectangular and polar coordinates. Design a program that will test this class template for integer and floating point values.

10.2 Use the class template designed in Project 10.1 as a base class template, from which another class template will be derived. In addition to members inherited from the base class template, the derived class template should contain functions that can be used to add and subtract two ac currents, as well as a function that can be used to multiply an ac current by a floating point value.

10.3 Design a program that uses two *vector* containers to store integer numbers and strings, respectively. The program should use *stack* and *queue* adaptors to insert into and remove objects from each container.

10.4 Design a program that uses a *map* container to store days (integer numbers from 1 to 31) and corresponding temperatures for each day (floating point numbers). The program should use a user-defined function to load values into the container. It should also instantiate an iterator and use this iterator to access and display temperatures for one week, as well as to compute and display the average monthly temperature.

10.5 Design a program that uses *vector* containers to store three sets of floating point numbers. The program should use the STL algorithms to perform the following operations:

- Sort numbers within a range specified by the user
- Merge sorted numbers of two containers and put into the third container
- Swap numbers between two containers, as specified by the user
- Search for a number based on the user's input
- Find the largest number within a container
- Compute and display the sum of all numbers within a range specified by the user

CHAPTER 11

Exception Handling

INTRODUCTION

One of the most challenging tasks for programmers is to anticipate all of the possible errors that may occur during the execution of their programs. These errors may be caused by the computer system used to run the program or by the user. Well-designed programs contain code that handles various types of run-time errors and prevents these programs from crashing or producing incorrect results if an error occurs. Unlike most other programming languages, C++ provides very sophisticated and efficient tools for processing run-time errors (exception-handling tools). This chapter will introduce and discuss a variety of C++ exception-handling tools and techniques and demonstrate their use in structured, as well as object-oriented, programs.

11.1 FUNDAMENTALS OF EXCEPTION HANDLING

An **exception** is an occurrence that causes abnormal program termination. These abnormal occurrences may be caused by hardware failures (e.g. insufficient resources, or errors in peripheral devices) or by the user (*garbage* data input). When designing programs used in critical applications such as nuclear power plants, medical devices, or aircraft guidance systems, it is important that these programs are robust and not prone to errors. Programs must therefore efficiently process (handle) exceptions.

An **exception** can be also defined as an **object** that is *thrown* at the location in a program where a run-time error occurs. This object must be *caught* and handled by code called the **exception handler**, which is designed to process that particular type of run-time error.

When processing exceptions, the following two tasks must be successfully completed:

- Detecting and **throwing** (raising) an exception
- **Handling** an exception

Run-time errors, such as a division by 0, an even root of a negative number, insufficient memory in the heap, or errors in peripheral devices, are common examples of exceptions that may cause abnormal program termination. If an exception is detected during program execution, it is thrown to the code (exception handler) that handles that particular type of exception. Programmers should anticipate various kinds of exceptions that may interrupt their programs at execution time and design code that detects, throws, and handles these exceptions. Programs that include the exception-handling code are more robust, less error-prone, and less likely to crash than programs without this code.

Programming languages that do not provide C++-like, exception-handling tools use techniques that perform error checking and error handling at the locations in the code where errors may occur during program execution. The disadvantage of this approach is that program readability may be decreased due to the interspersing of error-checking and handling code within the main code. C++ exception-handling techniques enable programmers to design exception-handling code that executes an alternate path if a run-time error occurs. This approach does not require interspersing error and exception-handling code with the rest of the code. The general structure of a program that contains the exception-handling code separated from the rest of the code is shown in Figure 11.1.

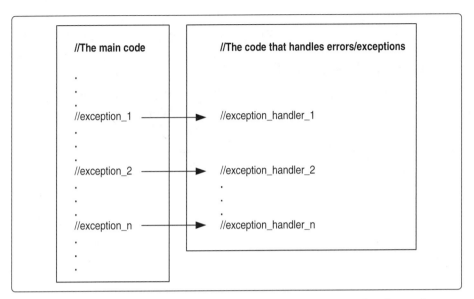

Figure 11.1 *General structure of a program that contains exception-handling code.*

During the execution of the main code, `exception_1`, `exception_2`,..., `exception_n` exceptions may occur. Each exception is processed by the respective exception-handling code named in Figure 11.1 as `exception_handler_1`, `exception_handler_2`,..., and `exception_handler_n`. If an exception occurs, the program control is transferred to an appropriate exception handler that processes that particular type of exception. This mechanism is similar to calling functions. After the exception is caught and handled, the program may recover from the error situation or normally terminate without crashing.

C++ exception-handling tools should be used in the following situations:

- To separate the error-handling code from the main code, to improve program readability and maintainability

- To process exceptions in a uniform way

- To process exceptions before they cause a system failure

- To separate the exception processing from the error detection section of a program (this is particularly appropriate when developing large projects by a team of programmers)

- To properly terminate a program in situations when it cannot recover

- To process errors caused by library functions

Programs that contain exception-handling code generally consume more memory than programs without this code. Due to this increased memory usage and resultant degradation of performance, C++ exception-handling tools should only be used for the purpose of processing run-time errors. These tools should not be used for other purposes, such as normal program control.

11.2 USING *try-throw-catch*

C++ provides a structure that uses the *try*, *throw*, and *catch* keywords to process run-time errors. The general format of the *try-throw-catch* structure is shown in Figure 11.2.

```
try {
        //code fragment
        throw exception_1;
        //code fragment
        throw exception_2;
        .

        .

        .

        //code fragment
        throw exception_n;
        //code fragment
}   //end of try block
catch(data_type1 argument)  {
        //exception handler
}

catch(data_type2 argument)  {
        //exception handler
}
        .

        .

        .

catch(data_typeN argument)  {
        //exception handler
}
```

Figure 11.2 *General format of the* **try-throw-catch** *structure.*

The **try** keyword is used to mark a code segment (**try** block), which will be monitored for errors. A **try** block can contain any part (small or large) of a program, as well as the code of the entire **main()** function. A program can have as many **try** blocks as necessary, including nested **try** blocks. If an error (exception) is detected within a **try** block during program execution, the exception is thrown by the **throw** keyword to a **catch** block following the **try** block. Throwing an exception results in transferring control from the **try** block to the appropriate exception handler code within a **catch** block that is designed to process that particular type of exception.

The logic of a **try-throw-catch** structure that handles two exceptions is demonstrated in the flow chart shown in Figure 11.3.

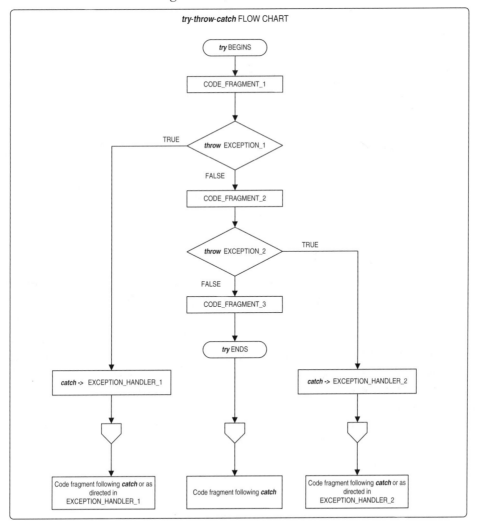

Figure 11.3 *Flowchart of a* **try-throw-catch** *structure with two exceptions.*

In the example shown in Figure 11.3, one of the following three situations could occur at the execution time:

1. `exception_1` occurs.

   The code sequence that executes:
   - `code_fragment_1`
   - `exception_handler_1`

2. `exception_2` **occurs (but not** `exception_1`**).**

   The code sequence that executes:
   - `code_fragment_1`
   - `code_fragment_2`
   - `exception_handler_2`

3. None of the exceptions occurs.

   The code sequence that executes:
   - `code_fragment_1`
   - `code_fragment_2`
   - `code_fragment_3`

 NOTE: A **try** block must be followed by at least one (or as many as necessary) **catch** statement, or a syntax error will be generated.

11.2.1 Throwing and Handling an Exception

Throwing an exception transfers control to an exception handler within a **catch** block. This process commonly involves passing an object from the point where the exception occurs to the exception-handler code, which can use that object to process the exception.

A selection of a **catch** block contains appropriate exception-handler code based on the type of the object passed (thrown). The type of the object thrown by **throw** must match the type of the argument in one of the **catch** statements following the **try** block, or the exception will not be handled. Throwing an unhandled exception—i.e., there is no appropriate **catch** statement for this type of exception—automatically invokes the **terminate()** function, which terminates the program by calling the **abort()** function.

The following code demonstrates examples of **throw** statements:

```
//Assume the following declarations:
class Exception {
```

```
        //private class members
public:
        Exception(int, float, char);      //class constructor
        //public class members
};
float fun(int);
int a;
//Examples of throw statements:
throw a;          //throws an integer
throw 1;          //throws an integer constant
throw a*0.1;      //throws a floating point value
throw "string";   //throws a string constant
throw Exception(1,3.3,'E'); //throws an object of Exception
throw fun(a);     //throws a value returned by fun()
throw;            //rethrows exception
```

Note that the *throw* keyword can be followed by a variable (object), constant, expression, or a function call, including a class constructor. The expression that follows *throw* is evaluated first and then its value (object) is thrown to a corresponding *catch* statement containing an argument—the type of which matches the type of the value (object) thrown. A *throw* expression can be omitted; that is, the *throw* keyword can be followed directly by a semicolon indicating the end of the *throw* statement. In this case, the current exception will be passed (**rethrown**) to an outer *try/catch* block.

PROG11_1 demonstrates the use of a *try-throw-catch* structure to process run-time errors when computing the nth root of any number entered by the user. This program implements the logic shown in Figure 11.3.

To find the nth root of a number, the following relationship between roots and exponents can be used:

$$\sqrt[n]{a} = a^{1/n}$$

Please note that an even root of a negative number is imaginary and an odd root of a negative number is a real, negative number. The expression $a^{1/n}$ is not valid if $n = 0$, or when n is even and a is a negative number. In Program Example 11.1, PROG11_1 should handle these two exceptions.

PROGRAM EXAMPLE 11.1: PROG11_1

```
1   //PROG11_1: Program computes and displays the nth root of any
2   //          number entered by the user and uses C++ exception
3   //          handling to prevent run-time errors.
4   #include <iostream>
5   #include <cmath>
6   using namespace std;
7
8   double roots(int n, double a)   //returns the nth root of a number
9   {
10      double e=(double)1/n;
11      return pow(a,e);
12  }
13
14  int main()
15  {
16      int n;
17      double a, b;
18      char c;
19      do {
20          cout<<"Enter root => ";
21          cin>>n;
22          cout<<"Enter number => ";
23          cin>>a;
24          try {                //try block begins
25              if(n==0)         //division by 0
26                  throw 1;     //throws an integer constant
27              if((n%2==0)&&(a<0)) //even root from a negative number
28                  throw "an even root of a negative number!";
29                              //throws a string constant
30              if((n%2!=0)&&(a<0)) //odd root from a negative number
31                  {
```

```
32                    b=roots(n,-a);
33                    cout<<n<<". root of "<<a<<" is "<<-b<<endl;
34                }
35            else                //nth root from a positive number
36            {
37                    b=roots(n,a);
38                    cout<<n<<". root of "<<a<<" is "<<b<<endl;
39            }
40        } //try block ends
41
42        catch (int x) {         //handles an integer exception
43            cout<<"Exception # "<<x<<" occurred!"<<endl;
44            cout<<"Cannot be 0 root!"<<endl;
45        }
46        catch (char *exc2) { //handles a string exception
47            cout<<"Exception # 2"<<" occurred!"<<endl;
48            cout<<"Cannot be "<<exc2<<endl;
49        }
50
51        cout<<"\tTo exit enter X or any key to continue => ";
52        cin>>c;
53    }while (c!='X');
54    return 0;
55 }
```

This program contains a *try* block within the *main()* function between lines 24 and 40. The code within the *try* block calls the roots() function that computes the nth root of a number a, where n and a are entered by the user (lines 21 and 23). The values of n and a are checked, and if n is equal to 0 or n is even and a is a negative number, exceptions are thrown in lines 26 and 28, respectively. The exception in line 26 throws an integer constant. This exception is caught by the *catch* statement containing an integer argument (line 42). The exception is first processed by the handler (lines 43 and 44) and then the program execution resumes in line 51. Notice that the second *catch* statement (lines 46–49) is ignored in this case. The exception in line 28 throws a string constant, an even root and a negative number!, and is caught by the *catch* statement with a string argument (lines 46–49). If this exception is thrown, the program will resume in line 51 after the exception is processed by the handler (lines 47 and 48).

Note that the roots() function is called from the *try* block to compute and return a root (lines 32 and 37) only if neither of the two exceptions occurs at run-time. Using the exception-handling tool in this program protects the roots() function against possible run-time errors. A sample run of PROG11_1 is shown in Figure 11.4.

```
Enter root => 5
Enter number => 234
5. root of 234 is 2.97744
        To exit enter X or any key to continue => 1
Enter root => 0
Enter number => 67
Exception # 1 occurred!
Cannot be 0 root!
        To exit enter X or any key to continue => 2
Enter root => 6
Enter number => -84.7
Exception # 2 occurred!
Cannot be an even root of a negative number!
        To exit enter X or any key to continue => 3
Enter root => 5
Enter number => -875.3
  5. root of -875.3 is -3.87642
        To exit enter X or any key to continue => X
```

Figure 11.4 *Sample run of PROG11_1.*

In PROG11_1, exceptions are thrown directly from the *try* block within the *main()* function. Exceptions can also be thrown from any function that is called directly or indirectly from a *try* block. Program Example 11.2 illustrates PROG11_2, which is a modified version of PROG11_1; in which the two exceptions are thrown from the roots() function that is called from the *try* block.

PROGRAM EXAMPLE 11.2: PROG11_2

```
1  //PROG11_2: A modified version of PROG11_1 to demonstrate
2  //          exceptions thrown from a function called within a
```

```
3   //           try block.
4   #include <iostream>
5   #include <cmath>
6   using namespace std;
7   double roots(int n, double a)  //function that throws exceptions
8   {
9     if(n==0)                //division by 0
10        throw 1;  //throws an integer constant
11    if((n%2==0)&&(a<0))  //even root from a negative number
12        throw "an even root and a negative number!";
13        //throws a string constant
14    double e=(double)1/n;
15    return pow(a,e);
16  }
17
18  int main()
19  {
20    int n;
21    double a,b;
22    char c;
23    do{
24    cout<<"Enter root => ";
25    cin>>n;
26    cout<<"Enter number => ";
27    cin>>a;
28    try {    //try block begins
29        if((n%2!=0)&&(a<0)) //an odd root of a negative number
30        {
31                b=roots(n,-a);
32                cout<<n<<". root of "<<a<<" is "<<-b<<endl;
33        }
34        else              //a root of a positive number
35        {
36                b=roots(n,a);
```

```
37                         cout<<n<<". root of "<<a<<" is "<<b<<endl;
38                  }
39          }    //try block ends
40
41      catch (int x) {          //catches an integer exception
42          cout<<"Exception # "<<x<<" occurred!"<<endl;
43          cout<<"Cannot be the 0th root!"<<endl;
44      }
45      catch (char *exc2) {   //catches a string exception
46          cout<<"Exception # 2"<<" occurred!"<<endl;
47          cout<<"Cannot be "<<exc2<<endl;
48      }
49
50      cout<<"\tTo exit enter X or any key to continue => ";
51      cin>>c;
52      }while (c!='X');
53      return 0;
54 }
```

Unlike PROG11_1, the *try* block in PROG11_2 (lines 28–39) does not directly contain *throw* statements. Instead, these statements are within the roots() function (lines 10 and 12), which is called from the *try* block (lines 31 and 36). This function computes and returns a root only if no exception is thrown. Error checking is done within the function in this example, instead of prior to calling the function, which is the case in PROG11_1. PROG11_2 produces the same output as PROG11_1 (Figure 11.4).

After an exception is thrown from a function, the function terminates and locally declared, *non-static* variables are destroyed (same as when a function returns). When the function is called again, the exception-handling mechanism is reset.

 TIP: Use exception handling to process exceptions generated in library functions in order to prevent certain types of run-time errors when using these functions.

Throwing an exception transfers control from a *try* block to an exception handler. This action results in the destruction of each variable declared in the *try* block. In addition to a *throw* statement, program control can be transferred out of a *try* block (or exception handler) by using *break*, *return*, *continue*, or *goto* statements. This will also result in the destruction of all variables declared within the *try* block or exception handler.

The following code fragment demonstrates a nested *try* block, and uses a *goto* statement to transfer control from the inner *try* block to the beginning of the outer *try* block:

```
lab1: try {
            int x;
            try {
                double y;
                if(condition)
                    goto lab1;
        } //inner try block ends
        //catch statement(s) following inner try block
    } //outer try block ends
    //catch statement(s) following outer try block
```

Executing goto lab1; in this example, will first destroy y and then x.

C++ provides a special kind of a *catch* statement that can be used to catch an exception of any type. The general format of this statement is shown in Figure 11.5.

```
catch(...)  {

        //exception handler

    }
```

Figure 11.5 *General format of a* **catch** *statement that can catch an exception of any type.*

A substitution of an argument declaration of a specific type by **ellipses** within a *catch* statement enables using a single *catch* statement for exceptions of any type. In Program Example 11.3, PROG11_3 demonstrates the use of this statement.

PROGRAM EXAMPLE 11.3: PROG11_3

```
1 //PROG11_3:  Program demonstrates a function with a try-throw-catch
2 //           structure as well as catching an exception of any
3 //           type by using catch(...).
```

```
4   #include <iostream>
5   using namespace std;
6
7   void temperature(int t)
8   {
9     try {
10          if(t==100)    throw "BOILING";
11          else if(t==0) throw "FREEZING";
12          else if((t<-100)||(t>200)) throw 0.1;
13          else throw t;
14    } //end of try block
15    catch(char *str) {
16        cout<<str<<endl;
17    }
18    catch(int x) {
19        cout<<"Temperature = "<<x<<" deg C"<<endl;
20    }
21    catch(...) {
22        cout<<"Incorrect value!";
23    }
24  }
25
26  int main()
27  {
28    temperature(0);
29    temperature(47);
30    temperature(100);
31    temperature(-155);
32    return 0;
33  }
```

Unlike the previous two program examples, in which a *try* block is placed within the *main()* function, this program contains a *try* block (lines 9–14) within a user-defined function called temperature() (lines 7–24). Four exceptions are thrown from the *try* block: two string constants (lines 10 and 11), a floating point constant (line 12), and an integer (line 13). These exceptions are caught by the *catch* statements as follows:

- A *catch* statement with a string argument (lines 15–17) catches the exceptions thrown in lines 10 and 11.

- A *catch* statement with an integer argument (lines 18–20) catches the exception thrown in line 13.

- As there is no *catch* statement with a *float* argument, a *catch* statement with ellipses (lines 21–23) catches the exception thrown in line 12.

The output produced by PROG11_3 is shown in Figure 11.6.

```
FREEZING
Temperature = 47 deg C
BOILING
Incorrect value!
```

Figure 11.6 *Output produced by PROG11_3.*

When an exception is thrown, C++ searches for the first *catch* statement that could handle the exception—that is, a *catch* statement with an argument type that matches the type of the object thrown, or a *catch* statement with ellipses. *A catch statement with ellipses has to be the last catch statement that follows a try block* (after all other *catch* statements with arguments of specific types), or a syntax error will be generated. This is logical as C++ searches for the first match when handling exceptions and *catch(...)* can handle all exceptions.

The *catch(...)* statement (also known as a *catch all* statement) should be used as a default exception handler (similar to *default* in a *switch* statement) to process exceptions that cannot be handled by other *catch* statements. Notice that throwing an unhandled exception causes abnormal program termination.

 TIP: When an exception is thrown that cannot be handled by other *catch* statements, use *catch(...)* to prevent abnormal program termination.

11.2.2 Exception Specifications

A function that is called from within a *try* block, or any other function called from that function, can throw exceptions. C++ uses an **exception-specification list** to restrict types of exceptions that can be thrown directly or indirectly from a function. An exception specification has the general format shown in Figure 11.7.

```
throw ( list_of_types )
```

Figure 11.7 *General format of an exception specification.*

An exception specification can appear only on a function declaration/definition or a function pointer (or reference) declaration, as shown in the following example:

```
void fun(int) throw(double, char *); //function prototype
void (*ptr)() throw (int); //function pointer declaration
                           //with an exception specification
```

The `fun()` function in this example can throw exceptions with types restricted to **double** and **char ***, while a function pointed to by the `ptr` pointer can throw only **int** exceptions as specified in their exception-specification lists.

An attempt to throw an exception from a function where the exception type is not listed in the function exception-specification list, will cause abnormal program termination. C++ automatically invokes the **unexpected()** function in this case; which, by default, calls the **terminate()** function to terminate the program. Programmers, however, can design their own code to handle unexpected exceptions. That code would execute (instead of the default **unexpected()** function) when an unexpected exception occurs.

An exception-specification list can be empty, specifying that a function cannot throw any exception. For example,

```
float compute(int, float) throw();   //cannot throw exceptions
```

The `compute()` function cannot throw any exception, and any attempt to do so would result in an automatic call of the **unexpected()** function—either default, or user defined.

In Program Example 11.4, PROG11_4 demonstrates a function with an exception specification.

PROGRAM EXAMPLE 11.4: PROG11_4

```
1  //PROG11_4: Program demonstrates a function with an exception
2  //          specification.
3  #include <iostream>
4  using namespace std;
5
```

```
6   void temperature(int t)throw(char *,int) //exception-specification
7   {                                        //list
8     if(t==100)    throw "BOILING";
9     else if(t==0) throw "FREEZING";
10    else throw t;
11  }
12
13  int main()
14  {
15    try {
16        try {
17           temperature(13);
18        } //inner try ends
19        catch(int x) {
20           cout<<"Temperature = "<<x<<" deg C"<<endl;
21        }
22        temperature(0);
23    } //outter try ends
24    catch(char *str) {
25        cout<<str<<endl;
26    }
27    return 0;
28  }
```

The `temperature()` function in PROG11_4 contains an exception-specification list (line 6) that restricts the types of exceptions that can be thrown from this function to *char** and *int*. The three exceptions thrown from `temperature()` in lines 8, 9, and 10 match one of these two types, and as a result, no unexpected exceptions will occur at run-time. The output produced by PROG11_4 is shown in Figure 11.8.

```
Temperature = 13 deg C
FREEZING
```

Figure 11.8 *Output produced by PROG11_4.*

C++ does not check types of exceptions at compile time. Should a function contain an exception that is not listed in its exception-specification list, no syntax error is generated. Instead, an unexpected exception will be generated at run-time by invoking the *unexpected()* function.

By default, the *unexpected()* function terminates the program by calling the *abort()* function. In some cases, however, program termination is not desired. To prevent an automatic call to the default *unexpected()* function, programmers might want to design their own function that will be invoked each time an unexpected exception occurs. To set up a user-defined function as a handler of unexpected exceptions in a program, the *set_unexpected()* function (defined in the *exception* header file) is used. The following code segment demonstrates this technique:

```
void myUnexpected()
{
        //Code that handles unexpected exceptions
}
int main()
{
        set_unexpected(myUnexpected);//Sets up myUnexpected() as
        //a handler of unexpected exceptions
        //.............................
}
```

The myUnexpected() user-defined function is used to process unexpected exceptions in this example. To set up myUnexpected() as an unexpected exception handler, the *set_unexpected()* function is called. Note that *set_unexpected()* takes as its argument a pointer to a function that will be invoked when an unexpected exception occurs. The pointer in this example is myUnexpected (reminder: a function name serves as a pointer to the function).

The technique demonstrated in the previous example can be used to create and set up a user-defined function that will be invoked instead of the default *terminate()* function to take care of unhandled (uncaught) exceptions. The *set_terminate()* function (defined in *exception*) is used to set up the user-defined function that replaces *terminate()* as an uncaught exception handler.

 NOTE: A function without an exception-specification list can throw any exception.

It is important to check the compiler manual before using C++ exception-handling tools and techniques. Most of the exception-handling tools have been recently added to C++ and some of the compilers may not comply with the current C++ standard.

11.3 HANDLING MEMORY ALLOCATION ERRORS

C++ dynamic memory allocation (run-time memory allocation), which uses *new* and *delete* operators, is a very powerful and frequently used tool. The *new* operator, however, may fail to successfully allocate memory (insufficient resources), thus causing a run-time error. C++ provides a variety of tools and techniques to handle memory allocation failures—some of which are discussed in this section.

A simple method to handle a memory allocation error is to check for a null pointer returned by *new* when memory allocation fails. The following code fragment demonstrates this method:

```
double *dptr = new double[100];   //Allocates 100 double variables
if(dptr==0)                //checks for a null pointer
{
    cout<<"Memory allocation error";
    exit(1);
}
```

If *new* fails to allocate 100 *double* variables as requested, it will return a null pointer (0) to dptr. The message Memory allocation error will be printed on the standard output device to notify the user, and the program will terminate.

Similar results can be achieved with less coding by using the *assert()* macro that is defined in the *cassert* header file. The following code fragment demonstrates the use of *assert()* when processing new failures:

```
double *dptr = new double[100]; //Allocates 100 double variables
assert(dptr!=0);               //Handles a memory allocation error
```

The *assert()* macro tests the value of the expression (condition) that is passed to the macro as an argument. If the value is *false, assert()* displays an error message and invokes the *abort()* function (similar to *exit()*) to terminate the program. This macro can also be used as a powerful debugging tool when testing variables and expressions.

C++ enables programmers to design their own recovery routine (a user-defined function) to handle memory allocation errors. To register a user-defined function as a default handler of *new* failures, the *set_new_handler()* function (defined in the *new* header file) is called. For example, the following statement placed at the beginning of the *main()* function will register the my_handler() user-defined function as a default handler of *new* failures:

```
set_new_handler(my_handler);
```

A call to *set_new_handler()* with the 0 argument removes the current *new* handler, resulting in a program without a default *new* handler.

The *set_new_handler()* function takes a function pointer as an argument. A function pointed to by the pointer will automatically be invoked each time *new* fails. Program Example 11.5 demonstrates this technique.

PROGRAM EXAMPLE 11.5: PROG11_5

```
1   //PROG11_5: Program demonstrates a user-defined function as a
2   //          handler that processes memory allocation errors.
3   #include <iostream>
4   #include <new>
5   using namespace std;
6   const int n=20;
7   const int size=20;
8
9   void memError()   //user-defined new handler
10  {
11      cout<<"Memory allocation error!"<<endl;
12      cout<<"Program will terminate!";
13      exit(1);
14  }
15  typedef char Mbyte[1000000]; //defines a type of 1000000 bytes
16
17  int main()
18  {
19      set_new_handler(memError);    //Sets new handler
20      Mbyte *ptr[n];                //an array of pointers
21      for(int i=0; i<n;i++)
22      {
23          ptr[i]=new Mbyte[size];    //Allocates an array dynamically
24          cout<<((i+1)*20)<<" Mb allocated successfully!"<<endl;
25      }
26      return 0;
27  }
```

The memError() user-defined function (lines 9–14) is registered by the ***set_new_han-dler()*** function as a default handler that processes ***new*** failures (line 19). The program uses ***typedef*** to define the Mbyte type, whose size is 1000000 bytes (line 15). It then uses a ***for*** loop and the ***new*** operator to dynamically allocate arrays of size variables of type Mbyte (line 23). The amount of memory allocated to store each array is approximately 20 Mb. This program is intended to allocate a large amount of memory in the heap, causing a run-time memory allocation error when the size of free memory is exceeded. When the ***new*** operator fails, the memError() function will be invoked as the default ***new*** handler.

A sample run of PROG11_5 is shown in Figure 11.9. The output produced by this program may differ depending on the compiler and computer system (available storage resources) used to run the program.

```
20 Mb allocated successfully!
40 Mb allocated successfully!
60 Mb allocated successfully!
80 Mb allocated successfully!
Memory allocation error!
Program will terminate!
```

Figure 11.9 *Sample run of PROG11_5.*

Note that a ***new*** handler could contain a recovery routine that frees memory in the heap, instead of terminating the program when ***new*** fails as demonstrated in PROG11_5.

11.4 EXCEPTIONS AND CLASSES

A class object can be thrown when an exception occurs. The C++ library (***exception*** header file) contains classes that are used to handle exceptions. A standard library class named ***exception*** is commonly used. This class serves as the base class for all exceptions thrown by certain expressions. The skeleton of the standard ***exception*** class is shown in Figure 11.10.

Note that all member functions of the ***exception*** class contain an exception-specification list with no types specified (throw()), and as a result, these functions cannot throw any exception. The ***exception*** class is used as the base class for other classes that handle specific types of exceptions. The ***what() virtual*** function, which returns a constant string (an exception description), can be overridden by any class derived from ***exception***.

```
class exception {

public:

  exception() throw();           //class constructor

  exception(const exception & rhs) throw(); //copy constructor

  exception & operator=(const exception & rhs) throw();

  virtual ~exception() throw();           //class destructor

  virtual const char*  what() const throw();

};
```

Figure 11.10 *Skeleton of the standard* **exception** *class.*

Program Example 11.6 demonstrates an example of using the standard *exception* class to process exceptions.

PROGRAM EXAMPLE 11.6: PROG11_6

```
1   //PROG11_6: Program demonstrates the use of the standard
2   //          exception class.
3   #include <iostream>
4   #include <exception>
5   using namespace std;
6
7   class Sample {
8   private:
9     int n;
10  public:
11    Sample(int x=0) { n=x;}
12    ~Sample(){ cout<<"Sample destructor is called.\n";}
13    int getN(){ return n;}
```

```
14 };
15
16 int main()
17 {
18    try {
19        Sample obj(-1);
20        if(obj.getN()<0)
21            throw exception();//throws an exception's object
22        else
23            cout<<obj.getN();
24    }
25    catch(exception exc) {
26        cout<<"Cannot be a negative value!";
27    }
28    return 0;
29 }
```

This program example uses the Sample user-defined class (lines 7–14) and the *exception* library class. The *main()* function contains a *try* block between lines 18 and 24. An object of Sample is instantiated within the *try* block (line 19). The *if* condition in line 20 is *true*, and therefore an exception in line 21 will be thrown at runtime. The exception thrown is an object that is constructed and returned by the *exception* constructor. This constructor is called explicitly in line 21 as a regular function (exception()). The thrown *exception's* object is caught by the *catch* statement (lines 25–27), an argument of which is an object of *exception*, named exc. The exc object is a copy (created by the *exception's* copy constructor) of the object thrown when the exception in line 21 occurs. Before the exception is thrown, the Sample destructor is called to destroy obj, instantiated within the *try* block. The output produced by this program is shown in Figure 11.11.

```
Sample destructor is called.
Cannot be a negative value!
```

Figure 11.11 *Output produced by PROG11_6.*

> **NOTE:** Destructors are called to destroy all objects instantiated within a **try** block before any exception is thrown from the block.

The exc object of the *exception* class in PROG11_6, which serves as an argument of the *catch* statement (line 25), can be used to invoke the *what( )* library member function when handling an exception, as follows:

```
catch(exception exc) {
    cout<<exc.what();
}
```

By default, a string constant Unexpected exception is returned by *what( )*. The *what( )* function, however, can be redefined (overridden) by classes derived from *exception* and return different string constants.

In addition to standard classes defined in the C++ library, user-defined classes can also be used to process exceptions. Exception classes can have data members and member functions as normal classes do. They can use constructors, destructors, *virtual* functions, and can be organized into an inheritance hierarchy of classes. In Program Example 11.7, PROG11_7 uses user-defined exception classes to process the exceptions demonstrated in PROG11_1.

PROGRAM EXAMPLE 11.7: PROG11_7

```
1   //PROG11_7: Program demonstrates user-defined exception classes.
2   #include <iostream>
3   #include <cmath>
4   using namespace std;
5
6   class RootExceptionZero {            //base exception class
7   protected:
8      char *errMessage;
9   public:
10     RootExceptionZero()        //base constructor
11     {
12         errMessage="Cannot be 0 root!";
13     }
14     char * getError()  { return errMessage; }
15   };
```

```
16
17  class RootExceptionNeg:public RootExceptionZero { //derived class
18  public:
19    RootExceptionNeg()              //derived constructor
20    {
21    errMessage="An even root of a negative number is imaginary!";
22    }
23  };
24
25  double roots(int n, double a)      //returns the nth root of a number
26  {
27      double e=(double)1/n;
28      return pow(a,e);
29  }
30  int main()
31  {
32      int n;
33      double a, b;
34      char c;
35      do {
36          cout<<"Enter root => ";
37          cin>>n;
38          cout<<"Enter number => ";
39          cin>>a;
40          try {                 //try block begins
41            if(n==0)     //division by 0
42                  throw RootExceptionZero(); //throws a base object
43            if((n%2==0)&&(a<0)) //even root from a negative number
44                  throw RootExceptionNeg();   //throws a derived object
45            if((n%2!=0)&&(a<0)) //odd root from a negative number
46            {
47                  b=roots(n,-a);
48                  cout<<n<<". root of "<<a<<" is "<<-b<<endl;
```

```
49              }
50           else            //nth root from a positive number
51           {
52              b=roots(n,a);
53              cout<<n<<". root of "<<a<<" is "<<b<<endl;
54           }
55        }                    //try block ends
56     catch (RootExceptionNeg &obj1) {  //catches a derived object
57        cout<<obj1.getError()<<endl;
58     }
59     catch (RootExceptionZero &obj2) {   //catches a base object
60        cout<<obj2.getError()<<endl;
61     }
62     cout<<"\tTo exit enter X or any key to continue => ";
63     cin>>c;
64  }while (c!='X');
65  return 0;
66 }
```

PROG11_7 uses RootExceptionZero (lines 6–15) and RootExceptionNeg (lines 17–23) classes to process exceptions that may occur when computing a root. The RootExceptionNeg class is derived from the RootExceptionZero class. Each class has its own constructor that is used to initialize a string data member errMessage to a message that will be displayed when an exception occurs (lines 10–13 and 19–22, respectively). An exception thrown in line 42 is an object constructed by the RootExceptionZero constructor. A *catch* block between lines 59 and 61 catches this exception. When an exception in line 44 occurs, an object of RootExceptionNeg is thrown and caught by a *catch* block (lines 56–58).

A *catch* block that catches a base-type exception can also catch all exceptions derived from the base type. The C++ exception-handling mechanism searches for the first *catch* after *try* that can handle an exception. A *catch* block with a base-type argument should therefore be placed last, after all other *catch* blocks that handle types derived from the base type. In PROG11_7, the RootExceptionZero *catch* is placed after the RootExceptionNeg *catch*. A sample run of PROG11_7 is shown in Figure 11.12.

TIP: Using an inheritance hierarchy of exception classes enables all related errors to be caught by a single exception handler, which catches a pointer or reference to a base-type object.

```
Enter root => 3
Enter number => 23.4
3. root of 23.4 is 2.86026
   To exit enter X or any key to continue => 1
Enter root => 0
Enter number => 53
Cannot be 0 root!
   To exit enter X or any key to continue => 2
Enter root => 4
Enter number => -60.78
An even root of a negative number is imaginary!
   To exit enter X or any key to continue => 3
Enter root => 3
Enter number => -60.78
3. root of -60.78 is -3.93176
   To exit enter X or any key to continue => X
```

Figure 11.12 *Sample run of PROG11_7.*

SUMMARY

1. C++ provides powerful exception-handling tools to process various types of errors that may occur at run-time and to create programs that are more robust and less prone to errors.

2. An exception causes abnormal program termination. Well-designed programs should have code that processes various types of exceptions.

3. Processing exceptions involves the following two tasks: raising (detecting and throwing) and handling exceptions.

4. C++ exception handling enables programmers to separate code that handles errors from the main code, thus improving the program readability and maintainability.

5. A structure that uses the **try**, **throw**, and **catch** keywords is a commonly used exception-handling tool.

6. A **try** block encloses a code segment, which can **throw** an exception when a run-time error occurs. An exception can be caught and handled by a **catch** block, whose argument matches the type of the exception, or by **catch(...)**, which can catch any exception.

7. If there is no appropriate **catch** block that can handle a specific type of exception (unhandled exception), the **terminate()** library function will be automatically invoked to terminate the program by calling **abort()**.

8. Any function called from within a **try** block, or a function called from this function, can throw exceptions.

9. C++ exception handling should be used to process exceptions generated in library functions, in order to prevent certain types of run-time errors when using these functions.

10. An exception-specification list is used to restrict the types of exceptions that can be thrown by a function. A function can only throw exception types listed in the function's exception-specification list. A function cannot throw any exception if **throw()** (list with no types specified) is placed in the function's header. A function without an exception specification can throw any exception.

11. Unexpected exceptions (exceptions that are not listed in the function's exception-specification list) are handled by the **unexpected()** function, which by default invokes **abort()** to terminate a program. The **set_unexpected()** function can be used to register a user-defined function as the unexpected exception handler.

12. When using C++ dynamic memory allocation with **new** and **delete**, code that handles **new** failures should be designed to prevent run-time errors.

13. The **assert()** macro can be used as a handler of memory allocation errors.

14. The programmer can design his/her own function and register this function as a default handler of **new** failures by using the **set_new_handler()** function.

15. Exception classes can be designed as regular classes and used to process exceptions. The **exception** library class is commonly used as the base class, from which classes that handle specific types of exceptions are derived.

16. A handler that catches a pointer/reference to an object of a base class can catch pointers/references to objects of all classes derived from the base class.

EXERCISES

State the output produced by the code fragments in Exercises 11.1 through 11.4.

11.1
```cpp
try {
    int x=3, y=5;
    if(x<y) throw x;
    else throw y;
    throw "End of try block";
}
catch(int n) {
    cout<<n<<" is caught!"<<endl;
}
catch(char *str) {
    cout<<str;
}
```

11.2
```cpp
try {
    int x=3, y=5;
    if(x<y) throw x;
    else throw y;
    throw "End of try block";
}
catch(...) {
    cout<<"An exception is caught!"<<endl;
}
```

11.3
```cpp
int x=1, y=0;
try {
    if(!(x&&y))
        try {
            if(x||y)
                throw 1;
        } //end of inner try block
```

```
        catch(...) {
             throw;
        }
    } //end of outer try block
    catch(int a) {
        cout<<a<<" is caught!";
    }
```

11.4
```
    try {
        cout<<"The exception library class is used."<<endl;
        throw exception();
        cout<<"End of try block.";
    }
    catch(exception exc) {
        cout<<exc.what();        //default what()
    }
```

11.5 Declare a function named fun that can only throw the following exceptions: a string, an integer pointer, and a floating point value.

11.6 Declare a function named fun that cannot throw any exception.

11.7 Write a statement that sets up the myHandler() user-defined function as a default handler of memory allocation errors.

Identify and correct the errors in the code fragments in Exercises 11.8 through 11.11.

11.8
```
    try {
        if(x%2==0) throw 1;
    }
    cout<<x;
    catch(int a) {
        cout<<" is an even number.";
    }
```

11.9
```
void calc(float y) throw()
{
    if(y>999.99) throw y;
    else throw 1;
}
```

11.10
```
try {
    throw exception();
    if(x<0)
        throw "Negative value!";
}
catch(char *st) {
    cout<<st;
}
cout<<"No more catch blocks!";
```

11.11
```
void isEven(int a) throw(int)
{
    if(a%2==0) throw "is even";
}
```

PROGRAMMING PROJECTS

11.1 Modify PROG11_7 such that both exceptions (the base-type and derived-type exception) are handled and processed by a base-type handler.

11.2 Design two functions with an exception-specification list as follows:

    a. A function which can throw only an integer exception

    b. A function which can throw only a string exception

Design the **main()** function with a **try** block that is used to test and handle exceptions thrown by these two functions.

11.3 Write a program that uses a two-dimensional dynamic array to store daily temperatures for as many weeks as requested by the user. The **assert()** macro should be used to process memory allocation errors. The program should display all daily temperatures as well as average weekly temperatures in a table-like format.

11.4 Modify the previous program (Project 11.3) and use a user-defined function as a handler of memory allocation errors. The user-defined function should be registered as a default handler of *new* failures.

11.5 Create a program that can be used as a trigonometric functions calculator. The program should use library functions to compute the sine, cosine, and tangent of any angle entered by the user. It should also contain the exception-handling code to ensure 100% accurate results for the following angles:

      a. $\sin(\theta)$, where θ is $\pm\,\pi,\pm\,2\pi$

      b. $\cos(\theta)$, where θ is $\pm\,\pi/2,\pm\,3\pi/2$

      c. $\tan(\theta)$, where θ is $\pm\,\pi/2,\pm\,\pi,\pm\,3\pi/2,\pm\,2\pi$

The exception-handling code should be designed as an inheritance hierarchy of exception classes.

EXERCISE

CHAPTER 12

File I/O

INTRODUCTION

Program examples in previous chapters used standard console input/output stream objects (the keyboard and the screen) to obtain data to be processed, or to display results after processing. In many practical problems, data must be organized into files and stored externally (outside of a program) for future use and processing. C++ uses object-oriented tools when processing files for input or output (file I/O). This chapter will discuss the steps in C++ file I/O processing. It will also demonstrate commonly used C++ techniques when processing files as sequential and random-access files.

12.1 STEPS IN FILE I/O PROCESSING

File I/O in C++ uses file streams and file objects. This concept is similar to the concept of standard console I/O. A **file stream** connects a program to a file stored externally on a device such as a disk or CD-ROM. File streams can be text or binary streams. Please note that a **text stream** is a sequence of ASCII coded characters, while a **binary stream** is a sequence of bytes that are not translated into ASCII characters.

When processing text or binary files in C++, the following four steps are performed:

1. Create a file object.
2. Open a file.
3. Use a file for input and/or output.
4. Close a file.

12.1.1 Creating a File Object

The first step in file I/O processing in C++ is creating (instantiating) a **file object**. The file object also serves as a **logical file name**. A logical file name is used in code to refer to a file when processing (opening, reading, writing, or closing) the file. In C, a file pointer is used as a logical file name.

A file object is instantiated from one of the following classes that are defined in the standard *fstream* header file:

1. The *ifstream* class for input operations
2. The *ofstream* class for output operations
3. The *fstream* class for input/output operations

The standard C++ library provides a variety of classes that can be used to create and process input/output streams. Figure 12.1 shows an inheritance hierarchy of standard C++ I/O classes which includes file I/O classes.

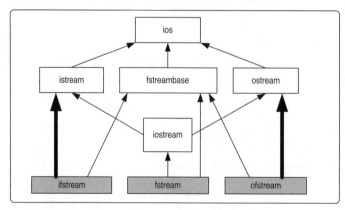

Figure 12.1 *Inheritance hierarchy of I/O classes.*

Unlike most of the other I/O classes that are defined in the ***iostream*** header file, file I/O classes are defined in the ***fstream*** header file. Note that a directive that includes ***fstream*** (***#include <fstream>***) will also automatically include ***iostream***. It is common practice, however, to explicitly include ***iostream*** if non-file I/O objects such as ***cout*** and ***cin*** are used in addition to file objects.

A parent-child relationship between the ***istream*** and ***ifstream***, as well as ***ostream*** and ***ofstream*** classes, is emphasized in Figure 12.1. This relationship is important when using the stream insertion operator << and the stream extraction operator (>>) to write data to a file and read data from a file, respectively (Section 12.2).

The following code segment instantiates (creates) three file objects:

```
ifstream fin;   //fin can be used for input (reading) operations
ofstream fout;  //fout can be used for output (writing) operations
fstream fio;    //fio can be used for input/output operations
```

The fin object in this example behaves like ***cin***. Please note that ***cin*** is an object of ***istream***, which is a parent class of ***ifstream*** that is used to instantiate fin. The fout object is instantiated from the ***ofstream*** class. This object behaves like ***cout***, which is instantiated from ***ostream***—a parent class of ***ofstream***. The fio object can be used for both input and output, thus behaving like an object composed of ***cin*** and ***cout***.

12.1.2 Opening a File

After a file object has been created, the next step in file I/O processing is to open a file.

C++ provides the following two methods to open a file:

- Using a file object to invoke the ***open( )*** member function
- Passing appropriate arguments to a constructor function when instantiating a file object

When opening a file, a file object (logical file name) must be associated with a **physical file** name, which is the actual file name that is recognized and used by the operating system to access the file. C++ naming rules are applied when creating a logical file name, while a physical file name must comply with the file naming rules of a specific operating system. Depending on the method used to open a file, a physical file name must be passed either to the ***open( )*** function or a constructor function as an argument. In addition to passing a physical file name to a function that opens a file, a specific file **mode** should also be passed or the file will be opened in a **default mode**. A file mode determines how a file is opened as well as what function is being performed on the file (e.g., reading, writing, appending, or truncating). Commonly used file I/O modes, with a brief description of each mode, are shown in Table 12.1.

Table 12.1 File I/O Modes

Mode identifier	Description
ios::in	Input mode (default for objects of *ifstream*)
ios::out	Output mode (default for objects of *ofstream*)
ios::trunc	Deleting the existing file content (also default for *ofstream*)
ios::binary	Input and output binary mode
ios::app	Output mode — appending the file starting at its end
ios::ate	Output and input mode — starting at the end of the file

Each of the three classes from which a file object can be instantiated (*ifstream*, *ofstream*, and *fstream*) has its version of the *open()* function. This function is defined as a member function in each class and has two arguments. The first argument is a *const char* pointer that points to a specific physical file name. The second argument (declared as a default argument) represents the mode in which a file is opened. The default value (default mode) that is assigned to the second argument is different in each of the three file I/O classes. Table 12.2 shows file I/O classes and their respective default modes.

Table 12.2 The Default File I/O Modes

Class	Default mode
ifstream	*ios::in*
ofstream	*ios::out* | *ios::trunc*
fstream	*ios::in* | *ios::out*

Please note that a file can be opened in more than one mode separated by a pipe (\|). By default, a file stream is created as a text stream (text file). The following code segment demonstrates some examples of the *open()* function calls.

```
ifstream file1;
file1.open("parts.dat");      //file opened in ios::in
ofstrem file2;
file2.open("A:\\report.dat",ios::binary|ios::app);
                              //file opened in appending binary mode
fstream file3;
file3.open("sales.dat");  //file opened in ios::in and ios::out
```

A physical file name must contain a path specification if a file is not stored on the same device or directory (folder) where a program that processes the file is stored. The report.dat file that is associated with the file2 object, for example, is stored in the root directory of the **A** drive, while a program that processes this file can be stored in any other directory or drive. Two files in this example (file1 and file3) are opened in default modes *ios::in* and *ios::in|ios::out*, respectively.

In addition to using *open()*, a file can also be opened by using a constructor function when instantiating a file object. The following code segment demonstrates this method:

```
ifstream file1("parts.dat");   //file opened in ios::in
ofstrem file2("A:\\report.dat",ios::binary|ios::app);
fstrem file3("sales.dat");   //file opened in ios::in and ios::out
```

A constructor function, in this case, performs two tasks: it creates a file object and opens a file. The *open()* function enables programmers to attach a specific file to a file object after the object has been created. By using a constructor function, both tasks can be done at the same time.

It is important to check for possible run-time errors that may occur when opening a file. An attempt to open a file that cannot be located by the operating system for reading, for example, may cause abnormal program termination. A run-time error also occurs when attempting to open a file in output mode (writing to a file) if no space is available on the specified disk. The following two methods are commonly used when designing a file-opening error checker:

- Passing a file object to the **operator!()** function (overloaded in the **ios** class) and checking its return value (**true** or **false**)
- Using a file object to invoke the **fail()** function and checking its return value (**true** or **false**)

A *true* value returned by either of the two functions indicates that the file was not successfully opened. The following code segment demonstrates the first method that uses *operator!()*:

```
ifstream file1("C:\\parts.dat",ios::in);
if(!file1)          //file-opening error checker
{
     cerr<<"Error in opening file for input!";

     exit(1);
}
```

This code segment attempts to open the parts.dat file stored on the **C** drive for reading. The file1 object (instantiated from *ifstream*) is associated with the file and passed to **operator!()**. A value returned by **operator!()** is used as the **if** condition. If parts.dat cannot be located on the **C** drive, **operator!()** returns **true** (the **if** condition !file1 is **true**). An error message, Error in opening file for input!, is displayed and the program will properly terminate by calling the **exit()** function. Please note that the error message is inserted into the standard error stream called cerr, which is normally connected to the screen.

The following code segment demonstrates a method that uses the **fail()** function to check for an error in file opening:

```
ofstream cmpFile("cmpinfo.dat");  //file opened in ios::out
if(cmpFile.fail())                //file opening error checker
{
    cerr<<"Error in opening file for writing!";
    exit(1);
}
```

The **fail()** function (defined in **ios**) returns a nonzero value if any I/O error has occurred. In this example, the cmpFile object that is associated with cmpinfo.dat is used to invoke **fail()**. If cmpinfo.dat has not been successfully opened for output (**ios::out**), **fail()** will return **true** and code that handles this error will execute.

12.1.3 Using a File

After a file has been successfully opened in a specified mode, the I/O operations (reading or writing) can be performed. C++ supports the following two methods of reading data from or writing data to a file:

1. Using the >> operator and << operator to extract data from a file stream, and to insert data to a file stream, respectively

2. Using a file object to invoke a member function that reads data from, or writes data to, a file associated with the file object.

Table 12.3 shows commonly used stream I/O member functions. Both methods of reading/writing data from or to a file are demonstrated in Section 12.2 (using the >> and << operators) and Section 12.3 (using I/O member functions).

Table 12.3 Stream I/O Member Functions

Input Functions	
Function	**Description**
read()	Reads a specified number of bytes from a file
get()	Reads a character or a sequence of characters (3 versions of *get()*)
getline()	Reads a specified number of characters or until \n
peek()	Reads the next character, but does not remove the character
Output Functions	
write()	Writes a specified number of bytes to a file
put()	Writes a character to a file

12.1.4 Closing a File

When a file object goes out of scope, an appropriate destructor will be automatically invoked to close a file associated with the file object and *destroy* the object. In addition to closing the file by using the destructor function, the file can also be closed explicitly by calling the *close()* member function. Closing a file using *close()* disconnects the file from a file object that is used to invoke *close()*.

For example,

```
cmpFile.close();          //closes file
```

closes a file associated with the cmpFile file object. This object can be used again to open and process another file.

A file should be explicitly closed with *close()*. It improves program readability and frees some resources that a program can reuse.

12.2 SEQUENTIAL FILES

When writing programs that create and process files for I/O, it is important to properly organize data stored in a file. Please note that a file can be organized as a collection of data records. A **data record** is a collection of related data items called **fields**. A file that stores an inventory of computer components, for example, consists of records with each record representing a specific computer component. A data record could consist of fields such as a component's description, quantity, and price. Each record must have a field that can be used to uniquely identify the record (**record primary key**).

A file can be processed as a sequential or random-access file. Data records in a **sequential file** are written to, or read from, the file in a specific order and they are typically sorted by the field that is used as the record primary key. In Program Example 12.1, PROG12_1 demonstrates a simple method of creating a sequential file and writing data sequentially to the file.

PROGRAM EXAMPLE 12.1: PROG12_1

```
1   //PROG12_1: Program demonstrates sequential file output.
2   #include <iostream>
3   #include <fstream>
4   #include <cstdlib>
5   using namespace std;
6
7   int main()
8   {
9       char part[10];
10      int quantity;
11      float price;
12      char *fname="comparts.dat";          //physical file name
13      ofstream fout(fname,ios::out);        //opening file for output
14      if(!fout)                             //handles errors in file opening
15      {
16          cerr<<"Error in opening file for output!";
17          exit(1);
18      }
19      cout<<"Enter components' data and CTRL-Z to stop =>"<<endl;
20      cout<<"\nComponent description -> quantity -> price =>"<<endl;
21
22      while(cin>>part>>quantity>>price)
23      {
24          fout<<part<<' '<<quantity<<' '<<price<<'\n';   //file output
25      }
26      return 0;
27  }
```

A `fout` file object is created by using the ***ofstream*** constructor, indicating that a file associated with `fout` will be processed for output. When instantiating `fout`, a `comparts.dat` physical file name and a ***ios::out*** mode are passed to the ***ofstream*** constructor as arguments (line 13). The constructor opens the file (connects `fout` to `comparts.dat`) in the requested ***ios::out*** mode. This mode specifies that the program will create the `comparts.dat` file if the file does not exist, and the data will be written to the file starting from the beginning of the file. If the file exists, data stored in the file will be truncated and replaced by the data that the program writes to the file. Note that the ***ios::app*** mode is used when it is necessary to preserve the existing data and add new data starting from the end of the file. An error checker (lines 14–18) handles errors that may occur when opening `comparts.dat`.

The program obtains data (a component's description, quantity, and price) from the user by using ***cin*** and the `>>` operator (line 22). In addition to performing input, `cin>>part>>quantity>>price` also serves as a condition of the ***while*** loop (lines 22–25), which writes data entered by the user to the file. The `>>` operator returns ***false*** to ***cin*** if *bad data*, or the end-of-file key combination, is entered. The <Ctrl>Z key combination is used to indicate the end of file on IBM PCs and compatible systems. The user, therefore, can stop data entry and ***break*** the loop by entering <Ctrl>Z.

Data entered by the user is written to the file by using the `<<` operator (line 24). The `fout` file object is located on the left side of `<<`, while data to be written to `comparts.dat` associated with `fout` is on the right side of `<<`. The concept of using `<<` to produce output to a file (i.e., write data to a file) is the same as the concept used to produce output on a display screen (***cout***). The only difference between these two output operations is the type of output object that is located on the left side of the `<<` operator.

A sample run of PROG12_1 is shown in Figure 12.2. The output in Figure 12.2 also shows the contents of the `comparts.dat` file that is processed by PROG12_1. Line 24 that produces output to the file specifies how the data records appear in the file. Note that a space is inserted between data items (fields), and a new line character is inserted at the end of each record.

```
Enter components' data and Ctrl-Z to stop =>

Component description -> quantity -> price =>
cdrw 18 168.50
hdrive 15 188.99
modem 17 65.00
mouse 30 21.50
sdram 25 55.90
sndcard 12 95.00 <Ctrl-Z>
```

Figure 12.2 *Sample run of PROG12_1.*

After the execution of PROG12_1, the comparts.dat file has been created and the data records entered by the user have been stored in the file. This file can be opened and its data can be read and processed by another program.

PROG12_2 is used to manipulate data stored in comparts.dat. This program, illustrated in Program Example 12.2, demonstrates a method of reading data sequentially from a file.

PROGRAM EXAMPLE 12.2: PROG12_2

```
1   //PROG12_2: Program demonstrates sequential reading.
2   #include <iostream>
3   #include <iomanip>
4   #include <fstream>
5   #include <cstdlib>
6   using namespace std;
7
8   int main()
9   {
10      char part[10];
11      int quantity,qmin;
12      float price;
13      char *fname="comparts.dat";
14      ifstream fin(fname,ios::in);
```

```
15    if(!fin)
16    {
17       cerr<<"Error in openning file!";
18       exit(1);
19    }
20    cout<<"Enter a minimum quantity => ";
21    cin>>qmin;
22    cout<<"\nComponents where quantity is less than "<<qmin<<endl;
23    cout<<"Quantity   Component    Price"<<endl;
24    cout<<setiosflags(ios::fixed)<<setprecision(2);
25    while(fin>>part>>quantity>>price)
26    {
27       if(quantity<qmin)
28       {
29          cout<<setiosflags(ios::left);
30          cout<<setw(11)<<quantity<<setw(10)<<part;
31          cout<<resetiosflags(ios::left);
32          cout<<" $"<<setw(6)<<price<<'\n';
33       }
34    }
35    return 0;
36 }
```

This program invokes the *ifstream* constructor to create a file object named `fin` and to connect `fin` to `comparts.dat` (line 14). Notice that the *ios::in* mode is passed to the constructor, which opens the file for reading. This mode is the default for *ifstream* and therefore does not have to be explicitly passed to the *ifstream* constructor. Explicitly specifying a mode in which a file is opened, however, improves the clarity of a program.

The program obtains a `qmin` integer value (line 21) from the user, which represents a minimum quantity of a component in `comparts.dat` to search for. The data records stored in `comparts.dat` are read by using the >> operator (line 25). After a data record is extracted by >> (that is, copied from the file to memory allocated to store the record), its `quantity` is compared to `qmin` (line 27). If `quantity` is less than `qmin`, the data record is displayed on the screen (lines 29–32). This operation is repeated until the end of the file is reached. The >> operator returns 0 when the end of the file has been reached and the *while* loop stops.

If the data records stored in comparts.dat are those shown in Figure 12.2, a sample run of PROG12_2 would display the output shown in Figure 12.3. The program only displays records in which quantity is less than the quantity entered by the user.

```
Enter a minimum quantity => 20

Components where quantity is less than 20
Quantity   Component   Price
   18       cdrw       $168.50
   15       hdrive     $188.99
   17       modem      $ 65.00
   12       sndcard    $ 95.00
```

Figure 12.3 *Sample run of PROG12_2.*

PROG12_1 and PROG12_2 demonstrate sequential writing and reading of data items of built-in data types. The << operator and the >> operator have been used to perform I/O operations. In addition to the writing/reading of data of built-in types, user-defined class objects can also be written to or read from a file by using << and >>.

The << and >> operators must be overloaded relative to the class(es) when writing or reading class objects to or from a file. This technique is similar to that used when inserting/extracting class objects into or from the standard I/O stream objects—*cout* and *cin* (demonstrated in Chapter 6). In Program Example 12.3, PROG12_3 demonstrates this technique.

PROGRAM EXAMPLE 12.3: PROG12_3

```
1  //PROG12_3: Program demonstrates sequential file input/output
2  //           of user-defined class objects.
3  #include <iostream>
4  #include <iomanip>
5  #include <fstream>
6  #include <cstdlib>
7  using namespace std;
8  int const SIZE=4;
9
10 class Compart {
```

```
11 private:
12    char part[10];
13    int quantity;
14    float price;
15 public:
16    Compart(){ strcpy(part," "); quantity=0; price=0; }
17    friend istream &operator>>(istream &ist, Compart &obj)
18    {
19        ist>>obj.part>>obj.quantity>>obj.price;
20        return ist;
21    }
22    friend ostream &operator<<(ostream &ost, const Compart &obj)
23    {
24        ost<<obj.part<<' '<<obj.quantity<<' '<<obj.price<<'\n';
25        return ost;
26    }
27 };
28 int main()
29 {
30    Compart cp1[SIZE];
31    int i;
32    char *fname="comparts.dat";
33
34    ofstream fout(fname,ios::out);      //Creates a file object for
35    if(!fout)                           //output
36    {
37        cerr<<"Error in opening file for output!";
38        exit(1);
39    }
40    cout<<"Enter part -> quantity -> price => \n";
41    for(i=0;i<SIZE;i++)
42    {
43        cout<<"Part #"<<(i+1)<<" => ";
```

E
X
A
M
P
L
E

```
44        cin>>cp1[i];           //Extracts objects from the keyboard
45        fout<<cp1[i];          //Inserts objects into the file
46     }
47     fout.close();             //Closes the file
48
49     ifstream fin(fname,ios::in);  //Creates a file object for input
50     if(!fin)
51     {
52        cerr<<"Error in opening file for input!";
53        exit(1);
54     }
55     Compart cp2[SIZE];
56     cout<<"\nContents of the file "<<fname<<endl;
57     cout<<setiosflags(ios::fixed)<<setprecision(2);
58     for(i=0;i<SIZE;i++)
59     {
60        fin>>cp2[i];   //Extracts objects from the file
61        cout<<cp2[i];  //Inserts objects onto the screen
62     }
63     return 0;
64 }
```

This program creates a Compart class (lines 10–27) whose objects are written to or read from the comparts.dat file. The Compart class overloads both the stream extraction operator (lines 17–21) and the stream insertion operator (lines 22–26). Objects of Compart can therefore be inserted to or extracted from the standard I/O stream objects (*cout* and *cin*) as well as from the file objects by using the stream extraction and stream insertion operators. Remember that file objects are instantiated from the classes derived from *istream* and *ostream* from which *cout* and *cin* are instantiated.

The program first instantiates an array of objects named cp1 from Compart (line 30). A fout file object is instantiated and connected to comparts.dat, which is opened for output (line 34). The program uses the stream extraction operator to extract objects' data from *cin* (line 44) and then uses the stream insertion operator to write the objects' data to the file (line 45). The file is closed after the objects have been written to it (line 47).

Another file object named `fin` is instantiated and connected to the same `com-parts.dat` file, which is now opened for input (line 49). A `cp2` array of `Compart` objects is instantiated (line 55) and used to store data that is read from the file by using the `>>` operator (line 60). The program outputs data that is read from the file on the screen by inserting `cp2` elements into *cout* (line 61). A sample run of PROG12_3 is shown in Figure 12.4.

```
Enter part -> quantity -> price =>
Part #1 => cdrw 27 210.90
Part #2 => hdrw 19 230.00
Part #3 => memc 53 110.50
Part #4 => mthb 11 650.10

Contents of the file comparts.dat
cdrw 27 210.90
hdrw 19 230.00
memc 53 110.50
mthb 11 650.10
```

Figure 12.4 *Sample run of PROG12_3.*

PROG12_3 writes to and reads objects of the same `Compart` class type from a file. Unlike data stored in memory, data stored in a disk file lose their data types. The data stored in `cp1` and `cp2` arrays in PROG12_3, for example, is stored in memory as `Compart` objects. The same data stored in `comparts.dat`, however, is not treated as a sequence of objects of a specific class type, but as a sequence of bytes. This raises the following question: is it possible to write objects of different types to a file; and if it is possible, how are these different types distinguished when reading data from the file into memory allocated for a specific type of data?

One method for distinguishing this data requires the *operator<<()* and *operator>>()* functions to be overloaded relative to each class whose objects are written to or read from a file. This method also requires an object's type identifier to be inserted into a file stream before inserting the actual object's data. The type identifier is then used as a selector of the *switch* statement that will invoke the appropriate *operator>>()* function to read data (i.e., copy data from the file into memory).

Sequential files (sequential writing and reading) are simple to implement and process. Updating sequential files, however, could be a challenging task. Changing a record that is stored in a sequential file, for example, may destroy other data records, thus causing an error when reading incorrect data into a program. To prevent errors when updating sequential files, all data records preceding the record to be updated should first be written to a new file. Next, the modified record(s), as well as all remaining records, should be written to the new file. Random-access files provide a much more efficient way of updating and processing files than sequential files. Random-access file handling, however, requires more skill than sequential file handling.

12.3 RANDOM-ACCESS FILES

Unlike sequential files, reading from and writing to **random-access files** can start from any location in the file, and data records can be read from or written to in any order.

C++ uses the **file position indicator (FPI)** to determine the position in a file at which the next read or write operation will occur. There are two types of FPIs—the first type is for reading and the second is for writing. A first step in random-access file processing is to position FPI to the desired location in the file. To accomplish this, the two standard library functions shown in Figure 12.5 are commonly used.

```
istream & seekg(streamoff offset, seek_dir origin);

ostream & seekp(streamoff offset, seek_dir origin);
```

Figure 12.5 *Standard library functions used to position FPI within a file.*

The *seekg()* function positions the FPI for reading, while the *seekp()* determines the position of FPI for writing. Both functions take two arguments. A first argument, called offset, specifies the new position of the FPI. This position is expressed in bytes starting from the specified origin. A second argument, called origin, can have one of the following values:

- *ios::beg* (beginning of the file)
- *ios::cur* (current position within the file)
- *ios::end* (end of file)

The following code segment demonstrates some examples of *seekp()* and *seekg()* calls:

```
ofstream fout("orders.dat");
ifstream fin("comparts.dat");
fout.seekp(100,ios::beg);              //Positions FPI for writing
fin.seekg(-count*sizeof(compart),ios::end);  //Positions FPI
                                             //for reading
```

The *seekp()* function in this example positions the FPI for writing at the location 100 bytes away from the beginning of the file — "orders.dat". The *seekg()* function moves the FPI for reading count*sizeof(compart) bytes toward the beginning of the file, starting from the end of the "comparts.dat". Note that the offset value can be positive or negative, indicating the direction away from or toward the beginning of the file.

After the FPI has been successfully positioned at the location where reading or writing should take place, one of the I/O member functions shown in Table 12.3 should be used to perform reading/writing operations. When reading/writing a block of data to or from a random-access file, the *write()* and *read()* functions are commonly used. PROG12_4 demonstrates this technique in Program Example 12.4.

PROGRAM EXAMPLE 12.4: PROG12_4

```
1  //PROG12_4: Program demonstrates random-access file processing.
2  #include <iostream>
3  #include <iomanip>
4  #include <fstream>
5  #include <cstdlib>
6  using namespace std;
7
8  struct compart {
9     char part[10];
10    int qty;
11 };
12
13 int main()
14 {
15    int count=0;
16    compart newpart;
17    ofstream fcout("comparts.dat",ios::out|ios::binary);
18    if(!fcout)
19    {
20       cerr<<"Error in file opening for writing!";
21       exit(1);
```

```
22    }
23    cout<<"Enter part and quantity or Ctrl-Z to stop=>"<<endl;
24
25    while(cin>>newpart.part>>newpart.qty)
26    {
27        fcout.seekp(count*sizeof(compart));
28        fcout.write((char*)&newpart, sizeof(compart));
29        count++;
30        cout<<"Record #"<<count<<" written to the file."<<endl;
31    }
32    fcout.close();
33
34    ifstream fcin("comparts.dat",ios::in|ios::binary);
35    if(!fcin)
36    {
37        cerr<<"Error in file opening for reading!";
38        exit(1);
39    }
40    if(count>=3)
41    {
42        cout<<"\nLast 3 records written to the file =>"<<endl;
43        cout<<"\nPart  Quantity"<<setiosflags(ios::left)<<endl;
44        fcin.seekg((count-3)*sizeof(compart),ios::beg);
45        int c=0;
46        while(c<3 && !fcin.eof())
47        {
48            fcin.read((char*)&newpart, sizeof(compart));
49            c++;
50            if(c<=3)
51            cout<<setw(10)<<newpart.part<<setw(5)<<newpart.qty<<endl;
52        }
53    }
54    else
```

```
55          cout<<"Less than 3 records written to file";
56     return 0;
57 }
```

This program writes and reads data records of the `compart` structure type. The program first opens the `comparts.dat` file for binary writing and connects it to the `fcout` file object (line 17). A *while* loop is used to read data records until the user enters the <Ctrl>Z end-of-file key combination (line 25). The FPI for writing is positioned by *seekp()* at the location `count*sizeof(compart)`bytes away from the beginning of the file `comparts.dat` (line 27). The `count` variable counts the number of `compart` data records recorded in the file. The *write()* function writes a data record stored in `newpart` to the file (line 28). Note that the *(char *)* type cast must be applied to the address of `newpart` before passing it to *write()*, because this pointer is declared as a *char** pointer in the definition of the standard *write()* function. After the number of records specified by `count` have been successfully written to the file, the file is closed (line 32).

The same file is then opened for binary reading and connected to the `fcin` file object (line 34). The file position indicator for reading is positioned at the location `(count-3)*sizeof(compart)` bytes away from the beginning of `comparts.dat` by the *seekg()* function (line 44). This location is positioned at the beginning of the third data record from the end of the file. A *while* loop (lines 46–52) reads the last three records in the file by *read()* (line 48) and displays these data records on the screen (line 51). The standard *read()* library function also requires that the *(char*)* type be cast prior to the pointer that stores an address in the memory to which a data record read from the file will be copied. A sample run of PROG12_4 is shown in Figure 12.6.

452

```
    Enter part and quantity or Ctrl-Z to stop =>
    cpu 12
    Record #1 written to the file.
    hdisk 25
    Record #2 written to the file.
    modem 41
    Record #3 written to the file.
    ram 35
    Record #4 written to the file.
    sndcard 15
    Record #5 written to the file.
    <Ctrl-Z>

    Last 3 records written to the file =>

    Part            Quantity
    modem              41
    ram                35
    sndcard            15
```

Figure 12.6 *Output produced by PROG12_4.*

It is much easier to update a random-access file (modify, delete, or add data records) than a sequential file. Random-access files allow programmers to specify where the location of a data record to be modified is within a file. This approach does not require reading or writing over the data records located before or after the record(s) to be modified.

SUMMARY

1. C++ uses file objects (file streams) when processing file I/O. A file object is instantiated from one of the three classes (*ifstream*, *ofstream*, or *fstream*) defined in the standard *fstream* header file.

2. A file can be opened either by invoking the *open()* member function, or by passing appropriate arguments to a constructor function when instantiating a file object.

3. A physical file name that is used by the operating system to access the file must be passed to a function that opens the file.

4. A file mode determines how a file is opened as well as the purpose of file processing. Each class used to instantiate a file object has its default file mode.

5. An error checker should be used to check for file opening errors before using the file.

6. In addition to class member functions, the >> operator and << operator can be used to read data from and write data to a file, respectively.

7. A file can be closed explicitly by invoking the **close()** member function, or automatically by the destructor function.

8. When performing reading or writing operations, a file can be processed as a sequential or random-access file.

9. Data records in a sequential file are read from or written to in a specific order starting from the beginning or the end of the file. A common method of sequentially reading/writing data uses the stream extraction and the stream insertion operators.

10. Data records in a random-access file can be read from or written to any location within a file that is specified by the file position indicator (FPI). To move the file position indicator to a specific location within the file, the **seekp()** (for writing) or **seekg()** (for reading) function is used.

11. To randomly write or read data records to or from a file, member functions (commonly **read()** and **write()**) should be invoked on file objects.

12. It is much easier to update data records stored in a file by using the random-access file-processing techniques rather than the sequential file-processing techniques.

EXERCISES

Identify and correct the errors in the code segments in Exercises 12.1 through 12.6.

12.1
```
fstream myfile("info.dat");
if(myfile)
{
  cout<<"Error in file opening.";
  exit(1);
}
```

12.2
```
ifstream fstr;
fstr.open("A:\info.dat",ios::out);
```

12.3
```
ofstream fout("comparts.dat");
if(fout.fail())
{
    cerr<<"Error in file opening.";
    exit(1);
}
fout.seekp(-2*sizeof(compart),ios::end);
fout.read((char*)&part,sizeof(compart));
```

12.4
```
ifstream fin("info.dat",ios::app);
fin<<obj;
fin.close();
```

12.5
```
ofstream fstr("info.dat");
fstr>>x>>y;
fstr.close();
```

12.6
```
fout.seekg(n*sizeof(int),ios::cur);
fout<<a;
```

12.7 State the output produced by the following program.
```
#include <iostream>
#include <fstream>
using namespace std;
int main()
{
    char *course="OOP USING C++", ch;
    ofstream ftest1("test.dat");
    ftest1<<course;
    ftest1.close();
    ifstream ftest2("test.dat");
```

```
    ftest2.seekg(-8,ios::end);
    ch=ftest2.get();    //reads a character
    cout<<ch<<endl;
    ftest2.seekg(2,ios::cur);
    ch=ftest2.get();    //reads a character
    cout<<ch;
    return 0;
}
```

PROGRAMMING PROJECTS

12.1   Design a program that creates a sequential file and writes 50 random integer numbers, in the range from 0 to 100, to the file. The program should first create the file and then open the file for reading and display the numbers greater than and equal to 60 on the screen.

12.2   A file is required to record a city's daily temperature, humidity, and barometric pressure for one month. Design a program which first creates this file. It should then open the file for reading and compute and display the largest, smallest, and average values of the temperature, humidity, and barometric pressure data that are recorded in the file.

12.3   Two files are used to control access to a laboratory. The first file stores ID numbers of engineers and technicians who are permitted to use the lab and the second file records data of the personnel who entered the lab on a specific day. Each record in the second file should contain an ID number and time when an engineer or technician entered the lab. Design a program that allows a lab manager, who is identified by his/her ID number and password, to create and name both files.

The program should also provide the following two options:
- Get permission to enter the lab (for engineers and technicians)
- Check the personnel in the lab (for the lab manager)

When the first option is selected, the user is prompted to enter his/her ID number. If the ID number is found in the first file, the program should display the message: `ACCESS TO THE LAB IS PERMITTED!`. If the ID is not found, the program should display: `ACCESS DENIED!` If permission is granted, the program should record the ID number and the time an engineer or technician entered the lab in the second file.

The second option should allow the lab manager to check the list of engineers and technicians who were in the lab at a specified time.

12.4 Design a program that creates and uses a file to process an inventory of computer components. The program should use a class with data members that store a component's description, quantity, and price.

The program should provide the following menu options to the user:

1. Create a file and store inventory
2. Add a component to the list
3. Display the current list of components
4. Delete a component from the list
5. Update (edit) a component
6. Sort components by description or quantity
7. Exit program

If any of the first six options is selected and executed, the program control should go back to the main menu.

Options 1 through 6 should open and process the file for writing or reading based on the option selected. All files should be processed as random-access files. The first option (*Create a file and store inventory*) should enable the user to name the file.

C++ Keywords and Synonyms

C++ provides 63 standard keywords (reserved identifiers), 32 of which are also used by the C programming language. Table A.1 shows a complete list of C++ keywords with a description of each keyword. The 32 keywords common to both the C++ and C programming languages are *underlined* in Table A.1.

Table A.1 C++ Keywords

Keyword	Description
asm	Enables information to be passed directly to the assembler
auto	Default storage class for local variables (objects)
bool	A Boolean data type
break	Terminates a loop or *switch* statement
case	Specifies a control expression in a *switch* statement
catch	Specifies an exception handler
char	A character (integer) data type
class	Used to declare classes and template type parameters
const	Used to declare constants
const_cast	A type-cast operator for casting *const* or *volatile*
continue	Executes the next iteration of a loop from the beginning
default	Specifies a code segment that executes if no match occurs in *switch*
delete	Frees memory dynamically allocated by *new*
do	Specifies a *do/while* loop
double	A floating-point data type
dynamic_cast	A type-cast operator for casting pointers
else	Specifies a *false* expression in an *if* statement
enum	Declares an enumerated data type
explicit	Prevents a constructor from being invoked for an implicit conversion
export	Enables access from another compilation unit
extern	Default storage class for global variables (objects)

Keyword	Description
false	A Boolean value
float	A floating-point data type
for	Specifies a *for* loop
friend	Declares *friend* functions and classes
goto	Transfers a program control to a labeled statement
if	Specifies an *if* statement
inline	Declares *inline* functions
int	An integer data type
long	A data type prefix for *int* and *double*
mutable	A storage class specifier that allows class members to be modified
namespace	Declares program entities with the same scope
new	Allocates memory dynamically
operator	Declares functions that overload operators
private	An access specifier for class members (specifies *private* access)
protected	An access specifier for class members (specifies *protected* access)
public	An access specifier for class members (specifies *public* access)
register	A storage class for variables stored in CPU registers
reinterpret_cast	A type-cast operator for nonstandard type conversions
return	A statement that terminates a function and returns a value
short	An integer data type
signed	A data type prefix for *int*
sizeof	An operator that returns the size of an object in bytes
static	A storage class for objects that exist until the end of the program
static_cast	A type-cast operator for standard type conversions
struct	Used to declare structures
switch	Specifies a *switch* statement
template	Used to declare function and class templates
this	A pointer that points to the object that invokes a member function
throw	Throws an exception
true	A Boolean value
try	Specifies a code segment to be monitored for exceptions
typedef	Used to declare user-defined types
typeid	A run-time type information (RTTI) operator
typename	Used to declare template type parameters
union	Used to declare structures in which all members use the same storage
unsigned	A data type prefix for *int*
using	A directive used to omit a namespace prefix

Keyword	Description
virtual	Used to declare virtual member functions and classes
void	A *no-type* data type
volatile	Used to declare objects that may be altered from outside the program
wchar_t	A character type that stores wide characters (e.g. 2-byte, 4-byte)
while	Specifies a ***while*** loop or precedes the condition of a ***do/while*** loop

In addition to keywords, C++ also provides 11 standard synonyms (alternative representations) for certain operators. Synonyms for bitwise operators (&, |, ^, ~, <<, >>), for example, can be used if a keyboard does not support characters that represent these operators. The use of synonyms may also improve a program's readability. Like keywords, synonyms are reserved and cannot be used for any other purpose. Table A.2 shows a complete list of C++ standard synonyms.

Table A.2 C++ Synonyms

Synonym	Description
and	A synonym for the logical AND operator (&&)
and_eq	A synonym for the bitwise AND assignment operator (& =)
bitand	A synonym for the bitwise AND operator (&)
bitor	A synonym for the bitwise inclusive OR operator (|)
compl	A synonym for the bitwise complement operator (~)
not	A synonym for the logical NOT operator (!)
not_eq	A synonym for the inequality operator (! =)
or	A synonym for the logical OR operator (||)
or_eq	A synonym for the bitwise inclusive OR assignment operator (| =)
xor	A synonym for the bitwise exclusive OR operator (^)
xor_eq	A synonym for the bitwise exclusive OR assignment operator (^ =)

APPENDIX b

C++ Operators

C++ provides a large collection of operators. Table B.1 shows standard C++ operators in a decreasing order of **precedence** (from highest to lowest). The higher-level precedence operators are evaluated before the lower-level precedence operators. Table B.1 also shows the **associativity** of each operator. The addition operator (+), for example, associates from left to right; therefore, the expression a+b+c is evaluated as (a+b)+c, where the expression enclosed in brackets will be evaluated first. The assignment operator (=) is an example of the operator that has the right-to-left associativity; therefore the expression a=b=1 is evaluated as a=(b=1) (1 is first assigned to b, and then 1 is assigned to a).

Table B.1 Standard C++ Operators

Operator	Name	Precedence	Associativity
::	Binary scope resolution	17	left to right
::	Unary scope resolution	17	left to right
( )	Parentheses	16	left to right
[ ]	Array subscript	16	left to right
.	Direct member selection	16	left to right
->	Indirect member selection	16	left to right
++	Postincrement	16	left to right
- -	Postdecrement	16	left to right
typeid	Run-time type information	16	left to right
dynamic_cast	Run-time type-checked cast	16	left to right
static_cast	Compile-time type-checked cast	16	left to right
reinterpret_cast	Nonstandard conversions cast	16	left to right
const_cast	*const* cast	16	left to right
++	Preincrement	15	right to left
- -	Predecrement	15	right to left
+	Unary plus	15	right to left

Operator	Name	Precedence	Associativity
-	Unary minus	15	right to left
!	Logical negation	15	right to left
~	Bitwise complement	15	right to left
( )	Type cast	15	right to left
sizeof	Size of object	15	right to left
&	Address	15	right to left
*	Dereference	15	right to left
new	Dynamic memory allocation	15	right to left
new[ ]	Dynamic array allocation	15	right to left
delete	Dynamic memory deallocation	15	right to left
delete[ ]	Dynamic array deallocation	15	right to left
.*	Pointer to member via object	14	left to right
->*	Pointer to member via pointer	14	left to right
*	Multiplication	13	left to right
/	Division	13	left to right
%	Modulus	13	left to right
+	Addition	12	left to right
-	Subtraction	12	left to right
<<	Bitwise left shift	11	left to right
>>	Bitwise right shift	11	left to right
<	Less than	10	left to right
<=	Less than or equal to	10	left to right
>	Greater than	10	left to right
>=	Greater than or equal to	10	left to right
==	Equal to	9	left to right
!=	Not equal to	9	left to right
&	Bitwise AND	8	left to right
^	Bitwise exclusive OR	7	left to right
|	Bitwise inclusive OR	6	left to right
&&	Logical AND	5	left to right
||	Logical OR	4	left to right
?:	Conditional	3	right to left
=	Assignment	2	right to left
+=	Addition assignment	2	right to left
-=	Subtraction assignment	2	right to left
*=	Multiplication assignment	2	right to left
/=	Division assignment	2	right to left

Operator	Name	Precedence	Associativity
%=	Modulus assignment	2	right to left
&=	Bitwise AND assignment	2	right to left
^=	Bitwise exclusive OR assignment	2	right to left
|=	Bitwise inclusive OR assignment	2	right to left
<<=	Bitwise left shift assignment	2	right to left
>>=	Bitwise right shift assignment	2	right to left
,	Comma	1	left to right

APPENDIX C

Standard C++ Library

The C++ library contains the following components:

- **Language support** components (required by certain parts of C++, such as memory allocation and exception handling)
- **Diagnostics** components (provides tools for reporting errors, including exception classes)
- **General utilities** components (includes components used by other elements of the library, such as a storage allocator for dynamic storage management)
- **String** components (provides support for manipulating sequences of characters)
- **Localization** components (extends internationalization support for text processing)
- **Containers** (STL components)
- **Iterators** (STL components)
- **Algorithms** (STL components)
- **Numeric** components (extends support for numeric processing, including complex number processing)
- **Input/output** components

The C++ Standard Library provides 32 **C++ header files** shown in Table C.1.

Table C.1 C++ Standard Header Files

Header File	Description
algorithm	Defines numerous function templates that perform useful algorithms
bitset	Defines the *bitset* class template and two supporting templates
complex	Defines the *complex* class template and supporting function templates
deque	Defines the *deque* container class template and three supporting templates
exception	Defines function and class templates for exception handling

Header File	Description
fstream	Defines class templates for file I/O
functional	Defines class templates that are used to instantiate function objects
iomanip	Defines I/O manipulators, such as *setw()*, *setprecision()*, etc.
ios	Defines I/O types and functions (typically included by other I/O headers)
iosfwd	Defines forward references to class templates for I/O
iostream	Defines objects used to perform standard I/O, such as *cin*, *cout*, *cerr*, etc.
istream	Defines the *basic_istream* class template for input operations
iterator	Defines templates that are used to create and manipulate iterators
limits	Defines the *numeric_limits* class template
list	Defines the *list* container and three supporting containers
locale	Defines class and function templates that manipulate locales
map	Defines the *map* and *multimap* container class templates
memory	Defines an operator and templates that help allocate and free objects
new	Defines classes and functions that support dynamic memory management
numeric	Defines several function templates used for numeric operations
ostream	Defines the *basic_ostream* class template and related manipulators
queue	Defines the *queue* class template and its supporting templates
set	Defines the *set* and *multiset* class templates and their supporting templates
sstream	Defines class templates that support I/O operations on sequences
stack	Defines the *stack* class template and two supporting templates
stdexcept	Defines several classes that are used for reporting exceptions
streambuf	Defines the *basic_streambuf* class template
string	Defines the *basic_string* class template and supporting templates
typeinfo	Defines classes and functions used for type identification
utility	Defines several templates of general use throughout the library
valarray	Defines the *valarray* class template and supporting templates
vector	Defines the *vector* class template and three supporting templates

Some header files are seldom directly included in a program (for example, *ios*, *iosfwd*, *istream*, *ostream*, etc.). These header files are typically included by another header file(s).

C++ provides the facilities of the Standard C Library organized into 18 additional header files (shown in Table C.2). Each header file of the Standard C Library that is included in the Standard C++ Library starts with the character "c". The C++ standard requires that each header file cname is the same as the corresponding name.h header file as specified by the C standard. For example, the *cstdio* header file in the Standard C++ Library must be the same as the *stdio.h* header file in the Standard C Library.

Table C.2 C++ Header Files for C Library Facilities

cassert	*cctype*	*cerrno*	*cfloat*
ciso646	*climits*	*clocale*	*cmath*
csetjmp	*csignal*	*cstdarg*	*cstddef*
cstdio	*cstdlib*	*cstring*	*ctime*
cwchar	*cwctype*		

APPENDIX d

Standard C++ Algorithms

In addition to containers, iterators, function objects, and adaptors, the Standard Template Library (STL) also contains approximately 70 algorithms that are designed as non-member function templates. These function templates (algorithms) can operate on containers; however, they do not depend on the implementation of the containers on which they operate. Algorithms are separated from containers in the STL. This enables the addition of new algorithms to the STL without modifying the existing container classes. Note that the STL algorithms can also operate on regular (C-style) arrays.

STL algorithms can be categorized into the following groups:

1. Sorting and searching algorithms (in the *algorithm* header file)

2. Comparison algorithms (in the *algorithm* header file)

3. Permutation algorithms (in the *algorithm* header file)

4. Numeric algorithms (in the *numeric* header file)

5. Algorithms on sequences (in the *algorithm* header file)

6. Algorithms on sets (in the *algorithm* header file)

7. Algorithms on heaps (in the *algorithm* header file)

Table D.1 shows a list of standard C++ algorithms with a brief description of each algorithm.

Table D.1 STL Algorithms

Algorithm	Description
accumulate()	Sums the values in a sequence
adjacent_difference()	Loads the differences of adjacent values into a segment
adjacent_find()	Finds the first adjacent pair of values in a segment

Algorithm	Description
binary_search()	Determines if a value is in a sorted sequence
copy()	Copies a segment to a new location
copy_backward()	Copies a segment in reverse order to a new location
count()	Counts the number of elements with a given value
count_if()	Counts the number of elements that satisfy a predicate
equal()	Compares two sequences of values by equality
fill()	Sets every element in a segment to a specific value
fill_n()	Sets *n* elements in a segment to a specific value
find()	Locates a value in a sequence
find_end()	Locates the last occurrence of a given substring
find_first_of()	Locates the first occurrence of an element in a segment
find_if()	Locates the first element that satisfies a predicate
for_each()	Applies a general function to every element in a sequence
generate()	Generates values for every element in a segment
generate_n()	Generates *n* values in a specified segment
includes()	Compares two sorted sets of values
inner_product()	Computes the inner product of two sets of values
inplace_merge()	Merges two sorted segments into one
iter_swap()	Swaps two values referred to by iterators
lexicographical_compare()	Compares two sequences alphabetically
lower_bound()	Locates the first element in a segment with a given value
make_heap()	Reorganizes a sequence of values into a heap
max()	Returns the largest value in a segment
max_element()	Locates the largest value in a segment
merge()	Merges two sorted segments into a third segment
min()	Returns the smallest value in a segment
min_element()	Locates the smallest value in a segment
mismatch()	Finds the first position where two segments do not match
next_permutation()	Permutes a segment of values
nth_element()	Finds the first occurrence of a given value
partial_sort()	Sorts the first *n* values in a segment
partial_sort_copy()	Copies *n* smallest sorted values into another segment
partial_sum()	Computes partial sums and loads into a segment
partition()	Partitions a segment
pop_heap()	Removes the top element of a heap
push_heap()	Adds a new value into a heap

Algorithm	Description
prev_permutation()	Permutes a segment of values
random_shuffle()	Randomly orders values in a sequence
remove()	Deletes all elements in a sequence that match a given value
remove_copy()	Deletes all elements with a given value and copies to a segment
remove_copy_if()	Deletes and copies all elements that satisfy a predicate
remove_if()	Deletes all elements in a sequence that satisfy a predicate
replace()	Replaces all elements that match a specified value
replace_copy()	Replaces and copies all elements that match a specified value
replace_copy_if()	Replaces and copies all elements that satisfy a predicate
replace_if()	Replaces all elements in a sequence that satisfy a predicate
reverse()	Reverses the elements in a segment
reverse_copy()	Copies the elements to a new segment in reverse order
rotate()	Rotates the elements
rotate_copy()	Rotates the elements and copies to a new segment
search()	Searches for a given subset
search_n()	Searches for a given subset of *n* values
set_difference()	Copies the relative complement of two sets to a third set
set_intersection()	Copies the intersection of two sets to a third set
set_symmetric_difference()	Copies the symmetric difference of two sets to a third set
set_union()	Copies the union of two sets to a third set
sort()	Sorts the elements in a segment
sort_heap()	Sorts a sequence of values that are arranged in a heap
swap()	Swaps two values
swap_ranges()	Swaps the elements in two sequences
transform()	Applies a general function to every element in a sequence
unique()	Removes all duplicate elements from a sorted sequence
unique_copy()	Copies all unique elements from a sorted sequence to a segment
upper_bound()	Finds the last element in a segment that matches a given value

Answers to
Odd-Numbered Questions

CHAPTER I

1.1   //a precision is missing
cout<<setprecision(2)<<x<<y;

1.3   //the stream insertion operator is missing
cout<<setprecision(4)<<setw(10)<<x;

1.5   //the array subscript operator is missing
const char PLANGUAGE[] = "C++";

1.7   //b is not declared within **sample**
//missing '}' after the body of print()
//a namespace declaration cannot be completed by a semicolon
namespace sample
{
    int a, b;
    print() { cout<<a<<b; }
}

1.9   _ _ _13_ _ _ _d   //'_' represents a space

1.11 B
          F

CHAPTER 2

2.1
```
inline double perimeter(double width, double length)
{
    return (2*width+2*length);
}
```

2.3
```
inline int max(int x, int y)
{
    return (x>y?x:y);
}
```

2.5
```
inline double magnitude(double x, double y)
{
    return (sqrt(x*x+y*y));
}
```

2.7
```
void fun2(double, int, float=0.0);
```

2.9
```
void fun4(char *, int=1);
```

2.11
```
void fun2(int, ...);         //function prototype
    fun2(1);    //function call #1 (an argument is missing)
    fun2(3, "C/C++");        //function call #2
    fun2(-1, '$', 3.9);    //function call #3
```

2.13
```
double fun4(int, float=0);    //function prototype
    cout<<fun4(1);               //function call #1
    double x=fun4(1,3.3)         //function call #2
    double y=fun4(5); //function call #3 (an argument is missing)
```

2.15
```
int fun5(float,int=0);
int fun5();             //function overloading is incorrect
int fun5(int);
```

2.17
```
template<class T>
int counter(T a[], T x, int n)
{
    int count=0;
    for(int j=0; j<n; j++)
    {
        if(a[j]==x)
            count++;
    }
    return count;
}
```

2.19
```
template<class T>
T average(T a[], int n)
{
    T total=0;
    for(int k=0; k<n; k++)
        total=total+a[k];
    return total/n;
}
```

CHAPTER 3

3.1   An array of references cannot be created.

3.3
```
int x=13;
int &ref1=x;
int &ref2=ref1;        //cannot be '&&' before ref2
cout<<ref1<<endl;
cout<<ref2;
```

3.5   The address stored in a constant pointer cannot be changed, therefore, the **dp=&v2**; statement generates an error.

3.7 `float *fp;`

`fp=new float;   //data type after `*new*` must match the pointer type`

3.9 `char* stfun(char* pstr, int n)    //Function returns a `*char*`
`{                                //pointer`

```
    int i;
    char* cp = new char[n+1];
    if(!cp)     //Memory allocation error checker - good practice
    {
        cout<<"Memory allocation error";
        exit(1);
    }
    for(i=0; i<n; i++)
        cp[i] = pstr[i];
    cp[i+1]='\0';
    return cp;
}
```

3.11 d

d

3.13 The following output is produced by invoking the **output()** function:

```
    2.3   3.4
    3.4   2.3
```

CHAPTER 4

4.1 `Pixel 1,0 is deleted.`

4.3
```
#include <iostream>
using namespace std;
class Circuit {
    float res, vol;
public:
    void set(float r, float v){ res=r, vol=v; }
```

```
        float current();
    };
    float Circuit::current()
    {
        return vol/res;
    }
    int main()
    {
        float r,v;
        Circuit crc;
        cout<<"Enter resistance => ";
        cin>>r;
        cout<<"\nEnter voltage => ";
        cin>>v;
        crc.set(r,v);
        cout<<"\n\nThe current is => "<<crc.current()<<" A";
        return 0;
    }
```

4.5
```
    class NumsHex {
        int n1, n2;
    public:
        NumsHex(int a, int b){n1=a; n2=b;} //Overloaded constructors
        NumsHex(){n1=0; n2=0;}       //cannot have the same parameters.
        void showHex(){ cout<<hex<<n1<<n2;}
    };
```

4.7
```
    #include <iostream>
    using namespace std;
    class Nums {
        int x, y;
    public:
        void set(int a){ x=a; y=x*2; }
```

```
        void display(){ cout<<x<<' '<<y<<endl; }
};
int main()
{
    Nums *nptr;
    int x=10;
    nptr=new Nums[x];
    if(nptr==0)
    {
        cout<<"Memory allocation error.";
        exit(1);
    }
    for(int i=0; i<x; i++)
    {
        nptr[i].set(i);
        nptr[i].display();
    }
    delete []nptr;
    return 0;
}
```

CHAPTER 5

5.1
```
class Point {
    int a, b;
public:
    Point(Point &x) { a=x.a; b=x.b; }
    Point(int x) { a=b=x; }
    int calc(int c) { return (a * c + b); }
    friend void display(Point p);
    static int s;
};
int Point::s=1;
void display(Point p)
```

```
    {
        cout<<p.a<<p.b;
    }
```

5.3
```
    class Nums {
        int x, y;
    public:
        Nums(){ x=3; y=5; }
        Nums inc()     //Function returns a class object
        {
            x++;        //It is not necessary to explicitly use this
            y++;             //in order to access x and y.
            return *this;
        }
    };
```

5.5
```
    class Power {
        float voltage;
        float frequency;
    public:
        Power(){ voltage=110; frequency=60; }  //cannot be const
        void display() const { cout<<voltage<<frequency; }
        float getVolt() const { return voltage; }
        void setVolt()                          //cannot be const
        {
            cout<<"Enter voltage:";
            cin>>voltage;
        }
    };
```

5.7
```
    #include <iostream>
    using namespace std;
    class Circle {
```

```
        float radius;
public:
    Circle(float r) { radius = r; }
    friend float area(Circle c);
};
//definition of the area() friend function
float area(Circle c)
{
    return 3.14159*c.radius*c.radius;
}
int main()
{
    float r;
    cout<<"Enter radius ==> ";
    cin>>r;
    Circle c1(r);
    cout<<"\nThe area is: ";
    cout<<area(c1);              //friend function call
    return 0;
}
```

5.9   12

CHAPTER 6

6.1
```
//The operator+() member function has too many arguments.
//This function could be redefined as follows:
Pixel Pixel::operator+(int a)
{
    Pixel p;
    p.x = x + a;
    p.y = y + a;
    return p;
}
```

6.3   //The assignment operator can only be overloaded by a member
//operator function.
//**operator=()** member function prototype
const Impedance &operator=(const Impedance &);

6.5   //This operator function must be defined as a friend function.
Pixel operator-(int a, Pixel &p)
{
    Pixel temp;
    temp.x = a - p.x;
    temp.y = a - p.y;
    return temp;
}

6.7   Pixel Pixel::operator--()   //pre-decrement
{
    --x;
    --y;
    return *this;
}
Pixel Pixel::operator--(int)   //post-decrement
{
    Pixel temp=*this;
    --x;
    --y;
    return temp;
}

6.9   //A binary operator function requires two arguments if declared
//as a **friend** function.
friend float operator/(float v, ACcurrent &c1);

6.11
```
ACcurrent operator-(const ACcurrent &c1, const ACcurrent &c2)
{
    ACcurrent temp;
    float real, imag;
    real=c1.mag*cos(c1.phase*D2R)-c2.mag*cos(c2.phase*D2R);
    imag=c1.mag*sin(c1.phase*D2R)-c2.mag*sin(c2.phase*D2R);
    temp.mag=sqrt(real*real+imag*imag);
    if(!((real==0)&&(imag==0)))
        temp.phase=atan(imag/real)*R2D;
    else
        temp.phase = 0;
    return temp;
}
```

6.13
```
//function prototype
void operator<<(float);
//function definition
void ACcurrent::operator<<(float p)
{
    phase=phase+p;
}
```

6.15
```
//function prototype
Pixel operator+(const Pixel &);
//function definition
Pixel Pixel::operator+(const Pixel &p2)
{
    Pixel temp;
    temp.x = x + p2.x;
    temp.y = y + p2.y;
    return temp;
}
```

CHAPTER 7

7.1   Single inheritance is implemented.

*Table 7.1 Members of the **A** Class*

Member Name	Access Status
count	*private*
x	*protected*
A()	*public*
~A()	*public*
display()	*public*

*Table 7.2 Members of the **B** Class*

Member Name	Access Status
y	*private*
x	*protected*
B()	*public*
get()	*public*
display()	*public*

7.3   Multiple-direct inheritance is implemented.

*Table 7.3 Members of the **Base1** Class*

Member Name	Access Status
x	*protected*
y	*protected*
A()	*public*
Base1()	*public*
get()	*public*

*Table 7.4 Members of the **Base2** Class*

Member Name	Access Status
z	*private*
w	*protected*
Base2()	*public*
compute()	*public*

*Table 7.5 Members of the **Derived** Class*

Member Name	Access Status
v	*private*
w	*private*

```
    compute()      private
    x              protected
    y              protected
    Derived()      public
    display()      public
    get()          public
```

7.5
```
class Circuit : public Resistor {
private:
    float ind;        //inductance
    float frq;        //frequency
public:
    //Circuit constructor invokes the Resistor constructor
    Circuit(float i, float f, float x):Resistor(x)
    {
        ind=i;
        frq=f;
    }
    float getImpedance();
};
float Circuit::getImpedance()
{
    float r=get_r();
    float x=2*3.14*frq*ind;
    return  sqrt( r*r + x*x );
}
```

7.7
```
//Inheritance must be public in order to call the get_current()
//inherited member function in main()
class Circuit : public Resistor {
    // Body of the Circuit class
};
int main()
```

```
{
    Circuit c(100, 0.001, 60);
    cout<<"Current   = "<<c.get_current(20);
    Resistor res(100);
    Circuit *cptr=&c;
    //getImpedance() is not a member of Resistor, therefore cptr
    //must point to c to invoke this function
    cout<<"Impedance = "<<cptr->getImpedance();
    return 0;
}
```

7.9   4 2 3 1
        45

CHAPTER 8

8.1   The order of the constructor calls: A,C,D,B
        The order of the destructor calls: B,D,C,A

8.3   The order of the constructor calls: A,B,D,C,F,E
        The order of the destructor calls: E,F,C,D,B,A

8.5
```
#include <iostream>
using namespace std;
class Point {
public:
    int x, y;
    Point(int a, int b) {x=a; y=b;}
};
class Rectangle {
    int perimeter;
    Point p1, p2;
public:
    Rectangle(int a, int b, int c, int d):p1(a,b), p2(c,d)
    {
```

```
                perimeter=2*((p2.y-p1.y)+(p2.x-p1.x));
        }
        void display(){ cout<<"Perimeter: "<<perimeter; }
    };
    int main()
    {
        Rectangle r(1,2,3,4);
        r.display();
        return 0;

    }
```

CHAPTER 9

9.1   13

f

9.3   The output produced by Program 9.1:

```
13
15
```

The output produced by Program 9.2:

```
1
3
4
```

9.5
```
class Dryer : public Device {
public:
    Dryer();                //A constructor cannot be virtual
    virtual ~Dryer();
    void print()
    {
        cout<<"Description: "<<description<<endl;
        cout<<power<<" W "<<voltage<<" V";
    }
```

```
    //Derived class must redefine pure virtual functions
    void getValues();
};
```

9.7   There are no errors.

CHAPTER 10

10.1
```
//The keyword class, or the keyword typename must precede a
//template type parameter in a template header.
template<class Tc, int n=10>
class Circuit {
    //body of the template
};
```

10.3
```
//A non-type parameter cannot be a floating point type.
template<int, char>
class X {
    //body of the template
};
```

10.5
```
template<class T>
class X {
    friend int fun1(int);
    friend class Y;
    friend void Z<T>::fun2();
};
```

10.7
```
template<class Ttype>
class X {
    static Ttype num;
    //non-static members
};
template<class Ttype> Ttype X<Ttype>::num=0;
```

10.9
```
vector<int> v;
v.push_back(1);
cout<<v.size()<<" objects in container";
```

10.11 TEMLATCES

10.13 4 3 2 1 0

CHAPTER 11

11.1 3 is caught!

11.3 1 is caught!

11.5 `void fun() throw(char*,int*,float);`

11.7 `set_new_handler(myHandler);`

11.9
```
void calc(float y) throw(float, int)
{
    if(y>999.99) throw y;
    else throw 1;
}
```

11.11
```
void isEven(int a) throw(char *)
{
    if(a%2==0) throw "is even";
}
```

CHAPTER 12

12.1
```
fstream myfile("info.dat");
if(!myfile)
{
    cout<<"Error in file opening.";
    exit(1);
```

```
    }

12.3  ofstream fout("comparts.dat");
      if(fout.fail())
      {
          cerr<<"Error in file opening.";
          exit(1);
      }
      fout.seekp(-2*sizeof(compart),ios::end);
      fout.write((char*)&part,sizeof(compart));

12.5  ofstream fstr("info.dat");
      fstr<<x<<y;
      fstr.close();

12.7  S
      G
```